Nina Speransky

Transitivity and Aspect in Sahidic Coptic:
Studies in the Morphosyntax
of Native and Greek-Origin Verbs

Lingua Aegyptia

Studia Monographica

Herausgegeben von

Frank Kammerzell, Gerald Moers und Kai Widmaier

Band 26

Institut für Archäologie
Humboldt Universität
Berlin

Widmaier Verlag
Hamburg

Institut für Ägyptologie
Universität Wien
Wien

Transitivity and Aspect in Sahidic Coptic: Studies in the Morphosyntax of Native and Greek-Origin Verbs

DDGLC Working Papers 2

Nina Speransky

Widmaier Verlag · Hamburg
2022

Die Publikation wurde ermöglicht durch eine Ko-Finanzierung
für Open-Access-Monografien und -Sammelbände
der Freien Universität Berlin.

Titelaufnahme:
Nina Speransky,
Transitivity and Aspect in Sahidic Coptic.
Studies in the Morphosyntax
of Native and Greek-Origin Verbs
Hamburg: Widmaier Verlag, 2022
(Lingua Aegyptia – Studia Monographica; Bd. 26)
ISSN 0946-8641
ISBN (paperback): 978-3-943955-26-2
ISBN (PDF): 978-3-943955-91-0
DOI: https://doi.org/10.37011/studmon.26

Druck und Verarbeitung: Hubert & Co., Göttingen
Printed in Germany

In loving memory of Brakha (Beatrice) Avigad

Contents

Editorial

It is a great pleasure for the undersigned to present, as a second installment of *DDGLC Working Papers*, the volume "Transitivity and Aspect in Sahidic Coptic – Studies in the Morphosyntax of Native and Greek-Origin Verbs". Its author Nina Speransky studied linguistics at the Hebrew University of Jerusalem with Haim Baruch Rosen and Ariel Shisha-Halevy. Proselytized by the latter, her MA supervisor, she became an ardent devotee of Coptic whose glow has not stopped sparking her curiosity ever since. A PhD fellowship of the *German Israeli Foundation* project "Transitivity and Valency in Language Contact: The Case of Coptic" (2016-2019)[1] brought her in touch with the DFG long-term project *Database and Dictionary of Greek Loanwords in Coptic* (*DDGLC*) at Freie Universität Berlin where she received her PhD in 2021.

"Transitivity and Aspect in Sahidic Coptic" is a landmark in the linguistic description, interpretation, and typological comparison of Coptic language data. The main thread of its first part "Transitivity and aspect in native Sahidic verbal system" goes along, and eventually beyond previous observations and thoughts by Ludwig Stern, Petr Ernstedt, and Wolf-Peter Funk and results in a revised model of the Coptic conjugation system, supplemented by what the author calls, the Aspect-Diathesis Grid. A bit (though not exceedingly) complicated than the one we know, it displays a neat structural equilibrium, explains some hitherto poorly understood observations and helps disambiguating what had until now looked like homonymies. A crucial point is the discovery of the regular function of the difference between the Coptic bipartite and tripartite pattern for voice marking. While parts of the rediscovered system, such as the compatibility rules of the stative, were already known, and others, such as the passive semantics of objectless transitive verbs in the tripartite pattern, had already been observed but not fully understood, the overall compatibility limitations of intransitive infinitives have thus far been partly overlooked, partly mistaken as a peculiarity of the verbs of motion. The Aspect-Diathesis Grid model now provides a fuller account of the entanglement of all these phenomena and shows the fundamentally templatic character of voice marking in Coptic.

The posterior part of the book, "Greek loan verbs in Coptic: diathesis and grammatical voice marking", is a major contribution to the study of Greek-Egyptian language contact and an expedition into still uncharted territory. Research in borrowability and borrowing strategies of Greek verbs in Coptic has until now mostly concentrated on the morphology of Greek input forms and their syntactic integration with or without light verb. The issue of the adaptation of loaned verbs to recipient language patterns of valency and transitivity and the question how Greek verbs were marked for voice within the Coptic matrix system have barely been raised so far.[2] Based on thorough analysis of the data accessible in the

---

1 Conceived by Eitan Grossman, this project (*GIF* Grant No. I-1343-110.4/2016) was conducted at Jerusalem and Berlin with professor Grossman and the undersigned as principal investigators.

2 The question was explored by aforesaid *GIF* project, see E. Grossman, "Language-Specific Transitivities in Contact: The Case of Coptic," *Journal of Language Contact* 12, 89-115; see also W.-P. Funk, "Differential Loan across the Coptic Literary Dialects", in E. Grossman, P. Dils, T.S. Richter & W. Schenkel (eds), *Greek Influence on Egyptian-Coptic: Contact-Induced Change in an Ancient*

DDGLC database and on a sophisticated differentiation of loan verbs along their morphological and diathesis variation, the author has discovered a transition from (relics of) the donor language system of morphological voice marking, including evidence for parallel system borrowing, towards the recipient-language system of templatic voice marking. Her conclusions help profoundly to brighten up the twilight of this transitory situation and lead to new findings, such as the hitherto unnoticed productivity of the Greek middle-passive suffix in Coptic as a means of valency reduction of loan verbs.

"Transitivity and Aspect in Sahidic Coptic" was granted the *Award for Academic Excellence* of the *International Association for Coptic Studies* on its congress at Brussels in July 2022. It is delightful to see the lexicographical data of the *DDGLC* project bear rich fruit already before their public release. I am particularly grateful to the Freie Universität Berlin for funding the *Gold Open Access* publication of this book.

Berlin, 31 October 2022   Tonio Sebastian Richter

African Language (DDGLC Working Papers I), LingAegStudMon 17, Hamburg: Widmaier, 369-397, and E.D. Zakrzewska, "Complex verbs in Bohairic Coptic: language contact and valency," in: B. Nolan & E. Diedrichsen (eds), *Argument Realisation in Complex Predicates and Complex Events: Verb-Verb Constructions at the Syntax-Semantic Interface*, Studies in Language Companion Series 180, Amsterdam: Benjamins, 213-243.

Acknowledgements

Completing this work, I find myself hardly able to express all the gratitude I owe the people who by their concern, patience, and support enabled me to conduct the research. From the very hatching of the idea developed here, my supervisor, Professor Sebastian Richter was the person who inspired and guarded my every step, being the most generous and open-minded listener and critic, I ever had the good chance to meet. I am deeply grateful for every one of our stimulating conversations, as well as for his brilliant seminars that imbued the Coptic history and culture with such a lively shine.

I am very thankful to my second advisor, Dr. Alexander Letuchiy, whose papers served to me as a long-desired textbook on verbal typology.

I shall always gratefully remember my teachers at the Hebrew University, Hannah and Haim Baruch Rosen. And of course, my heartfelt thanks go to my teacher of general and Coptic linguistics, Ariel Shisha-Halevy.

I owe special thanks to Prof. Heike Behlmer who practically ordered me to start my PhD study. I am extremely grateful to my fantastic colleagues, Dr. Diliana Atanassova, Dr. Frank Feder, Theresa Kohl, Julien Delhez and So Miyagawa, without whom I could never cope with the many difficulties the process involves. I sincerely thank the whole team of the DDGLC project for assisting me with their expertise, as well as for providing the actual material the study is based upon. I am also deeply grateful to all my colleagues at the Digital Edition of the Coptic Old Testament project of the Göttingen Academy of Sciences and Humanities. Special thanks are due to Prof. Andréas Stauder. The present research could be not conceived without the existence of the digital databases of the Coptic Scriptorium (http:// copticscriptorium.org), http://coptot.manuscriptroom.com, and DDGLC (https://refubium.fu-berlin.de/handle/fub188/27813).

I really cannot thank enough my dear friend and colleague Sina Becker, who has always been there for me in every little need. The present work owes much to her expertise in the world of Coptic literature. I am also deeply grateful for the privilege of using her still unpublished dissertation.

With deep love and gratitude, I name my friends whose kindness and patience supported me all this time through: Natacha Descombes, Anna Sergeeva, Julia Braverman. My dear parents, my husband, my children, Sarah, Seva, Yasha, Joseph, and Leah, and my nieces and nephew, Julia, Galia, Vadim were the support team I could not do without.

The work was supported by German Israeli Foundation [I-1343-110.4/2016 "Valency and Transitivity in Contact: The Case of Coptic" and Deutsche Forschungsgemeinschaft [DFG-Langzeitprojekt Database and Dictionary of Greek Loanwords in Coptic].

Abstract

Despite the relatively long history of grammatical descriptions, certain details of the Coptic verbal system have not yet been sufficiently clarified. Diathetic classes of labile verbs, semantic classes of non-labile mutable verbs, *stative: infinitive* opposition, the functional range of the periphrastic construction, integration of Greek loan verbs into Coptic valency alternation system and the role of the loaned morphology in that system are some of the pressing problems the present study aims to investigate. In Coptic, all these problems belong to the domain of the interaction between two grammatical categories, transitivity and aspect.

Apart from the introductory chapter that briefly states the research objectives and gives a general overview of the linguistic material and theory employed, the present study consists of three chapters. The first chapter studies major regularities in the transitivity alternations of native Egyptian verbs. Defining the Coptic conjugation system by two parameters, those of aspect and transitivity, I examine the functions of the absolute infinitive as the only unmarked form opposed, on the one hand, to transitive eventive construct forms, and on the other hand, to intransitive stative. The system of conjugation patterns is analyzed as a templatic system where a specific conjugation pattern ascribes not only tense, aspect, and modus, but also voice to an unmarked verbal form. Finally, the native verbs are classified into four groups based on the formal criteria of mutability and lability, and this classification is found to correlate with the semantic one based on the agentivity and telicity of verbal lexemes. I also look into the diachrony of the aspect-transitivity cluster and use the two-parameter model to explain various synchronic anomalies of Coptic verbal valency.

The second chapter looks into semantic and grammatical factors triggering the use of the periphrastic pattern <ϣⲱⲡⲉ + circumstantial clause> which is shown to fulfil the whole range of functions, from punctual passive to resultative, depending on the lexical properties of the verb.

The third chapter explores the diathesis of Greek loan verbs in Sahidic. Valency-changing devices for Greek verbs are examined and compared with those operating on native verbs. The occasional use of Greek middle-passive suffix is analyzed as the vestige of parallel system borrowing.

Zusammenfassung

Trotz der relativ langen Geschichte der grammatikalischen Beschreibungen sind bestimmte Details des koptischen verbalen Systems noch nicht ausreichend geklärt. Diathetische Klassen labiler Verben, semantische Klassen nicht labiler veränderlicher Verben, die Opposition <Stativ: Infinitiv>, Funktionsbereich der periphrastischen Konstruktion, Integration griechischer Lehnverben in das koptische Valenzalternationsystem und die Rolle der entlehnten Morphologie in diesem System sind einige von den dringenden Problemen, die die vorliegende Studie untersuchen soll. In der koptischen Sprache gehören alle diese Probleme zum Bereich der Interaktion zwischen zwei grammatikalischen Kategorien, Transitivität und Aspekt.

Neben dem Einführungskapitel, in dem die Forschungsschwerpunkte kurz dargestellt und ein allgemeiner Überblick über das verwendete sprachliche Material und die Theorie gegeben werden, besteht die vorliegende Studie aus drei Kapiteln. Das erste Kapitel befasst sich mit wichtigen Regelmäßigkeiten bei den Transitivitätswechseln von ägyptischen Verben. Indem ich das koptische Konjugationssystem durch zwei Parameter definiere, nämlich Aspekt und Transitivität, untersuche ich die Funktionen des absoluten Infinitivs als der einzigen unmarkierten Form, die auf der einen Seite transitiven eventiven Konstruktformen und auf der anderen Seite intransitiven Stativen entgegengesetzt ist. Das System der Konjugationsmuster wird als ein templatisches System analysiert, bei dem ein bestimmtes Konjugationsmuster nicht nur Zeitform, Aspekt und Modus, sondern auch Diathese einer unmarkierten verbalen Form zuschreibt. Schließlich werden die nativen Verben aufgrund der formalen Kriterien der Veränderlichkeit und Labilität in vier Gruppen eingeteilt, und es wird festgestellt, dass diese Klassifizierung mit der semantischen korreliert, die auf der Agentivität und Telizität verbaler Lexeme basiert. Ich untersuche auch die Diachronie des Aspekt-Transitivitäts-Clusters und verwende das Zwei-Parameter-Modell, um verschiedene synchrone Anomalien der koptischen verbalen Valenz zu erklären.

Das zweite Kapitel befasst sich mit semantischen und grammatikalischen Faktoren, die die Verwendung des periphrastischen Musters <ϣⲱⲡⲉ + Umstandssatz> auslösen, von dem gezeigt wird, dass es den gesamten Funktionsumfang erfüllt, von punktuellem Passiv bis Resultativ, je nach den lexikalischen Eigenschaften des verbalen Lexems.

Das dritte Kapitel befasst sich mit der Diathese der griechischen Lehnverben im Sahidischen. Die Mechanismen der Valenzalternation für griechische Verben werden untersucht und mit denen verglichen, die mit nativen Verben fungieren. Die gelegentliche Verwendung des griechischen medial-passiven Suffix wird als ein Rudiment von „parallel system borrowing" analysiert.

Tables

Table 1 Aspectual-diathetic distribution of verbal morphs.

Table 2. Aspect / diathesis / form of unaccusatives: instances
Table 2a. ⲱⲛϩ 'to live'
Table 2b. ⲡⲱϩ 'to reach'
Table 2c. ⲥⲣϥⲉ 'to be at leisure'
Table 2d. ⲣⲱⲧ 'to grow, sprout'
Table 2e. ⲕⲛⲛⲉ 'to grow fat'
Table 2f. ⲁϣⲁⲓ 'to multiply'
Table 2g. ⲙⲟⲩⲛ ⲉⲃⲟⲗ 'to remain'

Table 3. Aspect / diathesis / form of labile verbs: instances
Table 3a. ⲙⲟⲩϩ 'to fill / be filled'
Table 3b. ⲡⲱⲣϣ 'to spread'
Table 3c. ⲡⲱϩ 'to divide / be divided, burst out'
Table 3d. ⲣⲱⲕϩ 'to incinerate / burn'
Table 3e. ⲧⲁⲕⲟ 'to destroy / perish'
Table 3f. ⲧⲁⲗϭⲟ 'to heal, make calm / be healed, calm down'
Table 3g. ⲟⲩⲱⲛϩ ⲉⲃⲟⲗ 'to show / appear'
Table 3h. ⲱⲡ 'to count / to be counted, belong to'

Table 4. Diathesis of absolute infinitive: specific instances
Table 4a. ⲃⲱⲗ (ⲉⲃⲟⲗ)
Table 4b. ⲛⲟⲩϩⲙ
Table 4c. ϣⲱⲱϭⲉ
Table 4d. ⲥⲱⲟⲩϩ

Table 5. Syntactic-semantic classification of native Coptic verbs
Table 6. ⲥⲟⲟⲩⲛ and ⲉⲓⲙⲉ in the Old Testament (sample)
Table 7. Form-meaning distribution of the verbs of class A
Table 8. Middle-passive morpheme in the detransitivized predicate
Table 9. Deponent morphology dating
Table 10. Greek-Coptic correlates for 'witness'
Table 11. Non-causative token ratio for labile and non-labile Greek loan verbs
Table 12. Diathetic patterns of Koine verbs.

Abbreviations

Abbreviations of documentary texts follow those listed in the *Checklist of Editions of Greek, Latin, Demotic and Coptic papyri, ostraca and tablets*. This ressource can be currently found at https://library.duke.edu/rubenstein/scriptorium/papyrus/texts/clist.html.

Amel. 1 = Amélineau (1914), vol. 1
Amel. 2 = Amélineau (1914), vol. 2
BASP = Bulletin of the American Society of Papyrologists
BCNH.T = Bibliothèque copte de Nag Hammadi, Section "Textes"
CSCO / CS = Corpus Scriptorum Christianorum Orientalium / Scriptores Coptici
DDGLC = Database and Dictionary of Greek Loanwords in Coptic (https://www.geschkult.fu-berlin.de/en/e/ddglc/index.html)
LBG = Lexikon zur byzantinischen Gräzität
MONB. = Monasterio Bianco (White Monastery)
NHC = Nag Hammadi Codices
NHMS = Nag Hammadi and Manichaean Studies
NHS = Nag Hammadi Studies
Pier.Morg. = Pierpont Morgan Library
Shen. Can. = Shenoute Canon
TLA = Thesaurus Linguae Aegyptiae (https://aaew.bbaw.de/tla/servlet/TlaLogin)

Quoted sources

The Greek texts of the Old Testament are quoted according to Rahlfs-Hanhart (2006), those of the New Testament follow Nestle-Aland (2012). Unless otherwise specified, I use the English Standard Version (ESV) for the English translation. The standard abbreviations for the Bible books can be found at https://www.esv.org/resources/esv-global-study-bible/list-of-abbreviations/. The Sahidic text of the Old and the New Testament is quoted according to the Coptic Scriptorium database (Caroline T. Schroeder, Amir Zeldes, et al., Coptic SCRIPTORIUM, 2013-2021, http://copticscriptorium.org).

Greek and Egyptian papyri

Canopus Kom el-Hisn, CG 22186	Simpson (1996)
Canopus Tanis, CG 22187	Simpson (1996)
HGV BASP	BASP 48 (2011)
HGV O.Frange 188	Boud'hors/ Heurtel (2016)
HGV PSI	Vitelli / Norsa (1917)
HGV SB	Ruprecht / Hengstl (1997)
P Carlsberg	Smith (2002)
P. Berlin P 15530	Zauzich (1993)
P. Boulaq	Töpfer (2013)
P. Cair. Masp. 1	Maspero (1911)
P. Cair. Masp. 2	Maspero (1913)
P. Cair. Masp. 3	Maspero (1916)
P. Harkness	Smith (2005)
P. Insinger	Lexa (1926)
P. Leiden I 348,	
Vso. 9,6-10,8, Bakenptah's letter	Caminos (1954)
P. Leiden I 384	Spiegelberg (1917)
P. Lond. 4	Crum (1910)
P. London BM EA 10477 (P.Nu)	Lapp (1997)
P. London-Leiden	Griffith-Thompson (1921)
P. Oxy 54	Coles, Maehler, Parsons (1987)
P. Petese Tebt. A, The Story of Petese	Ryholt (1999)
P. Rylands	Vittmann (1998)
P. Spiegelberg	Spiegelberg (1910)
P.Ant	Barns / Ziliacus (1960)
P.Berlin P 13548	Zauzich (1993)
P.Berlin P 3022, Sinuhe	Gardiner (1909)
P.Bodl.	Salomons (1996)
P.Flor.	Vitelli (1906)
P.Heid.	Duttenhöfer (1994)
P.Kairo CG 51189 (P.Juja)	Munro (1994)
P.Oxy. 8	Grenfell, Hunt (1898)
pMMA Heqanakht II	Allen (2002)
Sakkara Necropole	
The Tomb of Tjy the ship convoy lord	Steindorf (1913)
Stela of Hor (Kairo JE 71901)	Landgrafova / Dils, TLA
Stela of Nesmontu (Louvre C 1 = N 155)	Landgrafova / Dils, TLA
Tomb of Si-renpowet I	Gardiner (1908)

Coptic texts

Abbaton
Timothy, Archbishop of Alexandria,
    Discourse on Abbaton, BL Or. 7025   Budge (1914)

Abraham of Farshut
First Panegyric on Abraham of Farshut,
    White Monastery codex CG   Goehring (2012)

Ad Phil. Gent.
Shenoute, Ad Philosophum Gentilem   Leipoldt (1955)

Amazed
MONB. HB 28 b:24-29 ("I am amazed")   Cristea (2011)

Antiphonary
Pier.Morg. M575, Antiphonary   Cramer/Krause (2008)

Apocalypse of Adam
NHC V, The Apocalypse of Adam   MacRae (1979)

Apocalypse of James
NHC V, The (Second) Apocalypse of James   Hedrick/Parrott (1979)

Apocr.John
NHC II, The Apocryphon of John   Waldstein/Wisse (1995)

Apologia de incrudelitate
Fondation Bodmer 58, Apologia de incrudelitate   Crum (1915)

Asclepius
NHC VI, Asclepius 21-29   Dirkse/Parrott (1979)

Berliner "Koptisches Buch"
Berlin, Ägyptisches Museum P.20915,
    Berliner „Koptisches Buch"   Schenke Robinson (2004)

Besa on Theft
Besa Codex A: On Theft and Deceitful Behaviour   Kuhn (1956)

Colluthus
Encomium on St. Colluthus, Pier.Morg. M.591   Chapman/Depuydt (1993), Schenke (2013)

Concept of Power
NHC V, The Concept of our Great Power   Wisse/Parrott (1979)

Cyprianus
Legend of Cyprianus, Pier.Morg. M.609   Bilabel (1934)

Encomium on John the Baptist
British Library Or. 7024,
        Encomium on John the Baptist   Budge (1913)

Epima
Martyrdom of Apa Epima, Pier.Morg. M.580   Mina (1937)

Evod.rossi
Homily on the Passion and the Resurrection
        Attributed to Evodius of Rome   Rossi (1892)

Exegesis on the Soul
NHC II, The Exegesis on the Soul   Lundhaug (2010)

Festal Letter 16
Vienna Nationalbibliothek K 9241, K 9242, MONB.DS   Cristea (2011)

Four Creatures
John Chrysostom, Encomium on the
        Four Bodiless Creatures, Pier.Morg. M.612   Wansink(1991)

Gabriel
Installation of Gabriel, Pier.Morg. M.593

Great Mysterious
Book of the Great Mysterious Discourse,
        Bodleian Library MS Bruce 96   Crégheur (2013)

Historia Ecclesiastica
MONB.FY - Historia Ecclesiastica Coptica   Orlandi (1968-1970)
FY 158 Volume II
FY 49 Volume I

Hochzeit zu Kana
Benjamin of Alexandria, Hochzeit zu Kana   Müller (1968)

Hom. Pass. Res. (M.595)
Homily on the Passion and the Resurrection
        Attributed to Evodius of Rome, P.Morgan M.595   Chapman (1993)

Matthew/Scheide
Princeton, Private collection Scheide MS 144
        Gospel of Matthew   Schenke (1981)

Michael
Installation of Michael, Pier.Morg. M.593   Müller (1962)

O.Crum 22
Cairo, Egyptian Museum CG 8138 - O.Crum 22   Crum (1902)

On the Punishment
MONB.BB, Fr. 3 On the punishment of sinners   Kuhn (1956)

P.Budge
Columbia University P.600, SB Kopt. 1 036,
    papyrus Budge   Schiller (1968)

P.CLT
New York, Metropolitan Museum of Arts,
    Accession 24.2.7   Schiller (1932)

P.KRU
HGV P.RKU, Koptische Rechtsurkunden aus Djeme   Crum/Steindorf (1912)

P.Méd.Copt. IFAO
Cairo IFAO, Coptic Medical Papyrus   Chassinat (1921)

P.Mon.Epiph.
Papyri of the Monastery of Epiphanius at Thebes   Crum/Evelyn-White (1926)

P.MoscowCopt.
Coptic texts of Pushkin Museum, Moscow   Jernstedt (1959)

ParShem
NHC VII, Paraphrase of Shem   Wisse/Pearson (1996)

Pepper Receipt
London, British Museum Or. 8903, 20-26   Crum (1925)

Pistis Sophia
Pistis Sophia, British Library Add MS 5114   Schmidt/MacDermot (1978)

Protennoia
NHC XIII, Trimorphic Protennoia   Poirier (2006)

Rufus
Rufus of Shotep Homilies on Luke and Matthew   Sheridan (1998)

Shen.Can. 1
Shenoute, Canon 1   Emmel (2021)

Shen.Can. 2
Shenoute, Canon 2   Kuhn (1956)

Shen.Can. 3 YA
Shenoute, Canon 3 MS. YA   Layton (2014)

Shen.Can. 3
Shenoute, Canon 3   Leipoldt (1954)

Shen.Can. 4
Shenoute, Canon 4   Wessely (1909), Leipoldt (1955)

Shen.Can. 6
Shenoute, Canon 6   Leipoldt (1954, 1955), Amelineau 1,2
   (1914)

Shen.Can. 7
Shenoute, Canon 7   Leipoldt (1954); Crum Cat. 194 f.3

Shen.Can. 8
Shenoute, Canon 8   Boud'hors (2013)

Shen.Can. 9
Shenoute, Canon 9   Pleyte / Boeser (1897)

Spiteful Monk
Catechesis against a spiteful monk,
   British Museum Or. 7024   Lefort (1956)

St. Antony
New York, Pier.Morg. M.579,
   Encomium on St. Antony   Garitte (1943)

Teachings of Silvanus
NHC VII, Teachings of Silvanus   Peel (1996)

Theodore
Martyrdom of Theodore the Anatolian,
   Leontios the Arab, and Panigeros the Persian,
   Pier.Morg. M.583   Müller/Uljas (2019)

Thomas
NHC II, The Gospel of Thomas   Layton (1989)

To Herai
MONB.BA, Fr. 30 To Herai   Kuhn (1956)

White Mon.
Great Prayerbook of White Monastery   Lanne (1958)

Wisdom of Jesus Christ
Berlin, Ägyptisches Museum 8502,
   Wisdom of Jesus Christ   Till /Schenke (1972)

Zostrianos
NHC VIII, Zostrianos   Barry, et al. (2000)

0 Introduction

0.1 Research objectives

The present work includes three papers that deal, from different angles, with one and the same vast issue of transitivity and diathetic alternation in Sahidic Coptic. Although one of the central questions of the present-day typological studies, this issue is also – quite surprisingly, – one of the weakest points in the modern Coptic linguistics. Not that it has always been so. Transitive, intransitive, and passive forms and patterns received much attention in the works by Stern and Jernstedt who formulated, with an admirable mixture of accuracy and inspiration, the basic rules governing the syntax of direct object in Coptic. In doing so, they boldly crossed the border between two syntactic domains that were, since the days of antique grammarians and almost up to the present, strictly divided, the domains of *genus verbi* (voice) and verbal aspect. Indeed, for a mind trained on Greek and Latin conjugation tables, Coptic with its Moebius strip of grammatical categories opens an entirely new and wonderful perspective. However, the line of research laid down by these scientists has not been continued. Despite much meticulous work of the masters of today's Egyptian and Coptic philology, such as Shisha-Halevy, Depuydt, Emmel, Funk, Layton, Engsheden, Reintges, Grossman, we have not grown much wiser regarding the Coptic *active: non-active* opposition, as a whole, nor regarding the relation between this opposition and the opposition of *eventive: durative* aspect. As long back as in 1978, Funk called the attention of Coptologists to the pertinent problem with the treatment of "those Coptic verbs that are Active in meaning when they have a direct complement but are approximately "Passive" or "Middle" when used in the tripartite pattern without a direct complement".[1] Yet, that very problem is hardly even stated, not to mention systematically treated or explained in the newest Sahidic grammars, Layton (2000) and Reintges (2004). Transitive or intransitive use of the absolute infinitive form, alternations of infinitive and stative, a holistic understanding of stative, grammatical distinctions between passive and anticausative, the opposition of simple and periphrastic constructions are the topics very much in need of a caring hand. Many phenomena that we take at face value, as mere stylistic or rhetorical variations, could turn to be essential for the language structure, if correctly analyzed.

Our current state of knowledge concerning the morphosyntax of Greek loan verbs in Coptic is in no way more advanced than that of native verbs. Several studies discussing the integration of Greek verbs into Coptic, such as Böhlig (1953, 1955, 1995), Girgis (1955), are mainly interested in the morphophonetic changes occurring to the loan verbs, others (e.g., Almond 2010, Grossman & Richter 2017) consider insertion strategies of Greek infinitives which oscillate between light-verb insertion and direct insertion. Finally, one recent contribution (Grossman 2019) briefly sketches the integration of Greek verbs into Coptic transitivity and valency patterns comparing the most general morphosyntactic properties of native Coptic and Greek verbs. The issue that remains completely unaddressed

---

1   Funk (1978b:120).

is the interplay of diathesis and aspect, as reflected in the semantic and syntactic behavior of loan verbs. This issue, however, is of primary importance for our understanding of the loan verb integration in Coptic. Whether the aspectual split that is so crucial for the native verb paradigm does or does not play the same role for loan verbs, is the question to be answered before we can make any meaningful comparison between the transitivity models of loan and native verbs.

This study addresses the following questions: 1) the distribution of native verb forms in terms of diathesis and aspect; 2) semantic and syntactic properties of the periphrastic circumstantial construction; 3) transitivity alternations in Greek loan verbs and their connection to aspect realization. In the first part, the Coptic conjugation system is defined as a diathesis-aspect grid where some verbal forms (*status constructus, status pronominalis,* stative) are marked for both diathesis and aspect, whereas the absolute infinitive is unmarked for either and thus functions as a contrastive opposition to the marked form in each conjugation pattern. This approach allows to specify the functional load of several oppositions: eventive absolute infinitive vs. durative infinitive; durative infinitive vs. stative; eventive absolute infinitive vs. construct forms. An interesting corollary is the conclusion that the non-causative / intransitive use of absolute infinitives was, in fact, far more reduced and semantically specific than commonly assumed now. Further on, I try to pursue the development of the aspect-diathesis system throughout the course of the attested history of Egyptian, in order to verify the hypothesis of a causative split that could have shaped the system, as we see it in Coptic. Another diachronic excursus deals with the history of the durative transitive pattern. In particular, I examine and try to explain the exceptions to the Stern-Jernstedt rule discussed in Simpson (1996) and Depuydt (2009). The last section describes various syntactic and lexical phenomena that might arise as a result of the causative split in Coptic, most of them previously disregarded.

The second chapter focuses on the periphrastic circumstantial construction specifying the place of periphrasis in the verb paradigm, the semantic values associated with it, and the classes of verbs participating in that construction.

The third chapter is dedicated to the syntactic integration of Greek loan verbs into the diathesis-aspect grid. I explore the use of Greek voice morphology concluding that the integration of the Greek middle-passive voice marker into Sahidic represents a specific case of parallel system borrowing. Further on, I delimit the group of loan verbs capable of labile alternation and examine various factors that could be responsible for this behavior.

However tempting it was to conduct the intended research on the material of all the attested dialects of Coptic, in the end to choose Sahidic as the sole object of examination looked like the only reasonable option. Attested infinitely better than the minor dialects, Sahidic offers a singularly diverse body of corpora including literary texts of different times and genres and a rich collection of documentaries. Some of these corpora, such as the Biblical corpus or Shenoute's Canons, are large enough to gather even some kind of (very thin and tentative) statistics, which seems to be impossible to do in any other dialect, perhaps except Bohairic. However, Bohairic is so different from Sahidic in many aspects of valency patterning, not to mention the treatment of the loan verbs, that it obviously calls for a separate study.

At the same time, I did not deem it sensible to confine the research to a single text corpus of Sahidic. The variance we find inside this dialect does not prevent us from conceiving a holistic idea of the verbal system. Rather, it demonstrates the potential of that system.

Far from being in any way exhaustive, this study is an attempt to make the Coptic verbal grammar more adequate for a typological comparison and the semantic categories behind it more pulpable for the readers of Coptic.

0.2 Coptic language: an outline of the verbal system

Coptic[2] is the last language phase of the Egyptian language, the native language of the population of the Northern Nile valley, which constitutes an autonomous branch of Afro-Asiatic language family. The first written attestations of Egyptian come from ca. 3000 BC. The onset of Coptic is marked with the transfer of written Egyptian to an alphabet based on the Greek script, with an addition of some six or seven Demotic consonantal signs. The lifetime of Coptic encompasses the period from ca. the 4th CE to ca. 14th CE,[3] when the last Coptic speakers shifted to Arabic, as a result of the Arabic conquest of Egypt in the 7th CE.

The standardization of the Coptic script coincided with (and possibly resulted from) the spread of Christianity in Egypt when the Bible and other important Christian literary texts were translated into the native language. Containing a large corpus of religious literature, such as homilies, monastic rules, vitae of holy fathers etc., Coptic belongs to the main languages of the Christian East. Alongside Christian writings, Coptic contains Gnostic and Manichean texts, as well as a large number of documentary texts — private letters, legal documents, medical prescriptions, and ritual or magical spells. All that makes Coptic a medium of precious information on the early Christian history and the everyday life in Late Antique Egypt.

The pre-Coptic data gives pretty little opportunity to trace regional language varieties, but in Coptic one already discerns more than ten standardized written dialects. The best attested are Sahidic, a southern dialect that for a certain period served as a literary standard for Coptic, Bohairic, originally spoken in the western part of Lower Egypt, Fayyumic, Akhmimic, Oxyrhynchitic (otherwise called Mesokemic or Middle Egyptian), and Lycopolitan. Less standardized texts may show local linguistic traits. Thus, the Hermopolitan Sahidic is relatively easily recognizable by the lenition of final plosives. The most conspicuous differences between the dialects lie on the phonetic and lexical level, but it is possible to observe also minor morphosyntactic and word order variations, such as changes in valency patterns, different distribution of conjugation bases or placement of clitic elements.[4]

---

2   A detailed linguistic description of Egyptian in its continuity may be found in Grossman & Richter (2015), a grammatical overview is presented in Haspelmath (2015b). Richter (2015) gives a profound account on the early history of Egyptian-Coptic linguistics.

3   Different sources give various dates, from the 11th to the 14th CE. Here I follow the data presented in Grossman & Richter (2015).

4   For a selective list of Bohairic isoglosses, see, e.g., Shisha-Halevy (1981).

Due to the close and prolonged contact with Koine Greek, the *lingua franca* of a multiethnic population of Ptolemaic and Roman Egypt, Coptic language became enriched with Greek vocabulary to such a degree, as to allow some researchers call it a 'bilingual language variety'.[5] The estimated percentage of Greek loan words in Coptic varies from 20% to 40%, comprising ca. 3000 nouns (among them nominalized adjectives), ca. 600-700 verbs, and remarkably many functional elements, viz., prepositions, conjunctions, discourse markers.

There is, however, a slight inaccuracy in saying that Coptic borrowed the Greek parts of speech. As distinct from Greek, Coptic is not an inflectional language and has almost no part-of-speech morphology. The structural elements of Coptic are sequences of morphs, in all probability, bound by a common stress, some of them bearing a grammatical meaning, and the others a lexical one.[6] The order of constituents in a group is fixed and determined by their dependency classes. The order of clause constituents is also fixed, which allows to distinguish several models of predication called ***conjugation patterns***. Since Polotsky (1960), two major conjugation patterns are recognized in Coptic, the ***Tripartite / Non-durative*** (eventive) pattern and the ***Bipartite / Durative*** pattern. The distinctive element of the Tripartite conjugation is the tense-aspect-modus-polarity marker occupying the first position in the predicate base. It is followed by a nominal subject and a verbal lexeme in form of ***absolute infinitive*** or else in one of the two pre-object forms, ***status constructus*** that is immediately followed by a substantival object, or ***status pronominalis*** that is immediately followed by a pronominal object.

Tripartite (eventive) conjugation

ⲁϥⲥⲱⲧⲙ / ⲁⲡⲣⲱⲙⲉ ⲥⲱⲧⲙ   ϣⲁⲩⲟⲩⲱⲛϩ ⲉⲃⲟⲗ / ϣⲁⲡⲛⲟⲩⲧⲉ ⲟⲩⲱⲛϩ ⲉⲃⲟⲗ
a-f-sôtm / a-p-rôme sôtm   ša-u-ouônh ebol / ša-p-noute ouônh ebol
pret-3sgm-hear /
pret-Art.MSG-man-hear   hab-3pl-show outside / hab-Art.MSG-God-show outside
'He / The man heard'   *'They appear (habitually) / The God appears'*

ⲙⲡⲟⲩⲥⲉⲧⲙⲗⲁⲁⲩ (verb in form of *status constructus*)
mp-ou-setm-laau
pret.neg-3pl-hear-anyone
'They did not hear anyone.'

ϣⲁⲓⲥⲟⲧⲙϥ (verb in form of *status pronominalis*)
ša-i-sotm-f
hab-1sgl-hear-3sgm
'I hear him (habitually)'

Some of the categories marked by the TAM markers of the Tripartite are tense (past), relative tense ('not yet', 'after', 'until'), modus (jussive, optative).

---

5   Reintges (2001:233). See Zakrzewska (2017) for a discussion.
6   See Layton (2011:22, §27), Haspelmath (2015b).

The Bipartite conjugation has no conjugation base. The first position is filled by a pronominal prefix or, much less often, by a nominal subject. The second position is filled either by an adverb, or by a verb in one of the two forms, absolute infinitive or *stative*. Stative (formerly also termed qualitative) is a verbal form that predicates a state in some way related to the action or event named by the verb.

Bipartite (durative) conjugation

п-ϫⲟⲉⲓⲥ ⲧⲁⲭⲣⲟ ⲙ-ⲡⲉϥ-ϭⲃⲟⲓ   ⲥⲉ-ⲧⲁⲭⲣⲏⲩ ⲅ̄ⲛ ϩⲉⲛⲉⲓϥⲧ
p-čoeis tačro m-pef-cboi   se-tačrêu hn hen-eift
DEF.M.-lord strengthen.INF ACC.-POSS.3S-arm 3P-strengthen.STAT with IDF.P-nails
'The Lord strengthens his arm'   *'They are strengthened with nails'*

The Bipartite pattern is associated with one tense (general or actual present) and one aspect (durative).

Not every verbal root can occur in each of the four above-mentioned forms (absolute infinitive, *status constructus & pronominalis*, and stative). A significant number of verbs are attested only in infinitive. Such verbs are called ***immutable***, as opposed to ***mutable*** verbs that possess, at least, two forms distinguished by different vocalization. ⲡⲱϩⲧ 'strike / fall' is an example of a mutable verb, ϩⲁⲣⲉϩ 'guard' represents the immutable class.

Absolute infinitive	ⲡⲱϩⲧ	ϩⲁⲣⲉϩ
Status constructus	ⲡⲉϩⲧ-	—
Status pronominalis	ⲡⲁϩⲧ=	—
Stative	ⲡⲁϩⲧ	—

0.3 Argument structure; transitive clause type

The major clause type in every language consists of a predicate and a number of dependent noun phrases called predicate arguments. Each argument is associated with a distinct semantic role, such as agent, patient, experiencer, goal, recipient etc. The semantic roles in a clause satisfy the condition of uniqueness: every argument is assigned one and only one semantic role. The set of semantic (or thematic) roles developed in comparative linguistics[7] proves to be more or less finite, which makes it possible to base further analysis on some general definitions. The most common are:

Agent: The 'doer' of the action denoted by the predicate.

Patient: The 'undergoer' of the change denoted by the predicate.

Experiencer: The living entity that experiences the event denoted by the predicate.

Goal: The location or entity indicating the end of the movement denoted by the predicate.

---

7   The system of semantic valency was first outlined in the works of J.Gruber (1965), Ch. Fillmore (1969), Ju. Apresjan (1974).

Source: The location or entity indicating the origin of the movement denoted by the predicate.

Recipient /Benefactive: The entity that benefits from the action or event denoted by the predicate.

Every semantic role tends to correlate with some consistent syntactic coding type.

Not all roles are equally important for a sentence to be complete and understandable. The arguments that bear the essential semantic roles are called **core arguments**. They must either be overtly stated, or be retrievable from the context. Their omission makes the clause ungrammatical. Other arguments are called peripheral. A specific configuration of core and peripheral arguments is called an argument structure, or, in more venerable, but still used terms, a **valency pattern**.

Depending on the number of core arguments, verbs are divided into univalent or monadic, bivalent, and ditransitive. A **monadic** verb has a single core argument, which may bear the semantic role of an agent (as, e.g., 'dance', 'work'), or of a patient ('sleep', 'fall'). A **bivalent** verb has two arguments, most often an agent and a patient ('bite', 'take'), a **ditransitive** verb has three arguments, the third mostly a recipient ('give', 'pay').

Introducing the notion of **transitivity**, a recent authoritative study, Dixon & Aikhenvald (2000), recognizes two universal clause types:

- *intransitive* clause, with an intransitive predicate and a single core argument which is in S (intransitive subject) function
- *transitive* clause, with a transitive predicate and two core arguments which are in A (transitive subject) and O (transitive object) functions

Transitivity is understood as a property of a bivalent clause whose arguments have the following specific semantic traits:

A - the argument whose referent "does (or potentially could) initiate or control the activity"[8] (i.e., has the semantic role of agent)

O - the argument whose referent is affected by the activity (i.e., has the semantic role of patient)

Whereas monadic clauses are unambiguously defined as intransitive, bivalent clauses present something more of a problem. There is a more or less general consensus among the linguists that there are two-argument clauses that are intransitive. However, the above definition offers no clear criteria that would help to distinguish between these two types of clauses.[9] In fact, it gives no cross-linguistically applicable criteria of transitivity,[10] nor does it explicitly state that transitivity is a linguistic universal to be found in any specific language.

---

8   Dixon & Aikhenvald (2000:3).
9   Affectedness of the second argument's referent cannot be considered a clear criterion, since most non-agentive referents are in this or the other way affected.
10 The most widely accepted recent approaches to transitivity are discussed in Haspelmath (2011).

Now, in many cases, the ambiguity surrounding the category of transitivity is no great impediment. As observed in Haspelmath (2011), in most languages transitive clauses are such a prominent type that they can easily be selected intuitively.[11] However, Coptic, with its rather unconventional (for a European eye) valency and voice system, prepares many traps for anyone who would like to replace a strict grammatical analysis with his intuitions. Therefore, it appears necessary, at the very outset, to explore the deep semantic content of the notion of transitivity in order to prove it indispensable for a reasonable analysis of the Coptic verbal system, and to establish connections between transitivity and other domains of verbal grammar, most importantly, with aspect.

---

11 Haspelmath (2011:545).

1 Transitivity and aspect in native Sahidic verbal system

1.1 Transitivity: towards a working definition

1.1.1 Transitivity: a lexical property or a grammatical cluster category?

In Shisha-Halevy's "Coptic Grammatical Categories", the chapter dealing with different models of argument expansion bears the eloquent title of "The **so-called** direct object" (emphasis mine). This reserved term is not accidental. An amazing fact about Coptic linguistics is that the applicability of the notion of transitivity to the Coptic verbal system is far from being an established fact. The source of this ambiguity is not only our insufficient knowledge of the intricate grammatical mechanisms of Coptic, but also the somewhat dubious nature of the notion itself. For, despite multiple elaborate treatments of various parameters of transitivity in the works by authors such as Aikhenvald, Borer, Comrie, Dixon, Dowty, Fillmore, Givón, Kittilä, Kulikov, Lakoff, Lazard, Levin and Rappaport Hovav, Letuchiy, Mal'chukov, Mel'čuk, Næss, Nedjalkov, Polinsky, Testelec, Tsunoda, to name just the most authoritative ones, it is difficult to find a comprehensive description of the phenomenon that would have universal validity. Indeed, it is not even claimed that transitivity in the sense of encoding specific semantic relations by a specific syntactic pattern is a universally valid phenomenon. Consequently, as a researcher of a particular language, you have full freedom to incorporate or not this category in your grammatical descriptions. To quote G.Lazard,

> "Within the limits of the description of an individual language, the question of transitivity is not so difficult, and not so interesting. 'Transitive' is a label the descriptive linguist gives to a certain class of verbs which, for some reason, he sets apart from other kinds of verbs, because he deems them worthy of special treatment. He is always free to choose a certain verb class and to decide that this shall be the transitive class. He is also free to make no use of the notion of transitivity and only to classify verbs according to whatever criteria he finds relevant. Both choices are licit.[12]"

Is then transitivity a language-specific descriptive category or a cross-linguistic comparative concept?[13] Though Lazard's definition sounds more like the first option, it is obvious that transitivity is based on some fundamental semantic distinctions and should therefore be represented in that or other form all across the languages. In order to provide a working definition of transitivity that might be used in the analysis of Coptic data, and also to try to gain a more precise understanding of the phenomenon as a whole, it might be helpful to re-examine the origins of the notion and to track down possible misapprehensions that might have distorted our view of it.

---

12 Lazard (2002:150).
13 The distinction is proposed and discussed in Haspelmath (2010).

Excursus. The history of the concept of transitivity

The concept of transitivity has entered the Indo-European grammar in the second century C.E., in the works of the Alexandrian school. In his treatise on Greek verbal voice system, the alleged author of the term, Apollonios Dyscolos has set aside the class of verbs taking prepositionless accusative objects as the one capable of regular voice alternation. Hierarchizing the basic bivalent patterns, Apollonios regards the accusative pattern as the basic one, from which all others deviate, both in form and in meaning. His logic can be captured from the fragment below where Apollonios discusses the semantic and the syntactic divergence between the two verbs denoting 'love': φιλέω and ἐράω:

φαίνεται δ᾽ ὅτι καὶ τὸ *φιλεῖν* τοῦ *ἐρᾶν* διοίσει, καθότι ἡ μὲν ἐκ τοῦ *φιλεῖν* ἐγγινομένη διάθεσις ἐνεργείας ὄνομα σημαίνει· οἱ γοῦν φιλοῦντες παιδεύουσιν, πάλιν τῆς διαθέσεως κοινῆς τοῖς προκειμένοις ἐπ᾽ αἰτιατικὴν συντεινούσης…2.2.419 τό γε μὴν *ἐρᾶν* ὁμολογεῖ τὸ προσδιατίθεσθαι ὑπὸ τοῦ ἐρωμένου… καὶ σαφές ἐστιν ὡς συνετοῦ μέν ἐστι καὶ ἀγαθοῦ τὸ *φιλεῖν*, καθάπερ καὶ πατέρες παῖδας φιλοῦσιν, οὐ μὴν συνετοῦ τὸ *ἐρᾶν*, ἀλλ᾽ ἤδη παρεφθορότος τὸ λογιστικόν. Οὐ χρὴ ἄρα ἀπορεῖν ἕνεκα τίνος τὸ μὲν *φιλῶ* ἐπ᾽ αἰτιατικὴν φέρεται, τὸ δὲ *ἐρῶ* ἐπὶ γενικήν.[14]

The basic sense conveyed in the accusative pattern is defined by Apollonios as 'transitive' (διαβιβαστικόν), featuring a transfer of the active force (ἐνέργεια) from the referent of the nominative to the referent of the accusative argument.[15] Thus, starting from Apollonios, transitivity has been understood as a linguistic sign with a very specific signifier and a very imprecise meaning. Accusative object (termed *direct object*) and double voice morphology were signs of a transitive verb for classical grammarians who understood transitivity as a property of a verbal lexeme. Yet, with the flourishing of non-Indo-European linguistics, it has become pretty clear that, whereas the notion of transitivity seems to be efficient for the description of manifold grammatical phenomena, the formal properties alone do not suffice to identify the domain of transitivity in languages with essentially different Case and Voice systems. On the other hand, traditional semantically based definitions largely following the one given by Apollonios do not provide criteria for any meaningful grammatical distinction.[16] Starting from late 1970s, these definitions became essentially

---

14 "Es scheint sich aber auch 'φιλεῖν' von 'ἐρᾶν' in der Weise zu unterscheiden, dass das dem 'φιλεῖν' entspringende Verhalten (des Subjekts) vorzugsweise eine Thätigkeit in sich schliesst; denn die 'φιλοῦντες' erziehen, und beide Thätigkeiten (sowohl die des 'φιλεῖν' wie die des 'παιδεύειν') erstrecken sich gleicherweise auf einen (Objekts)Akkusativ… Das 'ἐρᾶν' aber setzt zugleich ein von dem Geliebten verursachtes Affiziertsein (der Seele) voraus… Es ist einleuchtend, dass das 'φιλεῖν' das Zeichen eines Guten und Verständigen ist, welcher liebt wie Väter ihre Kinder lieben, dass 'ἐρᾶν' aber das Zeichen eines nicht verständigen Mannes, dessen Vernunft bereits Schaden gelitten. Man darf also nicht in Zweifel sein und fragen, warum φιλῶ den Akkusativ, ἐρῶ den Genitiv regiert." (Transl. Buttmann 1877).

15 "χρὴ γὰρ νοεῖν ὅτι ἡ ἐνέργεια ὡς πρὸς ὑποκείμενόν τι διαβιβάζεται, ὡς τὸ *τέμνει, τύπτει,* τὰ τούτοις παραπλήσια· ἧς καὶ τὸ παθητικὸν ἐκ προϋφεστώσης ἐνεργητικῆς διαθέσεως ἀνάγεται, *δέρεται, τύπτεται.*" (Ap.Disc. III 148).

16 Cf. Kittilä (2002:26-27).

refined in typological studies. The far-reaching similarities in the semantics of transitive verb classes between various languages made it possible to eventually grasp the main semantic components of transitivity. It has been observed, for example, that verbs of an immediate effect ('break', 'shoot', 'boil' etc.), as well as verbs denoting solicitation ('ask', 'threaten') or pursuit ('follow', 'search') tend to be encoded by transitive structures, while verbs of symmetric actions ('fight with', 'talk to') mostly take indirect objects. Verbs of perception ('hear', 'smell') and emotion ('love', 'like', 'hate') may participate in the transitive pattern, or else take indirect objects. Moreover, it became clear that transitivity is not simply a lexical feature, but rather the property of the whole clause, influenced, inter alia, by factors outside the verbal lexeme as such. That opened a new perspective: the opposition 'transitive vs. intransitive' was no longer analyzed as a clear-cut dichotomy, but rather as a scalar property that can be more or less expressed in a clause, depending on the values of certain semantic parameters. Various proposals were made regarding the exact nature of these parameters, such as the very extensive list presented in Lakoff (1977):

1) There is an agent who does something

2) There is a patient who undergoes a change to a new state

3) The change in the patient results from the action by the agent

4) The agent's action is volitional

5) The agent is in control of what he does

6) The agent is primarily responsible for what happens

7) The agent is the energy source in the action

8) There is a spacio-temporal overlap between the agent's action and the change in the patient

9) There is a single definite agent

10) There is a single definite patient

11) The agent uses his hands, body or some instrument

12) The change in the patient is perceptible

13) The agent perceives the change

and even

14) The agent is looking at the patient.[17]

The somewhat excessive granularity of this list blurs the general idea. A more targeted list of parameters is provided in the fundamental study of Hopper and Thompson (Hopper & Thompson 1980). Here, the cluster of features includes: the number of participants; kinesis (action); aspect (telicity vs. atelicity); punctuality; volitionality; polarity (affirmative or negative nexus); mode (realis vs. irrealis); agency; affectedness and individuation of the

---

17 Lakoff (1977:244).

object. Each parameter yields a scale on which clauses may rank higher or lower; the combinations of these parameters characterize clauses as more or less transitive.

There is a cardinal difference between this approach and the one in Lakoff (1977). Hopper and Thompson extend the repertory of the verbal features relevant for transitivity to include non-lexical ones, such as telicity, punctuality, mode and polarity. In doing so, they combine two lines of research that are usually separated. The first one (Verkuyl, 1972, 1993, 1999, Comrie, 1981, Tenny, 1987, 1994, Paducheva and Pentus 2008, Rothstein 2008, Borer 2005 and others) considers transitivity, along with other types of argument structuring, as a tool of grammatical (mainly, aspectual) construal of a clause.

The other line of research, on the contrary, explores transitivity as a lexical property. The arguments of a verb are ascribed semantic proto-roles of agent, patient, experiencer[18] etc. which are characterized in terms of volition, control and affectedness. It is studied, in what way specific configurations of these features determine the argument structure of a verb. Thus, Testelec (1998) argues that different combinations of control and affectedness in the two arguments yield a semantic classification of verbs closely corresponding to the formal *intransitive : middle : transitive* classification.[19] Along the same lines, Naess suggests that maximal distinction of participants with respect to the features of volition, control (in Naess' terms, instigation) and affectedness is the semantic trigger of syntactic transitivity.[20] Control and volition of the agent, affectedness of the patient together with the real mood and affirmative polarity of the verb are taken to constitute a prototype of transitivity, a limiting case which has the highest chances to be encoded by a syntactically transitive construction, if it exists in the language. (As was mentioned before, the universality of transitivity is hypothesized, but not yet proven.)

1.1.2 Prototypical transitive construction: definitions and problems

A notion of prototypical transitive construction (PTC) is a convenient instrument for identifying transitive patterns in languages of different morphosyntactic profile and / or different types of argument linking (ergative or nominative-accusative). The definitions of PTC can be either more empirical, or more generalized, but their application yields identical results. The empirical approach proposed – seemingly independently, – by Kozinsky in 1980 and Tsunoda in 1985 defines prototypically transitive verbs based on a specific class of meanings that assume transitive case frames in all languages. These are the verbs "which describe an action that not only impinges on the patient, but necessarily creates a change in it"[21], i.e., verbs of destruction, such as 'kill', 'destroy', 'break', 'bend'".[22] Recently, the same idea was advocated in Haspelmath (2015):

---

18 See the discussion in Dowty (1991).

19 Testelec (1998:44).

20 Naess (2007).

21 Tsunoda (1985:387).

22 Cf. Kozinsky: "… A small semantic class of verbs, viz. verbs of destruction and creation, is assumed to be transitive in its basic voice in all languages. Further, any verb which requires the same construction(s) as the verbs in the core class do, may be called transitive. " (Quoted from Testelec 1998:29).

"A verb is considered transitive if it contains an A and a P argument. A and P are defined as the arguments of a verb with at least two arguments that are coded like the 'breaker'and the 'broken thing' micro-roles of the 'break'".[23]

Once the transitive core class is thus identified, all the verbs using the same valency pattern are pronounced transitive.

In a generalized way, the same identification pattern is presented in Lazard (2002):

"A PROTOTYPICAL ACTION is an effective volitional discrete action performed by a controlling agent and actually affecting a well individuated patient. The MAJOR BIACTANT CONSTRUCTION, in any language, is the construction used to express a prototypical action.[24]"

Givón (1995) provides a list of basic features of any PTC, which, besides the lexical properties of volitionality and control, include grammatical parameters of aspect and modus.

"a. **Agent**: The prototypical transitive clause involves a volitional, controlling, actively initiating
agent who is responsible for the event, thus its **salient cause**.
b. **Patient**: The prototypical transitive event involves a non-volitional, inactive noncontrolling
patient who registers the event's changes-of-state, thus it has **salient effect**.
c. **Verbal modality**: The verb of the prototypical transitive clause codes an event that
is *compact* (non-durative), *bounded* (non-lingering), *sequential* (non-perfect) and
realis (non-hypothetical). The prototype transitive event is thus fast-paced, completed,
real, and **perceptually and/or cognitively salient**."[25]

The concept of the transitive prototype makes it possible to match syntactic alternations of a bivalent clause with their semantic proximity to the prototype or deviation from it, as with partitive case of direct objects in the imperfective aspect in Finnish (1) or genitive of negated transitive clauses in Russian (2).

(1)   a. Liikemies kirjotti   kirjeen   valiokunnalle.
        Businessman wrote   letter-ACC.   committee-to
        'The businessman wrote a letter to a committee.'

        b. Liikemies kirjotti   kirjettä   valiokunnalle.
        Businessman wrote   letter-PART.   committee-to
        'The businessman was writing a letter to a committee.'
        (Hopper and Thompson 1980:262)

---

23 Haspelmath (2015:5).
24 Lazard 2002:152
25 Givón 1995:76

(2)   a. Ja   chital   vashu   knigu.
       I   read-PST   your-ACC   book-ACC
       'I have read your book.'

       b. Ja   vashej   knigi   ne chital.
       I   your-GEN   book-GEN   not read-PST
       'I have not read your book.'

Conversely, it is somewhat more difficult to use the prototype theory to account for multiple verb classes that are compatible with transitive case frames, but do not match the semantic prototype. The claim is that all the non-prototypical transitive clauses are formed by analogy or, in Givón's wording, **metaphorical extension** of the transitive sense[26]. Metaphorical extension, according to Givón, covers verbs with a locative direct object ("enter the house'), locative direct object and implied patient ('feed the cows' = 'give food to the cows', 'they robbed her' = 'took something from her'), with a moving part of the subject ('kick'), with a dative-experiencer subject (verbs of cognition, sensation, volition), verbs with a reciprocal/ associative object ("He met Sylvia." – "He met with Sylvia."), the verb 'have', verbs with cognate objects ('sing a song'). However, the concept of metaphorical extension does not suffice to account for crosslinguistic systemic similarities and distinctions outside the core class, such as, e.g., invariably transitive alignment of possession-transfer verbs ('sell', 'lose' etc.).[27] Yet another weakness of the prototype theory is its inability to grasp the formal distinction between different surface-syntactic (active and passive) representations of a transitive event.

1.1.3 What does transitivity stand for?

Finally, it is easy to notice that the transitive prototype is a descriptive model, without any explanatory force.[28] Neither the list of transitivity parameters, nor the prototype theory provide any conceptual frame for the grammaticalization of the prototypical action. There is, as yet, no general agreement concerning the factors that could be responsible for the phenomenon of transitivity. Hopper and Thompson suggest that transitivity may be one of the strategies used for information structuring[29], perfective / transitive clauses being usually more rhematic (or foregrounding), than imperfective / intransitive ones. For Kittilä, morphosyntactic or structural transitivity is an iconic reflection of the ontological transitivity of events.[30] Næss, as has been mentioned above, takes the principle of the

---

26 Givón (1984:98).
27 See Testelets (1998:30).
28 Cf. Naess (2007:16).
29 Hopper & Thompson (1980:283 ff.).
30 Kittilä (2002:44 ff.): "Ontological transitivity (as for linguistic manifestation of transitivity) is best defined as our idea about different events in the non-linguistic world. Based on the recurrence of events, we are able to make generalizations about their relevant properties. Only the bare nature of events is relevant is this respect. This information is employed in the description of events and in the interpretation of constructions. The features of ontological transitivity are usually absolute in nature and the ontological information about the nature of events is common for all language users

maximum role distinction between the agent and the patient to be the superordinate semantic idea of transitivity.[31] Comparing valency alternations with TAM-splits, Tsunoda concludes that both phenomena belong to the domain of transitivity and are operated by the superordinate notion of effectiveness of the action.[32] For all their outward difference, the ideas of Næss and Tsunoda seem to point to one and the same thing: transitive structure serves to distinguish the agent as an effective performer of an action from the undergoer (patient) or experiencer.

A more profound version of the same idea has been suggested in DeLancey (1987). According to DeLancey, "the cluster of attributes associated with transitivity define a semantic construct which approximates the notion of EVENT as opposed to STATE".[33] Assuming now that the opposition is not binary, but scalar, it can be most closely defined as STATE vs. NON-STATE opposition. Indeed, the most salient semantic feature of an effective action is that it is not a state. To make my point, I shall briefly return to the list of transitivity parameters in Hopper & Thompson (1980).[34] As was first observed by Tsunoda, the ten parameters constituting this list are not equally relevant in triggering the transitive encoding[35], and what is more, none of them seems to be crucial for it.[36] One obvious exception from this principle seems to be the number of participants. Indeed, the point on which the parameter theory is most often criticized consists precisely in that it effectively includes the one-participant clauses into the scope of transitivity.[37] Moreover, Hopper and Thompson's hypothesis licences the view that one-argument constructions might be ascribed some degree of transitivity or even surpass in transitivity some less lucky bivalent constructions, given the univalents possessed more transitivity features. Lazard illustrates the awkwardness of such an analysis with the following examples:

(regardless of the language they speak). The absolute nature of these features means that we all are able to distinguish 'killing' from 'hearing' and we all agree on this distinction (provided that we behave rationally)." The idea seems to be unwarranted. The nature of events is not structured, it is our analysis that structures them, and the analysis is performed through linguistic means. Thus, we cannot witness anything like "a pure event of beating", we rather witness a sequence of situations that we can analyze as an event of beating. Saying 'John beat Harry' is only a specific way of reflecting the situation that could possibly be expressed in a series of intransitive clauses, such as 'John pushed hard', 'Harry fell to the ground' and so on. Kittilä's logic, therefore, seems to pull linguistic categories on the extra-linguistic reality. This shows, however, how deeply is the notion of transitivity rooted in our consciousness.

31 Næss (2007:22).
32 Tsunoda (1981:392 ff.).
33 DeLancey (1987:58).
34 To this list of parameters, one probably has to add that of tense. The past tense must be considered more transitive, than the non-past tense. This would explain such phenomena as the split causativity described in Kulikov (1999) or the Coptic data that shall be discussed below.
35 See Tsunoda (1985:386).
36 As stated, e.g., by DeLancey (1987:58) for Lhasa.
37 See, e.g., Tsunoda, Lazard (2002), Kittila (2007).

(3)   Susan left.

(4)   John likes beer.[38]

Whereas the second clause has only one feature of transitivity (2 participants), the first clause has four: it is active, telic, punctual and volitional. If one understands Hopper and Thompson's theory literally, it must follow that the first clause will enjoy transitive encoding with much more probability than the second one, which looks quite contrary to linguistic facts, at least, in the limits of the English grammar[39]. Lazard offers a solution for this problem suggesting that the two-participancy should rather be regarded as a basic condition of transitivity.[40]

Let us, however, assume that the analysis in Hopper & Thompson is more correct and that one-argument stative predicates belong to the domain of transitivity forming the negative pole of the transitivity scale. On the other pole, there would stand two-argument predicates denoting a causation of a certain change in the patient.[41] The patient-like argument can be regarded as the measure of the non-stativity of the predication. Under such view, transitivity is one of the instruments that are used to denote the temporary, non-permanent character of the nexus.

Unlike the prototype theory, this view is clearly based on a grammatical constant, the difference between states and non-states being a universal one. Moreover, it does not prescribe any *a priori* features to the transitive model, but it can explain some features of the prototype, such as volitionality or control. As observed by Vendler, states are treated in the language as non-volitional predicates, or to put it more precisely, the semantic component of volition is neutralized for states:

> "When I say that I could run if my legs were not tied, I do not imply that I would run if my legs were not tied. On the other hand, there is a sense of "can" in which "He could know the answer if he had read Kant" does mean that in that case he would know the answer. Similarly, in an obvious sense, to say that I could like her if she were not selfish is to say that I would like her if she were not selfish. One feels something strange in "Even if I could like her, I would not like her". It appears, therefore, that in conditionals "could" is often interchangeable with "would" in connection with states. For the same reason, "can" might become redundant in indicative sentences of this kind. Hence the airy feeling about "I can know", "I can love", "I can like" and so forth."[42]

Thus, the feature of volitionality is a contrastive feature in the opposition of a stative and a non-stative predicate. Such conclusion is but a paraphrase of DeLancey's idea

---

38 Lazard (2002:178).

39 As shown in Hopper and Thompson (1980:268 ff.), the data of ergative languages confirm their analysis.

40 Lazard (2002:180).

41 Cf. Testelets (1998:33): "The purest case of an Agent with no characteristics of a Patient is probably that participant of many-place predicates which is linked to them via the causative relation and bears no other relation of a more specific kind."

42 Vendler (1957:148).

that volitionality is an inalienable part of the causative semantics and as such enters the cognitive scheme of CAUSE and EFFECT expressed in transitive constructions.[43]

At the level of parts of speech, the scale STATE-> ACTION would probably equal the spontaneity scale of verbs (3), from passives (or, in Haspelmath's term, agentful) and unaccusatives through unergatives and transitives to causatives.

The spontaneity scale (from Haspelmath 2016)

transitive	>	unergative	>	automatic	>	costly	>	agentful
('cut')		('talk')		('freeze (intr.)')		('break (intr.)')		('be cut')

<—— more causatives   more anticausatives ——>

But one might as well suggest a broader view which would include in this stativity-activity scale also nominal, adjectival and adverbial predicates as denoting qualities and permanent, stable and temporary states.[44] A continuum leading from the most stable nexus to the least stable one could look as follows: he is a doctor -> he is young -> he is in denial -> he is sleeping -> he is reading a book -> he broke the glass.

An example from Chukchee (Mel'čuk 1993) may serve as an illustration of the link between intransitivity and stativization.

(5)   a. Γəm-nan tə-ret-ərkən-ø kimitʔ- ə n (tom-etə).
       I-INSTR 1SG.SUB-transport-PRES-3SG.OBJ load-SG.NOM friend-SG/PL.DAT
       'I [= I] transport a-load [= II] (to-friend(s) [= III])': I actually do this.

       b. Γəm-ø t-ine-ret-ərkən (kimitʔ-e) (tom-etə).
       I-NOM 1SG.SUB-'antipassive'-transport-PRES load-SG.INSTR friend-SG/PL.DAT
       'I [= I] transport (a-load [= II]) (to-friend(s) [= III])': I am a transporter (this is my occupation).

(5a) is a transitive / ergative clause with the nominative direct object. The antipassive marker in the example (5b) lowers the syntactic rank of the second argument, it becomes an indirect object, whereas the initial ergative subject ('I') changes the case to nominative / absolutive. The change in the surface structure brings about the change in the meaning. The initially active predicate ("I am transporting") is reinterpreted as a permanent state ("I am a transporter of loads").[45]

Understanding transitivity as a mechanism of the (non-)stative characterization of the predicate, it is easy to see why aspect is one of its crucial components and is taken by

---

43 DeLancey (1987:61 ff.).
44 Cf. Nedjalkov & Jaxontov (1988:3): "It is assumed here that actions (e.g., 'to build', 'to break'), states (e.g., 'to stand', 'to be broken'), and qualities (e.g., 'to be long', 'to be kind') are the basic types of predicated properties irrespective of the formal means of their expression in individual languages." See also Wunderlich (2006).
45 Mel'čuk (1993:35).

some researchers (e.g., Tenny 1994) to be the decisive factor in (in)transitive encoding. Indeed, various alternations of transitivity are directly bound to the aspectual properties of the predicate. So, as has been suggested by Verkuyl (1972 et al.), for some groups of verbs, a specific object may characterize the clause as telic (6a), whereas a bare plural noun determines the atelic interpretation (6b):

(6a)   Joan ate an apple.

(6b)   Joan ate apples.

Another case of interdependence between the aspect and the form of the object may be illustrated by (7a,b):

(7a)   Taylor ate the apricot.

(7b)   Taylor ate at the apricot.

The above examples display homomorphism from the spatial extent of the second participant to the temporal progress of the event it participates in. The terms 'incremental theme'[46] and 'incremental theme verbs' are applied to objects and verbs that allow for such homomorphism, respectively. As the above examples show, the contrast between the transitive and the intransitive structure corresponds to the difference in semantics: the transitive pattern denotes an accomplished action, whereas the intransitive pattern denotes an action with an unspecified outcome.

In both situations of (6) and in (7a), the object appears to be a quantificator of the event (in Borer's term, "subject-of-quantity"[47]). This provides us with the important characteristics of a transitive pattern. To put it quite simply, transitive pattern does not tell us HOW the object is affected, but about HOW MUCH it is affected. While different semantic roles of non-patient participants, e.g., benefactive, instrument, source and so on, are signaled by cases and/or prepositions with their own range of meanings, the patient-valency tends to be the least morphologically marked (at times being coded just by immediate adjacency, as in Nivkh, Hebrew or Coptic) and semantically charged.[48]

This 'orthogonal to semantics' role of the non-agent participant in a transitive clause is probably the factor ensuring this pattern's overwhelming frequency and productivity throughout languages. It would not seem improbable, - though I am not aware of any statistical study to that purpose, - if transitive verbs would prove to constitute the majority of the verbal lexicon in most languages. The productivity of the transitive pattern also depends on its property to form a causative counterpart to non-causatives, sometimes by morphological derivation (e.g., German 'be'-prefix word formation), sometimes by

---

46 See Dowty (1991) etc.

47 See Borer (2005).

48 Cf. Testelec (1998:32): "Much work has been done to characterize the role of Agent explicitly... By contrast, I am aware of no convincing semantic definition of the role of Patient, i.e., of the most affected argument of a verb... Agent, or Instrument, or Benefactive are semantic roles which are the same or similar with different verb predicates, whereas Patient semantics cannot be generalized but is rather a role installed individually by every particular verb."

creating a labile use for a previously non-causative verb (e.g., spoken Russian "гулять собаку" 'walk the dog', "меня улыбнуло" 'it has smiled me', Spanish "lo desapareció el Estado" 'The State has 'disappeared' him'). Frequency, productivity, transparency, autonomy, and naturalness are the properties often invoked for defining prototypical syntactic transitivity.[49]

Thus, there is every reason to treat transitivity as a universal grammatical category understanding it as a manifestation of the STATE vs. NON-STATE character of the predicate through the argument linking pattern. Crucially, transitive diagnostics is not confined to the morphologically marked passive voice or the differential flagging of agents and patients, the factors that are irrelevant for an analytic language, such as Coptic. Rather, a valency pattern with two core arguments demonstrating some correlation with the individuation features of the non-agentive argument, correlation with tense-aspect-mood categories of the verb, semantic transparency, frequency, and productivity should be regarded as *bona fide* transitive.

1.1.4 Transitivity alternations; anticausatives; resultatives

Whereas the above-mentioned secondary symptoms help in identifying a transitive pattern, an even more important feature, in fact, the hallmark of a transitive verb is that it can undergo diathesis alternations. The term '**diathesis**', introduced in Xolodovič (1970), refers to the possible patterns of mapping the semantic arguments of the verb (agent, patient, goal etc.) onto syntactic functions (subject, object etc.).[50] Different diathetic patterns are represented, for instance, in

(8a)   He cooked soup for the homeless.
(8b)   He cooked for the homeless.

(9a)   The blast of wind broke the window.
(9b)   The window broke.

(10a) You rub the body with mud.
(10b) You rub mud on the body.

Diathetic distinctions may or may not be morphologically marked on the verb. Grammatical voice, such as Ancient Greek middle-passive τέμνει ~ τέμνεται 'cuts ~ is being cut' can be defined as diathetic distinctions marked in verbal morphology.[51] As our examples show, in the absence of morphological marking, diathesis may be expressed through syntactic means, such as word order.

---

49 Cf. Winters (1990).
50 Xolodovič (1970:13), cf. Mel'čuk (1993).
51 Mel'čuk, I., Xolodovič, A. (1970:117).

One salient feature of the transitive class is a specific diathesis alternation that involves the syntactic promotion of the patient and the demotion or elimination of the agent.[52] The ensuing intransitive clause may belong to one of the four following types:

Passive *stricto sensu*: the original agent becomes a peripheral argument and may be either realized as an oblique object, or omitted:

(11) Η δήλωση υπογράφηκε από όλους τους συμμετέχοντες
      i dhilosi ipoghrafike apo olus tus simetexondes
      the.NOM statement.NOM sign.NACT.PAST.PRFV.3SG by all the participants
      'The statement was signed by all the participants'

Middle (Dixon & Aikhenvald's 'agentless passive'): the original agent is implied, but not specified:

(12) Αυτό το βιβλίο διαβάζεται πολύ ευχάριστα
      afto to vivlio dhiavazete poli efxarista
      this.NOM the.NOM book.NOM read.NACT.PRES.3SG very pleasantly
      'This book reads very pleasantly'

Noncausal (Anticausative): there is no agent stated or implied, the event is conceived as spontaneous:[53]

(13) Η πόρτα άνοιξε ξαφνικά
      i porta anikse ksafnika
      the.NOM door.NOM open.ACT.PAST.PRFV.3SG suddenly
      'The door opened suddenly'[54]

Statal passive / objective resultative: the state reached by the patient as a result of the core event, irrespective of there being an agent implied, or not.

(14) Окно разбито
      okno razbito
      window.NOM break.PAST.PRFV.PRTCP.NOM
      'The window is broken'

The above diathesis types share a number of common features: each type relates to the corresponding transitive structure as effect to cause; all of them involve valency reduction, with Agent suppressed and Patient promoted to the subject position.[55] The functional overlap between these categories results in them often sharing the same morphological

---

52 The list does not include the reflexive and the reciprocal diathesis, since they are not agent-suppressive. The term 'middle' is not unproblematic, but it will not be play any role in the subsequent discussion concerning Coptic and is mentioned here for the sake of exhaustiveness only.

53 Cf. Dixon & Aikhenvald (2000:7).

54 The exx. (11) through (13) are taken from Lavidas (2009:19).

55 This formula captures prototypical traits of passive; as shown in Abraham (2006), languages vary with respect to specific parameters of passive structures.

marking[56] which is why they remained undetected for a long time, subsumed under the cover notion of passive. In particular, anticausative and resultative were not recognized by grammarians until the recent works of Leningrad / St. Petersburg typological school (Nedjalkov & Sil'nickij 1969, Nedjalkov & Jaxontov 1988 and others). The grammatical and semantic properties of these categories, as well as the distinctions between them and passive, are far from being clearly grasped, let alone finalized, but since both notions are indispensable for the correct grammatical analysis, I shall try to briefly summarize the most essential properties of each.

The term '**anticausative**' can be employed in a narrower sense based on semantics and morphology, or in a broader, purely semantic sense.[57] As a morphological term, it refers to intransitive verbal forms that are derived from the corresponding causatives by means of a decausativizing morpheme, as *aç-il-di* in (15):

(15) Turkish Annem   kapi-yi   aç-ti
            Mother   door-ACC   open-PAST
            "My mother opened the door"
            Kapi   aç-**il**-di
            Door   open-ANTICAUS-PAST
            "The door opened" (Haspelmath 1987)

In this sense, the term is conceived as a structural counterpart to **causative verbs** where the valency increase is marked by a causativizing affix, e.g., Estonian *-ta-* (*õppida* 'learn' / *õpetama* 'teach', *kasvama* 'grow (intr.)', *kasvatama* 'grow (tr.)').

Understood semantically, anticausative denotes any verb (or verbal form) which fulfills three conditions:

1) the anticausative verb X has a synthetic counterpart X_1, such that the meaning of X_1 is [to CAUSE X];

2) X denotes an event that occurs spontaneously, without an agent implied;[58]

3) the subject of X has the semantic role of *patient*.

It is evident that the semantic definition of anticausatives comprises a larger number of verb classes, than just morphological anticausatives. In fact, the [CAUSE – EFFECT] relation between the members of *anticausative~causative* pairs may have different morphological realizations across the languages. Following the classification introduced in Nedjalkov & Sil'nickij (1969), typologists distinguish between directed and non-directed causativity

---

56 Cf. Haspelmath (1987:30): "… there are quite a number of languages in which one and the same morpheme has reflexive, anticausative and passive meaning. In other language, the morpheme has only reflexive and anticausative meaning (German, Qechua, Nivkh…), and yet in other languages it has only anticausative and passive meaning… There do not seem to be any languages in which one morpheme has reflexive and passive meaning, but no anticausative meaning."

57 On the necessary differentiation of the two meanings see Haspelmath (1987), 2.2.

58 See Comrie (1985:326): "Passive and anticausative differ in that, even where the former has no agentive phrase, the existence of some person or thing bringing about the situation is implied, whereas the anti causative is consistent with the situation coming about spontaneously."

alternations. Directed alternations are further divided into causative and anticausative alternations, where one of the alternants is morphologically derived from the other one by means of a causativizing or decausativizing morpheme. Both causative and anticausative types of alternation have been instantiated above.

The non-directed alternations fall into three different types, equipollent, suppletive and labile. According to Haspelmath (1993), "in **equipollent** alternations, both are derived from the same stem which expresses the basic situation, by means of different affixes (16a), different auxiliary verbs (16b), or different stem modifications (16c)."[59]

> (16)   a. Japanese atum-aru 'gather (intr.)'
>   atum-eru 'gather (tr.)'
>   b. Hindi-Urdu šuruu honaa 'begin (intr.)'
>   šuruu karnaa 'begin (tr.)'
>   c. Lithuanian lūžti 'break (intr.)'
>   laužti 'break (tr.)'

Further on, in **suppletive** alternations, the causal opposition is represented by different stems, as in:

> (17)   Russian goret' 'burn' (intr.) ~ žeč 'burn' (trans.)

Finally, in **labile** alternations, one and the same verbal lexeme can be used in both causal and noncausal sense, without any formal change. That type of causative alternation is characteristic of Coptic verbal grammar.

Finding a common semantic denominator of the whole anticausative class and proposing strict criteria for distinguishing morphologically marked anticausatives from passives is as yet an unsolved problem.[60] The crucial distinction is that anticausative verbs denote processes that are spontaneous (Comrie, Haspelmath), occur without a volitional intervention of an agent (Levin & Rappaport Hovav 1995:102), tend to increase the entropy (Kulikov 1998:147 ff.). The absence of an 'agent-oriented meaning component'[61] rules out the use of an agentive prepositional phrase or agent-oriented adverbs (e.g., "on purpose") with anticausative predicates. On the contrary, an intransitive predicate modified by an adverb with the sense of '*sua sponte*' is usually anticausative.

The above criteria, however, are not universally applicable, neither do they always yield unambiguous results. The adverbial modifiers are so infrequent that one cannot possibly use them for anticausative diagnostics in dead languages. Further on, the prepositional phrase introducing agent in passive can cover other meanings, as well, often instrumental. Thus, if present, it does not always denote an agent; yet the absence of such phrase does not necessarily mean that no agent has been implied. Morphological marking is not decisive, either. As stated in Kulikov (1998:141), some languages use the same marking for both categories, and in languages with different marking, the distinction is not carried out in a systematic way. Finally, the semantic definitions are too vague to rely upon.

---

59 Haspelmath (1993:91 ff.).
60 See Kulikov (1998:140 ff.).
61 Haspelmath (1993:92 ff.).

Nevertheless, the two categories must be set apart in an accurate grammatical analysis. One reason for that is their unequal distribution: whereas every transitive verb can be passivized, the causative / anticausative alternation is available for a subset of the transitive class only.[62] Even more importantly, the TAM behavior of anticausative verbs may differ from that of passive forms. Though this topic is as yet largely unexplored, it seems that, at least in some languages, anticausatives behave as an eventive form, whereas passives are aspect-neutral. This issue will be addressed in some detail in the section 3.5.3.3 of the present work.

In order to avoid terminological confusion, I shall henceforth follow M. Haspelmath's proposal in using the terms '**causal**' and '**noncausal**' for the respective members of a semantic causativity alternation.[63] This definition of 'noncausal' applies to any semantic entity that has a causal correlate. Thus, our notion of 'noncausal' comprises also passive meanings. Where it will be necessary to maintain the distinction between the anticausative and passive semantics, I shall use the respective terms.

Anticausatives form a subset of the **unaccusative**[64] class of intransitive verbs. An unaccusative verb (e.g., 'fall', 'burn', 'languish', 'trip', 'collapse') is a univalent verb whose syntactic subject is semantically a patient. Unaccusatives are contrasted to **unergative** verbs ('dance', 'work', 'call') that predicate volitional actions of an agent subject. In Coptic, as in many other languages, this semantic difference has far-reaching syntactic implications.

It is easy to see that unaccusatives share two properties of anticausative verbs, namely, they denote a spontaneous action affecting the patient subject. However, the notion of unaccusative is broader since it does not imply the existence of a causative counterpart. Thus, Levin & Rappaport Hovav (1995, section 3.3) have convincingly shown that languages usually do not have any synthetic causative for the unaccusative verbs of existence and appearance.[65] The term 'anticausative' is convenient to use when discussing valency alternations of a causative verb, whereas 'unaccusative' usually applies to lexical classes.

The term '**resultative**' refers to a verbal form used to denote a state resulting from a previous action or implying a previous event.[66] The subject of resultative may be co-referential with various participants of the core event, yielding different diathetic types of resultative. The two basic types are subjective and objective resultative, where the subject of resultative corresponds to the subject or the object of the underlying clause, respectively. The objective resultative is only derived from transitive verbs and involves the change in diathesis identical to that of passive: the agent is demoted, the patient subjectivized. This results in the partial intersection of functions between resultative and passive: statal passive is frequently combined with resultative, being used to express the

---

62 I refer the reader to the thorough discussion in Haspelmath (1987:13 ff.).
63 Haspelmath (2016:37).
64 For details, see Perlmutter (1978).
65 Interestingly, Coptic might be an example to the contrary: the labile verb ογωνϩ ⲉⲃⲟⲗ has both the anticausative reading 'appear' and the causative reading 'reveal'.
66 Nedjalkov & Jaxontov (1988:6).

result of a previous action, or is interchangeable with it, with a very slight change in meaning.[67] Further on, both are contrasted to actional passive: referring to one and the same situation, actional and statal passive stress different temporal planes of that situation. Actional passive emphasizes the action that preceded and caused the observed state, statal passive / resultative is focused on the resulting state itself. Accordingly, objective resultative / statal passive may formally differ from actional passive, as in German (18a), or may be identical with it, as in English (18b).

(18)   a. Der Brief war bereits versiegelt, aber ich kann nicht sagen, von wem er versiegelt wurde.
        b. The letter was already sealed, but I cannot say by whom it was sealed.

It is suggested that there may exist a genetic relation between resultative and passive, resultative being an older category.[68] Thus, Arkadiev (2018) suggests a graduate transition from resultative through statal passive to actional passive by means of adverbial extensions with temporal or instrumental meaning, or alternatively by intercalation of an inceptive verb, such as English 'get' or German 'werden'. Such path of "dynamicization" (to use Arkadiev's term) of resultative is instantiated in German, Baltic, and Slavic languages.

(19)   a. Gestern noch war dort ein Schild angebracht. (resultative)
           'Yesterday, a signboard was still attached there.'
        b. Gestern noch wurde dort ein Schild angebracht. (actional passive)
           'Only yesterday someone attached a signboard there.'

In the grammar of Coptic, the term 'resultative' is sometimes applied to the form known as 'stative'.[69] The two notions are very close, indeed, yet with a difference between them which is most accurately described in Nedjalkov & Jaxontov (1988): "…The stative expresses a state of a thing without any implication of its origin, while the resultative expresses both a state and the preceding action it has resulted from."[70]

1.2 Transitivity in Coptic: previous research

The necessity to revise the notion of transitivity before applying it to the Coptic grammar is due to the remarkable lack of agreement on that issue among the linguists of Coptic. The disagreement stems not so much from different understanding of the observable linguistic data, as from the barely comparable ways of systematizing this data. Depending on the method of defining transitivity, the attempted approaches can be loosely divided into pure lexico-semantic (Steindorff, Till, Spiegelberg, recently Layton), formal syntactical (Crum, Jernstedt, Polotsky, Shisha-Halevy, Engsheden), diachronic-syntactical (Stern, recently Reintges), and formalized semantic ones (Grossmann). An important methodological distinction (not always explicitly stated) is whether transitivity is regarded as a property

---

67 Nedjalkov & Jaxontov (1988:45 ff.).
68 Nedjalkov & Jaxontov (1988:49).
69 See Reintges (2011), Haspelmath (2015b).
70 Nedjalkov & Jaxontov (1988:6).

of a verbal lexeme (as in Till, Layton, partly Polotsky) or as a property of a specific valency construction (Jernstedt 1986, Crum). Since none of the approaches has proven to be convincing enough, the valid definition of Coptic transitive pattern still remains a matter of personal preference, though in nearly all the recent work on the topic (Layton's Grammar excepted), the label of 'transitive' refers to the alternation of immediate object attachment and <ⲛ-/ⲙⲙⲟ=>-pattern. Below I shall briefly address the main difficulties that arise from applying the transitivity theory to Coptic.

1.2.1 Semantic equivalents to Indo-European transitive verbs use different valency patterns in Coptic

The lexico-semantic approach is characterized by the initial presupposition that transitivity is an inherent property of a verbal lexeme as a semantic unit. For the first authors of Coptic grammars, this idea was so self-evident that the usefulness of the notions 'direct object' or 'accusative' for Coptic was never questioned; moreover, these authors obviously did not see any need to theoretically justify the grammatical choices they made. The procedure of selecting transitive valency patterns thus consisted in determining semantically transitive verb classes and listing their valences. In this selection, the Coptologists seem to have been guided by their sense of language which was based on the transitive pattern distribution in their native European language, i.e., German or French.[71] Since there is no one-to-one match between the inventory of the European transitives and the inventory of Coptic mutable or, broader, ⲛ-governing verbs (the most obvious difference being the verbs of perception which are mostly transitive in European languages, but immutable and ⲉ-governing in Coptic), the result of this selection was a set of 'accusative' prepositions, slightly different for each author. Thus, Steindorff relates the notion of the direct object (or 'accusative object') to the following three valency options:

1) Immediate object attachment pattern (henceforth IP) with the object immediately following one of the construct forms of the infinitive (*status constructus* or *status pronominalis*, respectively)

2) ⲛ- (ⲙⲙⲟ=) valency pattern

3) ⲉ- (ⲉⲣⲟ=) valency pattern[72]

The last subgroup is further specified by Steindorff as containing verbs of sensual perception (ⲛⲁⲩ 'see', ϭⲱϣⲧ 'watch', ⲥⲱⲧⲙ̄ 'hear, listen', ϣⲱⲗⲙ̄ 'smell' etc.), verbs of speech (ⲙⲟⲩⲧⲉ 'call', ⲥⲙⲟⲩ 'bless', ⲥⲁϩⲟⲩ 'curse') and a group without any common semantic denominator (ⲕⲓⲙ 'move', ϩⲓⲟⲩⲉ 'hit', ϫⲣⲟ 'win', equivalent to German 'besiegen'). It is pretty obvious that this selection of transitive lexemes is conditioned not so much by Coptic grammatical facts, as by aligning Coptic verbal inventory to the grammar of German.

Till, in his 'Koptische Grammatik', applies the same method even more generously:

---

71 Cf. Jernstedt (1986:399).
72 Steindorff 1904:165-167

"Bei bestimmten Verben wird das direkte Objekt mittelst der Präposition ε-, εϥο= bezeichnet. … Manche Verba können das Objekt mit ⲛ- oder mit ε- bezeichnen… Seltener werden die Präpositionen ⲛⲥⲁ-/ ⲛⲥⲱ= (wörtl. 'nach') und ϩⲁ-/ ϩⲁⲣⲟ= (wörtl. 'unter') verwendet, wo wir ein direktes Objekt haben."[73]

More recent treatises on transitivity, such as Layton's grammar, abandon this intuitive method of grammatical assortment, but not the idea that transitivity is a semantic property of a verbal lexeme and goes beyond any specific valency pattern in Coptic. In particular, Layton suggests the following definition of a transitive lexeme:

"'*Transitive*' infinitives are those which at the speaker's choice can be constructed so as to express action directed at a '*direct object*', i.e., at a receiver or goal of action."[74]

Based on meaning alone, this definition clearly is not meant to make any distinctions between various two-argument valency patterns: there are few types of the second core argument that cannot be interpreted as a receiver or a goal of an action.[75] To illustrate his point, Layton provides examples of 'transitive constructions' with the prepositions ⲛ-, ε-, ⲛⲥⲁ-:

(20)   Matt. 2:11 ⲁ-ⲩ-ⲛⲁⲩ **ε-ⲡϣⲏⲣⲉ** ϣⲏⲙ… ⲁⲩ-ⲟⲩⲱⲛ **ⲛ-ⲛⲉⲩⲁϩⲱⲱⲣ**
       '*They saw the child… They opened their treasures*'

(21)   Matt. 2:13 ϩⲏⲣⲱⲇⲏⲥ ⲅⲁⲣ ⲛⲁ-ϣⲓⲛⲉ **ⲛⲥⲁ-ⲡ-ϣⲏⲣⲉ** ϣⲏⲙ
       '*Herod is about to search for the child*'

Layton further states that "each transitive infinitive has its own particular preposition(s) that mark objects", setting apart the sub-class of mutable infinitives that "under certain conditions" allow the direct object to be immediately suffixed to the infinitive instead of being mediated by a preposition. But equating in such a way transitivity with bivalency, Layton does not only deprive the notion of transitivity of any sense. He also commits a huge 'oversmoothing' of the Coptic valency and diathesis grammar ignoring such significant properties of ⲛ-governing verbs as the capacity for differential object marking and valency reduction.[76] (For instance, whereas ⲟⲩⲟⲛϩ ⲉⲃⲟⲗ can mean both 'show' and 'appear' and ⲙⲟⲩϩ both 'fill' and 'be filled', it is impossible to find the verb ϩⲁⲣⲉϩ with the 'guarded' patient encoded as a subject, or ⲛⲁⲩ as a predicate to something 'seen'.) Hence, this method fully merits the reproach addressed by Jernstedt to its predecessors, namely

---

73 Till 1955:129-130
74 Layton (2004:127).
75 Eventually, such a broad definition would include even a recipient, which makes it *a priori* rather infelicitous.
76 On DOM in Coptic see Engsheden (2006), (2008), (2017). According to my observation (yet to be tested), the IP /ⲛ- (ⲙⲙⲟ=)- valency pattern is the only valency pattern compatible with the zero-article of the *nomen rectum*.

that being useful for didactic purposes, they still should be discarded as blurring important grammatical distinctions and preventing any meaningful systematization of data.[77]

Condemning the purely semantic view on the issue of transitive valency as dysfunctional in terms of grammatical description, Jernstedt, in his 'Study on Verbal Government', advocates a more formal approach[78]. He supports his choice of the pattern with the following criteria: the syntactic parallelism between the <ɴ-/ммо=>-pattern and Indo-European accusative patterns, the relative frequency of this pattern compared to other argument structure patterns of Coptic and, finally, its analogy to the direct object pattern in Semitic languages where one observes a similar alternation between the immediate and the prepositional object attachment through the *'nota accusativi'*.[79] Probably for reasons related to scientific communication problems, Jernstedt's arguments never became widely known or followed.

1.2.2 No uniform morphosyntactic passive in Coptic

As mentioned in 1.1, a significant trait of transitive verb usually is its markedness for voice. Voice is usually defined as an inflectional category that changes the diathesis of a verb without changing its propositional meaning[80]. More specifically, by means of a morphological alternation, passive voice allows to change the syntactic representation of semantic actants, so that *patiens* acquires grammatical characteristics of the subject, while *agens* is demoted to the position of an oblique object. Thus, logically, passivization should not bring any changes to such properties of the denoted action, as its aspect or tense:

(22)   a. The mourners have brought Mugabe's body home.

b. Mugabe's body has been brought home by the mourners.

c. The parents are beating the child.

d. The child is being beaten by the parents.

In Coptic, as stated by Shisha-Halevy,[81] there exists no single, unambiguous, and regular passive construction. The closest equivalent is the impersonal passive construction with a non-referential 3rd plural subject а-ɣ-coтπ=ч 'he was chosen' (lit., "they have chosen

---

77 Cf Jernstedt (1986:399): "Obviously, this kind of terminology is possible only as long, as the author aims at writing a practical grammar, not having the least intention of undertaking a thorough investigation which would most probably free him from the elementary biases and change his whole approach to the issue." (Translation- N.S.)

78 Jernstedt (1986: 398-399): "When defining the notion of the direct complement (object) in Coptic, I think it advisable to be guided almost exclusively by purely formal criteria, since the semantic criterion is too broad to define any such specific content of the term, as could be conveniently used in research. Judging by semantics alone, it would be equally justified to apply the term "direct object" not only to the above-mentioned <ɴ-/ммо=>, but also to the <e-/epo=> and several other prepositional phrases. For both ммо= and epo= imply a similar mode of the object's affectedness by the action" (translation – N.S.).

79 Jernstedt (1986:400).

80 As, e.g., in Geniušienė (2006:31).

81 Shisha-Halevy (1986:107, § 3.0.1.1).

him"), with or without the prepositional phrase ⲉⲃⲟⲗ ϩⲓⲧⲛ-, introducing the agent. But whereas semantically this construction resembles the canonical European passive clauses (the agent can be demoted, and the patient topicalized), the surface structure of the verbal phrase is identical to that of a regular active predicate in the respective tense / modus. Moreover, being syntactically active, the impersonal construction is not distinctive of the transitive pattern, but can be used with any non-monadic verb, e.g.,

(23)   Shen.Can. 6, Leipoldt (1954:43, 5)

ⲉⲩⲣ ⲙⲛⲧⲣⲉ ϩⲁⲣⲟϥ ⲉⲃⲟⲗ ϩⲓⲧⲛ ⲛⲉⲧⲟⲩⲏϩ ⲧⲏⲣⲟⲩ ϩⲛ ⲛⲉⲓⲥⲩⲛⲁⲅⲱⲅⲏ

'Him being witnessed by all who gathered in these synagogues…'

Finally, neither the use of the agentive complement, which otherwise may denote a source or an instrument, nor obviously the use of 3rd plural subject is confined to the impersonal passive construction. On the above grounds, Shisha-Halevy claims the impersonal construction to be "a passive-surrogate" or translation equivalent, not a true passive transform".[82] Largely the same view is held by Layton[83] and Reintges[84]. Importantly, the semantic bleaching of the formal pronominal subject shows that the construction underwent a certain degree of grammaticalization, which is all the more obvious, when the clause contains both the subject and the agentive prepositional phrase. Yet, it principally differs from the canonical passive in that it does not change the diathesis of the core verb.

Another Coptic passive equivalent is stative, a verbal form confined to the durative conjugation. As observed in Reintges (2004), this form is close in meaning to English adjectival passives which name a state or condition without necessarily implying an agent,[85] as in '*the air in the room was stuffed*'. In Nedjalkov's terms, this state can be either primary, or secondary, i.e., conceived as a result of a previous event. The first meaning is typical for the statives of intransitive verbs, such as ⲥⲣϥⲉ 'be at leisure'[86]:

---

82 Shisha-Halevy 1986:106, footnote 6.

83 Layton (2011:135-136, §175).

84 Reintges (2004:226).

85 Reintges (2004:228).

86 Such primary states (and not resultatives) are also the statives of the verbs of motion. This is explicitly stated in Polotsky (1957: 230): "… bei den Verben der Bewegung bezeichnet das Qualitativ keineswegs den erreichten Zustand, sondern die im Vollzug, im Fortgang, befindliche Bewegung. Es bedeutet also 'ϯⲃⲏⲕ' "ich gehe", nicht etwa "ich bin weggegangen und (schon) fort"; ϯϩⲏⲩ "ich falle, πίπτω"… nicht "ich bin gefallen und liege da, πέπτωκα". Common for primary and secondary states, i.e., for statives and resultatives is the non-terminative time schema (in Vendler's terms). The difference is that resultative implies an already terminated action, while stative presents the action itself as non-terminative: 2Sam 3:29 ⲁⲩⲱ ⲉⲣⲉ ⲛⲁⲓ ⲛⲁⲉⲓ ⲉϩⲣⲁⲓ ⲉⲝⲛ ⲧⲁⲡⲉ ⲛⲓⲱⲁⲃ … ⲛϥⲧⲉⲙⲱⲝⲛ ⲉⲃⲟⲗ ϩⲙ ⲡⲏⲓ ⲛⲓⲱⲁⲃ ⲉϥϫⲁϩⲙ ⲁⲩⲱ ⲉϥⲥⲟⲃϩ ⲉϥⲁⲙⲁϩⲧⲉ ⲛⲟⲩⲟⲩⲣⲁⲥ ⲁⲩⲱ **ⲉϥϩⲏⲩ** ϩⲛ ⲧⲥⲏϥⲉ ⲁⲩⲱ ⲉϥⲣϭⲣⲱϩ ⲛⲟⲉⲓⲕ
καταντησάτωσαν ἐπὶ κεφαλὴν Ιωαβ … καὶ μὴ ἐκλίποι ἐκ τοῦ οἴκου Ιωαβ γονορρυὴς καὶ λεπρὸς καὶ κρατῶν σκυτάλης καὶ **πίπτων** ἐν ῥομφαίᾳ καὶ ἐλασσούμενος ἄρτοις
"May it fall upon the head of Joab …, and may the house of Joab never be without one who has a discharge or who is leprous or who holds a spindle or **who falls** by the sword or who lacks bread!"

(24) Exod 5:8

ⲁⲩⲱ ⲧⲁⲡⲥ ⲛⲧⲱⲃⲉ ⲉⲧⲏⲡ ⲉϣⲁⲩⲧⲁⲙⲓⲟⲥ ⲉϣⲁⲩⲧⲁⲙⲓⲟⲥ ⲙⲙⲏⲛⲉ ⲉⲕⲉⲛⲟⲭⲥ ⲉϩⲣⲁⲓ ⲉϫⲱⲟⲩ ⲛⲛⲉⲕϥⲓ ⲗⲁⲁⲩ ⲉⲃⲟⲗ ⲛϩⲏⲧⲟⲩ **ⲥⲉⲥⲣⲟϥⲧ** ⲅⲁⲣ

καὶ τὴν σύνταξιν τῆς πλινθείας, ἧς αὐτοὶ ποιοῦσιν καθ᾽ ἑκάστην ἡμέραν, ἐπιβαλεῖς αὐτοῖς, οὐκ ἀφελεῖς οὐδέν· **σχολάζουσιν** γάρ·

'*But the number of bricks that they made in the past you shall impose on them, you shall by no means reduce it, for **they are idle**.*'

Transitive verbs, such as ⲧⲁⲗϭⲟ 'heal', on the contrary, often yield a resultative reading in stative:

(25) Matt. 15:31

ⲉⲩⲛⲁⲩ ⲉⲛϭⲁⲗⲉ ⲉⲩⲙⲟⲟϣⲉ ⲙⲛ ⲛϭⲁⲛⲁϩ ⲉⲩⲧⲁⲗϭⲏⲩ

'*When they saw the mute speaking, the crippled healthy (lit.: healed)*'

In 1.1.4, it has been shown that the functions of objective resultative and statal passive partly overlap. Yet, the question whether the Coptic stative must be termed a passive form, is not uncontroversial for Coptologists. For Till, the aspectual limitation of this form was an argument against equating it with passive, since in his opinion, only eventive forms are passive. In his review of Till's Coptic grammar, Polotsky considers this argument invalid and claims that the stative of transitive verbs is to be regarded as a passive form on account of the diathetic shift between this form and the corresponding infinitive:

"Bei transitiven Verben... hat das Qualitativ regelmäßig das reale Patiens, also das Objekt des Infinitivs, zum Subjekt, und bezeichnet den Zustand, in dem sich das reale Patiens nach Erleidung (*passio*) der durch den Infinitiv bezeichneten Handlung befindet. In solchen Fällen von "Passiv" zu reden, entspricht herkömmlichem Sprachgebrauch..."[87]

We should, however, stand up for Till here. Since the set of verbal participants does not change with the change in diathesis, one basic symptom of passive is the principal compatibility with an agentive phrase. However, a stative predicate with an agentive phrase <ⲉⲃⲟⲗ ϩⲓⲧⲛ̄ + Noun / Pronoun> are rather an exception. There are two such examples in the Old Testament (Psalm 37:13, Isaiah 51:20), and three (two of them identical) in the New Testament (Luke 6:18 = Acts 5:16, Romans 13:3). I managed to find only one clause of this type in the corpus of Shenoute's Canons:

(26) Shen.Can. 1, 21(1), YG 129:1[88]

ⲧⲁⲓ ⲧⲉ ⲑⲉ ⲉⲧⲥ̄ⲛⲁⲣⲁϣⲉ ⲉϫⲛ̄**ⲛⲉⲧⲥⲟⲛϩ̄** ⲛ̄ⲧⲟⲟⲧⲥ̄ ⲉⲃⲟⲗ ϩⲓⲧⲟⲟⲧⲟⲩ ⲙ̄ⲙⲓⲛ ⲙ̄ⲙⲟⲟⲩ

'*... thus will she rejoice on behalf of those **who are bound** to her through their own effort...*'

Moreover, even in this unique example, the sense of the prepositional phrase hovers on the border between agent, instrument, and source, so that the passive reading is not mandatory.

---

87 Polotsky (1957:230).
88 Funk (unpublished).

In other cases, Shenoute avoids using <stative + agentive PP> structure altogether; instead, in order to de-topicalize the agent of a durative predicate, he resorts to the impersonal passive pattern discussed above:

(27)   Shen.Can. 9, Leipoldt (1954:94, 18)

ⲡⲉⲧϣⲟⲣϣⲣ ⲇⲉ **ⲛⲛⲉⲧⲟⲩⲕⲱⲧ ⲙⲙⲟⲟⲩ ⲉⲃⲟⲗ ϩⲓⲧⲛ ⲓⲥ** ⲉϥϣⲟⲣϣⲣ ⲛⲧⲉϥⲯⲩⲭⲏ

'*He who destroys **what has been built by Jesus**, destroys his soul*'

(28)   Shen.Can. 4, Leipoldt (1955:171, 11)

ⲉⲩⲙⲉ ⲙ̄ⲙⲟⲟⲩ ⲉⲃⲟⲗ ϩⲓⲧⲛ̄ ⲛ̄ⲣⲱⲙⲉ ⲛⲁⲧⲥⲱⲧⲙ̄

'*...it is by disobedient people that **they are loved***'

Thus, passive stative constructions with animate agents seem to be barely acceptable in the biblical language and even less so in Shenoutean Coptic.

Finally, Till's idea of the overall function of stative does not deserve to be discarded lightly. Establishing a state-to-process relation between a stative and its infinitive, instead of a passive-to-active one,[89] Till creates a holistic concept of the morphological class of statives, a concept that accounts for the fact that the set of verbs with attested stative forms comprises intransitive monadic verbs, unaccusative, as well as unergative (ⲕⲛⲛⲉ 'become fat', ⲁϣⲁⲓ 'be multiplied', ⲡⲱϩ 'reach', ⲱⲛϩ 'live', ⲃⲱⲕ 'go'), and transitive verbs with alternating diathesis, i.e., verbs whose infinitive may have a causative, as well as a non-causative meaning (ⲟⲩⲱⲛϩ 'show / appear', ⲙⲟⲩϩ 'fill / be filled'). At the same time, for many, if not for most of non-alternating transitive verbs, e.g., ϥⲓ 'bear', ⲥⲟⲟⲩⲛ 'know', ⲧⲱⲙⲥ 'bury', a stative form is not attested, or is attested very poorly. So, even though the transitive infinitive of an alternating verb is diathetically opposed to its stative, it would be hardly justified to regard stative as a regular passive formation.

1.2.3 Verbal lexemes of the mutable class have both transitive and non-causative meaning

The most serious difficulty in establishing the category of transitivity in Coptic arises from the fact that the most part of the Coptic absolute infinitives are neutral in terms of *causative: non-causative* opposition, which means that one and the same <C¹ōC²C³>-form can code both transitive and intransitive meaning. This property, though not covering the whole of the mutable class (so, for instance, ⲙⲓϣⲉ 'to fight' will never be used non-causatively as 'to be fought against' or ⲥⲟⲃⲧⲉ 'to prepare' as 'to be prepared') is typical for roughly 70% of the Coptic verbal inventory. Steindorff attributes this feature to the originally nominal character of the absolute infinitive:

"Als Nominalform bezeichnet der Infinitiv kein bestimmtes Genus des Verbums, weder Aktivum, noch Passivum. ⲟⲩⲱⲛϩ bedeutet z.B. "öffnen" und "geöffnet sein", ⲙⲓϣⲉ "schlagen" und "geschlagen werden". In dieser Weise wird der Infinitiv bei den meisten transitiven Verben in aktivischer und passivischer Bedeutung gebraucht."[90]

---

89   Till (1955:257).
90   Steindorff 1904:92

The same observation (though without the reference to the nominal character of the infinitive) may be found in the works of Till, Polotsky, Grossman.[91] The diathetic neutrality of Coptic infinitives led Till to claim that the distinction between transitive and intransitive is "completely foreign to Egyptian affecting only the translation".[92] However, Funk in his survey of Coptic diathesis points out that Coptic grammatical mechanisms are perfectly able to perform the universal diathetic distinctions, such as the distinction between anticausative (ⲁϥϩⲱⲡ ϩⲛ ⲟⲩⲕⲗⲟⲟⲗⲉ 'he hid in a cloud'), passive (ⲁⲩϩⲟⲡϥ ϩⲛ ⲟⲩⲕⲗⲟⲟⲗⲉ 'he was hidden in a cloud'), reflexive (ⲁϥϩⲟⲡϥ ϩⲛ ⲟⲩⲕⲗⲟⲟⲗⲉ 'he hid himself in a cloud') and resultative (ϥϩⲏⲡ ϩⲛ ⲟⲩⲕⲗⲟⲟⲗⲉ 'he is hidden in a cloud') usages[93] which indicates a developed morphosyntactic diathesis-marking system. To combine the premise that each verbal lexeme is a bearer of an inherent (in)transitivity with the diathetic flexibility of most Coptic verbal lexemes, Funk suggests that in each pair of *non-causative: causative* homonyms, the causative counterpart is derived from the non-causative one by means of a zero causative element.[94] Thus, '*pōrč*' in *a-f- pōrč mmo=* 'he divided (something)' or *a-u- porč-f* 'he was divided' stands in derivational relationship to '*pōrč*' in *a-f- pōrč* 'he was divided'. This zero-derivation, according to Funk, would be parallel to overtly formed contrastive patterns of denominal verbs derived by means of ⲧ and ϫⲓ, respectively.

In the more recent research, the above-discussed diathetic flexibility of Coptic absolute infinitives is ascribed to the phenomenon of *lability*[95] defined as the property of a verb to show valency alternation without any formal change.[96] The relative merits of both explanatory models, the derivational one and the monolexemic one, will be discussed below.

1.2.4 ⲛ-/ⲙⲙⲟ=: question of identity

The prepositional phrase <ⲛ-/ⲙⲙⲟ=> stands apart from the rest of prepositional verb expansions being the only prepositional phrase to regularly alternate with the immediate object attachment pattern (IP). But whereas it is most often considered to be a functional equivalent of the IP, the distributional differences between these two constructions suggest that they are not necessarily to be subsumed under the same valency pattern. The distributional properties of the two constructions can be briefly sketched as follows:

---

91 Till (1955:122-123): "der Infinitiv im Koptischen ... einfach die Handlung als solche bezeichnet ohne Rücksicht darauf, ob sie vom Standpunkt des Handelnden (Subjekt) = aktiv, oder vom Standpunkt des Behandelnden (Objekt) = passiv betrachtet wird". Polotsky (1960:230): "... richtige Wahrnehmung, dass die Transitivität nicht am Infinitiv-Schema $C^1\bar{o}C^2C^3$ haftet". Grossman 2019:108: "Valency-reduction in Coptic is mostly marked via labile verbs, verbs that participate in alternations in which "the same verb is used both in the inchoative and in the causative sense" [without any formal change]... Coptic allows both A-preserving and P-preserving lability."

92 Till (1955:123-124): "diese Unterscheidung ist dem Ägyptischen vollkommen fremd; sie wirkt sich nur in der Übersetzung aus."

93 Funk (1978b:121).

94 Ibid.

95 Emmel (2006), Grossman (2019).

96 See 1.1.4.

a) The immediate pattern is usually the one more frequent in the non-durative conjugation;[97] my (not yet statistically verified) impression is that IP is also the prevailing construction for the imperative of the native Coptic verbs;

b) together, the immediate and the mediated constructions constitute a mechanism of *differential object marking* inside the non-durative conjugation which in some way correlates with the information packaging in the clause. According to Engsheden, high referentiality and thematicity of the object promotes the use of the mediated construction.[98] This (not too strict) interdependence is realized only in the non-durative conjugation, and only with native verbs: Greek verbal lexemes lack construct forms and cannot participate in the mediated / immediate alternation;[99]

c) On the contrary, in the durative conjugation, <ⲛ-/ⲙⲙⲟ=> is almost the only possible allomorph for a direct object construction. The only exception[100] is a zero-determinated object without a possessive suffix, i.e., the lowest specificity-grade object. This compatibility restriction is known in Coptology as 'Stern-Jernstedt rule'.

In the linguistic treatment of the prepositional pattern, one can often observe a mixture of synchronic and diachronic considerations. Thus, for Shisha-Halevy, this pattern is "on the one hand, a direct-object marker after transitives under given conditions, yet on the other hand an "adverbial", i.e. modifier signal... and is thus in fact an 'onset' of the 'indirect' object as rection of transitives."[101] According to Stern (who calls it a 'verbal genitive construction'[102]), Schenkel[103] and Reintges[104], the use of the genitive preposition is conditioned by the originally nominal or adverbial (for Schenkel) character of the durative infinitive. Both Schenkel and Reintges attempt to demonstrate that the use of the prepositional DO-pattern implies also slight semantic deviations from the sense coded by the IP. According to Schenkel,

"[a]ls charakteristisch für Verbaladverbien ist anzusehen, daß sie keine verbale Rektion besitzen... Die mit ⲛ-/ⲙⲙⲟ= eingeleiteten Ersatzkonstruktionen sind nicht als Präpositionalobjekte einzuschätzen, vielmehr als "freie" adverbiale Bestimmungen, die

---

97 The respective numbers of IP: PrepP for several test verbs in the biblical text are: ⲙⲟⲩϩ 'fill': 70:16; ⲡⲱⲣϣ 'spread': 23:23; ⲱⲡ 'count': 69:10; ⲟⲩⲱⲛϩ ⲉⲃⲟⲗ 'show': 68: 44; ⲧⲁⲕⲟ 'corrupt, destroy': 169:101. Appreciating these figures, one has to consider that according to Jernstedt, the use of <ⲛ-/ⲙⲙⲟ=> in the non-durative conjugation is more widespread in the Bible translations, than elsewhere in Sahidic, which suggests a Greek influence (Jernstedt 1986:441).

98 Engsheden (2008:34).

99 See Engsheden (2008:24) for other exceptions.

100 Apart from some very specific lexical cases, such as indefinite and interrogative pronomina (ⲟⲩ 'what', ϩⲁϩ 'many' etc.), complements of the verb ⲟⲩⲱϣ 'to wish' and a few other cases.

101 Shisha-Halevy (1986:107).

102 Stern (1880:312).

103 Schenkel (1978).

104 E.g., in Reintges (1995:195).

nicht in der Rektion des Verbs gesetzt sind. Ein ϯ ϫⲱ ⲙⲙⲟⲥ ist nicht als "ich sage es" zu analysieren, sondern, approximativ paraphrasiert, als "ich sage – mit dem Inhalt Es."[105]

This interpretation looks arbitrary. Seeing that ϫⲱ ⲙⲙⲟⲥ is a mandatory durative equivalent of the non-durative ϫⲟⲟⲥ, it is hardly reasonable to analyze the first verbal expansion as an adverbial modifier, and the second one as a direct object. Moreover, since this 'free adverbial modifier' cannot, in fact, be omitted without turning the clause unfinished or ungrammatical, it is simply wrong to call it a 'free modifier'. It is clearly a part of the argument structure of the verbal lexeme, which corroborates Polotsky's statement that "within the framework of Coptic, there is nothing 'adverbial' about the predicative Infinitive and the Qualitative".[106]

Reintges, in his turn, draws an analogy between the opposition <IP: ⲛ-/ⲙⲙⲟ=phrase> in Coptic and that of <*accusative: partitive case*> in Finnish:

> "In Finnish as well as in Coptic, a verb phrase with an accusative Case-marked object imposes a bound event reading on the entire clause, while an unbound event reading is obtained when the direct object is assigned oblique Case."[107]

Now, applied to Coptic, this precise wording suggests that in a contrastive environment which can only be the non-durative conjugation, the two different valency patterns yield the above difference in meaning. That contradicts Coptic data, since the boundedness / unboundedness of the verbal event is coded in the conjugation base, and not imposed by the object; the choice of this or the other object attachment construction has no impact on the aspectual characteristics of a non-durative clause. But it is nevertheless true that the oblique pattern being obligatory in the durative conjugation and the IP basically excluded of it, one may speak of a high correlation between the valency pattern and the aspectual type of the event. This, and the almost 100%-coinciding lexemic distribution[108] between the two patterns is a strong argument in favor of regarding them as allomorphs of one direct object supermorpheme, as Jernstedt does.

1.2.5 No transitivity in Coptic?

In view of all the above difficulties, it is easy to understand that for Coptic, the notion of transitivity remains, if possible, even more problematic than for the general theoretical linguistics. In two of the more recent studies, Shisha-Halevy and Emmel opt for abandoning this notion altogether, when dealing with the Coptic verbal system. An alternative approach proposed by Shisha-Halevy in his 'Coptic Grammatical Categories' suggests describing each verbal lexeme in terms of its obligatory valency to obtain classes of uni-, bi- and trivalent verbs. Under such approach, a lexeme compatible with various valency

---

105 Schenkel (1978:15).
106 Polotsky (1960:395).
107 Reintges (2001: 185).
108 Except in very few cases where the absolute form of a mutable verb has other valency (kōmš nsa-). Cf. Jernstedt 459.

patterns (e.g., ⲉⲓⲣⲉ ⲛ- 'make' vs. ⲉⲓⲣⲉ ⲛ- ⲛ- 'make into') is treated as a conglomerate of homonyms, and the task of elaborating the verbal system is basically reduced to making out an exhaustive list of all such homonyms with all the possible valency patterns.[109]

In a similar fashion, the analysis of various valency patterns of the verb ⲥⲱⲧⲙ and its allomorphs brings Emmel to the conclusion that "the phenomena that fall under the heading *transitivity* are far too complex…to warrant using the traditional transitive/intransitive dichotomy as a category for dividing all Coptic verbs into two large groups."[110] According to Emmel, the transitivity terminology should not be applied to Coptic, except for the purpose of making cross-references to other languages[111]. At the same time, he remarks that if Coptologists had to resort to making an "extensive and precise valency listing of all verb lexemes" instead of categorizing and describing valency as a system, such a list would not prove either descriptively adequate, or very elegant.[112] It would actually obfuscate verbal system regularities that are crucial for our understanding of Coptic.

1.3 Transitivity in Coptic: Systemic view

1.3.1 Redefining the transitive pattern

On theoretical grounds whose validity I tried to demonstrate in the section 1.1, a transitive pattern in a language is the one characterized by all or most of the following properties:

1) It denotes no specific semantic relation of the second argument to the verb (such as recipient, goal, benefactive, source etc.)

2) It correlates with the second argument's individuation features (such as definiteness, specificity, personal reference)

3) It correlates with the tense-aspect-modus categories

4) It may be subject to valency reduction, where either the first, or the second argument is demoted; this alternation may or may not be morphologically marked

5) It is particularly frequent and productive compared to other bivalent patterns

6) It most probably coincides with the valency pattern of the verb 'break' in its active diathesis

Such configuration of symptoms permits us: a) to establish beyond doubt that transitivity is a working grammatical category in Coptic; b) to unequivocally define the transitive valency pattern as the alternation of the immediate pattern with the ⲛ-/ⲙⲙⲟ=prepositional phrase. The relevance of (2), (3), (4) and (6) for this pattern needs no further comment. As for its frequency, a rough count based on the examination of the entire verb inventory in Crum's Dictionary reveals that the class of verbs employing the IP/ ⲛ-/ⲙⲙⲟ=alternation

---

109 Cf. Shisha-Halevy 1986:108
110 Emmel 2006:52
111 Ibid.
112 Ibid.

comprises some 70% of the verbs of Egyptian origin.[113] For Greek loan verbs, this percentage is much lower, only about 30%, but still significant. Finally, as far as the semantics of the pattern is concerned, the data allows two ways of interpretation. In Shisha-Halevy's opinion, obligatory (or rectional) expansions of the verb have no proper meaning, but contribute to the overall meaning of the verbal syntagm. For instance, "the preposition ⲉ- when non-commutable – i.e. after ⲛⲁⲩ or ⲅⲁⲣⲉⲅ – is as rectional, as devoid of meaning, as ⲛ-/ⲙⲙⲟ= or the immediate object-construction ⲥⲉⲧⲡ-/ⲥⲟⲧⲡ=".[114] On the other hand, the verbs compatible with ⲉ-/ⲉⲣⲟ= belong to a limited number of semantic classes compared to those compatible with ⲛ-/ⲙⲙⲟ=. According to Zakrzewska, the marker ⲉ-/ⲉⲣⲟ= "is preferably employed for the second argument... with the verbs of perception and cognition, characterized by low agency of the referent of the first argument, verbs denoting performative acts which demand a certain amount of instigation on the part of the referent of the second argument and verbs denoting either superficial affectedness or affectedness pertaining to that referent's sphere of influence."[115] The possibility of such delineation for ⲉ-/ⲉⲣⲟ= means that ⲛ-/ⲙⲙⲟ= (expanding, as previously mentioned, the most part of the verbal lexicon) imposes fewer restrictions on the semantics of its verbal head (or, in Borer's view which seems to be exceptionally appropriate for Coptic, its verbal modifier[116]) than ⲉ-/ⲉⲣⲟ=, i.e. is basically far more semantically loose.

1.3.2 Transitivity as a parameter of the conjugation patterns

1.3.2.1 Aspect-Diathesis Grid

The inner mechanism of direct object attachment in Coptic is defined by two rules, the Stern-Jernstedt rule (briefly referred to in 1.2.4) and the rule of the distribution of stative forms. Though the Stern-Jernstedt rule is sometimes taken to relate solely to the definiteness / animacy / specificity of the object[117], Jernstedt's own phrasing emphasizes not only the individuation features of the object, but also the distributional properties of verbal forms:

---

113 According to my calculations, the exact numbers are 590 transitive verbs to 266 intransitives or reflexives, i.e. 68,9 %. The examination included only such lexemes whose meaning is not marked by Crum as unknown. This is, of course, a very rough evaluation mixing up the data of different dialects, periods and genres. Thus, impressionistically, Bohairic seems to have gone furthest in the direction of replacing the transitive pattern with other valency patterns, predominantly with the prepositional phrase ⲉ-/ⲉⲣⲟ= (the issue of ⲉ- gradually superseding ⲛ- as a DO-marker is explored in Lincke 2018). For simplicity's sake, I disregard the fact that Coptic valency patterns are not completely rigid (e.g., ⲥⲱⲧⲙ 'to hear, listen' can use both the IP and the < ⲉ-/ⲉⲣⲟ=>-pattern, ⲥⲱⲃⲉ 'to laugh at' uses < ⲉ-/ⲉⲣⲟ=>, <ⲉⲝⲛ- /ⲉⲝⲱ=> and <ⲛⲥⲁ- / ⲛⲥⲱ=>-patterns with no observable difference in the meaning). The statistics here thus shows only the percentage of verbs that are compatible with the transitive pattern.
114 Shisha-Halevy (1986:108).
115 Zakrzewska (2017b: 230).
116 Borer (2005: 9).
117 So, e.g., in Winand (2015:534).

"... In the system of present tenses, the verb is never used in *status pronominalis*, while *status constructus* is permitted only with undetermined common nouns and undetermined pronouns (among them the demonstratives)."[118]

With some approximation, one can state that both construct forms are reserved for the eventive conjugation. Stative, on the other hand, is acceptable only in the durative pattern[119]. That means that of the four verbal morphs, three are marked for aspect: the construct forms are punctual/ eventive[120], whereas the stative is durative.

Another characteristic trait of these forms, also so trivial that it has been never to my knowledge taken into account, is their diathetic markedness. Indeed, both forms marked for non-durative aspect (*status constructus* and *status pronominalis*) are also necessarily transitive. Moreover, since one of them is reserved for substantival and the other for pronominal arguments, together they would suffice to exhaust the transitive valency of the verb covering the whole field of possible nominal arguments. Vice versa, the durative form (stative) is always intransitive.

This aspect-diathesis clustering is crucial for the Coptic verbal system, since it reveals an additional dimension in the grammatical opposition of *non-durative: durative* conjugation, the dimension of diathesis. Indeed, the absolute infinitive in the Tripartite conjugation is opposed to (and possibly stands in a complimentary distribution with) the transitive verbal forms. On the other hand, in the Bipartite, it contrasts with a characteristically intransitive form. It therefore stands to reason that the two absolute infinitives – that of the non-durative and that of the durative conjugation – do not have an identical function in the system. Even if liable to labile usage, an absolute form will primarily occupy the empty niche in the diathetic lattice. Thus, the present analysis of the properties of marked verbal forms predicts that in the Tripartite conjugation base, an absolute infinitive will mostly have a non-causative meaning, whereas in the Bipartite, it will rather be used causatively.

Table 1 | Aspectual-diathetic distribution of verbal morphs

Diathesis	Eventive (Tripartite) Conjugation	Durative (Bipartite) Conjugation
TRANSITIVE	STATUS CONSTRUCTUS STATUS PRONOMINALIS	***STATUS ABSOLUTUS***
INTRANSITIVE	***STATUS ABSOLUTUS***	STATIVE

1.3.2.2 Durative intransitive infinitive: a ghost form

As already discussed in 1.2.3, the majority of verbal lexemes in the transitive class can code the transitive-causative, as well as the non-causative meaning, seemingly just depending on the physical presence of the object. However, at least, as regards the inventory of native Coptic verbs, this general statement can be accepted as true with two caveats: of

---

118 Jernstedt (1986:390, translation – N.S.).
119 See Funk (1978a) for the explanations of possible exceptions.
120 With the exception of the *status constructus* combined with Ø-object which is aspectually neutral.

all the verbal forms, it refers **only** to absolute infinitives; and for them, the term 'lability' applies to either one of the two oppositions: non-durative intransitive vs. non-durative transitive infinitive, or non-durative intransitive vs. durative transitive infinitive. The third theoretically possible opposition: durative intransitive infinitive vs. durative transitive infinitive – is not a full-fledged grammatical opposition in Coptic.

The first restriction is so self-evident that one often omits mentioning it and speaks about the lability of the Coptic verb, in general, as one sees in the introductory remark in Funk (1978b):

> "Another pertinent problem of some importance would be the treatment of those Coptic verbs that are Active in meaning when they have a direct complement but are approximately "Passive" or "Middle" when used in the tripartite pattern without a direct complement.[121]"

But we lose vital structural facts if we ignore the fact that out of the four morphs of one and the same verb, only one displays lability.

The second condition – lability absent from the Bipartite conjugation base – was first mentioned by Stern in his 'Koptische Grammatik':

> "Neutropassivische verba können, sofern sie veränderlich sind, im stat. absol. nicht in allen verbalformen als solche gebraucht werden, namentlich nicht in den dauerzeiten, dem präsens, imperfectum und participium, welche… das qualitativum erheischen. In den präterita und futura, im conjunctiv, imperativ und infinitiv dagegen vertreten sie das passiv häufig, z.b. ⲁⲩⲟⲩⲱⲛ ⲛⲭⲉ ⲛⲓⲣⲱⲟⲩ ⲧⲏⲣⲟⲩ ⲟⲩⲟϩ ⲛⲓⲥⲛⲁⲩϩ ⲧⲏⲣⲟⲩ ⲁⲩⲃⲱⲗ ⲉⲃⲟⲗ : ⲁ ⲛⲣⲟ ⲇⲉ ⲧⲏⲣⲟⲩ ⲟⲩⲱⲛ ⲛⲧⲉⲩⲛⲟⲩ ⲁⲩⲱ ⲙⲙⲣⲣⲉ ⲛⲟⲩⲟⲛ ⲛⲓⲙ ⲁⲩⲃⲱⲗ ⲉⲃⲟⲗ (es wurden alle thüren geöffnet, öffneten sich, und alle fesseln wurden gelöst, lösten sich) Act 16:26[122]".

An identical observation, namely, that the intransitive absolute infinitive is practically ruled out from the durative conjugation, was made by Jernstedt:

> "…a significant number of intransitive verbs positively must have the form of stative, if used in the durative conjugation'[123]"

Polotsky associates this morphosyntactic function pattern first and foremost with the verbs of motion:

> "Ergänzend wäre zu bemerken gewesen, dass bei den Verben der Bewegung in den Dauerzeiten der Infinitiv mit einigen bestimmten Ausnahmen überhaupt unzulässig ist."[124]

---

121 Funk (1978b:120).
122 Stern (1880:301-302).
123 Jernstedt (1986:401).
124 Polotsky (1957:229).

However, Polotsky admits that verbs of motion may not be the only class displaying such idiosyncrasy:

> "The possibility of having the same actor for the Infinitive as well as for the Qualitative is limited to intransitive verbs, but the number of such verbs actually admitting both forms in the Bipartite Pattern is none too great… With many intransitive verbs, like ϩⲕⲟ "to be hungry" and ⲉⲓⲃⲉ "to be thirsty" the Infinitive is hardly found in the Bipartite Pattern.[125]"

As for the verbs of motion, this verb class constitutes, indeed, the most conspicuous instance of the principle discovered by Stern and Jernstedt, because the stative form in this case denotes an action in progress,[126] the meaning supposed to be rendered by infinitive:

> "In so far as the Infinitive and the Qualitative of the same verb can both be used in the Bipartite Conjugation Pattern, they form a contrast: the Infinitive expresses an action in progress, while the Qualitative expresses a state."[127]

Rather surprisingly, the key words in this formula are "in so far". Although some verbs do, indeed, display the contrast in aspect (progressive vs. stative) indicated by Polotsky, such cases are too infrequent to form a notion of a consistent grammatical opposition. Stative may effectively capture the meaning of an ongoing process, as can be seen in the verbs of motion, as well as in many others:

(29)   Ps 24:15
       ⲉⲣⲉⲛⲁⲃⲁⲗ ⲉⲓⲟⲣⲙ ⲛⲟⲩⲟⲉⲓϣ ⲛⲓⲙ ⲉⲡϫⲟⲉⲓⲥ
       οἱ ὀφθαλμοί μου διὰ παντὸς πρὸς τὸν κύριον
       'My eyes are ever toward the Lord' (Coptic, lit.: 'my eyes are forever looking at the Lord')

Specific semantic conditions triggering the use of both forms for a non-causative durative meaning will be explored in 1.3.3.1. We should observe, however, that the notion 'action in progress' can be rather misleading, making one look at Coptic through the tenets of the European grammar. As far as it means nothing other than a continuing process, it will be treated in the Coptic verbal system not as an action, but as a state of being engaged in an action, i.e., will be expressed by a stative. The above misapprehension is the possible source of fallacy one finds in Layton's definition of the opposition between intransitive infinitive and stative in the durative conjugation. Layton claims that apart from some five verbs of motion, "the stative describes the enduring state of the subject after some process has come to an end or some quality has been acquired, ⲥⲉ-ϣⲟⲩⲱⲟⲩ "They are dry", and the infinitive expresses enduring, ongoing, or general process or entry into a state, ⲥⲉ-ϣⲟⲟⲩⲉ "They are becoming dry, they dry out".[128] Thus, according to Layton, Coptic stative

---

125 Polotsky (1960: 396-397).
126 Ibid.
127 Polotsky (1960: 396, §9).
128 Layton (2011:236-237).

has predominantly a resultative reading, which is too rough an approximation. On the other hand, an 'enduring, ongoing, or general process', from the point of view of Coptic grammar, is a state. So, the semantic distinction denoted by Layton seems to be illusionary.

To sum up, the observations made by Stern, Jernstedt and Polotsky suggest the following restrictions on the use of the absolute form in the durative tenses: with alternating verbs, apart from a relatively small number of exceptions, this form has a causative meaning and stands in a transitive construction. With non-alternating intransitive verbs, the absolute form is nearly always[129] excluded, making stative the only verbal form compatible with the durative tenses. Thus, for transitive verbs, the opposition <infinitive : stative> is in the first place an opposition of diathesis, while with intransitives, this opposition is most often suppressed,[130] or at least, does not have a consistent grammatical meaning.

1.3.3 Tense-base / Morphology / Diathesis distribution: sample statistic from Sahidic

I shall now proceed to check the above statements against the data of two large text corpora, namely, Shenoute's Canons as represented in Funk (unpublished) and the Bible. The test is conducted on a small sample of verbs, all meeting one basic requirement: the verb must appear in the corpora, at least, in the forms of absolute infinitive and stative. Now, based on the criteria of valency and transitivity, the Coptic verbal inventory can be divided into four groups: 'strong transitive' verbs which do not have any form with a non-causative meaning (e.g., ϫι 'take'); unergative verbs with non-transitive valency (e.g., ϩⲁⲣⲉϩ 'guard, preserve'); unaccusatives (e.g., ⲙⲟⲩⲛ ⲉⲃⲟⲗ 'remain')[131]; finally, verbs displaying labile alternation pattern (e.g., ⲧⲁⲕⲟ 'destroy / be destroyed'). Being semantically unalterable and having either a functionally limited stative or no stative at all[132], the verbs of the first two groups turn out to be irrelevant for the study of interdependencies between tense patterns and diathesis. The mechanisms of valency reduction for these verbs seem to be impersonal passive or reflexive construction. On the other hand, unaccusative verbs possess statives; therefore, a contrastive analysis of their stative vs. durative infinitive should reveal the aspectual distinction suggested in Layton (2000), if indeed such distinction is manifested grammatically. The group of unaccusatives is represented in the sample by the following

---

129 The exceptions are discussed in detail in 1.3.4.6 and 1.3.4.7.

130 See Shisha-Halevy (1986:106, fn.4).

131 Interestingly, my classification does not match the similar one presented in Reintges (2004:228-230). In particular, the class of verbs that I take to be unaccusatives is called 'variable behavior verbs' by Reintges who comments that "in the absolute state, they behave semantically as unergative verbs with agentive subjects. In the corresponding stative, variable behavior verbs behave more like unaccusatives, because the subject receives a non-agentive interpretation as the holder of some state or condition." (Reintges 2004:229-230). Now, to estimate the contrast between eventive and stative forms as a contrast between unergative and unaccusative subject linking seems to be an interpretation profoundly influenced by the desire to explain the formal opposition at whatever price. It is difficult to agree, e.g., that a referent that remained or will remain has some other semantic role than the one that remains.

132 Thus, for instance, the stative of ϫι (ϫⲏⲩ) occurs in the Bible only as a part of fixed lexical units, ϫⲏⲩ ⲛϭⲟⲛⲥ 'the oppressed ones' and ϫⲏⲩ ⲛⲕⲟⲧⲥ 'perverse' (Psalms 102:6, 145:7, Proverbs 2:15, 8:8, Sirach 32:12). In Shenoute's Canons this form is not used, at all.

verbs: ⲱⲛϩ 'live', ⲡⲱϩ 'reach', ⲥⲣϥⲉ 'be at leisure', ⲣⲱⲧ 'grow, sprout', ⲕⲛⲛⲉ 'grow fat', ⲁϣⲁⲓ 'multiply', ⲙⲟⲩⲛ ⲉⲃⲟⲗ 'remain'. The group of labile verbs allows for multiple comparisons: non-durative vs. durative absolute infinitive, non-durative transitive vs. non-durative intransitive infinitive, durative intransitive infinitive vs. stative. Included in the sample are labile verbs with a relatively high degree of frequency, such as ⲙⲟⲩϩ 'fill out / be filled out', ⲡⲱⲣϣ 'spread', ⲡⲱϩ 'divide / be divided, burst out', ⲱⲡ 'count / to be counted', ⲟⲩⲱⲛϩ ⲉⲃⲟⲗ 'show / appear', ⲧⲁⲕⲟ 'destroy / be destroyed', ⲣⲱⲕϩ 'incinerate / burn', ⲧⲁⲗϭⲟ 'heal, make calm / be healed, calm down'.

1.3.3.1 Unaccusatives: aspect / form distribution

Table 2a | ⲱⲛϩ 'to live'

Conjugation	Form	Bible	Shenoute - Canons
Eventive Tenses	non-causative infinitive	138	11
Durative Tenses	stative	231	31
	non-causative infinitive	–	–

Table 2b | ⲡⲱϩ 'to reach'

Conjugation	Form	Bible	Shenoute - Canons
Eventive Tenses	non-causative infinitive	62	5
Durative Tenses	stative	5	2
	non-causative infinitive	–	–

Table 2c | ⲥⲣϥⲉ 'to be at leisure'

Conjugation	Form	Bible	Shenoute - Canons
Eventive Tenses	non-causative infinitive	7	4
Durative Tenses	stative	3	2
	non-causative infinitive	–	–

Table 2d | ⲣⲱⲧ 'to grow, sprout'

Conjugation	Form	Bible	Shenoute - Canons
Eventive Tenses	non-causative infinitive	11	3
Durative Tenses	stative	12	3
	non-causative infinitive	1	2

Table 2e | ⲕⲛⲛⲉ 'to grow fat'

Conjugation	Form	Bible	Shenoute - Canons
Eventive Tenses	non-causative infinitive	5	–
Durative Tenses	stative	9	2
	non-causative infinitive	1	–

Table 2f | ⲁϣⲁⲓ 'to multiply'

Conjugation	Form	Bible	Shenoute - Canons
Eventive Tenses	non-causative infinitive	81	9
Durative Tenses	stative	63	14
	non-causative infinitive	4	–

Table 2g | ⲙⲟⲩⲛ ⲉⲃⲟⲗ 'to remain'

Conjugation	Form	Bible	Shenoute - Canons
Eventive Tenses	non-causative infinitive	26	7
Durative Tenses	stative	12	5
	non-causative infinitive	–	–

1.3.3.2 Labile verbs: aspect / diathesis / form distribution

Table 3a | ⲙⲟⲩϩ 'to fill / be filled'

Conjugation	Form	Bible	Shenoute - Canons
Eventive tenses	non-causative infinitive	73	7
	causative infinitive	16	1
	construct forms	70	16
Durative tenses	stative	78	32
	non-causative infinitive	1 (?)	1 (?)
	causative infinitive	5	3

Table 3b | ⲡⲱⲣϣ 'to spread'

Conjugation	Form	Bible	Shenoute - Canons
Eventive tenses	non-causative infinitive	18	–
	causative infinitive	23	4
	construct forms	23	8
Durative tenses	stative	13	3
	non-causative infinitive	1	–
	causative infinitive	1	1

Table 3c | ⲡⲱϩ 'to divide / be divided, burst out'

Conjugation	Form	Bible	Shenoute - Canons
Eventive tenses	non-causative infinitive	16	5
	causative infinitive	17	14
	construct forms	8	9
Durative tenses	stative	6	6
	non-causative infinitive	–	1
	causative infinitive	1	2

Table 3d | ⲣⲱⲕϩ 'to incinerate / burn'

Conjugation	Form	Bible	Shenoute - Canons
Eventive tenses	non-causative infinitive	10	3
	causative infinitive	36	3
	construct forms	73	8
Durative tenses	stative	9	7
	non-causative infinitive	2	–
	causative infinitive	6	3

Table 3e | ⲧⲁⲕⲟ 'to destroy / perish'

Conjugation	Form	Bible	Shenoute - Canons
Eventive tenses	non-causative infinitive	195	22
	causative infinitive	101	19
	construct forms	169	29
Durative tenses	stative	10	4
	non-causative infinitive	5 (of them 4 in the NT)	–
	causative infinitive	12	20

Table 3f | ⲧⲁⲗϭⲟ 'to heal, make calm / be healed, calm down'

Conjugation	Form	Bible	Shenoute - Canons
Eventive tenses	non-causative infinitive	4	1
	causative infinitive	14	–
	construct forms	57	2
Durative tenses	stative	1	–
	non-causative infinitive	–	–
	causative infinitive	5	2

Table 3g | ογωΝϩ εβολ[133] 'to show / appear'

Conjugation	Form	Bible	Shenoute - Canons
Eventive tenses	non-causative infinitive	170	21
	causative infinitive	44	4
	construct forms	68	10
Durative tenses	stative	56	54
	non-causative infinitive	6	–
	causative infinitive	17	8

Table 3h | ωπ 'to count / to be counted, belong to'

Conjugation	Form	Bible	Shenoute - Canons
Eventive tenses	non-causative infinitive	16	2
	causative infinitive	10	5
	construct forms	69	8
Durative tenses	stative	39	39
	non-causative infinitive	–	–
	causative infinitive	16	5

1.3.4 Analysis of statistical data and comments

1.3.4.1 Reduced use of intransitive infinitive in the Bipartite

The first rough estimate of the data not only confirms the above cited observations by Stern, Jernstedt and Polotsky, but also allows to rephrase them more precisely. Thus, it must first be stated that both corpora make very little (and with unaccusatives, almost none at all) use of intransitive infinitives in the durative tenses, so little indeed that it would be difficult to ascribe this form any single and permanent grammatical function. At the same time, transitive infinitives in the Bipartite are perfectly regular, if not numerous. Consequently, a zero-argument infinitive in the Bipartite must with high probability be interpreted as a case of agent-preserving valency reduction, as in

(30)   Rev. 9:11
        επεϥραΝ ΜΜΝΤϩεβραιος πε βαττωΝ ΜΜΝΤογεειεΝιΝ ϫε ϫε πεττακο
        ὄνομα αὐτῷ Ἑβραϊστί Ἀβαδδών καὶ ἐν τῇ Ἑλληνικῇ ὄνομα ἔχει Ἀπολλύων
        'His name in Hebrew is Abaddon, and in Greek he is called Apollyon' (lit., 'he who destroys')

---

133 Excluded from the present statistics are all the occurrences of the verb in the sense of ἐξομολογέομαι 'to sing praises, confess'. The semantic divergence between the two senses is wide enough to treat the verbs as homonyms.

(31)   Shen.Can. 7, Leipoldt (1954:16, 6)
        ⲉⲃⲟⲗ ⲇⲉ ⲥⲡⲁⲧⲁⲥⲥⲉ ⲥⲧⲁⲗϭⲟ ⲇⲉ ⲟⲛ
        'for it strikes, and then it heals'

For Shenoute's texts, where we do not have any non-Coptic source text and have to rely on our philological feeling for interpretation, the almost total absence of durative intransitive infinitives is sometimes a decisive argument in favor of a causative interpretation of an object-less infinitive, as in:

(32)   Shen.Can. 6, Amel. 2 (286:11)
        ⲧⲱⲟⲩⲛ ⲡϫⲟⲓⲥ ⲙⲡⲣⲧⲣⲉⲡⲣⲱⲙⲉ ⲛⲥⲁⲧⲁⲛⲁⲥ ϭⲙϭⲟⲙ ⲙⲡⲣⲧⲣⲉ ⲧⲉⲕⲃⲟⲏⲑⲉⲓⲁ ⲟⲩⲉ ⲙⲙⲟⲛ
        ⲙⲏⲡⲟⲧⲉ ⲛϥⲧⲱⲣⲡ ⲛⲧⲉⲛⲯⲩⲭⲏ ⲛⲑⲉ ⲛⲟⲩⲙⲟⲩⲓ **ⲉⲙⲛ ⲡⲉⲧⲥⲱⲧⲉ ⲟⲩⲧⲉ ⲙⲛ ⲡⲉⲧⲛⲟⲩϩⲙ**
        '*Arise, oh Lord, do not let the man of Satan overcome, do not let your help go away from us, lest he seizes our soul, like a lion, with nobody to redeem (us), nor anybody to save (us)...*'

The alternative interpretation of the phrase in bold, which is "while nobody will be redeemed, nor nobody saved", is perfectly possible from the point of view of the content, but must be rejected on the above grammatical grounds.

In view of these data, we can re-examine Polotsky's statement cited in 1.3.2.2 reproduced here for the reader's convenience:

> "The possibility of having the same actor for the Infinitive as well as for the Qualitative is limited to intransitive verbs."

As becomes clear from Polotsky's examples (ϣⲱⲡⲉ, ⲙⲟⲩ, ϩⲕⲟ, ⲉⲓⲃⲉ), the term 'intransitive' comprises here the set of monadic / unaccusative verbs. It follows, therefore, that according to Polotsky, bivalent infinitives can only have transitive meaning in the Bipartite which is close enough to what we observe in our statistics. However, sporadic intransitive durative infinitives occur with monadic, as well as with bivalent verbs.[134] In 1.3.4.6 and 1.3.4.7, I shall endeavor to specify the semantic load of these forms.

1.3.4.2 Eventive infinitive: an anticausative form

An intransitive eventive infinitive constitutes an anticausative counterpart to the transitive form, since they are used to "express the same basic situation… and differ only in that the causative verb meaning involves an agent participant who causes the situation, whereas the inchoative (i.e., anticausative – N.S.) verb meaning excludes a causing agent and presents the situation as occurring spontaneously."[135] Thus, the Coptic lability can be classified as anticausative, which is the most frequent lability type cross-linguistically, according to

---

134 I shall refrain from passing any judgement concerning the diachrony of these occurrences. It is, however, curious that the two researched corpora differ in their tolerance to intransitive durative infinitives of various verbs. Moreover, the language of the New Testament seems to differ in this respect from that of the Old Testament. A diachronic study of this phenomenon might perhaps be useful for approximative text-dating.

135 Haspelmath 1993:90

Letuchiy (2009). Based on this understanding of the mechanism of Coptic lability, we can correctly predict that verbs that denote human activity in a strict sense will not exhibit the property of lability, i.e., will usually belong to the 'strong transitive' class. Indeed, the property of lability is not displayed in any of the synonyms with the meaning 'cut' (ⲟⲩⲱϣⲝⲉ, ϣⲱⲗϭ, ϣⲱⲱⲧ, ϣⲟⲧϣⲧ, ⲝⲱⲗϩ, ϭⲟⲝϭⲉⲝ, ϭⲱⲱⲝⲉ), as well as in the Coptic verbs for 'building' (ⲕⲱⲧ), 'spinning' (ⲉⲓⲥⲉ), 'stealing' (ⲕⲱⲗⲡ, ϩⲱϥⲧ), 'ploughing' (ⲥⲕⲁⲓ). Whenever any of these and similar verbs have a note 'intr.' in Crum's dictionary, this refers to the instances of agent-preserving (i.e., patient-dropping) valency reduction.[136]

We can now address the problem posed in Funk (1978): how do we define the distinction between different forms of a Coptic verb with a roughly 'passive' function, i.e., the forms displaying this or the other kind of valency reduction as compared to their transitive counterpart.[137] The specific instances Funk mentions to illustrate his question are:

(33)   ⲁϥϩⲱⲡ ϩⲛ ⲟⲩⲕⲗⲟⲟⲗⲉ
         PST-3SGM-hide in-a-cloud
         'He hid in a cloud'
         ⲁⲩϩⲟⲡϥ ϩⲛ ⲟⲩⲕⲗⲟⲟⲗⲉ
         PST-3PL-hide-3SGM in-a-cloud
         'He became hidden in a cloud'
         ⲁϥϩⲟⲡϥ ϩⲛ ⲟⲩⲕⲗⲟⲟⲗⲉ
         PST-3SGM-hide-3SGM in-a-cloud
         'He hid himself in a cloud'

We are now in position to state a clear semantic distinction between all three constructions. The first one is anticausative, so denoting rather a spontaneously occurring event than a volitional action. This explains why the intransitive infinitive of ϩⲱⲡ most often predicates inanimate nouns, as can be seen in Crum's examples. The second construction refer to the same situation as the corresponding transitive, but the agent is semantically (not syntactically) demoted. Thus, it serves as an exact equivalent of passive model, where this model is morphologically marked. Finally, the third example instantiates a reflexive construction, an action volitionally performed by the agent on himself. As mentioned elsewhere, the stative of the same verb can denote a secondary, as well as a primary state, i.e., can either mean that an entity has been hidden, or else that an entity has not yet been uncovered.

How strictly were the functions of anticausative, resultative, and passive differentiated in Coptic? In other words, how often could an eventive infinitive or a stative be used in the passive function? According to my data, almost never: the agent expression introduced, e.g., by ⲉⲃⲟⲗ ϩⲓⲧⲛ is very infrequent with intransitive infinitives, and even more so with statives. Among the rare examples that can be interpreted as passive constructions are:

---

136 The ambiguity of the note 'intransitive' in Crum (1939) which may refer to anticausative semantics
     or to intransitive syntax of the verb is addressed in Emmel (2006).
137 See Funk (1978:121).

(34)   Deut 22:3

ⲁϥⲥⲱⲣⲙ ⲧⲏⲣϥ ⲛⲧⲟⲟⲧϥ ⲙⲡⲉⲕⲥⲟⲛ ⲛⲛⲉⲧⲛⲁⲥⲱⲣⲙ ⲛⲧⲟⲟⲧϥ ⲁⲩⲱ ⲛⲅϩⲉ ⲉⲣⲟⲟⲩ ⲛⲛⲉⲕⲙⲟⲟϣⲉ
ⲉⲕⲁⲁⲩ

ὅσα ἐὰν **ἀπόληται παρ᾽ αὐτοῦ** καὶ εὕρῃς· οὐ δυνήσῃ ὑπεριδεῖν;

'... with any lost thing of your brother's, which he loses and you find; you may not ignore it.'

(35)   Shenoute, Ad Phil. Gent. 264, Leipoldt (1955:46):

ⲛⲑⲉ ⲙⲡⲣⲣⲟ ⲉⲧⲙⲙⲁⲩ ⲛⲁⲡⲓⲥⲧⲟⲥ, ⲛⲧⲁϥⲕⲁϩⲧⲏϥ ⲉⲡⲁϥ, ⲡⲛⲟⲩⲧⲉ ⲛⲁⲕⲕⲁⲣⲱⲛ, **ⲉⲧⲣⲉϥⲧⲁⲗϭⲟ
ⲉⲃⲟⲗ ϩⲓⲧⲟⲟⲧϥ** ϩⲙ ⲡⲉϥϣⲱⲛⲉ

'... Like that faithless monarch who trusted in the fly, the god of the Accaronites, that **he might be cured (through him? by him? – N.S.) of his sickness.** '[138]

(36)   Shen.Can. 2 (Kuhn 1956:120, 12)

ⲛ̄ⲧⲉⲧⲛ̄ϩⲉ ⲉϩⲣⲁⲓ ⲁⲩⲱ ⲛ̄ⲧⲉⲧⲛ̄ⲣⲱϩⲧ̄ ⲉⲡⲉⲥⲏⲧ **ⲉⲃⲟⲗ ϩⲓⲧⲟⲟⲧⲟⲩ ⲛ̄ⲛⲇⲁⲓⲙⲱⲛ** ⲉⲧⲁⲡⲁⲧⲁ
ⲙ̄ⲙⲱⲧⲛ̄ ⲁⲩⲱ ⲉⲧⲥⲱⲃⲉ ⲛⲥⲱⲧⲛ̄

'And you will collapse and **be cast** to the ground **by the demons** who deceive and mock you'

(37)   Shen.Can. 8 XO 100:40-42

ⲛⲧⲁϥϣⲟⲟϭⲟⲩ ⲏ ⲛⲧⲁⲩϣⲱϣϭⲉ **ⲉⲃⲟⲗ ϩⲓⲧⲟⲟⲧϥ**

'Whom he smote, or who have been smitten by him (became smitten through him? – N.S.)'

The incompatibility of stative with such constructions invalidates Polotsky's opinion of stative as a passive form, at least, in terms of modern typological linguistics.[139]

1.3.4.3 Eventive paradigm: transitive infinitive replacing *status constructus*?

In the non-durative tenses, the ratio of transitive / causative and intransitive / anticausative use of the absolute infinitive depends, as it seems, on the lexical meaning of each specific verb. Importantly, the paradigm of verbal arguments occurring with transitive eventive infinitives in our sample does not seem to be unbiased: nominal arguments tend to occur more frequently than pronominal ones. On the other hand, forms of *status constructus* (pre-substantival forms), on average, are represented poorly, compared to *status pronominalis*. With some verbs, e.g., ⲟⲩⲱⲛϩ ⲉⲃⲟⲗ 'show / appear', the mutual ratio of the three forms, as attested in the biblical text, is such as to almost speak about complementary distribution between transitive absolute form and *status pronominalis*.

Transitive absolute infinitive with nominal arguments	42
Transitive absolute infinitive with pronominal arguments	0
Status constructus	14
Status pronominalis	54

---

138 Translation by A.Alcock (with agens omitted).
139 Polotsky 1957:228-229

It would be reasonable to suggest that the semantic factor underlying such distribution is not even definiteness[140] or specificity of the object – for substantival objects of infinitives are often definite and specific, too, – but the respective informational weight of the object. In this respect, pronouns differ from most nominal objects. By their very nature, they are anaphoric, which means that they refer to a previously mentioned entity and thus have smaller communicative importance. As such, they tend to not be prosodically prominent and usually form a single prosodic unit with their verbal head.[141] This idea may be further extended to explain the choice between *status absolutus* vs. *status constructus* with nominal arguments. Hence, by way of diachronic reconstruction, one could assume that the absolute form that had been initially reserved for the non-causative usage in the Tripartite at some point started to supplant the construct forms under specific conditions which demanded an accentual separation between the verb and its object, due to the informational importance of the latter.[142]

This explanation would be at variance with Jernstedt's suggestion that the use of the absolute form with pronominal objects in the non-durative tenses had been standard in the previous stages of Egyptian and that the remnants of this practice are preserved in the Scripture Coptic.[143] However, the Demotic data, as attested in the TLA database, rather support our theory: the examples of verbs governing *n-im=* in non-durative tenses are far less frequent than those with pronominal suffixes. There is, therefore, every reason to consider the transitive absolute infinitive an innovation. Whether it had been introduced into the language by analogy with the unchangeable loaned Greek infinitives, as Quack supposes[144], or by an intra-Coptic analogy (with the durative infinitive or with the

---

140 Cf. Engsheden "Verbal semantics and differential object marking in Lycopolitan Coptic" 2018:156: "It would thus seem as if Coptic DOM conforms to the definiteness hierarchy: personal pronoun > proper noun > definite NP > indefinite specific NP > nonspecific NP (e.g. Aissen 2003: 437). The cut-off point along this scale differs between the main two TAM categories (imperfective vs. non-imperfective), but the lowest ranked category (non-specific NPs) is excluded in both. As definiteness is an all-pervasive feature (irrespective of TAM), it can be said to be the single most important factor for the selection of *n*-marking in Coptic…". The author would like to express her deepest gratitude to Dr. Åke Engsheden for bringing his paper to her attention.

141 My impression, though not yet verified statistically, is that in imperative, native transitive verbs will mostly occur in their construct forms, most frequently status pronominalis. If true, this might give an additional weight to the hypothesis of respective communicative importance of the verb and the object as the decisive factor for the choice of form, because by its very essence, imperative tends to emphasize the action which is to be conducted.

142 Such representation would comply, e.g., with J.Haiman's thesis that the distance between morphemes is economically motivated: "X#Y is replaced by X+Y where Y is predictable" (Haiman 1983:782 ff.).

143 Jernstedt (1986: 403): "During the period of the compilation of the Coptic Bible, the use of *status absolutus* with personal pronouns-objects outside the present conjugation still existed in the language, but was on the verge of disappearance. The principle of word-by-word translation applied by the translators of the Bible did not therefore introduce anything new to Coptic syntax, but had just succeeded to take advantage of the vanishing rule reflecting it in such way that totally distorted its ratio compared to the spoken language." (Translation – N.S.)

144 Quack (2020: 70): "… durchgängige Verwendung der indirekten Objektanknüpfung [mit griechischen Verben – N.S.] vielleicht der Auslöser dafür ist, dass sie im Koptischen auch ausserhalb der Dauerzeiten fakultativ gebraucht wird."

intransitive infinitive of the non-durative conjugations), can hardly be established. But in all cases, its use seems to be secondary compared to that of the non-causative forms.

1.3.4.4 Eventive non-causative infinitive: a member of two transitivity oppositions

Let us now consider the two transitivity oppositions: the *eventive* intransitive vs. *eventive* transitive and the *eventive* intransitive vs. *durative* transitive infinitive. If, as assumed above, the transitive use of the eventive infinitive has been a later development, we might expect that these two oppositions will not always have identical semantics. And such, indeed, is the case of the verb ⲥⲱⲣⲙ. The eventive anticausative ⲥⲱⲣⲙ may denote either 'to get lost' or 'to go astray'. Its transitive counterparts do not share this double meaning. In all attestations I could find, the eventive transitive ⲥⲱⲣⲙ invariably means 'lose', while the durative transitive infinitive stands for 'lead astray'. In Crum's opinion, the meaning 'lose' is derived from the general sense of 'send astray',[145] but such semantic derivation does not look plausible. A more probable scenario is that the two oppositions developed independently of each other. Thus, if the original meaning of the verb had been 'lose / be lost', then there would be nothing unexpected about its non-causative component gradually acquiring the synonymic meaning of 'to go astray'. This, in its turn, could later have produced a transitive allomorph with the sense 'to lead astray' in the durative conjugation pattern, which would result in the mentioned divergence of the two transitive forms.

(38)   Wis 12:24

ⲕⲁⲓ ⲅⲁⲣ **ⲁⲩⲥⲱⲣⲙ** ⲙⲡⲟⲩⲉⲓ ⲉϩⲣⲁⲓ ϩⲛ̅ⲛⲉϩⲓⲟⲟⲩⲉ ⲛ̅ⲧⲉⲡⲗⲁⲛⲏ ⲉⲩⲙⲉⲉⲩⲉ ϫⲉ ϩⲛ̅ⲛⲟⲩⲧⲉ ⲛⲉ ⲛⲁⲓ ⲉⲧⲥⲛⲱ ⲛ̅ⲛⲍⲱⲟⲛ ⲛⲛ̅ⲕⲉϩⲉⲑⲛⲟⲥ

καὶ γὰρ τῶν πλάνης ὁδῶν μακρότερον **ἐπλανήθησαν** θεοὺς ὑπολαμβάνοντες τὰ καὶ ἐν ζῴοις τῶν αἰσχρῶν ἄτιμα

'*They **wandered** far even from the normal ways in which people err! They took horrible things to be gods, the worst forms of animal life.*'[146]

(39)   1Sam 9:3

ⲁⲩⲱ ⲛⲉⲟⲟⲩ ⲛ̅ϭⲓⲥ ⲡⲉⲓⲱⲧ ⲛ̅ⲥⲁⲟⲩⲗ **ⲁⲩⲥⲱⲣⲙ**

καὶ **ἀπώλοντο** αἱ ὄνοι Κις πατρὸς Σαουλ,

'*Now the donkeys of Kish, Saul's father, **were lost**.*'

---

145 Crum (1939:355a).
146 Translation: Common English Bible.

(40) 2Tim. 3:13

ⲛⲣⲱⲙⲉ ⲇⲉ ⲙⲡⲟⲛⲏⲣⲟⲥ ⲁⲩⲱ ⲙⲡⲗⲁⲛⲟⲥ ⲥⲉⲛⲁⲡⲣⲟⲕⲟⲡⲧⲉ ⲉⲡⲡⲉⲧ̅ϩⲟⲟⲩ ⲉⲩⲥⲟⲣⲙ ⲁⲩⲱ **ⲉⲩⲥⲱⲣⲙ**

ⲛϩⲉⲛⲕⲟⲟⲩⲉ

πονηροὶ δὲ ἄνθρωποι καὶ γόητες προκόψουσιν ἐπὶ τὸ χεῖρον, **πλανῶντες** καὶ πλανώμενοι.

'...while evil people and impostors will go on from bad to worse, being deceived and *deceiving* others.'[147]

(41) Matt. 10:39

ⲡⲉⲛⲧⲁϥϩⲉ ⲉⲧⲉϥⲯⲩⲭⲏ ϥⲛⲁⲥⲟⲣⲙⲉⲥ ⲁⲩⲱ ⲡⲉⲛⲧⲁϥ**ⲥⲱⲣⲙ** ⲛⲧⲉϥⲯⲩⲭⲏ ⲉⲧⲃⲏⲏⲧ ϥⲛⲁϩⲉ ⲉⲣⲟⲥ

ὁ εὑρὼν τὴν ψυχὴν αὐτοῦ ἀπολέσει αὐτήν, καὶ ὁ **ἀπολέσας** τὴν ψυχὴν αὐτοῦ ἕνεκεν ἐμοῦ εὑρήσει αὐτήν.

'Whoever finds his life will lose it, and whoever *loses* his life for my sake will find it.'

The interesting thing about these examples is that they instantiate the mixed, morphological-templatic, nature of the verbal derivation in Coptic. The meaning of the verbal lexeme depends not only on the verbal root involved, but also on the specific aspectual pattern it is used in.

1.3.4.5 Conjugation bases as a mechanism of valency alternation

By using the term 'morphological-templatic derivation' I mean that for the infinitives of alternating verbs, the Coptic two-conjugation system constitutes a seemingly productive mechanism of valency alternation where the non-durative objectless matrix serves as an operator of valency reduction, and vice versa, the durative matrix is used for causativization. (The presence of an overtly expressed ⲛ-object in the non-durative matrix overrules its voice characteristics.) The conjugation base may therefore be regarded not only as the tense-aspect-mode-head of the infinitival form expanded by the indexes of person and number, but also as its voice head. The tables below illustrate the diathetic distribution across the conjugation patterns for the verbs **ⲃⲱⲗ ⲉⲃⲟⲗ** 'be loosened / loosen', **ⲛⲟⲩϩⲙ** 'be saved / save', **ϣⲱⲱϭⲉ** 'be wounded / wound' and **ⲥⲱⲟⲩϩ** 'gather (intr.) / gather (tr.)'. The examples which are taken from Shenoute's Canons cover all the tokens of the above verbs in the concordance.[148]

147　In Sahidic version, the order of the two epithets differs from that in the Septuagint. The ESV translation has been changed by me accordingly.

148　For lack of published editions, I supplied my own translations. These are approximative and only serve the purpose of intelligibility of the examples. – N.S.

Table 4a. ⲃⲱⲗ (ⲉⲃⲟⲗ)

	be loosened, released	loosen; interpret
Eventive	**C1** ⲙⲡⲉⲡⲟⲩⲁ ⲡⲟⲩⲁ ⲙⲙⲟⲛ ⲃⲱⲗ ⲉⲃⲟⲗ ⲟⲛ ⲡⲏⲇⲟⲛⲏ *none of us has been released from pleasures* **C1** ⲧⲉⲱⲣⲝ ⲙⲙⲟ ⲟⲙ ⲡϭⲟⲗ ⲉⲧⲛⲁⲃⲱⲗ ⲉⲃⲟⲗ *you strengthen yourself through the lie that will be dissolved* **C1** ϣⲁⲣⲉⲧⲥⲓⲟ ⲙ̄ⲡⲟⲉⲓⲕ ⲙ̄ⲡ̄ⲙⲟⲟⲩ ⲉⲣϣⲁⲛⲃⲱⲗ ⲉⲃⲟⲗ *You feed yourself on bread and water, when you stop fasting (lit.: "you are absolved")* **C4** ⲉⲁⲩⲃⲱⲗ ⲉⲃⲟⲗ ⲟⲣⲁⲓ ⲛⲟⲏⲧⲟⲩ ⲛⲙⲣⲣⲉ ⲛⲓⲙ ⲙⲛ ⲕⲁⲕⲓⲁ ⲛⲓⲙ *while they were released from all chains and all evils* **C6** ⲛⲑⲉ ⲛⲧⲁϥⲃⲱⲗ ⲉⲃⲟⲗ ⲁϥⲟⲩⲱϣϥ ⲧⲏⲣϥ *the way he broke down, was crushed altogether* **C6** ⲉⲧⲃⲉ ⲟⲩ ⲁϥⲡⲱⲟ ⲛⲛⲉϥⲟⲟⲉⲓⲧⲉ ⲏ ⲁⲟⲣⲟϥ ⲁϥⲃⲱⲗ ⲉⲃⲟⲗ *why did he tear his clothes or why did he break down?* **C6** ⲉⲙⲡⲁⲧϥⲃⲱⲗ ⲉⲃⲟⲗ ⲛⲙⲙⲁⲛ *when he did not yet come to terms with us* **C6** ϣⲁⲣⲉⲛⲉⲓⲕⲉⲙⲉⲗⲟⲥ ⲃⲱⲗ ⲉⲃⲟⲗ *the other members get weak (lit., dissolved)* **C7** ⲥⲉⲛⲁⲃⲱⲗ ⲉⲃⲟⲗ ⲛⲥⲉϥⲓ ⲙⲙⲁⲩ *they will be dissolved and carried away* **C8** ⲙⲡⲁⲧϥⲃⲱⲗ ⲏ ⲙⲡⲁⲧϥϥⲓ ⲙⲙⲁⲩ ⲟⲓϫⲱⲛ ⲛϭⲓ ⲡϭⲱⲛⲧ *until the wrath is released and comes upon us*	**C6** ⲁⲩⲱ ⲡⲉϥⲥⲁⲧ ⲛⲁⲃⲱⲗ ⲉⲃⲟⲗ ⲛⲙⲙⲣⲣⲉ *his tail will release the chains* **C9** ⲡⲉⲧⲛⲁⲃⲱⲗ ⲉⲃⲟⲗ ⲛⲧⲉⲓⲉⲛⲧⲟⲗⲏ *whoever will dissolve this order…* **C9** ⲉϥⲉⲃⲱⲗ ⲉⲃⲟⲗ ⲛⲧⲉⲯⲩⲭⲏ ⲛⲛⲉⲧⲣⲛⲟⲃⲉ *so that he releases the souls of the sinners*
Durative	**C7** ⲥⲟⲡ ⲉⲛⲃⲱⲗ ⲉⲃⲟⲗ ⲛⲑⲉ ⲛⲟⲩⲟⲙⲉ *sometimes we get dissolved like clay*	**C3** ⲉⲩⲃⲱⲗ ⲙⲙⲟϥ ⲉϫⲙ ⲡⲟⲩⲱϣ ⲙⲡⲉⲩⲟⲏⲧ *while they interpret it at will* **C3** ⲉⲧⲉⲣⲉⲛⲓⲁⲧⲥⲃⲱ ⲃⲱⲗ ⲙⲡⲉϥϣⲁϫⲉ ⲉϫⲙ ⲡⲉⲩⲟⲩⲱϣ *while the unlearned interpret his words at will* **C4** ⲧⲛⲃⲱⲗ ⲙⲙⲟϥ ⲉⲃⲟⲗ ⲉϫⲱⲧⲛ *we disclaim it on your behalf* **C4** ⲁⲩⲱ ⲧⲛⲃⲱⲗ ⲙⲡⲉⲧⲛⲟⲁⲡ ⲉⲃⲟⲗ ⲟⲓϫⲱⲛ *and we disclaim your opinion on us* **C7** ϥⲃⲱⲗ ⲉⲃⲟⲗ ⲛⲛⲉⲟⲃⲏⲩⲉ ⲙⲡⲥⲁⲇⲁⲛⲁⲥ *he destroys the deeds of Satan* **C8** ⲉⲩⲃⲱⲗ ⲉⲣⲟⲟⲩ ⲛⲟⲉⲛⲣⲁⲥⲟⲩ *while they interpret their dreams for them*

Table 4b | ⲛⲟⲩⲋⲙ

	be saved	save
Eventive	**C6** ⲙⲏⲧ ⲛⲉⲛⲧⲁⲩⲛⲟⲩⲋⲙ ⲋⲛ ϣⲉ *ten will be saved out of a hundred* **C6** ⲛⲧⲛⲛⲟⲩⲋⲙ ⲉⲛϭⲓϫ ⲙⲡⲛⲟⲩⲧⲉ *and we shall be saved to the hand of God* **C6** ⲁⲩⲛⲟⲩⲋⲙ ⲏ ⲁⲩⲡⲱⲧ ⲉⲃⲟⲗ ⲛⲙⲡⲉⲑⲟⲟⲩ *they were saved or they eloped from the evil* **C6** ⲛⲉⲛⲧⲁⲩⲛⲟⲩⲋⲙ ⲏ ⲛⲉⲛⲧⲁⲩⲛⲁⲋⲙⲟⲩ ⲉⲃⲟⲗ ⲋⲙ ⲡϣⲏⲓ *those who saved or were saved from the pit* **XR** ⲉⲧⲣⲉⲛⲛⲟⲩⲋⲙ ⲉⲧⲉⲋⲣⲱ ⲛⲕⲱϩⲧ *so that we shall be saved from the flame of fire*	**C1** ⲡⲛⲟⲩⲧⲉ ⲛⲁⲛⲟⲩⲋⲙ̄ ⲛ̄ⲧⲉⲩⲯⲩⲭⲏ *God will save their soul* **C1** ϥⲛⲁⲛⲟⲩⲋⲙ ⲙⲡⲉⲩⲑⲃⲃⲓⲟ *and he will save their humility*
Durative		**C6** ⲉⲙⲛ ⲡⲉⲧⲥⲱⲧⲉ ⲟⲩⲧⲉ ⲙⲛ ⲡⲉⲧⲛⲟⲩⲋⲙ *while there will be no one who rescues or who saves*

Table 4c | ϣⲱⲱϭⲉ

	be wounded	wound
Eventive	**C6** ⲁⲩϣⲱⲱϭⲉ ⲏ ⲉⲁⲧⲁⲡⲉ ϣⲱⲱϭⲉ *they were wounded, or the head was wounded* **C6** ⲏ ⲉⲧⲃⲉ ⲟⲩ ⲙⲡϥϣⲱⲱϭⲉ *why was he not wounded?* **C8** ⲛⲉⲛⲧⲁⲩϣⲱⲱϭⲉ ⲏ ⲛⲉⲛⲧⲁⲧⲉⲧⲛϣⲟⲟϭⲟⲩ *those who were wounded or whom you have wounded* **C8** ⲏ ⲛⲧⲁⲧⲉⲧⲛϣⲱⲱϭⲉ *or who are (2Pl.) wounded* **C8** ⲛⲧⲁϥϣⲟⲟϭⲟⲩ ⲏ ⲛⲧⲁⲩϣⲱⲱϭⲉ ⲉⲃⲟⲗ ⲋⲓⲧⲟⲟⲧϥ *whom he wounded or who were wounded by him* **C9** ⲏ ⲉⲁⲩϣⲱⲱϭⲉ *who were wounded* **C9** ⲉϣⲁⲩϣⲱⲱϭⲉ ⲛⲧⲟⲟⲩ ⲉⲃⲟⲗ ⲋⲓⲧⲟⲟⲧϥ *who were wounded by him*	**C6** ⲙⲏⲡⲟⲧⲉ ⲛⲧⲁϣⲱⲱϭⲉ ⲏ ⲧⲁⲃⲗⲁⲡⲧⲉⲓ ⲙⲡⲁⲓ *lest I shall hurt or harm this one* **C9** ⲉϣⲁⲩϣⲱⲱϭⲉ ⲙⲡⲱⲛⲉ ⲁⲛ *(those who stumble upon a stone), they do not hurt the stone*
Durative	**C8** ⲉⲧⲃⲉ ⲛⲉⲧϣⲟⲟϭⲉ ⲏ ⲛⲉⲧϣⲱⲱϭⲉ ⲛⲟⲩⲟⲉⲓϣ ⲛⲓⲙ	**C7** ⲥϣⲱⲱϭⲉ ⲥⲣ ⲡⲁϩⲣⲉ ⲉⲛⲉⲧⲥⲡⲗⲏⲅⲏ ⲙⲙⲟⲟⲩ *she wounds, (but) she heals those whom she hurts*

Table 4d | cⲱⲟⲩϩ

	be gathered	gather (trans.)
Eventive	**C3** ⲉⲩⲉⲥⲱⲟⲩϩ ϩⲱⲟⲩ ⲟⲛ ⲉϩⲟⲩⲛ ⲙⲛ ⲛⲉⲥⲛⲏⲩ *they will gather together with the brothers*	**C3** ⲟⲩⲛ ⲛⲉⲧⲥⲱⲟⲩϩ ϩⲱⲟⲩ ⲉϩⲟⲩⲛ ⲁⲩⲱ ⲉⲩϣⲁⲁⲧ *there are those who hoard for themselves (lit.: inside), but are still in need*
	C3 ⲉⲛⲁⲥⲱⲟⲩϩ ⲛⲧⲛⲃⲱⲕ *we shall gather and go*	
	C4 ⲛⲧⲁⲧⲉⲧⲛⲥⲱⲟⲩϩ ⲉϩⲟⲩⲛ ϩⲁϩⲧⲉⲧⲏⲩⲧⲛ *you have gathered among yourselves*	**C4** ⲉⲧⲣⲉⲧⲛⲥⲱⲟⲩϩ ⲛⲁⲓ ⲉϩⲟⲩⲛ ⲛⲛⲁⲥⲱϣⲉ *that you harvest my fields for me*
	C6 ⲙⲡⲟⲩⲥⲱⲟⲩϩ ⲉϩⲟⲩⲛ ϩⲓ ⲟⲩⲥⲟⲡ *They did not gather all at once*	**C4** ⲛⲧⲛⲥⲱⲟⲩϩ ⲛⲁⲛ ⲉϩⲟⲩⲛ ⲛⲟⲩⲛⲁ *and let us seek mercy for us*
	C6 ⲥⲱⲟⲩϩ ⲉϩⲟⲩⲛ ⲛⲧⲉⲕⲣⲓⲛⲉ ⲙⲙⲟⲟⲩ *come together and judge them*	**C4** ⲁⲧⲉⲧⲛⲥⲱⲟⲩϩ ⲟⲛ ⲉϩⲟⲩⲛ ⲛϩⲉⲛϣⲁϫⲉ ⲙ̄ⲡⲗⲁⲛⲏ *you collect deceitful words*
	C6 ⲉⲣⲉⲛⲉⲥⲛⲏⲩ ⲧⲏⲣⲟⲩ ⲛⲁⲥⲱⲟⲩϩ ⲉⲛⲉⲩⲉⲣⲏⲩ *when all the brothers will come together*	**C6** ⲙⲡⲛⲧ̄ ⲥⲟ ⲉⲥⲱⲟⲩϩ ⲛⲁⲛ ⲉϩⲟⲩⲛ ⲛⲟⲩϩⲁⲡ ϩⲛ ⲛⲉⲛⲙⲛⲧϣⲁⲩⲧⲉ ⲧⲏⲣⲟⲩ *I willingly collected sentences for all our evil deeds*
	C6 ⲉⲙⲡⲁⲧⲉⲛⲉⲥⲛⲏⲩ ⲧⲏⲣⲟⲩ ⲥⲱⲟⲩϩ *while not all the brothers are gathered*	
	C7 ⲉⲁⲩⲥⲱⲟⲩϩ ⲉϫⲱϥ ϣⲁⲛⲧϥⲙⲟⲩ *gathering upon him until he died*	
	C7 ⲛⲧⲁⲛⲁⲓ ⲧⲏⲣⲟⲩ ⲥⲱⲟⲩϩ ⲉⲣⲟⲥ *into which they all assemble*	
	C7 ⲛⲧⲁⲩⲥⲱⲟⲩϩ ⲉⲛⲉⲩⲉⲣⲏⲩ ϩⲛ ⲧⲁⲫⲟⲣⲙⲏ *which are gathered in the depository*	
	C8 ⲉⲧⲉⲙⲡⲉⲓⲥⲱⲟⲩϩ ⲉϩⲟⲩⲛ ⲛⲙⲙⲏⲧⲛ *I did not gather with you*	
	C8 ϯⲛⲁⲥⲱⲟⲩϩ ⲁⲛ ⲟⲛ ⲧⲉⲛⲟⲩ *I shall not gather now*	
	C9 ⲉϣⲁⲛⲥⲱⲟⲩϩ ⲉϩⲟⲩⲛ ⲛϩⲏⲧⲟⲩ *if you are gathered on them (sci., on Sabbaths)*	
	C9 ⲛⲧⲁⲛⲥⲱⲟⲩϩ ⲁⲛ ⲉϩⲟⲩⲛ ⲉⲛⲉⲓⲧⲟⲡⲟⲥ *it is not in those places that we gather*	
	C9 ⲉⲩϣⲁⲛⲥⲱⲟⲩϩ ⲉⲡⲙⲁ ⲉⲧⲟⲩⲣ ϩⲱⲃ ⲛϩⲏⲧϥ *if they are gathered in their working place*	
	C9 ϣⲁⲛⲧⲟⲩⲥⲱⲟⲩϩ ⲧⲏⲣⲟⲩ *until they are all gathered*	

be gathered	gather (trans.)
Durative	**C5** ⲉⲛⲥⲱⲟⲩϩ ⲛⲁⲛ ⲉϩⲟⲩⲛ ⲛⲟⲩϩⲟⲩⲟ
	as we gather a surplus for us
	C5 ⲉⲩⲥⲱⲟⲩϩ ⲙⲙⲟⲟⲩ ⲛⲁⲩ ⲉϩⲟⲩⲛ
	ⲉⲛⲉⲩϩⲛⲁⲁⲩ
	as they keep amassing their property
	C6 ⲉϥⲥⲱⲟⲩϩ ⲉϩⲟⲩⲛ ⲉⲣⲟⲥ ⲛϩⲉⲛⲁϣⲏ ⲛϥⲛⲧ
	as he gathers lots of worms inside it
	C6 ⲉⲩⲥⲱⲟⲩϩ ⲉϩⲟⲩⲛ ⲉⲧⲟⲟⲧⲥ ⲛⲧⲙⲛⲧⲁⲧⲥⲓ
	while they gather (property) driven by the
	insatiability
	C6 ⲉⲩⲥⲱⲟⲩϩ ⲛⲁⲩ ⲉϩⲟⲩⲛ ⲛⲟⲩϣⲱϣⲉ
	as they pile up poverty for themselves
	C8 ⲉϥⲥⲱⲟⲩϩ ⲉϩⲟⲩⲛ ⲉⲣⲟϥ ⲙⲡⲉϥⲧⲁⲕⲟ
	*Preparing (*lit.*: collecting) his own ruin*
	C8 ⲉⲛⲥⲱⲟⲩϩ ⲛⲧⲉⲭⲣⲓⲁ ⲧⲏⲣⲥ ⲛⲥⲱⲙⲁⲧⲓⲕⲟⲛ
	as we collect every corporeal need

The above tables show that the interpretation of a verb in infinitive emerges as a result of the interplay of the two following factors:

1) the overall meaning of the lexeme proper

2) the morphosyntactic framework the lexeme is incorporated into.

Thus, similarly to Semitic languages,[149] the Coptic verbal system is based on inflectional patterns, the difference being that Semitic templates are discontinuous morphemes consisting of specific vowel sequences the lexical component (verbal root) is combined with, whereas in Coptic the cluster of grammatical elements precedes the lexical component. It therefore has little sense to analyze one specific (transitive or intransitive) facet of a Coptic labile verb as basic, and the other one as derived from it, which is the analysis suggested in Funk (1978). Rather, each conjugation constitutes a derivation pattern in its own right, and infinitival stems serve as derivation bases. Thus, the pair like ⲡⲱⲣϫ 'be divided' vs. ⲡⲱⲣϫ 'divide' are not "two separate lexemes, one of which stands in derivational relationship to the other"[150], but rather two realizations of a single macro-lexeme with the general meaning of division. A description presenting such a pair as a pair of homonyms would be uneconomical.

Interestingly, lability is not a permanent property of a verbal lexeme throughout a dialect. So, in Shenoute's lexicon, ϩⲱⲛ is a non-causative monadic verb with the sense of 'approach':

---

149 See, e.g., Doron (2003) for Modern Hebrew, Arkhipov, Kalinin & Loesov (2021) for Accadian.
150 Funk (1978b:121)

(42)   Shen.Can. 6, Leipoldt (1955:190, 13)

ⲡⲉⲥⲙⲟⲩ ⲉϥⲟⲩⲱⲛϩ ⲉⲃⲟⲗ ⲙⲡⲣⲱⲙⲉ ⲛⲇⲓⲕⲁⲓⲟⲥ ⲛⲙⲡϣⲁ ⲉⲧⲣⲉϥϩⲱⲛ ⲉϩⲟⲩⲛ ⲉⲡϫⲟⲉⲓⲥ

*'The blessing reveals a virtuous man as worthy to **come closer** to the Lord.'*

For the causative counterpart, Shenoute uses the synthetic form ⲧϩⲛⲟ 'make approach', which is also strictly non-labile, at least, in the corpus of the Canons.

(43)   Shen.Can. 1, 14.5

ⲙⲏ ⲙ̄ⲡϫⲟⲉⲓⲥ ⲁⲛ ⲡⲉⲛⲧⲁϥⲥⲟⲧⲡⲉ ⲉⲃⲟⲗ ⲟⲩⲧⲉⲛⲉⲧϩⲓⲧⲟⲩϣ ⲧⲏⲣⲟⲩ ⲉⲁϥⲑⲛⲟ ⲉϩⲟⲩⲛ ⲉⲣⲟϥ·

'War es etwa nicht der Herr, der dich von all deinen Nächsten auserwählt und sich dir genähert hat' (lit.: 'made you come closer to him')

In the Bible, however, the same simplex lexeme may be found in the causative sense of 'make closer' (although 3 times out of 4 occur in one and the same book, Isaiah):

(44)   Isa 5:8

ⲟⲩⲟⲓ ⲛⲛⲉⲧⲧⲱϭⲉ ⲛⲟⲩⲏⲓ ⲉⲩⲏⲓ ⲉⲧϩⲱⲛ ⲛⲟⲩⲥⲱϣⲉ ⲉⲩⲥⲱϣⲉ

Οὐαὶ οἱ συνάπτοντες οἰκίαν πρὸς οἰκίαν καὶ ἀγρὸν πρὸς ἀγρὸν **ἐγγίζοντες**

*'Woe to those who join house to house, who **add** field to field'*

(45)   Isa 5:19

ⲙⲁⲣⲉⲡⲣⲉϥϭⲉⲡⲏ ϩⲱⲛ ⲉϩⲟⲩⲛ ⲛⲛⲉⲧϥⲛⲁⲁⲁⲩ ϫⲉ ⲉⲛⲉⲛⲁⲩ ⲉⲣⲟⲟⲩ

Τὸ τάχος ἐγγισάτω ἃ ποιήσει, ἵνα ἴδωμεν

'Let him be quick, let him speed his work that we may see it'

(46)   Isa 46:13

ⲁⲓϩⲱⲛ ⲉϩⲟⲩⲛ ⲛⲧⲁⲇⲓⲕⲁⲓⲟⲥⲩⲛⲏ

ἤγγισα τὴν δικαιοσύνην μου

'I bring near my righteousness'

On the other hand, ⲧϩⲛⲟ is almost entirely unattested in the Bible. In the case of this verb, the two corpora display alternative ways of causativization. The biblical Coptic causativizes by means of the conjugation pattern, in Shenoute morphological causativization is applied.

1.3.4.6 Classes of mutable verbs: strong transitives, labile verbs, monadic verbs

Cases of unstable lability like the above-described case of ϩⲱⲛ should be kept in mind when dividing Coptic morphologically mutable verbs into diathetic classes. Yet, such cases are rather exceptional. Upon the whole, it is possible to establish one labile and two unalterable classes of Coptic verbs based on the criteria of agency and lexical aspect.[151]

---

151 The same criteria are used for the classification of Akkadian verbs in Arkhipov, Kalinin & Loesov (2021).

Table 5 | Syntactic-semantic classification of native Coptic verbs

	Strong transitive verbs	Labile verbs	Non-labile intransitive verbs
Obligatory agent	+	-	-
Telic aspect[a]	+	+	-

a   This term is used here as a property of an aspectual pair combined in a labile verb, in the sense explained in Paducheva & Pentus (2008:192).

The class of agentive monodiathetic verbs has been identified in Stern (1880). Stern refers to this class as 'verbs of strong active meaning'[152] observing that these verbs never have the anticausative (in Stern's terms, passive) reading. Stern's list of these verbs comprises ϯ 'give', ϫι 'take', ειρε 'do', ϩι 'throw', ειɴε 'bring', ϭιɴε 'cross', ϭιɴε 'find', ⲥϩⲁⲓ 'write', ϣⲱⲡ 'receive', ⲟⲩⲱⲙ 'eat', ⲕⲱⲧ 'build', ⲕⲱ 'put, let, leave', ϫⲱ 'say', and several others. The verb ⲥⲟⲃⲧⲉ 'prepare' most often displays the behavior of a strong transitive verb, although isolated cases of labile use are attested, too. Importantly, this class also includes verbs of perception (ⲥⲱⲧⲙ 'hear, listen', ⲧⲱⲡⲉ 'taste', ϭⲱϣⲧ 'look, see') and a verb of cognition (ⲥⲟⲟⲩⲛ 'know'). [153]Some specific morphosyntactic features of these verbs which are here termed 'strong transitives' are discussed in the chapter 2 of the present work.

At the other extreme we find one-argument unaccusative verbs that do not undergo labile causativization. Semantically, this class consists of verbs predicating a state (ⲥⲣϥⲉ 'be at leisure', ⲙⲟⲩⲛ ⲉⲃⲟⲗ 'remain'), verbs predicating a feature (ⲕⲙⲟⲙ 'be black', ϩⲟⲣϣ 'be heavy', ϩⲱⲱⲙⲉ 'be thin, lean', ϫⲱⲙⲥ 'be foul, stink', ⲕⲣⲟⲙⲣⲙ 'be dark' etc.), certain verbs of emotional state (ⲣⲟⲉⲓⲥ 'care') and verbs whose core event[154] is a change of state (ⲁϣⲁⲓ, ⲣⲱⲧ 'grow', ⲁⲗⲉ 'rise' ϣⲱⲡⲉ 'become').[155] The mechanisms of valency increase for such verbs are morphological and morphosyntactic. Thus, some of them (ⲁⲗⲉ, ⲥⲃⲟⲕ, ⲁϣⲁⲓ) form ⲧ-causatives (ⲧⲁⲗⲟ, ⲧⲥⲃⲕⲟ, ⲧⲁϣⲟ), which, in their turn, are liable to the "standard", conjugation-based valency alternations. Another, productive and therefore more regular mechanism of causativization for the group of univalent verbs is the use of the causative construction with ⲧⲣⲉ-.

_____

152 "verba von stark activer bedeutung", see Stern (1880:302-303).

153 Several other verbs of perception and cognition (ⲛⲁⲩ 'see', ⲙⲟⲩϩ 'look, watch', ⲉⲓⲙⲉ 'learn') are not only monodiathetic, but also morphologically immutable.

154 In Haspelmath et al.(2014:590), the term 'core event' is defined as "the meaning component that is shared by both verbs of a causal - noncausal pair". Defined in this way, the term is, of course, inapplicable to the group of monadic verbs that do not have any causative counterpart. Yet, I would like to preserve it to denote the single most important component of the verbal semantics. Of course, the component of change is present in the semantics of all eventive (i.e., non-stative) verbs. For instance, the intransitive 'break' roughly means 'to pass from the state of wholeness to the state of non-wholeness'. But for such verbs as 'to grow', change is the key semantic component, for the verb does not include any understanding of previous smallness or ensuing greatness. It only states that a change in this direction occurs. The etalon verb with the change as core event is 'to become'.

155 In the more specific analysis in Reintges (2004:230), the following lexical groups are mentioned: verbs of smell emission, verbs of light emission, verbs of inherently directed motion, internally caused verbs of change of state, verbs of existence, occurrence and (dis)appearance.

(47)   Gen 48:4

ειс ϩннте †ναтреκαϣαι νгαιαι

Ἰδοὺ ἐγὼ αὐξανῶ σε καὶ πληθυνῶ σε

'*Behold, I will make you fruitful and multiply you*'

The multiple mechanisms of valency alternation generate two oppositions (monadic simplex vs. т-causative in its non-causative usage and т-causative vs. the causative тре-construction). The semantic or perhaps extra-linguistic factors influencing these oppositions are as yet an open question in the Coptic linguistics; their clarification lies outside the scope of the present work.

As can be seen in the statistical tables, almost all verbs of the mutable monodiathetic class have a TAM-complementary distribution of forms: infinitive for the non-durative tenses and stative for present and imperfect. A notable exception is the subgroup of verbs whose core event includes the semantic component of change. This subgroup uses infinitive in the Bipartite to express various kinds of **non-stative** meaning, which might be:

a)   iterative meaning

(48)   Shen.Can. 8 (XO 286:21-25)

εϣϣε ερϩнвε ннетϣιвε ϩнтεγϩγπομονн κατα καιρος

'*s'il convient de s'affliger pour ceux d'entre nous dont la constance **varie** au gré des circonstances...*'[156]

as opposed to the stative meaning in:

(49)   Shen.Can. 1, 10.3 (XC 16-17)

εϣχε καταπετςнϩ нтαει εвολ ϩнϩενπεθοογ εϩενπεθοογ ειϭερεϣ
ο
вε ноγ нто ενρεϥρνοвε тнρογ

'*Wenn, gemäß der Schrift, du hervorgegangen bist aus Schlechtigkeiten hinein in Schlechtigkeiten, was **unterscheidet** dich dann von allen (anderen) Sündern?*'

b)   dynamic (progressive) meaning

(50)   Ezek 17:8

ϩν ογςϣϣε εναнογς ϩιχν ογνοϭ ммоογ нтος **ςκннвε** ετρεςταγο εвολ нϩεн†ογϣ

εἰς πεδίον καλὸν ἐφ' ὕδατι πολλῷ αὔτη **πιαίνεται** τοῦ ποιεῖν βλαστοὺς

'*It had been planted (lit.: **'grows fat'** – N.S.) on good soil by abundant waters, that it might produce branches*'

vs. the stative

(51)   Num 13:21

αγϣ χε ογ πε πκαϩ χε νεϥ**κιϣ**ογ χε νεϥχαχϣ

Num 13:20 καὶ τίς ἡ γῆ, εἰ **πίων** ἢ παρειμένη

'*and whether the land is rich (lit.: **is fat**) or poor*'

---

156 A. Boud'hors (2013).

(52) Exod 1:12

ⲕⲁⲧⲁ ⲑⲉ ⲇⲉ ⲉⲧⲟⲩⲑⲃⲃⲓⲟ ⲙⲙⲟⲟⲩ ⲧⲁⲓ ⲧⲉ ⲑⲉ ⲉⲛⲉⲩⲁϣⲁⲓ ⲛϩⲟⲩⲟ

καθότι δὲ αὐτοὺς ἐταπείνουν, τοσούτῳ **πλείους ἐγίνοντο**

'*But the more they were oppressed, the more they* **multiplied**...'

vs. stative

(53) Num 22:3

ⲁⲙϣⲁⲃ ⲉⲣϩⲟⲧⲉ ϩⲏⲧϥ ⲙⲡⲗⲁⲟⲥ ⲙⲡϫⲟⲉⲓⲥ ⲛⲉϥⲟϣ ⲅⲁⲣ ⲙⲙⲁⲧⲉ ⲡⲉ

καὶ ἐφοβήθη Μωαβ τὸν λαὸν σφόδρα, ὅτι **πολλοὶ** ἦσαν

'*And Moab was in great dread of the people because they were* **many**.'

The past progressive meaning of these verbs could obviously be expressed by the absolute infinitive with the perfect or imperfect base, without any pronounced difference between them.

(54) Acts 9:31

ⲁⲩⲱ ϩⲙ ⲡⲥⲟⲡⲥ ⲙⲡⲉⲡⲛⲁ ⲉⲧⲟⲩⲁⲁⲃ **ⲛⲉⲥⲁϣⲁⲓ**

καὶ τῇ παρακλήσει τοῦ ἁγίου πνεύματος **ἐπληθύνετο**

'*... and in the comfort of the Holy Spirit, it* **multiplied**'

(55) Acts 12:24

ⲡϣⲁϫⲉ ⲇⲉ ⲙⲡⲛⲟⲩⲧⲉ ⲁϥⲁⲩⲝⲁⲛⲉ ⲁⲩⲱ **ⲁϥⲁϣⲁⲓ**

Ὁ δὲ λόγος τοῦ Θεοῦ ηὔξανε καὶ **ἐπληθύνετο**.

'*but the word of God increased and* **multiplied**'

The distinctions between infinitive and stative forms in the durative conjugation will be further discussed in section 1.3.4.7.

The nucleus of the class of labile verbs consists of telic lexemes with a non-obligatory agent actant in the event scheme, such as ⲡⲱϩ 'break, burst, tear', ⲱϭⲣ 'freeze', ⲥⲱⲕ 'draw, flow', ⲥⲟⲟⲩⲧⲛ 'stretch', ⲥⲱⲟⲩϩ 'gather', ⲡⲱⲱⲛⲉ 'turn', ⲡⲱϣ 'divide', ⲟⲩⲱⲛ 'open', etc. Occasionally, however, the verbs that do not comply with one of the two criteria may nevertheless demonstrate lability. So, ⲙⲟⲟⲛⲉ 'graze, pasture' is labile and atelic, ⲥⲱⲛⲧ 'create / be created', ⲱϣⲱϭⲉ 'wound / be wounded' have an obligatory agent but can be used in a clause with a patient subject. Yet, such cases are presumably rather infrequent.

Apart from these three classes of mutable verbs, Coptic verbal vocabulary includes the immutable class consisting of unergative verbs, such as verbs of movement and posture, verbs of sound emission (ⲟⲩⲉⲗⲟⲩⲉⲗⲉ 'howl', ⲕⲁⲥⲕⲥ 'whisper', ϩⲙϩⲙ 'neigh', ϩⲱⲥ 'sing'), communication (ϣⲗⲏⲗ 'pray', ϣⲟϫⲛⲉ 'take counsel', ⲙⲟⲩⲧⲉ 'call', ⲥⲙⲙⲉ 'appeal' and others).[157]

---

157 A very similar classification of unergatives can be found in Reintges (2004:229). The semantic groups mentioned by Reintges are: sound emission, bodily activity or expression, manner of motion.

1.3.4.7   The opposition <infinitive: stative> in the Bipartite conjugation

Let us now come back to the issue of the respective status of infinitive and stative forms in the durative tenses. As a start, I shall try to summarize the conditions bringing about the use of the Bipartite intransitive infinitive.

In 1.3.4.6, it has been demonstrated that a specific lexical group of unaccusatives (verbs lexicalizing change of state) use durative infinitive to express the meaning of a progressive non-causative present. Such meaning combining the semantics of process and of change of state is, on the ontological grounds, rather rare.

Beside the sporadic occurrences with non-labile monadic verbs, intransitive infinitives may also surface with labile verbs. Thus, in Shenoute's Canons, a Bipartite intransitive infinitive appears to be bound to the idea of *iterativity*, which can be dictated by the context or else constitute a part of the proper lexical meaning of a verb. The context-bound iterativity may be illustrated by the following examples:

(56)   Shen.Can. 7 GN381, Crum (1905, frag.194 f.3)[158]

ⲁⲛⲟⲛ ⲇⲉ ⲁⲛⲟⲛ ⲅⲉⲛⲕⲁⲅ · ⲥⲟⲡ ⲉⲛ**ⲃⲱⲗ ⲉⲃⲟⲗ** ⲛⲑⲉ ⲛⲟⲩⲟⲙⲉ · ⲥⲟⲡ ⲉⲛ**ⲡⲱⲟⲃ** ⲛ̄ⲑⲉ ⲛⲟⲩⲭⲟⲣⲧⲟⲥ ⲉⲙⲛ̄ ⲙⲟⲟⲩ ⲅⲁⲣⲟϥ

'*As for us, we are but earth. Sometimes we **dissolve** like clay, sometimes we **wither** like grass devoid of water.*'

(57)   Shen.Can 6, Amel. 2 (317:2)

ⲅⲉⲛⲥⲩⲛⲁⲅⲱⲅⲏ ⲉⲁⲩⲣⲱⲙⲉ ⲡⲱⲅ ⲛⲛⲉϥⲅⲟⲉⲓⲧⲉ ⲅⲣⲁⲓ ⲛⲅⲏⲧⲟⲩ ⲛⲅⲁⲅ ⲛⲥⲟⲡ ⲉⲙⲁⲧⲉ ⲉϥⲅⲓⲟⲩⲉ ⲉⲅⲟⲩⲛ ⲅⲙ ⲡⲉϥⲅⲟ ⲅⲛ ⲧⲉϥϭⲟⲙ ⲁⲩⲱ ⲉϥⲅⲉ ⲉϥ**ⲣⲱⲟⲧ** ⲉⲅⲣⲁⲓ ⲉⲝⲙ ⲡⲕⲁⲅ ⲝⲉ ⲙⲛ ϭⲟⲙ ⲙⲙⲟϥ ⲉⲁⲅⲉⲣⲁⲧϥ

'*…monastic communities where one would often tear his clothes hitting himself on the face with all his might, and fall, **collapsing** to the ground, because he does not have strength enough to stand*'

The infinitives in bold represent unique occurrences of their lexemes in a non-stative form in the Bipartite. Besides the form of the verb as such, iterativity is signaled by characteristic adverbials, such as ⲥⲟⲡ ⲉ-… ⲥⲟⲡ ⲉ- 'at times, now… again', ⲅⲁⲅ ⲛⲥⲟⲡ 'many times'.

On the other hand, for the lexically coded iteration, this durative form would be a standard one. This can be observed on such verbs as ⲅⲓⲧⲉ 'move to and fro' or ⲡⲱⲱⲛⲉ 'toss and turn'.

(58)   Shen.Can. 9 DF 113:16-17, Pleyte & Boeser (1897)

ⲟⲩⲛ̄ ⲟⲩⲁ ⲙⲉⲛ ⲅⲟⲥⲉ ⲉϥⲧⲁⲗⲁⲓⲡⲟⲣⲉⲓ ⲝⲓⲛ ⲅⲧⲟⲟⲩⲉ ⳉⲁ ⲣⲟⲩⲅⲉ ⲅⲙ̄ ⲡⲉⲣⲅⲱⲃ ⲕⲉⲟⲩⲁ ⲇⲉ ⲉϥ**ⲅⲓⲧⲉ** ⲝⲓⲛ ⲅⲧⲟⲟⲩⲉ ⳉⲁ ⲣⲟⲩⲅⲉ

'*There is one who toileth miserably from dawn till evening, while some other loiters (lit.: '**walks hither and thither**') from dawn till evening.*'

---

158 Crum's translation ("we are but earth and wither as grass") deviates slightly from the Coptic text. Translation – N.S.

(59)   Shen.Can. 6, Amel. 2 (322:7-8)

ϯⲡⲱⲱⲛⲉ ⲛ̅ϩⲏⲧⲟⲩ ϩⲛ ⲟⲩⲙⲁ ⲉⲩⲙⲁ ⲉⲩⲙⲁ ⲉⲓⲥⲟⲛⲧ ⲉⲃⲟⲗ ⲛ̅ⲧⲉⲩϣⲏ ⲧⲏⲣⲥ ⲉⲓⲉⲡⲓⲑⲩⲙⲉⲓ
ⲉⲧⲣⲉⲡⲟⲩⲟⲉⲓⲛ ⲉⲓ ⲉϩⲣⲁⲓ

'*I toss and turn* inside it (i.e., my bed – N.S.) from side to side waiting the whole
night through for the light to come out'

As a matter of fact, the infinitive form of these verbs is not opposed to any stative. For ϩⲓⲧⲉ,
there is no stative attested in Crum's dictionary. The entry for ⲡⲱⲱⲛⲉ does include the
stative ⲡⲟⲟⲛⲉ, but it is not used in the Canons. Since both verbs have construct allomorphs,
they can still be considered mutable; but there is a reason to suppose that their stative form
was gradually supplanted by infinitive precisely because of the iterative character of the
lexeme as such.[159]

Funnily enough, such is also the case of the verb of movement *par excellence*, ⲕⲓⲙ
'move, make movements'. Being a mutable verb, in as much as its construct allomorphs
are attested in the Bible, it is used as infinitive in the Bipartite and for all we know, does not
possess any stative form, which probably must be explained by the idea of the repetition of
movement contributing to its semantics.

An intransitive use of a causative morpheme to denote iteration is not unusual, from the
typological point of view. In Nedyalkov & Sil'nickij (1973), the meaning of intensity or
iterativity is claimed to be one of the cross-linguistically attested outcomes of a causative
derivation that does not increase original valency. Thus, in Zulu, the form *enz-isa* derived
from *enza* 'work' by means of a causative suffix has the meaning of 'work persistently', if
there is no direct object present. Further on, according to Nedyalkov, "it is apparently no
coincidence that in some languages synchronically primary V^{tr} (and even V^{in}) designating
actions which are *iterative by nature* and seemingly composed of a set of similar actions
contain a causative morpheme, e.g., Abkhazian *a-r-x-ra* 'mow'… Georgian *i-c-in-i*
'laugh'".[160] Of course, the similarity between Zulu and Coptic does not immediately strike
the eye, Coptic having no derivational causative morpheme. If, however, we take into
account that in the Bipartite infinitive itself is a marked transitive form, then its location
in an objectless paradigm equals to the non-valency increasing causative derivation.[161]
Again, the observed cases of lexical iteratives with the same alternation pattern echo the
instances mentioned by Nedyalkov for Abkhazian and Georgian.

In all other cases, except the two discussed above (dynamic interpretation with
the change-of-state verbs and iterative interpretation with labile verbs), the use of an
intransitive infinitive form where one would rather expect a stative must, in all likelihood,

---

159 Neither is the stative of ⲡⲱⲱⲛⲉ attested in the Bible. Durative intransitive infinitive occurs in Sir.
      18:25 and Gal. 1:6.

160 Nedjalkov & Sil'nickij (1973:20).

161 Interestingly, what looks like an exactly opposite phenomenon, namely, iterative sense conveyed
      through a reflexive form, may be a slightly different reflexion of the same underlying factor:
      non-valency changing, i.e., non-directed transitivity interpreted as an enhancement of the action,
      multiplying its objects or its occurrences. Examples of that may be found in Doron (2003).

be considered a formal variation without any functional meaning. Consider, e.g., the total semantic, even textual identity of the Greek *Vorlage* for the following examples:

(60) Joel 2:31

ⲉⲙⲡⲁⲧϥⲉⲓ ⲛϭⲓ ⲡⲛⲟϭ ⲛϩⲟⲟⲩ ⲙⲡⲭⲟⲉⲓⲥ ⲉⲧⲟⲩⲱⲛϩ ⲉⲃⲟⲗ

Joel 3:4 πρὶν ἐλθεῖν ἡμέραν κυρίου τὴν μεγάλην καὶ ἐπιφανῆ

and

Acts 2:20

ⲙⲡⲁⲧϥⲉⲓ ⲛϭⲓ ⲡⲉϩⲟⲟⲩ ⲙⲡⲭⲟⲉⲓⲥ ⲡⲛⲟϭ ⲉⲧⲟⲩⲟⲛϩ ⲉⲃⲟⲗ

πρὶν ἐλθεῖν ἡμέραν Κυρίου τὴν μεγάλην καὶ ἐπιφανῆ

'*before the day of the Lord comes, the great and magnificent*'

Another example of the free variation between stative and infinitive is the treatment of the verb ϩⲱⲛ 'approach'. In Luke 15:1, it translates the same Greek form (auxiliary εἰμί + present participle of ἐγγίζω), as in Jer 23:23.

(61) Luke 15:1

ⲛⲉⲣⲉⲛⲧⲉⲗⲱⲛⲏⲥ ⲇⲉ ⲧⲏⲣⲟⲩ ⲛⲙ ⲣⲣⲉϥⲣⲛⲟⲃⲉ **ϩⲱⲛ ⲉϩⲟⲩⲛ** ⲉⲣⲟϥ ⲉⲥⲱⲧⲙ ⲉⲣⲟϥ

Ἦσαν δὲ αὐτῷ ἐγγίζοντες πάντες οἱ τελῶναι καὶ οἱ ἁμαρτωλοὶ ἀκούειν αὐτοῦ.

'*Now the tax collectors and sinners were all drawing near to hear him*'

(62) Jer. 23:23

ⲁⲛⲟⲕ ⲡⲉ ⲡⲛⲟⲩⲧⲉ ⲉⲧϩⲏⲛ **ⲉϩⲟⲩⲛ**

θεὸς ἐγγίζων ἐγώ εἰμι

'*I am a God at hand*'

In both cases, the stative ϩⲏⲛ is to be expected. Indeed, as is expected for a verb of movement, ϩⲏⲛ occurs 101 times in the Bible, as opposed to 4 tokens of the durative intransitive ϩⲱⲛ, without any aspectual difference traceable. Both forms can translate the periphrastic participle construction, as in (61) and (62) above, and the adjectival phrase ἐγγύς εἰμι, as in (63) and (64):

(63) Rev. 22:10

ⲙⲡⲣⲧⲱⲱⲃⲉ ⲛⲛϣⲁϫⲉ ⲛⲧⲉⲓⲡⲣⲟⲫⲏⲧⲓⲁ ⲙⲡⲉⲓϫⲱⲱⲙⲉ ϫⲉ ⲡⲉⲟⲩⲟⲉⲓϣ ⲅⲁⲣ **ϩⲱⲛ** ⲉϩⲟⲩⲛ

Μὴ σφραγίσῃς τοὺς λόγους τῆς προφητείας τοῦ βιβλίου τούτου· ὁ καιρὸς γὰρ **ἐγγύς ἐστιν**

'*Do not seal up the words of the prophecy of this book, for the time **is near***'

(64) Rom. 10:8

ⲡϣⲁϫⲉ **ϩⲏⲛ** ⲉϩⲟⲩⲛ ⲉⲣⲟⲕ ϩⲛ ⲧⲉⲕⲧⲁⲡⲣⲟ ⲁⲩⲱ ϩⲣⲁⲓ ϩⲙ ⲡⲉⲕϩⲏⲧ

Ἐγγύς σου τὸ ῥῆμά **ἐστιν**, ἐν τῷ στόματί σου καὶ ἐν τῇ καρδίᾳ σου·

'*The message **is very close at hand**; it is on your lips and in your heart*'

Besides, stative is also used to convey the dynamic meaning expressed in Greek by a finite verb:

(65)   Isa 41:21

ⲡⲉⲧⲛ̄ϩⲁⲡ ϩⲏⲛ ⲉϩⲟⲩⲛ ⲡⲉϫⲉ ⲡϫⲟⲉⲓⲥ ⲛⲟⲩⲧⲉ ⲁⲛⲉⲧⲛϣⲁⲭⲛⲉ[162] ϩⲱⲛ ⲉϩⲟⲩⲛ ⲡⲉϫⲉ ⲡⲣⲣⲟ
ⲛⲓⲁⲕⲱⲃ

Ἐγγίζει ἡ κρίσις ὑμῶν, λέγει κύριος ὁ θεός· ἤγγισαν αἱ βουλαὶ ὑμῶν, λέγει ὁ
βασιλεὺς Ιακωβ.

'*Your judgement **comes close**, says the Lord God. Your arguments have come, says
the King Jacob*'[163]

The free variation or competition of semantically equal forms would usually result in
one form superseding the other, and indeed, various dialects of Coptic yield examples of
stative and infinitive replacing each other, as, for instance, in the case of the verb 'sit',
represented in both conjugations by the infinitive ⲃⲉⲙⲥⲓ in Bohairic and the stative ϩⲙⲟⲟⲥ
in Sahidic and other dialects.[164] The prevalence of that or the other form is individual
for each specific verb. So, for example, the stative ⲧⲁⲕⲏⲩ(ⲧ) of the verb ⲧⲁⲕⲟ 'destroy'
seems to have acquired adjectival character and is mostly used as an epithet ('spoilt,
κατεφθαρμένος) in Shenoute and in the Bible; the infinitive of this verb comes in not only
for iterative / habitual (2Cor. 4:9, 2Cor. 4:16, Jude 1:10), but also for resultative (Job 5:11)
usage which is characteristic of statives.

At the same time, the cases of stative used for dynamic meanings are evidently less
frequent than the reverse situation. In the biblical sample, there is at best one instance that
allows such an interpretation of stative.

(66)   Luke 2:40

ⲡϣⲏⲣⲉ ⲇⲉ ϣⲏⲙ ⲛⲉⲁϥⲁⲓⲁⲉⲓ ⲁⲩⲱ ⲛⲉϥϭⲙϭⲟⲙ ⲉϥⲙⲉϩ ⲛⲧⲥⲟⲫⲓⲁ
τὸ δὲ παιδίον ηὔξανεν καὶ ἐκραταιοῦτο **πληρούμενον** σοφίᾳ
And the child grew and became strong, **filled** with wisdom.

The use of the imperfective participle in Greek presents the action as progressive, as
opposed to the resultative sense conveyed in the English translation. But the uniqueness
of such an example in Coptic makes one think that the aspectual difference in this case
is neutralized, rather than expressed in an alternative way. In all other cases, stative is
reserved – both in Scriptures and in Shenoute – for resultative or stative meanings, as in

(67)   EpJer 16

ⲛⲉⲩⲃⲁⲗ ⲥⲉⲙⲉϩ ⲛ̄ϣⲟⲉⲓϣ
οἱ ὀφθαλμοὶ αὐτῶν **πλήρεις** εἰσὶν κονιορτοῦ
'*Their eyes are **full** of the dust*'

---

162 Read ϣⲟⲭⲛⲉ. Orthography according to Coptic Old Testament edition (http://data.
copticscriptorium.org/texts/old-testament/).

163 My translation deviates from the one in the ESV, so that it may more closely resemble the Coptic
text.

164 A detailed discussion of the functional neutralization between infinitive and stative can be found
in Funk (1978a:27 ff.).

(68)   Job 41:19

ⲉⲣⲉ ⲛⲃⲁⲕⲱⲛⲉ ⲏⲡ ⲛⲧⲟⲟⲧϥ ⲛⲧⲣⲉ ⲛⲟⲩⲭⲟⲣⲧⲟⲥ

Job 41:20 ἥγηται μὲν πετροβόλον χόρτον·

Job 41:28 '*for him, sling stones are turned to (lit.:* **count** *as) stubble*'

(69)   2Sam 11:11

ⲡⲁϫⲟⲉⲓⲥ ⲓⲱⲁⲃ ⲙⲛ ⲛⲉϩⲙϩⲁⲗ ⲙⲡⲁϫⲟⲉⲓⲥ ⲥⲉ**ⲡⲟⲣ(ϣ)** ⲉⲃⲟⲗ ϩⲓ ϩⲣⲁⲥ ⲛⲧⲥⲱ(ϣ)ⲉ

ὁ κύριός μου Ιωαβ καὶ οἱ δοῦλοι τοῦ κυρίου μου ἐπὶ πρόσωπον τοῦ ἀγροῦ **παρεμβάλλουσιν**

'*my lord Joab and the servants of my lord* **are camping** *(lit:* **spread**) *in the open field*'

(70)   Num 14:14

ⲁⲩⲱ ⲛⲧⲟⲕ ⲡϫⲟⲉⲓⲥ **ⲕⲟⲩⲟⲛϩ** ⲉⲃⲟⲗ ⲉⲣⲟϥ ⲛⲃⲁⲗ ϩⲓⲃⲁⲗ

ὅστις ὀφθαλμοῖς κατ᾽ ὀφθαλμοὺς **ὀπτάζῃ** κύριε

'*For you, O Lord,* **are seen** *face to face*'

The incompatibility of non-causative infinitives and infinitives of verbs of movement with the durative pattern, unless in the iterative sense, may occasionally be of use as an analytic tool for elucidation of homonyms. This logic can be applied to the lexeme ⲙⲟⲩϩ in:

(71)   P. Morgan Library M.593 Installation of Michael (Müller 1962:58,9-12)

ⲙ̄ⲡⲉⲣⲉⲛⲕⲟⲧⲕ̄ ⲟⲩⲇⲉ ⲙ̄ⲡⲉⲣϯⲛⲏⲃ, ⲁⲗⲗⲁ ϣⲱⲡⲉ ⲉ̄ⲣⲉⲛⲉⲧⲛϯ ⲙⲏⲣ **ⲉⲣⲉⲛⲉⲧⲉⲛϩⲏⲃ̄ⲥ̄ ⲙⲟⲩϩ**

Theoretically, two out of the three homonyms for ⲙⲟⲩϩ ('take a look', 'fill / be filled', 'burn') would fit in well as a predicate for ⲛⲉⲧⲉⲛϩⲏⲃ̄ⲥ̄ 'your lamps': 'be filled' as well as 'burn'. However, 'be filled' as a non-causative verb must be excluded from consideration. The correct translation, consequently, is 'burn':

'*Do not lie down nor do you fall asleep, but keep your loins girdled and your lamps burning.*'[165]

The data gathered in the above discussion make it possible to revise the scope of aspectual meanings the Coptic present tense can assume. According to Layton (2000), the present tense pattern expresses an enduring, ongoing or general action, process, state or situation.[166] Reintges (2004) distinguishes between the perceptive, performative, epistemic, habitual and generic types of present, whereas the aorist, in his opinion, can have multiple, iterative, frequentative, distributive, habitual or extensive reading. Our examples show that besides denoting primary or secondary states, the present can also have iterative or dynamic meaning that can be morphologically signaled through the infinitive of a mutable intransitive verb. Thus, the area of semantic intersection between aorist and present is greater than one can infer from grammars and calls for a further and more detailed research.

---

165 Of course, since the passage is a quotation from Luke 12:35, we do not have to recur to grammar analysis in order to understand the text. Yet, it is important to know that such analytic tool exists.

166 Layton (2011:233).

1.3.5 Diachrony

1.3.5.1 Attestations of causative split in pre-Coptic Egyptian

Although the huge life span of the documented Egyptian language[167] makes it possible to engage in the adventurous enterprise of 'linguistic archeology' speculating how different parts of the system changed over enormous periods of time, the sheer complexity of the pre-Coptic conjugation, not to mention limitations of the Egyptian writing system, work against all attempts at creating a concise and transparent diachronic survey. What follows should therefore be taken rather as a tentative sketch of such a survey, than as a final statement on "how everything has really happened". With that proviso, I shall venture the following analysis of the observable data.

As specified in 1.3.2.1, one can discern in the Coptic conjugation system two layers, that of morphologically marked forms (construct forms, stative) and that of the unmarked absolute infinitives. Let us imagine that the unmarked layer is a secondary one, that it has emerged in the process of paradigm readjustment after some categorial shift in the system. What we are left with is a paradigmatic system where the binary oppositions of tense (past vs. present), aspect (perfective vs. imperfective) and diathesis (transitive vs. intransitive) are not yet shaped in separate morphosyntactic paradigms, but rather merged in two categorial clusters: <transitive perfective past> and <imperfective intransitive present>. These two clusters may be thought of as the nucleus of the verbal system, while secondary forms expanding this nucleus filled the gaps where the category of tense disengaged itself from aspect and transitivity, such gaps as the intransitive past tense, the transitive present tense, the imperfective past tense. (Thus, our model, explains, inter alia, also the secondary derivation of the imperfective past tense by means of the preterite converter.)

The nucleus hypothesis conforms with Hopper & Thompson's generalizations regarding transitivity, since the perfective aspect is supposed to correlate with high degree of transitivity. Moreover, the clusterization of the three above categories as such is also not unheard of in linguistic typology. In this connection, one can recall the phenomenon of split ergativity which consists in the interdependence between different alignment patterns (ergative-absolutive or nominative-accusative) and tense-aspect (perfective / imperfective) characteristics of the clause. Even closer is the phenomenon of **split causativity** (predominant intransitivity of perfective forms for some verbs) described by Kulikov for Vedic Sanskrit and Ancient Greek. According to Kulikov,

"...the hypothesis of a genetic relatedness of these three categories appears quite plausible, notwithstanding the fact that they belong to three different classes: the perfect is a tense, the stative is usually considered an aspectual category, and the middle participates in the voice, or diathesis, opposition. In contemporary Indo-European studies these three categories are taken as associated with each other so intimately that some scholars even treat the perfect as one of the members of the diathesis opposition (active vs. perfect[-

---

167 See, e.g., Grossman and Richter (2015:70).

middle]), although, at first glance, the expression 'perfect diathesis' makes no more sense than, say, 'nominative number' or 'feminine case'."[168]

Split causativity is manifested in the older Indo-European languages, — Ancient Greek and Vedic Sanskrit, — through the phenomenon of the morphological tense-diathesis split. So, in Ancient Greek, active perfects of many verbs are intransitive non-causatives, whereas the corresponding present forms are transitive causative.

a. εἰ καί μιν Ὀλύμπιος αὐτὸς **ἐγείρει** (Iliad, N 58)
   if and him Olympian.Nom.SG self.Nom.SG awake.Pres-3SG.ACT
   'and if the Olympian himself awakes him ... '

b. οἱ δ'**ἐγρηγόρθασι** (Iliad, K 419)
   they awake.PF-3pL.ACT
   'They awoke.' (Example from Kulikov 1999:29)

Since perfectivity is supposed to be linked to a higher degree of transitivity, the anticausative perfects of Ancient Greek may seem puzzling. The unexpected combination can be explained by the semantic proximity between perfect and resultative stative. It is assumed that the intransitive form had originally functioned as a stative and later became reinterpreted as a past tense form.[169] If our interpretation of the Coptic data is correct, then Coptic represents an even more elegant instance of split causativity, where the three categories are clustered in a non-contradictory way.

At first sight, our model has an important drawback, because it seems to suggest that the above-described unfolding of the categories and emergence of the secondary forms has been a rather late, partly intra-Coptic phenomenon, which obviously cannot be true. However, one should take into account another possibility, namely, that some fundamental parts of the verbal mechanism, such as stative / transitive past patterns, were inherited through all the stages of the language, whereas the rest were configured around and adapted to this fundamental part in different ways.

Indeed, the Egyptian verbal system, the way it is represented in Old, Middle, Late Egyptian and Demotic grammars, has always had a tendency for a complementary distribution of transitive and intransitive verbs by various tense-aspect patterns with a following lifting of restrictions and reorganization of patterns. According to Edel (1955), the Old Egyptian perfect *sḏm=f* can be found solely with transitive verbs[170]. In Middle

---

168 Kulikov (1999:30 ff.).
169 Kulikov (1999:31).
170 Edel (1955:213). The description of the *sḏm=f* pattern in Malaise & Winand (1999) differs significantly from that given in Edel (1955). According to Malaise & Winand, this pattern underwent the change from Old Egyptian intransitive perfect tense to Middle Egyptian punctual past, which was compatible with transitive and intransitive verbs alike, though lexically restricted: "*En ancien egyptien*, dans les Textes des Pyramides, regulierement dote d'un sujet nominale, il est atteste avec les verbes intransitifs, comme contrepartie de la sdm.n.f des verbes transitifs... *En Egyptien classique*, le perfectif sdm.f est un accompli ponctuel... On trouve le perfectif sdm.f aussi bien avec des verbs transitifs qu'avec des verbes intransitifs." Interestingly, both contradicting descriptions mention diathesis restrictions in the distribution of the pattern.

Egyptian, the 'division of labor' between the two patterns — the *sḏm.n.f* and the stative pattern — is described as transitivity / intransitivity opposition[171], because both patterns are supposed to be identical in the denotation of tense and aspect. In Late Egyptian, the form *sḏm.n.f* becomes obsolete and falls out of use, but the same transitivity opposition resurfaces in the opposition of patterns *sḏm.f* and stative. So, according to Junge' Late Egyptian Grammar, "the Late Egyptian preterite *sḏm=f* ... (is) used exclusively with transitive verbs. Intransitive verbs, especially verbs of motion, use the First Present with the Old Perfective[172]". And again, in Demotic, the restriction on the compatibility of *sḏm=f* with intransitive verbs had slackened. Thus, according to Quack:

"Im Unterschied zum Neuägyptischen können auch intransitive Verben im *sḏm=f* der Vergangenheit konstruiert werden, speziell auch Bewegungsverben, bei denen das Vergangenheitstempus *sḏm=f* die ältere Vergangenheitsbildung mit dem Pseudopartizip im Präsens I ablöst.[173]"

At the same time, the form itself becomes slowly marginalized[174], replaced by the periphrastic form with the auxiliary *jrj* 'to do'.

Thus, it seems that in the whole course of Egyptian language, its verbal system tried to keep apart some kind of telic transitive and atelic intransitive structure, both given to an interpretation as a reference to a past action or to a present state resulting from that action. Thus, *pḥ.n.j ȝbw* can be both "I have travelled as far as to Elephantine" and "I am in Elephantine". The link between resultative forms and transitivity is explained by Kulikov as follows:

"In fact, the semantics of the PERFECT has two facets. One of them relates to an event in the past resulting in a certain state in the present. This part of the perfect semantics ('actional perfect') implies high effectiveness of an action and therefore must correspond to a high transitivity degree…The other facet is the meaning of an achieved state of affairs (resulting from some action in the past)[175], which belongs to the sphere of the present."

However, in order to avoid the danger of oversimplification, we have to bear in mind also the following. No Old or Middle Egyptian grammar describes the *sḏm=f* pattern as a transitive **structure**. Quite the contrary, it is underlined that this pattern is compatible with transitive **lexemes**, quite independently of whether they have an object. Thus, according to Edel (1955), "die Verwendung des *sḏmf* als historisches Perfekt… begegnet allerdings nur bei transitiven Verben (**mit oder ohne Objekt**)."[176]The important prerequisite for this

---

171 So, e.g., in Allen 2014: 247 with some examples, such as:
Xnt.kw pH.n.j Abw (Hatnub 14, 6) 'I have gone upstream and reached Elephantine.'
172 Junge-Warburton, Late Egyptian Grammar 3.5.1
173 Quack (2020: 78, § 12.4.1).
174 See ibid., p.73: "Im Spätdemotischen wird zunehmend das *sḏm=f* durch *irD=f sḏm* ersetzt."
175 Curiously, this resultative semantics of present rooted in the past was precisely the feature discerned by Young in Shenoute's use of present (Young 1961:116).
176 Edel (1955:213, § 467). Cf. Satzinger (1976:132), "unter den Verben, die im perfektischen *sḏm.f* belegt sind, sind nun auch solche, die zwar in gleicher oder ähnlicher Bedeutung transitiv

and the like statements is that the Egyptian finite forms, like the construct forms and the stative in Coptic, have a fixed diathesis. Hence, for transitive verbs, the opposition <*sḏm.f* : stative> pattern is valid and has the above-described sense (telic transitive vs. atelic intransitive):

(72)   Papyrus Nu, Tb 124, 2
       ḳd.n b3 =j ḫnr,t m ḏd,w
       '*My Ba has built a fortress in Busiris*'

vs.

(73)   P.Kairo CG 51189 (P.Juja), Tb 149, 860
       mn,w ḳd(.w)[177]
       '*Min is created*'

Or:

(74)   P. London BM EA 10477 (P.Nu), Tb 083, [2]
       sd.n =(j) wj m štw
       '*I have dressed / concealed myself as a turtle*'

vs.

(75)   P.Berlin P 3022, Sinuhe, 293-294
       sd.kw m p3ḳ,t gs.kw m tp,t sḏr.kw ḥr ḥnk,yt
       '*I was dressed in finest linen, anointed with oil, I lay on a bed*'

But for most intransitive verbs, this opposition is simply invalid. For them, the *sḏm=f* pattern is inaccessible, in much the same way, as the transitive part of the Coptic paradigm is inaccessible for monadic verbs. As follows from this analogy, this lexical constraint does not compromise the general model of tense-aspect-diathesis split.

Trying to reconstruct the details of the shift that transformed the earlier Egyptian diathetic system into the Coptic one, you inevitably stumble upon one more difficulty. As mentioned above, in the pre-Coptic stages of the language, the finite forms of the verb tended to have one diathesis. Incidentally, this was the reason for the remarkably frequent use of the causativizing *dj*-construction with monadic verbs, e.g., in Demotic. E.g., for a verb such as *wj* 'be (make) far', I have been able to find just one transitive example in the TLA database:

(76)   P.Berlin P 15530, x+13
       iw=f-ḫpr r rwḥ =f ḥD mj wj =w s r.r =f
       '*Wenn er Anstoß nimmt, soll man ihn von ihm (dem Heiligtum?!) entfernen!*'

---

gebraucht werden können, im speziellen Fall jedoch objektlos sind ("Objekttilgung")."

177 In the equivalent passage of Papyrus Nu, Tb 149, the identical phrase is interpreted as active: 'Min creates' (https://aaew.bbaw.de/tla/servlet/GetCtxt?u=guest&f=0&l=0&db=0&tc=25757&ws=101& mv=3, as of 07.03.2021). However, the passive reading seems to be more appropriate in the context.

On the other hand, the database contains about 150 instances of the *dj(.t) wj* construction, such as:

(77) P. Spiegelberg, XI,20

bw-ir =w dj,t wj ꜣḥ mḫl ḫI,21 iwḥ pꜣ mšꜥ n kmj

'*Sie pflegen nicht Kampf und Streit fernzuhalten unter dem Heer von Ägypten*'

(78) P. Petese Tebt. A, V 2

[bn]-iw =j dj,t wꜣj md,t pꜣj =(j) sn

'*Ich werde nicht zulassen, daß etwas fern ist (or: fehlt), mein Bruder!*'

What were the factors influencing the transition from this European-like, fixed-diathesis verbal system to the more Semitic-like labile one which we observe in Coptic, where the voice is a property not of the lexeme, but of the template? Should we look for these factors outside the native grammar – in other words, could the transition occur under the influence of the Greek voice grammar? I do not think such an explanation necessary or even likely. Instead, one could propose something like the following scenario.

In all the earlier stages of the language, from Old Egyptian through Demotic, tense-aspect templates, though not directly ascribing voice to a lexeme, demonstrate selective compatibility with the diathesis of the verb. This selective compatibility reaches the Coptic stage in form of the phenomenon captured by the Stern-Jernstedt rule and by the Stern's rule of the selective compatibility of stative. In Coptic, on the other hand, eventive patterns become re-structured so that the first argument is invariably indexed on the auxiliary verb, and the main verb expands the auxiliary in its construct or infinitival form. Now, the Egyptian infinitive is a form unmarked for voice. Edel reports this to be the case already in Old Egyptian, so it can hardly be viewed as a Coptic innovation caused by the language contact.[178] Once the objectless infinitive enters the Tripartite paradigm, the tense-aspect markers of the Tripartite become also its voice markers, in as much as they set the frame where it is opposed to construct forms and thus liable to a non-causative reading. Instances of this reading may be found already in Demotic, e.g., in negative periphrastic templates (which, one could suppose, served as a trigger for the switch of the whole of eventive conjugation to the periphrastic-tripartite structure)[179]:

(79) P. London-Leiden, 17, 30, Griffith-Thompson (1921:118-119)

iw =j r šꜥš =k nꜣj-ḥr pꜣ ntj ḥr pꜣ bhd ntj-iw **bw-ir =f htm**

'*I will glorify thee before him who is on the throne, who* **does not perish**'

(80) P. Leiden I 384, [XV,16]

bw-ir *pꜣj =w mtn[e] jꜥ m-sꜣ =w ꜥn sp-2*

"*Ihr Schandfleck (o.ä., wörtl. "ihre Spur") kann nie wieder von ihnen* **abgewaschen werden.**"

---

178 Edel (1955:351, § 695).

179 The diachronical table of verb forms in Quack (2020.:113) provides an excellent visualization of how the periphrasis enters the verbal paradigm in negations by the time of Late Egyptian and how it later becomes spread through the affirmative forms in the process of paradigm leveling.

Cross-linguistically, labile patterning can emerge or spread in different ways. Sometimes it is attained through the phonological merger of causative and anticausative counterparts (e.g., Old English *bærnan* 'kindle' and *biernan* 'burn (intr.)' melt into Modern English *burn*) or through the deletion of the reflexive pronoun, as in Germanic languages or Latin, or else through the multi-functionality of the middle voice, as in Classical Greek[180]. Among the mechanisms responsible for the rise of lability, the one suggested here, namely, the transfer of voice marking to the TAM-template by means of periphrasis manifests a singular and rather sophisticated linguistic phenomenon.

1.3.5.2 Excursus: Simpson-Depuydt Rule

Whereas it does not seem at all impossible to figure out the circumstances that have brought about the use of non-causative infinitive in the Tripartite conjugation, the dominance of the causative absolute infinitive in the Bipartite is much more difficult to account for. Ideally, two issues have to be clarified: what kind of 'natural selection' has left transitive infinitives, suppressing intransitive ones; and how did the original presuffixal *sḏm=f* form become supplanted in the Bipartite by the absolute infinitive with the prepositional phrase object. The second problem is by no means new; its answer would equal the explanation of the Stern-Jernstedt rule, a thing many Coptologists have made a try at. The first problem has, to my knowledge, never yet been posited, let alone answered.

It is an established fact in Egyptian linguistics that the Coptic First Present is the descendant of the Middle Egyptian *iw=f ḥr sḏm*[181], a form initially denoting progressive present. This construction is compatible with both intransitive (exx. 81 & 82) and transitive (exx. 83-86) verbs:

(81)   Tomb of Si-renpowet I. , [14-15])
*n',t =j m ḥb ḏ3m. =j **ḥr nhm** sḏm.t(w) ḥbb =(j) jm*
'*My city was in festival, my recruits rejoiced, when one heard (me) dancing there*'

(82)   Stela of Hor, Kairo JE 71901 [7]
*ḫ3s,t. <ḥr> ḥnk dw. **ḥr jm3** s,t nb.t ḏi.n =s sdḥ =s*
'*the foreign countries present gifts, the mountains are friendly, every place has given its secret*'

(83)   pMMA Heqanakht II, [rto30])
*ḏd =tn p3 ꜥk,w n r(m)ṯ.(Pl.) =j jw =sn **ḥr jri.t k3,t***
'*Ihr sollt diese Einkünfte meinen Leuten geben, wenn sie beim Verrichten der Arbeit sind*'

(84)   Stela of Nesmontu, (Louvre C 1 = N 155) [A.14])
*wr. **ḥr ḥzi.t =j***
'*The great ones praised me*'

---

180 Kulikov (2014), Gianollo (2014) etc.
181 Polotsky (1960:395).

(85)   Sakkara Necropole, the tomb of Tjy the ship convoy lord, [1]
       ...*sms,w-wḥr,t **ḥr wḏ^c=sn***
       '*Ein Ältester der Werft bei ihrem (= Schiffe/Klauentiere) Zuweisen/Entladen*'

(86)   P. Boulaq 3, x+7,5
       *jnp,w ḥr,w ḥr snfr **wt=k***
       '*Anubis und Horus verschönern deine Umwicklung*'

A cursory look at the tokens in the TLA database gives the impression that in this pattern, transitive verbs with overt direct objects are far more frequent than intransitive ones. However, this statement requires statistical verification which hopefully will be carried out through further research.[182] If this impression is correct, the opposition <stative : infinitive> in the present tense pattern must be interpreted as the opposition of diathesis, in the first place, in pre-Coptic Egyptian as well as in Coptic. In view of the above discussed interconnection between transitivity and aspect, it is not particularly difficult to reconcile this concept with Gardiner's treatment of the opposition as an aspectual one.[183]

In its further development, the <*ḥr*+ infinitive> pattern undergoes both formal and semantic changes. By the time of Late Egyptian or even earlier, it acquires the meaning of generic present, or aorist.[184] Starting from ca. 12th century B.C., the preposition *ḥr* is regularly omitted in writing,[185] and in Demotic texts, the pattern exhibits a new feature: in the overwhelming majority of cases, the direct object is not indexed on the verb in form of a personal suffix, but is attached (or flagged) by the preposition *n / n.im*. This has enabled Egyptologists to argue that the Stern-Jernstedt rule applies to Demotic grammar, as well.[186]

The attempts to explain the sudden flourishing of the prepositional phrase *n / n.im* in the transitive present initially focused on the adverbial status of the infinitive in the Bipartite. Thus, Elanskaya[187] claimed that as a member of the prepositional phrase, infinitive was necessarily indefinite and for that reason could not attach a suffix pronoun that would act as a determiner. This explanation looks confusing enough, since at the period when the bipartite predicate included the full prepositional phrase, direct objects were still coded by suffix pronouns.

---

182 For the sake of accuracy, one must add that the two examples without an overt DO cited here (81 and 82) do not contain non-causative verbs, either; *nhm* is not exactly 'rejoice' in the sense of 'be glad', but rather 'emit loud sounds of joy', which is unergative; *jm3* has the sense of 'honour somebody' and appears here exactly in that sense (as opposed to the passive 'be honoured').
183 Gardiner (1957:245), see above 1.3.3.7.
184 Satzinger (online:38), Depuydt (2002). However, there are reasons to believe that the functions of the bipartite pattern were not exhausted by the said two meanings, since it was also used, e.g., in the apodotical narrative perfect clauses, see Satzinger (1976:36 ff.).
185 Satzinger (online:27).
186 Parker (1961), Johnson (1976).
187 Elanskaya (2010:142).

(87)   P. Leiden I 348, Vso. 9,6-10,8, Bakenptah's letter, [9,9][188]

ptrj pȝy =k [DD] n shny.t n,tj **tw=k ḥr jrĪ =f**

'Siehe (?) dein [---] des Auftrags, das du ausführst'

(See also the examples 83-86.)

These examples suffice to demonstrate the futility of the part-of-speech approach to the Stern-Jernstedt rule attempted by Elanskaya and later by Schenkel[189]. Another, more promising path has been taken by Simpson and Depuydt. Their approach is based on the observation that in Demotic, the discussed pattern appears to sometimes violate the rule, yielding exceptions that would never hold in Coptic. In particular, Simpson claims that the language of Ptolemaic decrees contains very few examples conforming to Jernstedt's rule and that the choice between the immediate and the mediated (i.e., prepositional) object construction is affected by aspectual distinctions[190].

"[The object-suffixed] type of punctual durative infinitive has atemporal or 'aoristic' rather than simultaneous sense. A... parallel is provided by the 'gnomic' statements characteristic of wisdom texts. In relative clauses, these often imply conditions and can similarly combine atemporality with completed action, as in 'Ankhsheshonqy 21:19 *pA nt nq s-ḥm.t jw wn mtw=s ḥy* "he who lies with a married woman...[191]"

To illustrate the aspectual contrast, Simpson cites such examples as:

(88)   Canopus Tanis, CG 22187, 7/ 24 *n3 grṭ.w nt-jw=w fy=w*

'the rings they wear'

(89)   Canopus Tanis, CG 22187, 8/ 29 (the 25 priests) *nt-jw=w stp=w ḥr rnp.t*

'who are chosen each year'

as opposed to

(90)   Canopus Kom el-Hisn, CG 22186, 10 (the festival of Sothis) *nt-jw=w jr n-im=f n ḥ3,t-sp 9.t ibd-2 šmw sw 1*

'which is being held' (the current year, on a particular date)

Depuydt explains the correspondence between the use of the prepositional model and the imperfective meaning it conveys by referring to the partitive character of direct objects with imperfective verbs:

"The preposition *n-/n-jm=* (from earlier *m*) in origin had partitive meaning ("from, from among"). This partitive meaning is associated as follows with the continuous present. In the immediate present, an action only applies to *part* of a direct object. Thus, if one drinks a cup, one drinks only part of it right now. It does not surprise that, in the continuous present as expressed by the bipartite conjugation, a direct object is preceded by the preposition *n*... meaning "from". [...] In sum, a difference in tense is expressed by a difference in attachment of the direct object. This may seem unusual. But the bipartite

---

188 Translation: L.Popko.
189 Schenkel (1976), discussed above in 1.2.4.
190 Simpson (1996:152).
191 Simpson (1996:150).

conjugation does not leave room for distinctions elsewhere. The bipartite conjugation does not have auxiliaries.[192]"

We encounter here, as it seems, a sound explanation of the split in the object flagging with an ensuing preservation of the mediated form in the present tense. In this scenario, the prepositional phrase has germinated inside the Bipartite as a signal of progressive aspect. It is important to notice, however, that the split observed by Simpson and Depuydt is mainly restricted to one specific syntactic subtype of the bipartite pattern, viz., to its relative conversion. This might mean that in Demotic relative sub-pattern serves as a neutralization environment merging forms of relative aorist with those of relative present. This point of view seems not ungrounded, since the 'proper' aorist relative conversion <*ntj hr sdm.f s*> is extremely rare in Demotic. Thus, according to Quack (2020):

> "Aorist: Entweder *ntj ḫr sḏm=f s*, so *ꜣḫj nb ntj ḫr ꜥnḫ nṯr n.jm=w* „alle Dinge, von denen ein Gott lebt" pRhind I 9, 10, oder (meist) durch *ntj sḏm=f* „der es hört" bzw. *ntj.jw=f sḏm=f* „den er hört" ersetzt; so *pꜣ ntj bꜣk=s* „derjenige, der sie bearbeitet" Chascheschonqi 24, 20; *ibd 4 šmw ꜥrḳy ntj jw=w jr pꜣ hrw-ms pr-ꜥꜣ n.jm=f* „der 30. Mesore, an dem man den Geburtstag des Königs begeht" Rosettana 27f.[193]" etc.

The merger of aorist and present forms in the relative conversion is quite transparent in the following example, where the tense characteristics of the relative clause can be derived from its parallelism to aorist in the main clause.

(91) P. Insinger, IV,23, TM55918
      *pꜣ ntj **swn** ḥꜣtj =f ḥr-ir pꜣ šj swn =f*
      '*Wer sein Herz kennt, den kennt das Schicksal*'

The example of *swn* is illustrative, since in the durative conjugation this verb invariably combines with the prepositional phrase *n.im=*:

(92) P. Spiegelberg (line VIII,20)
      *tw =j **swn n.im =k** pꜣ mr-mšꜥ wr-ḥp-imn-nw,t*
      'Ich kenne dich, General Ur-di-imen-niut!'

Consequently, one could assume that the prepositional object first emerged inside the relative frame as a contrastive signal of imperfective aspect and then spread throughout the present tense pattern. Or, the other way round, the relative present was the last environment to resist the change by virtue of its overlapping with the aorist paradigm. While the exact order of grammatical events remains as yet unclear, the result is known: the older construct form is retained in the Bipartite in one case only, that of zero-determinated nominal object or indefinite pronoun. Like other cross-linguistically attested cases of noun incorporation, this phenomenon is associated with non-specificity of the noun and therefore with genericity. That is evident from examples such as:

---

192 Depuydt (2009: 107).
193 Quack (2020: 95).

(93) Shen.Can. 8 XO 235:22

ⲉⲛⲕⲉⲧⲏⲓ ⲛⲛⲓⲙ ⲉⲛϣⲉⲕϣⲏⲓ ⲛⲛⲓⲙ

'*Whom do we build houses for? Whom do we dig wells for?*' (Lit.: "For whom are we house-building / well-digging")

And yet, the use of *status constructus* in the present pattern is triggered by purely formal factors (i.e., noun determination) and not by semantic genericity of the clause. Generic statements not bearing the necessary formal feature are coded in exactly the same way as progressive ones:

(94) Shen.Can. 6, Amel. 1 (110:11)

ⲡⲃⲁⲗ ⲅⲱⲱϥ ⲛⲃⲗⲗⲉ ⲙⲉϥϣⲱⲡ ⲉⲣⲟϥ ⲙⲡⲟⲩⲟⲉⲓⲛ ⲉⲧⲃⲉ ⲡⲁϣⲁⲓ ⲙⲡⲕⲁⲕⲉ ⲉⲧⲛϩⲏⲧϥ· ⲡⲃⲁⲗ ⲏ ⲛⲃⲁⲗ ⲉⲧⲙⲉϩ ⲛⲟⲩⲟⲉⲓⲛ ⲛⲉⲧⲛⲁⲩ ⲉⲡⲟⲩⲟⲉⲓⲛ ⲏ **ⲉⲧϣⲱⲡ ⲉⲣⲟⲟⲩ ⲙⲡⲟⲩⲟⲉⲓⲛ**

'*As for the blind eye, it does not receive the light because of the abundance of darkness; the eye or eyes that are full of light, they are those that see the light and* **take the light into themselves**.'

As already mentioned in 1.3.4.7, aspectual values of the present tense and, inter alia, its use for generic present are a relatively virgin topic in Coptic linguistics. It is an established fact that both aorist and first present can code the generic meaning.[194] Moreover, Young has demonstrated that, at least, for Shenoute's Coptic, they are interchangeable in this meaning.[195] There is as yet no certainty as to the factors influencing the choice of either construction, but there can be no doubt that they go far beyond stylistic considerations suggested by Young for Shenoute's texts. So, for instance, the total absence of prenominal, pre-1 Pl. and pre-2 Pl. negative aorist in Shenoute must, in all probability, trigger (or at least signal) the use of negative present for generic tense with the subjects expressed by substantives or 1st and 2nd person plural pronouns. An additional factor could be the diathetic difference between present and aorist: it is possible that aorist was chosen for non-causative generic predicates, whereas present was preferred for causative ones. The issue of diathesis in Coptic generic statements is, at any rate, worth further examination.

1.3.6 Miscellaneous consequences of the asymmetrical diathesis

1.3.6.1 Discrepancies between absolute and construct forms

The principal dichotomy inside the Coptic verbal system, its split into eventive and durative paradigm, each one with its own set of forms and compatibilities, is most pronounced in the Stern-Jernstedt rule, as well as in the rule concerning the distribution of stative.

---

194 Layton (2011: 261-262, §337): "ϣⲁⲣⲉ- expresses nexus between actor and verbal action without reference to any particular range of time. It is a tenseless (generic, atemporal, extratemporal, omnitemporal) reference point next to the Coptic tense system. Sare- often co-occurs with the discourse perspective of timeless truth (gnomic/wisdom literature theology) so as to express generalizations and gnomic assertions about habitual actions or propensities, and about what does or does not, will or will not, can or cannot, did or did not, happen by nature... The Coptic durative present tense ϥ-ⲥⲱⲧⲡ also occurs in this kind of discourse." See also Layton (2011:436-437, §527).

195 Young (1961).

However, once this dichotomy is grasped as the opposition of diathesis, many more minor and intricate facts of Coptic verbal form distribution come into view and receive explanation. Among these, the least conspicuous problem is that of the missing infinitive. Indeed, according to the data from Crum's Dictionary, there exists a body of verbs attested solely in construct forms or in stative throughout the whole corpus of preserved Coptic texts (in all the dialects). Their absolute form is lacking and can be reconstructed on the basis of the common morphophonemic rules of Coptic. Computerized check of the verbal inventory in the Dictionary reveals that this is true for some 25 out of 590 native transitive verbs, such as (ⲛⲟϩⲛϩ) 'shake', (ⲥⲟⲣⲥⲣ) 'spread', (ⲥⲟⲩⲟⲗⲟⲩⲗ) 'wrap' etc. Now, the functions of an absolute infinitive are to provide an anticausative reading in the eventive conjugation and a causative / transitive progressive reading in the durative conjugation, and also to copy the eventive causative sense of construct forms. The last function is clearly supplementary. The causative progressive meaning tends to be statistically infrequent. So, if an anticausative reading is not applicable to the semantics of a particular lexeme, the chances to find that lexeme attested in the absolute form are significantly lower, and its total absence must not come as a surprise.

The same principle can have a milder consequence, when the absolute form is found in the durative, but not in the eventive conjugation. Such is the case of the verbs ⲙⲉ 'to love' and ⲙⲟⲥⲧⲉ 'to hate'. Both verbs do not have non-causative, 'spontaneous' semantic counterparts. In our terminology they are strong transitives, which means that they are practically never used without an overt direct object. In the Tripartite conjugation, these verbs appear solely in their construct forms. That is valid for the biblical corpus, as well as for Shenoute's Canons.

(95) Gen. 27:46

ⲡⲉϫⲉ ϩⲣⲉⲃⲉⲕⲕⲁ ⲇⲉ ⲛⲓⲥⲁⲁⲕ ϫⲉ ⲁⲓⲙⲟⲥⲧⲉ ⲡⲁⲁϩⲉ ⲉⲧⲃⲉ ⲛϭⲉⲉⲣⲉ ⲛⲛϣⲏⲣⲉ ⲛⲭⲉⲧ
'*Then Rebekah said to Isaac, "I loathe my life because of the Hittite women*'

(96) Deut. 22:12

ⲉⲣⲉϣⲁⲛⲟⲩⲁ ⲇⲉ ϫⲓ ⲛⲟⲩⲥϩⲓⲙⲉ ⲛϥϣⲱⲡⲉ ⲛⲉⲙⲁⲥ ⲁⲩⲱ ⲛϥⲙⲟⲥⲧⲱⲥ
'*If any man takes a wife and goes in to her and then hates her...*'

(97) 2Sam 13:22

ⲁⲩⲱ ⲛⲉⲣⲉ ⲁⲃⲏⲥⲁⲗⲱⲙ **ⲙⲟⲥⲧⲉ** ⲛⲁⲙⲛⲱⲛ ⲉⲧⲃⲉ ⲡϣⲁϫⲉ ⲛⲧⲁϥⲑⲃⲃⲓⲟ ⲛⲑⲁⲙⲁⲣ ⲧⲉϥⲥⲱⲛⲉ ⲛϩⲏⲧϥ
'*Absalom hated Amnon, because he had violated his sister Tamar*' (lit.: '*because of the word with which he humiliated Tamar, his sister*')

(98) Shen.Can. 1 9:3

ϫⲉⲕⲁⲁⲥ ⲉⲩⲙⲟⲥⲧⲱ[196] ⲉⲃⲟⲗ ϩⲓⲧⲛ ⲓ̅ⲥ̅ ⲙⲛⲛⲉϥⲁⲅⲅⲉⲗⲟⲥ ⲛⲑⲉ ⲛⲛⲣⲓⲣ ⲉⲧⲟⲩⲉⲛⲁⲕⲁⲑⲁⲣⲥⲓⲁ ⲉⲩⲙⲟⲥⲧⲉ ⲙ̅ⲙⲟⲟⲩ ⲉⲃⲟⲗ ϩⲓⲧⲛ̅ⲛⲉⲧⲛⲁⲩ ⲉⲣⲟⲟⲩ·
'*so dass du von Jesus und seinen Engeln gehasst wirst, wie die Schweine, die Unrat fressen, von denen gehasst werden, die sie sehen*'

---

196 Strictly speaking, this example is not illustrative, since (at least, in Shenoute) the 2-Sgl-fem. direct object cannot be coded with the prepositional phrase ⲙⲙⲟ=, unless after Greek loaned verbs. In

(99)   2Sam 19:6

ⲉⲧⲣⲉⲕⲙⲉⲣⲓ ⲛⲉⲧⲙⲟⲥⲧⲉ ⲙⲙⲟⲕ ⲁⲩⲱ ⲛⲅⲙⲉⲥⲧⲉ ⲛⲉⲧⲙⲉ ⲙⲙⲟⲕ

'because (lit.: *so that) you love those who hate you and hate those who love you*'

(100) Shen.Can. 3, Leipoldt 1954 128:26

ⲉⲧⲣⲉⲡⲣⲱⲙⲉ ⲙⲉⲣⲉⲛⲉϥϫⲓϫⲉⲉⲩ ⲉⲧⲃⲉ ⲡⲛⲟⲩⲧⲉ

'*so that the man loves his enemies for God's sake*'

(101) Shen.Can. 4 GH 33:60-34:2

ⲁⲩⲱ ⲧⲛⲛⲁⲙⲉⲣⲉ ⲛⲉⲧϫⲓ ⲥⲃⲱ ⲛⲧⲟⲟⲧⲟⲩ ⲛⲛⲉⲧϯ ⲥⲃⲱ ⲛⲁⲩ

'*And we shall love those who learn from those who teach them...*'

(102) Shen.Can. 6 Amelinau 1 57:9

ⲙⲏ ⲛⲧⲱⲧⲛ ⲧⲉⲛⲟⲩ ⲛⲉⲧⲙⲉ ⲛⲛⲉⲧϩⲓⲧⲟⲩⲱⲧⲛ ⲏ ⲛⲉⲧⲛⲕⲁⲧⲁⲥⲁⲣⲝ

'*Are you those who love their neighbors or their relatives*'

The discussed phenomena prove that construct forms are not morphological adaptations of the absolute infinitive, but independent forms with their own paradigmatic properties. The same principle is manifested in the verbs whose valency pattern varies according to the specific verb form employed. A textbook example of such verbs is ⲥⲱⲧⲙ 'hear, listen', but it is not at all unique in this respect, though the full list of verbs belonging to this type is yet to be made out. Attempts are made to explain the formal valency discrepancies at the semantic level, but the results obtained from semantic examinations are usually unsatisfying. Thus, in case of ⲥⲱⲧⲙ, Emmel deems it necessary to reject Shisha-Halevy's representation of ⲥⲱⲧⲙ as a set of homonymous verbs distinguished by their valency patterns:

> "... I must take issue with Shisha-Halevy's gloss of *sōtm e-* as "listen to", whereby he sought to distinguish it from *sōtm n-/mmo=, setm-, sotm=/sotme=*, which he glossed instead as "hear". But also in construction with the preposition *e-*, *sōtm* certainly can mean "hear", at least when the object of *e-* is a thing (such as a voice) rather than a person: for example, *mpou-sōtm e-tesmē* "they did not hear the voice" (Acts 22:9). I think it necessary... to admit – provisionally – that the distinction represented in English by "hear" versus "listen (to)" is not marked in Coptic by the opposition *sōtm -/n- : sōtm e-*..."[197]

In Emmel's opinion, consequently, the opposition between *sôtm₁* and *sôtm₂* cannot be reduced to the semantics of the verbal lexeme itself. An alternative explanation offered in Emmel (2006) is semantic, too, and focuses on the referentiality and semantic prominence of the object. It is claimed that the transitive allomorphs of *sôtm* are in most cases employed with a specific type of objects which is semantically void and not directly definable in terms of any other semantic case-role, such as SOURCE (sound emitter, typically a

---

all other cases, the meaning of this phrase is ablative. However, with ⲙⲟⲥⲧⲉ and ⲙⲉ, coding of any pronominal object with prepositional phrase is equally excluded.

197 Emmel (2006: 38).

person), AUDITIVE (sound or voice), FORM (text-type) or SPEECH (word). Emmel calls this type of object NEUTRAL. In the corpus of the Sahidic New Testament, this type of object is most frequently realized through the resumptive pronoun of a relative clause.[198] However, neutral objects are not confined to the transitive valency pattern; according to the statistics in Emmel (2006), they are, at least, as frequent with the prepositional phrase ε- / ερο-. Thus, the semantic type of object does not unambiguously define the valency pattern.

Since neutral objects are usually expressed by pronouns, one could imagine that *status pronominalis* of this verb stands in complementary distribution to *status absolutus* with respect to the type of object (direct pronominal vs. ε+ nominal object). This, however, is not quite true, because pronominal objects are also compatible, even frequent with the *sôtm e*-construction. A significant fact is that the absolute form of *sôtm* almost never comes with the prepositional phrase ммο=. Not a single example can be found in Shenoute's Canons, and there is only one such example in the Biblical corpus:

(103) Luke 16:2

    πεχαϥ ναϥ χε ογ πε παι εϯcωτм ммοϥ ετвнтк

    Τί τοῦτο ἀκούω περὶ σοῦ

    '(He) said to him 'What is this that I hear about you?''

Nor is <*status absolutus* + ν + Noun> a frequent combination. Again, Shenoute consistently abstains from using it, and the biblical Coptic provides not more than 4 examples: Job 9:16 (νϥcωτм ннειτανϩογτc), Jer 8:6 (ντετνcωτм ннεγϣαχε αν), Dan 3:29 (мпενcωτм ннεκντολн), Luke 9:9 εϯcωτм нναι ετвнтϥ). By way of comparison, the number of <cωтм ε>-tokens in the Bible amounts to some 600. Clearly, the absolute form of cωтм is as good as incompatible with the transitive pattern, which means that the two valency patterns are found in complementary sets of environments. These are also unevenly distributed. The construction of infinitive with the prepositional phrase seems to be unmarked, whereas the use of the transitive minority of construct forms is, in all probability, semantically conditioned by a specific type of object, namely, a resumptive or other pronoun. Thus, the functions of the two constructions partly overlap. This development can be construed as the gradual replacement of the transitive forms through the non-transitive infinitive in the process of paradigm levelling. Such diachronic model would mean that historically, the absolute infinitive of *sôtm* appeared in the eventive conjugation later than the transitive forms. Whether or not this pattern had originated in the durative conjugation and later spread on to the eventive one, could be clarified in the course of some further research.

Among the verbs with similar valency alternation pattern are, e.g., ϩιογε 'strike', κωρϣ 'request, persuade', πωϩ 'reach', κωмϣ 'mock, deride'.[199] Using κωмϣ as an example, we can once more verify that differences in valency are morphosyntactically conditioned and do not entail semantic differences. The absolute form of κωмϣ is expanded by the prepositional phrase νcα- 'after', which is compatible with both nominal and pronominal

---

198 Emmel (2006:49).
199 Emmel (2006) observes similar behavior in the verb ϩωн 'bid, order' (Emmel 2006:51).

objects and alternates with construct forms of the verb. Both the object of ⲛⲥⲁ- and the pronominal suffix object denote a person or an entity which is being derided.

(104) Shen.Can. 8 XO 51:10-16[200]

ⲏ ⲉⲕⲛⲁⲕⲱⲙ︦ⲱ︦ ⲛⲥⲁ ⲓⲱⲛⲁⲥ ⲡⲉⲡⲣⲟⲫⲏⲧⲏⲥ ⲉⲧⲥⲙⲁⲙⲁⲁⲧ· ⲡⲣⲱⲙⲉ ⲉⲧⲭⲁϩⲙ ⲁⲩⲱ ⲉⲧⲃⲏⲧ ϩⲙ ⲡⲓⲙⲁ

'Va-tu te moquer de Jonas, le prophète béni, ô homme souillé et abominé dans ce lieu?'

(105) Shen.Can. 8 XO 68:14

ⲛⲧⲁϥⲕⲟⲙ︦ⲱ︦ⲟⲩ ⲁⲛ ⲉⲧⲃⲉ ⲛⲧⲱⲱⲧⲉ ⲛⲛϩⲟⲓⲧⲉ ⲏ ⲛⲉⲣϣⲱ(ⲛ)·

'Ce n'est pas à cause des franges des vêtements ou des manteaux qu'il les a raillés...'

Both ⲕⲱⲙ︦ⲱ︦ ⲛⲥⲁ- and ⲕⲟⲙ︦ⲱ︦= are used to render identical or closely synonymous Greek verbs in the Bible: μυκτηρίζω 'turn up the nose, sneer at', ἐξουδενόω 'set at naught', ἀτιμάω 'disdain'.

(106) Psalm 2:4 ⲁⲩⲱ ⲡ︦ⲭⲟⲉⲓⲥ ⲛⲁ**ⲕⲟⲙ︦ⲱ︦ⲟⲩ**
καὶ ὁ κύριος **ἐκμυκτηριεῖ** αὐτούς

(107) Isa 37:22 ⲁϥⲥⲟϣⲉ ⲁⲩⲱ ⲁϥ**ⲕⲟⲙ︦ⲱ︦ⲉ** ⲧⲡⲁⲣⲑⲉⲛⲟⲥ ⲧϣⲉⲉⲣⲉ ⲛⲥⲓⲱⲛ
Ἐφαύλισέν σε καὶ **ἐμυκτήρισέν** σε παρθένος θυγάτηρ Σιων

(108) 2Sam 6:16 ⲁⲥ**ⲕⲱⲙ︦ⲱ︦ ⲛⲥⲱϥ** ϩⲙ ⲡⲉⲥϩⲏⲧ
καὶ **ἐξουδένωσεν** αὐτὸν ἐν τῇ καρδίᾳ αὐτῆς

(109) Ps 21:7 ⲟⲩⲟⲛ ⲛⲓⲙ ⲉⲧⲛⲁⲩ ⲉⲣⲟⲓ ⲁⲩ**ⲕⲱⲙ︦ⲱ︦ ⲛⲥⲱⲓ**
Ps 21:8 πάντες οἱ θεωροῦντές με **ἐξεμυκτήρισάν** με

(110) Ps 34:16 ⲁⲩⲡⲉⲓⲣⲁⲍⲉ ⲙⲙⲟⲓ ⲁⲩ**ⲕⲱⲙ︦ⲱ︦ ⲛⲥⲱⲓ** ϩⲛ ⲟⲩⲕⲱⲙ︦ⲱ︦
ἐπείρασάν με, **ἐξεμυκτήρισάν** με μυκτηρισμόν

The valency split of ⲕⲱⲙ︦ⲱ︦ looks therefore very similar to the previously discussed case of ⲥⲱⲧⲙ and can possibly be explained in the same vein, except that with ⲕⲱⲙ︦ⲱ︦, the referentiality of the object does not seem to make any difference for the choice of the absolute or the construct form.

1.3.6.2 Suppletive forms across the conjugation patterns: case of ⲉⲓⲙⲉ vs. ⲥⲟⲟⲩⲛ

The two Coptic verbs for 'know' – ⲉⲓⲙⲉ and ⲥⲟⲟⲩⲛ – have never as yet been regarded as suppletive forms. Moreover, the lexicologists of Coptic distinguish both verbs semantically. So, Crum translates ⲥⲟⲟⲩⲛ simply as 'know', whereas ⲉⲓⲙⲉ is both 'know' and 'understand'; similarly, Funk in his concordance to Shenoute translates them as "connaître" and "percevoir, comprendre", respectively. If I nevertheless suggest a relationship of suppletion between these two verbs, it is due to the fact that their distribution in the conjugation patterns is not identical. ⲉⲓⲙⲉ is almost without exception used in the non-

---

200 Translation of this and the next example: A. Boud'hors.

durative pattern, while the infinitive of cooyn seems to be compatible with the durative pattern only. In the table below, the first 50 occurrences of each verb in the Old Testament are listed with their conjugation base.

Table 6 | cooyn and eime in the Old Testament (sample)

cooyn	eime
1) Gen 3:5 ереппоуте гар cooyn хе	1) Gen 3:7 аүеіме хе
2) Gen 18:19 неісооүн гар хе	2) Gen 8:11 аqеіме де нбі нωге хе
3) Gen 19:35 ннеqсооүн ан пе етесбіненкотк	3) Gen 21:26 мпеіме хе
	4) Gen 24:14 гмпаі †наеіме хе
4) Gen 27:2 н†сооүн ан мпегооү мпамоу	5) Gen 24:44 гмпаі †наеіме хе
5) Gen 30:29 нток петсооүн етмнтгмгал	6) Exod 2:4 есбωшт мпоуе еіме енетнашωпе ммоq
6) Gen 31:6 нтωтн де гωттнүтн тетнсооүн хе	7) Exod 6:7 нтетнеіме хе (conj.)
	8) Exod 7:5 нсееіме нбі нрмнкнме тнроу хе
7) Gen 31:32 нереіакωв де cooyn ан пе хе	9) Exod 7:17 гм паі кнаеіме хе
8) Gen 48:19 †cooyn гω + clause	10) Exod 8:6 хекас екееіме хе
9) Exod 1:8 паі енqсооүн ан еіωснq	11) Exod 8:18 хекас екееіме хе
10) Exod 3:7 †cooyn гар мпеүгісе	12) Exod 9:29 хекас екееіме хе
11) Exod 3:19 анок наде †cooyn хе	13) Exod 10:2 граі нгнтоу нтетнеіме хе
12) Exod 4:14 †cooyn хе	14) Exod 10:7 коүωш еіме хе
13) Exod 5:2 н†сооүн ан мпхоеіс	15) Exod 14:4 нсееіме тнроу нбі нрмнкнме хе
14) Exod 6:12 анок наде н†сооүн ан ншахе	16) Exod 14:18 нсееіме тнроу нбі нрмнкнме хе
15) Exod 9:30 †cooyn хе	17) Num 11:23 епідн кнаеіме хе
16) Exod 10:26 анон наде нтнсооүн ан хе	18) Num 14:34 аүω тетнаеіме епбωнт нтаоргн
	19) Num 16:5 аqеіме нбі пноуте енетеноүq не
17) Num 11:16 нток етексооүн ммооу хе	20) Num 16:28 гм паі тетнаеіме хе
18) Num 14:23 наі ете нсесооүн ан мппетнаноуq мн ппегооу	21) Num 16:30 нтетнеіме хе
	22) Num 22:19 таеіме хе
19) Num 20:14 нток ксооүн епгісе тнрq	23) Deut 4:35 гωсте етрекеіме хе
20) Num 22:6 †cooyn анок хе	24) Deut 4:39 аүω екееіме мпооу нгкотк гм пекгнт хе
21) Num 22:34 неісооүн гар ан хе	25) Deut 7:9 аүω кнаеіме хе
22) Num 32:11 наі етсооүн мппегооу мн ппетнаноуq	26) Deut 8:5 аүω екееіме гм пекгнт хе
	27) Deut 9:3 аүω екееіме мпооу хе
23) Num 35:23 паі еqнамоу нгнтq нqсооүн ан	28) Deut 9:6 аүω екееіме мпооу хе
	29) Deut 11:2 аүω ететнеіме мпооу
24) Deut 1:39 етенqсооүн ан мпооу мппетнаноуq н мппегооу	30) Deut 11:2 наі **етенсееіме ан** оүте мпоүнау етесвω мпхоеіс
25) Deut 3:19 †cooyn хе	31) Deut 29:5 хекас ететнеіме хе
	32) Deut 29:8 хекас ететнеіме хе
	33) Josh 1:7 хекас екееіме егωв нім

ⲥⲟⲟⲩⲛ	ⲉⲓⲙⲉ
26) Deut 8:3 ⲉⲛⲥⲉⲥⲟⲟⲩⲛ ⲙⲙⲟϥ ⲁⲛ ⲛϭⲓ ⲛⲉⲕⲉⲓⲟⲧⲉ	34) Josh 1:8 ϫⲉⲕⲁⲥ ⲉⲕⲉⲉⲓⲙⲉ ⲉⲉⲓⲣⲉ ⲛϩⲱⲃ ⲛⲓⲙ
27) Deut 8:16 ⲉⲧⲉ ⲛⲥⲉⲥⲟⲟⲩⲛ ⲙⲙⲟϥ ⲁⲛ ⲛϭⲓ ⲛⲉⲕⲉⲓⲟⲧⲉ	35) Josh 3:7 ϫⲉⲕⲁⲥ ⲉⲩⲉⲉⲓⲙⲉ ϫⲉ
28) Deut 9:2 ⲛⲁⲓ ⲛⲧⲟⲕ ⲉⲧⲕⲥⲟⲟⲩⲛ ⲙⲙⲟⲟⲩ	36) Josh 3:10 ϩⲙⲡⲁⲓ ⲧⲉⲧⲛⲁⲉⲓⲙⲉ ϫⲉ
29) Deut 11:28 ⲉⲛⲧⲉⲧⲛⲥⲟⲟⲩⲛ ⲙⲙⲟⲟⲩ ⲁⲛ	37) Josh 4:24 ϫⲉ ⲉⲩⲉⲉⲓⲙⲉ ⲛϭⲓ ⲛϩⲉⲑⲛⲟⲥ ⲧⲏⲣⲟⲩ ⲙⲡⲕⲁϩ ϫⲉ
30) Deut 13:3 ⲉⲛⲧⲉⲧⲛⲥⲟⲟⲩⲛ ⲙⲙⲟⲟⲩ ⲁⲛ	38) Josh 22:22 ⲛⲧⲟϥ ϩⲱⲱϥ ϥⲛⲁⲉⲓⲙⲉ ϫⲉ
31) Deut 13:7 ⲉⲛⲅⲥⲟⲟⲩⲛ ⲙⲙⲟⲟⲩ ⲁⲛ	39) Josh 22:31 ⲙⲡⲟⲟⲩ ⲁⲛⲉⲓⲙⲉ ϫⲉ
32) Deut 13:14 ⲉⲛⲅⲥⲟⲟⲩⲛ ⲙⲙⲟⲟⲩ ⲁⲛ	40) Josh 23:13 ⲉⲓⲙⲉ ϫⲉ
33) Deut 14:21 ⲛⲡⲉⲧⲉ ⲛⲅⲥⲟⲟⲩⲛ ⲙⲙⲟϥ ⲁⲛ	41) Josh 23:14 ⲧⲉⲧⲛⲁⲉⲓⲙⲉ ϩⲙⲡⲉⲧⲛϩⲏⲧ ⲙⲛⲧⲉⲧⲛⲯⲩⲭⲏ ϫⲉ
34) Deut 19:4 ⲙⲡⲉⲧϩⲓⲧⲟⲩⲱϥ ⲉⲛϥⲥⲟⲟⲩⲛ ⲁⲛ	42) Judg 3:2 ϫⲉⲕⲁⲥ ⲉⲩⲉⲉⲓⲙⲉ ⲛϭⲓⲛⲅⲉⲛⲉⲁ ⲛⲛϣⲏⲣⲉ ⲙⲡⲓⲥⲣⲁⲏⲗ ⲉⲧⲥⲁⲃⲟⲟⲩ
35) Deut 28:33 ⲕⲉϩⲉⲑⲛⲟⲥ ⲉⲛϥⲥⲟⲟⲩⲛ ⲙⲙⲟϥ ⲁⲛ	43) Judg 3:2 ⲙⲡⲟⲩⲉⲓⲙⲉ ⲉⲣⲟⲟⲩ
36) Deut 28:64 ⲛⲁⲓ ⲛⲅⲥⲟⲟⲩⲛ ⲙⲙⲟⲟⲩ ⲁⲛ	44) Judg 3:4 ⲁⲩⲱ ⲁⲥϣⲱⲡⲉ ⲉⲕⲁⲁⲩ ⲉⲡⲁϩⲟⲩ ⲉⲡⲓⲣⲁⲍⲉ ⲙⲡⲓⲥⲣⲁⲏⲗ ⲛϩⲏⲧⲟⲩ ⲉⲉⲓⲙⲉ ϫⲉ
37) Deut 29:15 ⲛⲧⲱⲧⲛ ⲧⲉⲧⲛⲥⲟⲟⲩⲛ ⲛⲑⲉ…	45) Judg 4:9 ⲡⲗⲏⲛ ⲉⲓⲙⲉ ϫⲉ
38) Deut 29:25 ⲛⲁⲓ ⲉⲧⲉⲉⲛⲥⲉⲥⲟⲟⲩⲛ ⲙⲙⲟⲟⲩ ⲁⲛ	46) Judg 6:22 ⲁⲩⲱ ⲅⲉⲗⲉⲱⲛ ⲁϥⲉⲓⲙⲉ ϫⲉ
39) Deut 31:21 ⲁⲛⲟⲕ ⲅⲁⲣ ϯⲥⲟⲟⲩⲛ ⲛⲛⲉⲩⲡⲟⲛⲏⲣⲓⲁ	47) Judg 6:29 ⲁⲩⲉⲓⲙⲉ ϫⲉ
40) Deut 31:27 ϫⲉ ⲁⲛⲟⲕ ϯⲥⲟⲟⲩⲛ ⲛⲧⲉⲕⲙⲛⲧⲛⲁϣⲧ ⲛⲁⲕϩ	48) Judg 6:37 ϯⲛⲁⲉⲓⲙⲉ ϫⲉ
41) Deut 31:29 ϯⲥⲟⲟⲩⲛ ⲅⲁⲣ ϫⲉ	49) Judg 13:16 ⲙⲡϥⲉⲓⲙⲉ ϫⲉ
42) Deut 32:17 ⲉⲛⲥⲉⲥⲟⲟⲩⲛ ⲙⲙⲟⲟⲩ ⲁⲛ	50) Judg 13:21 ⲧⲟⲧⲉ ⲁⲙⲁⲛⲱϣⲉ ⲉⲓⲙⲉ ϫⲉ
43) Deut 32:17 ⲉⲛⲛⲉⲩⲉⲓⲟⲧⲉ ⲥⲟⲟⲩⲛ ⲙⲙⲟⲟⲩ ⲁⲛ	
44) Deut 34:6 ⲙⲛ ⲗⲁⲁⲩ ⲥⲟⲟⲩⲛ ⲛⲧⲉϥⲕⲁⲓⲥⲉ	
45) Josh 2:5 ⲛϯⲥⲟⲟⲩⲛ ⲁⲛ ϫⲉ	
46) Josh 2:9 ϯⲥⲟⲟⲩⲛ ϫⲉ	
47) Josh 8:14 ⲡⲣⲣⲟ ⲇⲉ ⲛⲉϥⲥⲟⲟⲩⲛ ⲁⲛ ϫⲉ	
48) Josh 10:2 ⲛⲉϥⲥⲟⲟⲩⲛ ⲅⲁⲣ ϫⲉ	
49) Josh 14:6 ⲛⲧⲟⲕ ⲕⲥⲟⲟⲩⲛ ⲙⲡϣⲁϫⲉ	
50) Josh 22:22 ⲁⲩⲱ ⲛⲧⲟϥ ⲡⲛⲟⲩⲧⲉ ϥⲥⲟⲟⲩⲛ	

This small sample providing a true-to-life picture of the distribution of the two verbs proves that the preference of each one towards a specific conjugation pattern is not accidental. It also shows that the choice of this or that verb is not conditioned by the type of the object, whether nominal phrase or clause, although ⲉⲓⲙⲉ may occur more frequently with a clause, than with a (pro)noun. The relationship between the two infinitives may thus be identified as suppletion in tense and aspect.

By way of illustration, let us consider the following example:

(111) Joshua 22:22

ПНОУТЄ ИТОЧ ОИ ПЄ ПНОУТЄ ЄИТОЧ ПЄ ПХОЄІС ПНОУТЄ ΑΥѠ ИТОЧ ПНОУТЄ **ЧСООУИ**
ΑΥѠ ПІСРАНΛ ИТОЧ ₂ѠѠЧ **ЧNΑЄΙΜЄ**

Ὁ θεὸς θεός ἐστιν κύριος, καὶ ὁ θεὸς θεὸς κύριος αὐτὸς **οἶδεν**, καὶ Ισραηλ αὐτὸς
γνώσεται·

'*The Mighty One, God, the Lord! He knows; and let Israel itself know!*'

Despite their being expressed by different lexemes in Coptic and in Greek, the two signs
for 'know' contain no difference in notion, but that of tense and aspect. This follows
not only from the parallelism of these two occurrences, but also from the fact that both
translate one and the same Hebrew verb יָדַע / יָדַע 'know'[201]:

אֵל אֱלֹהִים יְהוָה אֵל אֱלֹהִים יְהוָה הוּא יֹדֵעַ, וְיִשְׂרָאֵל, הוּא יֵדָע

El-Elohim-JHWH-El-Elohim-JHWH hu - **yode؟a** - ve - Israel – hu - **yeda؟**

'*God'(6) – 'he' – 'know'- 3 Sgl Pr – 'and' – 'Israel' – 'he' – 'know'- 3Sgl Fut*

One could argue that the feature <± telic> is an intrinsic property of each lexeme and
defines their respective compatibility with the conjugation patterns. Thus, in 1 John each
lexeme has a constant Greek counterpart, οἶδα for сооун and γιγνώσκω for єіΜє, the
second pair used with the telic sense even at the expense of the distribution regularity (in
the case of тєνєιΜє):

(112) 1John 2:3

ΑΥѠ ₂Μ ПΑΙ **ТЄNЄΙΜЄ** ХЄ ΑNСОУѠNЧ

καὶ ἐν τούτῳ **γινώσκομεν** ὅτι ἐγνώκαμεν αὐτόν

'*And by this we know that we have come to know him*'

(113) 1John 5:19-20

ТЄNСООУN ХЄ ΑNОN ₂ЄNΒОΛ ₂Μ ПNОУТЄ ΑΥѠ ПКОСМОС ТНРЧ ЄЧКН ₂Μ ПОNНРОС ΑΥѠ
ТЄNСООУN ХЄ ΑПѠΗРЄ ΜΠNОУТЄ ЄІ

οἴδαμεν ὅτι ἐκ τοῦ Θεοῦ ἐσμεν, καὶ ὁ κόσμος ὅλος ἐν τῷ πονηρῷ κεῖται. **οἴδαμεν**
δὲ ὅτι ὁ Υἱὸς τοῦ Θεοῦ ἥκει

'*We know that we are from God, and the whole world lies in the power of the evil
one. And we know that the Son of God has come*'

Interestingly, however, the feature <- telic> is characteristic of the absolute form of сооун,
but not of its construct forms which can render γιγνώσκω as can be seen from the example
112 (where ΑNСОУѠNЧ translates ἐγνώκαμεν). We may conclude that єіΜє plays a role
of a suppletive infinitive for construct forms of сооун. As also in the above discussed
case of сѠТΜ, this suppletive infinitive has lost the direct valency pattern in favor of the
prepositional phrase with є-. Since єіΜє is also capable of tackling (pro)nominal objects,
these types of objects form a contrastive environment where the difference between the
two 'know'-verbs becomes meaningful. To find out exact nuances of this difference is not
the task of the present paper, but the first impression is that the construct form of сооун

---

201 сооун translates γιγνωσκω, e.g., in Matt. 12:33 ЄΒОΛ ГΑР ₂Μ ПКΑРПОС NѠΑΥСОУNПѠΗN ἐκ γὰρ τοῦ
καρποῦ τὸ δένδρον γινώσκεται "For the tree is known by its fruit".

is preferred with pronominal objects over the ⲉⲓⲙⲉ ⲉⲣⲟ-construction. The ratio of ⲥⲟⲟⲩⲛ to ⲉⲓⲙⲉ occurrences with pronominal objects in the Bible is 99 / 35.

Aspect-bound stem suppletion with the verbs of knowing is a phenomenon that has parallels in Indo-European languages; in Classical Greek, as is well known, the verb οἶδα 'know' is morphologically related to εἶδον 'see', or more precisely, constitutes its morphological perfect / resultative. One could suspect a fundamental analogy in the way the notion of 'knowing' interacts with the category of aspect in both Greek and Demotic/ Coptic. In a most naïve way, that can be formulated as follows: some languages tend not to treat the resultative state of knowing something as a result of a process of acquiring knowledge. If you are sitting down, you will end up seated, but if you learn something, you will not necessarily end up knowing it. The process and the result lie, as it were, on different planes which is reflected in different lexemes being used for one and the other. Further, acquiring knowledge, either as a process or as a result, may be associated not with the idea of knowledge as such, but rather with the idea of experience gained by acts of perception or, in the case of Demotic, possibly even consumption.[202] In Greek, as already said, the consequence of this aspectual and notional split is that the resultative verb bears a genealogical similarity to the verb of perception, and not to the verb meaning 'learn, gain knowledge' - γιγνώσκω; in Demotic or in Coptic, on the contrary, the eventive forms for the resultative ⲥⲟⲟⲩⲛ are supplied by the verb that originally denoted a type of consumption (swallowing) and that came to denote the process of gaining knowledge, i.e. ⲉⲓⲙⲉ.

It is difficult to imagine in details the process by which this suppletion took place. The predecessors of the two lexemes are not abundant in Demotic. The TLA database contains 6 tokens of ꜥm-'eime' and about 25 of swn-'sooun'. This evidence is, of course, too scarce for any trustworthy reconstruction of events. One can at best try to mark some minor regularities in the usage of both forms. Thus, ꜥm participates in sḏm=f s constructions (4 tokens out of 6), whereas swn always comes in periphrastic patterns (3 tokens of aorist) or in present tense. ꜥm governs a clause (3 tokens), a noun introduced by the preposition n- (2 tokens) and once a pronoun introduced by r-r//. swn, on the other hand, strongly prefers nominal objects: nouns (8 tokens, no preposition), pronouns (4 tokens of pronominal suffix, 3 of n.im= with pronominal suffix 1 token of r-r=), as opposed to a single attestation with a clause as an object (Rosettana, line 31). It is not unthinkable that ꜥm and swn became fixed in the non-durative conjugation in their absolute and construct forms, respectively, in accordance with the type of object preferred in each case. It seems that later, this selectivity towards a specific object type became smoothed out, though it did not vanish altogether.

Whatever happened, it manifested a drastic conceptional change compared to the older stages of Egyptian that employed one and the same root rḫ for both the process of learning and the state of knowing something.

---

202 On the use of the verbs of tasting as metaphors for the process of cognition in Egyptian, see Steinbach-Eicke (2017).

1.3.7 Conclusion

The approach proposed in this chapter explores the association between transitivity and aspect in the Coptic conjugation system. Traditionally, this system is considered to be based on the binary aspectual distinction (eventive vs. durative tenses). I argue that the introduction of a new parameter, that of causativity /transitivity provides a more correct account of Coptic verbal grammar. My analysis is based on the fact that inherently transitive (construct) forms of the Coptic mutable verb are confined to the eventive conjugation, whereas the inherently intransitive stative is only compatible with the durative pattern. It is therefore reasonable to consider these forms aspectually marked. Thus, in conformity with the generalizations in Hopper & Thompson (1980), Coptic transitive forms are primarily associated with the telic (eventive) aspect, and vice versa, atelicity is linked to intransitivity, a phenomenon resembling the causative split described in Kulikov (1999) for Ancient Greek and Vedic Sanskrit. This model correctly predicts that the diathetically unmarked verbal form, the absolute infinitive, will be in the first place employed as the diathetic counterpart to the marked form in each conjugation. Indeed, in the eventive conjugation the free infinitive most often (with some verbs, in the vast majority of occurrences) has a non-causative reading. In the durative conjugation, on the other hand, the infinitive mainly serves as a transitive counterpart of stative. A durative intransitive infinitive occurs extremely infrequently, denoting an iterative event in present, or else a dynamic process with the verbs whose semantics includes the component of change, such as ⲁⲩϫⲁⲓ 'grow'. Many, if not most of the monadic unaccusative verbs do not allow the free infinitive form in the durative conjugation. The infinitive of such verbs is employed in the Tripartite conjugation only and thus stands in a complementary distribution to the stative.

The transitive use of the eventive infinitive is easy to construe as a secondary development. In fact, the statistically obvious tendency to use this form for nominal arguments suggests that the absolute infinitive gradually supplants *status constructus* as a prenominal transitive form, in course of the evolution of differential object marking in the Tripartite conjugation. The fact that infinitive supplanted *status constructus*, but not *status pronominalis* corroborates the idea that the differential object marking in Coptic is triggered by the information status of the object. The object with more informative value, e.g., referring to a newly introduced entity, is marked with a morphologically more elaborate construction of infinitive with the prepositional phrase ⲛ-.

Revising the traditional idea of the two construct forms as "mutated forms of infinitive" gives room for a better understanding of minor morphosyntactic facts of Coptic verbal grammar, such as a "valency split" shown by some lexemes having (transitive) construct forms along with an intransitive infinitive (ⲥⲱⲧⲙ, ϩⲓⲟⲩⲉ etc.). It also explains the absence of an absolute form with some lexemes, or suppletion of the missing absolute form with the form based on another verbal root, as in the case of ⲉⲓⲙⲉ / ⲥⲟⲟⲩⲛ 'know'.

Based on the features of morphological mutability, transitivity and lability, the inventory of Coptic native verbs can be divided into four classes: mutable transitive non-labile verbs (here labelled "strong transitives"), mutable labile verbs, mutable intransitive non-labile verbs, and immutable verbs. The members of each class have a common semantic denominator. Immutable verbs are unergative, mutable non-labile verbs are atelic unaccusatives, labile verbs are combinations of telic unaccusatives and their causatives. Finally, strong transitives are agentive telic verbs. Thus, a specific combination of two factors, agentivity and lexical (a)telicity, defines the morphosyntactic character of a native Coptic verb.

2 Periphrastic construction < ϣⲱⲡⲉ + circumstantial clause>

2.1 Problem description

As observed by Haspelmath, the concept of periphrasis has never belonged to central issues in either descriptive, or typological linguistics.[203] Though forming an essential part in the process of grammaticalization which repeats itself in cycles, each time using fresh periphrastic material for synthesizing new grammatical forms, periphrasis is perceived by grammarians as a marginal and haphazard phenomenon. The term is applied intuitively to designate multi-word expressions with some kind of grammatical meaning, either a basic one which is regularly signaled through morphological markers (e.g., Russian imperfective future, Latin present subjunctive), or a finer and more complex one (e.g., the Classical Greek periphrasis with τυγχάνω + participle 'I happen to do'). In the first case, the periphrastic form in question often fills a paradigmatic gap, usually marking the place of some categorial clash.[204] It is then opposed to synthetic members of the same inflectional paradigm (e.g., the Latin passive perfect is opposed to active perfect and present / imperfect passive). The second type of periphrasis has no synthetic grammatical counterparts and is consequently difficult to identify as a grammatical structure, rather than a coincidental co-occurrence of lexemes.[205] However, periphrastic constructions, as a rule, have specific features that help recognize them as such. Among these features, Haspelmath mentions idiomaticity (or, in Haspelmath's terms, 'semantic non-compositionality') and a limited range of grammatical contexts the auxiliary member is compatible with. This last feature is of special importance, since it provides a formal, not subjective and observer-dependent, criterion of grammatical function of the construction in question. To use Haspelmath's example, "in the German *werden*-future only present indicative (and perhaps subjunctive) forms of *werden* are allowed, but not past tense forms (e.g. *wird kommen* [becomes come] 'will come', but not **wurde kommen* [became come])."[206]

Sharing the common fate of periphrastic constructions, the Coptic periphrastic pattern <ϣⲱⲡⲉ ⲉϥⲥⲟⲧⲡ / ⲉϥⲥⲱⲧⲡ> has received very little attention until now. Being rather infrequent, it hovers in the eyes of a Coptologist halfway between a rhetorical device and a grammatical mechanism of an obscure function. As concerns the formal side, neither the distributional properties of its auxiliary, nor the commutation properties of the core verb have been adequately described. To my knowledge, no contrastive study compares this pattern with synthetic forms of a similar meaning. Consequently, our idea of its semantics may be but rough approximation.

Furthermore, it is unclear whether the criterion of semantic non-compositionality is at all applicable in this case: grammatical interpretations of the pattern usually focus on either one of its two parts, sometimes ignoring ϣⲱⲡⲉ and sometimes stressing it

---

203 Haspelmath (2000:654 ff.).
204 Haspelmath (2000:655): "…this kind of gap can only arise in inflectional systems in which more than one morphological category is combined".
205 Cf. the discussion in Bentein (2011).
206 Haspelmath (2000:661).

as the aspect-bearing element of the pattern, without any explicitly stated reason. This uncertainty is reflected in different ways periphrastic structures are translated. At times, they are rendered by a mere indicative passive, as in (114), or anticausative, as in (115):

(114) Shen.Can. 1 §6

ⲉⲩⲉϣⲱⲡⲉ ⲉⲩϣⲏⲡ ⲉϩⲣⲁⲓ̈ ⲉϫⲙ̄ⲡⲉⲑⲩⲥⲓⲁⲥⲧⲏⲣⲓⲟⲛ ⲛ̄ⲧⲉⲕⲕⲗⲏⲥⲓⲁ ⲛ̄ⲛ̄ϣⲣⲡⲙ̄ⲙⲓⲥⲉ

'Sie werden am Altar der Gemeinde der Erstgeborenen ... empfangen'

(115) Abbaton (Budge 1914:241, 30-31).

ⲉⲕⲉϣⲱⲡⲉ ⲉⲕⲁϣⲉ ϩⲛ̄ ⲧⲙⲏⲏⲧⲉ ⲉⲕⲣⲙⲟⲟⲥ ⲉϩⲣⲁⲓ̈ ⲉϫⲛ̄ ⲟⲩⲑⲣⲟⲛⲟⲥ ⲛ̄ⲕⲱϩⲧ̄

'You shall hang in the middle sitting upon a throne of fire'

In other cases, translators may choose to accentuate the durativity of the action suggested by the subordinate clause, e.g., with an adverb of duration as in:

(116) Benjamin of Alexandria, Hochzeit zu Kana 252:14

ⲁⲓϣⲱⲡⲓ ⲉⲓϯ ⲥⲑⲟⲓⲛⲟⲩϥⲓ ⲉϩⲣⲏⲓ

'Ich liess den Weihrauch *fortdauernd* aufsteigen'

Most frequently, however, periphrastic structures are rendered by an analytic construction with a verb denoting inchoativity, entry into a state:

(117) Hebrews 5:12[207]

ⲁⲩⲱ ⲁⲧⲉⲧⲛ̄ϣⲱⲡⲉ ⲉⲧⲉⲧⲛ̄ⲣⲭⲣⲉⲓⲁ ⲛⲟⲩⲉⲣⲱⲧⲉ ⲛⲟⲩϩⲣⲉ ⲁⲛ ⲉⲥϫⲟⲟⲣ

'You have come to need (*you-have-become you-needing*) milk, not the solid food'

(118) Benjamin of Alexandria, Hochzeit zu Kana 248:3-4

ⲟⲩⲟϩ ⲁϥϣⲱⲡⲓ ⲉϥⲡⲏⲧ ⲉⲡⲁⲓⲥⲁ ⲛⲉⲙ ⲫⲁⲓ ⲉϥϣⲑⲉⲣⲑⲱⲣ

'Und er begann zu fliehen nach dieser und jener Seite, indem er in Erregung geriet'

In cases like these, the translator must have relied upon the inchoative (i.e., change-of-state) component in the semantics of the auxiliary verb as the last resort for distinguishing the given sentence from its semantic *doppelganger* with a synthetic form (here, ⲁⲧⲉⲧⲛ̄ⲣ ⲭⲣⲓⲁ and ⲁϥⲡⲱⲧ, respectively).

Having no idea of either semantic, or formal triggers for the use of periphrasis, we are even less equipped to explain the absence of periphrasis in syntactic and semantic environment apparently suitable for it.[208]

---

207 Translation: B.Layton (Layton 2000:343).

208 So, e.g., we cannot validate Jernstedt's emendation of Sethe's 'misapplied stative' examples (see Sethe 1922, Jernstedt 1925). Jernstedt proposes obligatory use of periphrastic construction wherever the infinitive "would not fit due to its meaning" ("Wo der Infinitiv wegen seiner Bedeutung nicht hinpasste, da wurde allerdings das Qualitativ gesetzt, aber nie und nimmer in der Weise, dass man es dann einfach mit dem betreffenden nichtpräsentischen Hilfverbalpräfix zusammengab... Man bediente sich eben der Umschreibung durch das Verb 'sein, werden' im betreffendenfalls erforderlichen Tempus mit daran angeschlossenem präsentischen Umstandssatz, welcher das zum Ausdruck der Zustandsaktionsart unumgängliche Qualitativ selber enthielt"). Jernstedt obviously has in mind the use of the periphrastic construction as a suppletive form

Our uncertainty stems from a basic logical fault in the general approach to the periphrastic pattern. Strangely enough, it is usually regarded not as an autonomous grammatical form, but rather as a concatenation of forms, one of which (the auxiliary) is used to adapt the other (the core verb form) to the otherwise inaccessible grammatical environment. Thus, it is implied that grammatical means are the speaker's objectives. Under this interpretation, the speaker does not intend to find a proper linguistic form for the desired content, but rather wishes, for some obscure reason, to find whatever way there is to use the pre-conceived form where he should not use it. This approach is obviously fruitless as an instrument of linguistic analysis. Indeed, what would we learn of the English periphrastic form 'he will go', if the grammar would only tell us, it is used to combine the infinitive 'go' with the 3rd Sgl. personal pronoun?

Instead, I propose to apply the standard procedure that consists in:

a) verifying the categorial values suggested for the pattern by means of contrasting it with other entities with similar or identical values;
b) finding the formal restrictions imposed on each of its parts;
c) fine-tuning the definition of the pattern's grammatical functions to match its distributional properties.

2.2 Previous research

The most standard up-to-date description of Coptic periphrasis is provided in Layton (2011). In Layton's opinion, the periphrasis with ϣⲱⲡⲉ, as well as the periphrastic future with the auxiliary ⲉⲓ, serves to enlarge the range of tenses compatible with the verbal form used in the circumstantial clause.[209] For some reason, Layton does not extend this definition to include also the periphrastic *modi* of imperative and jussive which receive a separate brief mention. But even in this abridged version, Layton's explanation is problematic, since it cannot account for a substantial number of circumstantially converted infinitives occurring in the periphrastic construction, as in (119):

(119) Four Creatures, f.4v b (Wansink 1991: 29).

ⲁϥⲉⲓⲕⲟⲛⲟⲙⲉⲓ ϩⲛ ⲧⲉϥⲙⲛⲧⲙⲁⲓⲣⲱⲙⲉ ⲉⲧⲣⲉ ⲡⲟⲩⲁ ⲡⲟⲩⲁ ϩⲙ ⲡⲉϥⲧⲟⲟⲩ ⲛⲍⲱⲟⲛ **ϣⲱⲡⲉ ⲉϥⲉⲓⲛⲉ** ⲛϥⲧⲟⲟⲩ ⲛⲥⲧⲝⲓⲟⲛ ⲛⲛⲉⲧⲟⲛϩ

"(God) arranged in his benevolence that each of the four creatures would resemble four classes of the living"

Obviously aware of the problem, Layton adds to his formal explanation another one based on semantics. He claims that periphrastic conjugation may at times express an incipient meaning denoting "subject beginning to act, entering a state, beginning to participate in a process, acquiring a quality."[210] Given the extensive parallelism between Coptic periphrastic predications and Greek <γίγνομαι + adjective / participle> constructions

---

for a non-causal meaning, but he does not sufficiently clearly specify the conditions when this suppletion should be obligatory.
209 Layton (2011:342ff.).
210 Layton (2011:343)

in the Biblical corpus, such an idea certainly does not look ungrounded. However, the combination of formal and semantic factors in Layton's description of the pattern creates notional havoc reflected in the table of Coptic tenses where Layton summarizes his conclusions as follows (I reproduce here only the fragments that have a bearing on periphrasis):

Future:

(120) ϥ-ⲛⲁ-ⲕⲱⲧ 'he is going to build'
      ϥ-ⲛⲁ-ϣⲱⲡⲉ ⲉ-ϥ-ⲕⲱⲧ 'he will be building, he will build (*or* he will start building, he will get to building); *rare*

(121) ϥ-ⲛⲁ-ϣⲱⲡⲉ ⲉ-ϥ-ⲕⲏⲧ 'it is going to be/ become built' (describing a state)
      ⲥⲉ-ⲛⲁ-ⲕⲟⲧ-ϥ 'it is going to be built' (process)

Past:

(122) ⲁ-ϥ-ⲕⲱⲧ 'he built / has built; it became built / got built'

(123) ⲁ-ϥ-ϣⲱⲡⲉ ⲉ-ϥ-ⲕⲱⲧ 'he built, he started building, he got to building; *rare*

(124) ⲁ-ϥ-ϣⲱⲡⲉ ⲉ-ϥ-ⲕⲏⲧ 'it was built (describing a state) (*or* it came to be built)[211]

Aspectual values this table assigns to different members of the verbal paradigm seem to be impressionistic and not too clearly distinguished (for example, it is utterly incomprehensible how the process of going to be built can possibly differ from the state of going to become built).[212] That makes difficult rendering them through pulpable comparative concepts. Thus, the translation of the future tense periphrasis (ex.121) suggests the notion of a pre-resultative state, which would be a rare bird in typology. On the other hand, the past tense periphrasis (ex. 124) seems to refer to past progressive, past resultative or past inchoative, without any discrimination criteria suggested. So, for the moment, we can only cautiously state that according to Layton, the periphrastic pattern appears in predicates with conflicting tense / aspect / diathesis properties. This echoes the definition in Funk (1978a):

"Ein wesentlicher Zusatz zu dieser Regel (i.e., the rule of the incompatibility of stative with the Tripartite conjugation, -- N.S.) betrifft das Verfahren, das die koptische Spra-che für den Fall bereithält, dass die beiden inkompatiblen Bedingungen aufeinander treffen, d.h., wenn auf Grund semasiologischer Merkmale (Zustand und/oder Passiv)

---

211 Layton (2011:437-438).
212 Generally speaking, the given method of finding out aspects of verbal forms seems contrary to the usual procedures applied by linguists for this purpose. Whereas a standard aspectual test consists in finding out what aspect-marking elements, e.g., time adverbs, are compatible with the verbal form in question, the aspectual values represented in the above table seem to be derived from the meaning of different constituents of the patterns. So, for example, the translation 'he will start building' constitutes a word-for-word rendering of the Coptic phrase which does in no way guarantee the equivalence of grammatical meaning. Of course, the material of an extinct (and not abundantly documented) language does not yield enough opportunities to conduct all the necessary tests with precision.

einerseits für das Verb die Qualitativform gefordert ist, andererseits aber der syntakti-
sche Kontext eine Konjugation des Dreiteiligen Schemas vorschreibt. In diesem Fall
tritt normalerweise eine auf analytischem Wege gebildete Ersatzkonstruktion ein, die
sogenannte *Coniugatio periphrastica* mit ϣⲱⲡⲉ."[213]

Quack (2020) provides a similar explanation for the Demotic precursor of the pattern,
however, without any reference to the diathesis factor.

"Das Verb *ḫpr* „sein, werden" wird in verschiedenen Fällen als Hilfsverb gebraucht, um
Konstruktionen zu ermöglichen, die andernfalls ausgeschlossen wären. Sofern man die
Nuance des Qualitativs im Sinne des abgeschlossenen Zustandes einer Verbalhandlung
außerhalb des Systems der Dauerzeiten verwenden will, kann man das Verb *ḫpr* im
jeweiligen Tempus verwenden und daran einen Umstandssatz mit dem Qualitativ des
Hauptverbes anschließen…"[214]

The not too obvious common semantic denominator of the three definitions is that the
periphrastic pattern has some kind of bound stative or bound resultative reading. Now,
boundedness of a state can theoretically mean that this state is presented as having a
starting point or an end-point (if it has both, then it is punctual and therefore cannot be
regarded as a state). The second option must be excluded from consideration, because
there is no evidence of a periphrastic construction with ϣⲱⲡⲉ ever having a terminative
meaning analogical, e.g., to Russian derivatives with the prefix *do-*: *do-smotrel* "finished
watching".[215] Thus, the general meaning of periphrasis is assumed to be start-defined
stative, i.e., inchoative.

Two additional descriptions of the pattern, one in Demotic and one in Coptic, do not
refer to the feature of inchoativity or boundedness, but stress the ultimately imperfective
character of the pattern. Simpson (1999) claims that "the durative clauses in these
passages all express continuous or progressive actions, and the periphrastic construction
is presumably employed in order to link them with verbal bases which do not normally
have this sense."[216] In the same vein, contrasting forms like 'ⲕ-ⲛⲁ-ⲟⲩⲟⲡ' with 'ⲕ-ⲛⲁ-ϣⲱⲡⲉ
ⲉ-ⲕ-ⲟⲩⲁⲁⲃ' and 'ⲉ-ⲕ-ⲉ ⲕⲁ-ⲣⲱⲕ' with 'ⲉ-ⲕ-ⲉ-ϣⲱⲡⲉ ⲉ-ⲕ-ⲕⲱ ⲛ-ⲣⲱⲕ', Lambdin suggests that
the periphrastic circumstantial is employed, "when it is necessary to express a durative or
continuous process or state in the future".[217] Yet, he abstains from extending the validity of
his hypothesis to tenses other than the future.

Finally, Funk is the only author to explicitly propose passive diathesis for a possible
trigger of the periphrastic construction. His definition, however, is somewhat evasive and
does not specify the conditions under which diathesis could be considered the sole or main

---

213 Funk (1978a:25).
214 Quack (2018: 68).
215 For the terminative meaning, Coptic employs the periphrastic structure with the auxiliary ⲟⲩⲱ; but
     even that, strictly speaking, does not always have the meaning of termination of a state, but rather
     that of a state after the termination of an action, i.e., a resultative state, see Grossmann (2009).
216 Simpson (1996: 129).
217 Lambdin (1983: 30.9).

factor responsible for the use of periphrasis. Taken at face value, the idea that periphrasis serves to combine non-active forms with the tense base conjugation is not satisfactory. After all, a large number of verbs have a synthetic form (that of the absolute infinitive) which functions as a punctual passive or anticausative of the Tripartite conjugation. As can be seen from the following Biblical examples, neither an anticausative meaning, nor even a parallel periphrastic construction with the change-of-state meaning in the Greek original do necessarily bring about the use of periphrastic pattern in the Coptic translation:

(125) Matt. 17:2

ⲡⲉϥⲣⲟ ⲁϥⲧⲁⲁⲧⲉ ⲛⲧⲅⲉ ⲙⲡⲣⲏ ⲁⲩⲱ ⲛⲉϥⲣⲟⲓⲧⲉ **ⲁⲩⲟⲩⲃⲁϣ** ⲛⲧⲅⲉ ⲙⲡⲟⲩⲟⲉⲓⲛ

καὶ ἔλαμψεν τὸ πρόσωπον αὐτοῦ ὡς ὁ ἥλιος, τὰ δὲ ἱμάτια αὐτοῦ **ἐγένετο λευκὰ** ὡς **τὸ φῶς**

'*and his face shone like the sun, and his clothes became as white as the light*'

(126) John 5:9

ⲁⲩⲱ ⲛ̄ⲧⲉⲩⲛⲟⲩ **ⲁϥⲟⲩϫⲁⲓ** ⲛ̄ϭⲓ ⲡⲣⲱⲙⲉ

καὶ εὐθέως **ἐγένετο ὑγιὴς** ὁ ἄνθρωπος

'*and the man was immediately healed*'

(127) Acts 1:19

ⲁⲩⲱ **ⲁⲡⲉⲓϩⲱⲃ ϭⲱⲗⲡ̄ ⲉⲃⲟⲗ** ⲛ̄ⲟⲩⲟⲛ ⲛⲓⲙ

καὶ **γνωστὸν ἐγένετο** πᾶσιν'

'*and it was revealed to everyone*'

(128) Acts 8:1

ⲟⲩⲟⲛ ⲇⲉ ⲛⲓⲙ **ⲁⲩϫⲱⲱⲣⲉ** ⲉⲃⲟⲗ ⲉⲛⲉⲭⲱⲣⲁ ⲛ̄ⲧⲟⲩⲇⲁⲓⲁ ⲙⲛ ⲧⲥⲁⲙⲁⲣⲓⲁ

πάντες δὲ **διεσπάρησαν** κατὰ τὰς χώρας τῆς Ἰουδαίας καὶ Σαμαρίας

'*and they were all scattered throughout the regions of Judea and Samaria*'

It is therefore to be expected that the diathetically conditioned periphrasis, if indeed it exists, marks such cases where the use of a synthetic form is for some reason impossible, i.e., functions as a suppletive form filling an inflectional gap. Alternatively, one could perhaps argue that passive / non-causative is nowhere a single factor contributing to the use of periphrasis, but that it is invariably entwined with some other grammatical feature, e.g., with stative aspect, and it is precisely this combination that needs to be expressed analytically.

The sum total of our present-day ideas about the Coptic periphrasis looks as follows: this pattern must in most, if not all, cases have an imperfective value; it may, at least sometimes, convey the sense of change-of-state; it is often employed in future tenses, though not confined to them; finally, in some cases it might fill paradigmatic gaps created by collision of anticausative or passive sense with certain, as yet undefined, aspect-tense features of the Tripartite conjugation. In the following parts of the study, I shall try to elucidate this description.

2.3 Distributional properties of periphrasis

From the present-day descriptions of the pattern, one might conclude that no restrictions are imposed on the tense base of the auxiliary; indeed, Layton's above-cited wording suggests that the periphrastic pattern is aimed at employing as many tense bases, as possible, to enlarge the scope of stative. However, an examination of the distribution of periphrasis proves such ideas to be somewhat too loose. It turns out that some tense bases are involved in periphrasis much more often, than the others, some do not participate in the pattern, at all.

Unfortunately, the only text corpus allowing for exhaustive and significant statistics is a translated one, i.e., that of the Bible. The count below reflects the respective number of circumstantially converted infinitive or stative clauses expanding a Tripartite ϣⲱⲡⲉ-clause in the biblical corpus. It does not include circumstantial clauses with nominal predicates, with the predicates expressed by possessive verboid or adjectival verbs.

Tense base	Number of tokens
Optative	77
Future	76
Perfect	48
Conjunctive (mostly following future tense)	47
Imperative	19
Inflected Infinitive	14
Jussive	8
Conditional (future sense)	4
Aorist	1
All tokens	294

For reference, one can compare it with numbers obtained from Shenoute's Canon 1 and Canon 6:

Canon 1	
Perfect	4
Imperative	4
Optative	3
Conjunctive (following future)	2
Future	1
Inflected Infinitive	1
All tokens	15

Canon 6	
Perfect	4
Inflected Infinitive	3
Future	3
Conjunctive (following future)	2
Conjunctive (following present)	2
All tokens	14

Although there is a surprising variation in the data as to the ratio of perfect forms (in the biblical text, the tokens of periphrastic perfect constitute some 16% of the array, while in Shenoute's corpus they amount to some 30+%), in other respects, the statistics show much affinity. Thus, aorist forms are vanishingly rare in the Bible and virtually non-existent in the two selected canons. Importantly, in both corpora, there is no single occurrence of either limitative 'empat-f-sotm', or temporal 'ntere-f-sotm' with periphrasis. Later I shall try to account for the absence of these tense bases; suffice it here to observe that if the main semantic content of periphrasis would be to stress inchoative aspect of an action, its non-occurrence with the limitative base would be striking and rather unexplainable. At the same time, the majority of the overall occurrences of periphrasis are represented by tenses and moods with various shades of future meaning. The Demotic evidence, though extremely scarce, reveals roughly the same ratio of periphrastic future to past tense, as the biblical texts.[218] Thus, the temporal value of periphrasis may be either future or past, the modal meanings include indicative, optative and imperative.

In the next two sections, I intend to examine the opposition between periphrastic and synthetic temporal forms, to be able later to compare the results and find possible differences between them.

2.4 Periphrasis: future tenses / moods

In a most parsimonious way, the meaning of future periphrasis as a complex morpheme may be described as future resultative. In Nedjalkov (1988), one of the basic works on verbal resultative constructions, the term 'resultative' is defined as follows:

> "The term resultative is applied to those verb forms that express a state implying a previous event. The difference between the stative and the resultative is as follows: the stative expresses the state of a thing without any implication of its origin, while the resultative expresses both a state and the preceding action it has resulted from."

One has to bear in mind, though, that the distinction between the resultative and the stative pointed out by Nedjalkov is not unambiguous. This is reflected in the fact that both categories are oftentimes encoded by the same polysemous morpheme, which can also serve to denote the passive:

> The division was immediately surrounded by their opposite number. – Passive
> I saw Frank Sinatra surrounded by fans. – Resultative
> The village was surrounded by woods. – Stative[219]

In Coptic, too, these three categories are not strictly differentiated. Especially in the case of periphrasis, it is convenient to think of them as a continuum with fuzzy boundaries. With some lexemes (including complex ones, such as ϯ-ϩⲁⲡ 'judge'), the exact meaning of periphrasis may be closer to the 'pure', i.e., punctual passive, as in:

---

218 The Demotic data is discussed in 2.10.
219 This example is taken from Nedjalkov (1988).

(129) Shen.Can. 2 (Kuhn 1956:124, 24-25)

ⲁⲓϣⲁϫⲉ ⲛⲙⲙⲏⲧⲛ ϩⲙ ⲧⲁⲧⲁⲡⲣⲟ ⲙⲁⲣⲓϣⲱⲡⲉ ⲉⲧⲉⲧⲛϯ ϩⲁⲡ ⲉⲣⲟⲓ ϩⲙ ⲡⲙⲁ ⲉⲧⲙⲙⲁⲩ

'(I have come to you once, or two or three times), having spoken to you by word of mouth, let me be judged by you in that place.'

In this sentence, the adverbial expansion ϩⲙ ⲡⲙⲁ ⲉⲧⲙⲙⲁⲩ meaning roughly 'here and now', point rather to the punctual, than the statal interpretation ("let me be in the state of being judged by you"). From the structural point of view, the predicate here is opposed to the imperative pattern ϯ ϩⲁⲡ ⲉⲣⲟⲓ 'let you judge me'. Thus, the periphrastic structure serves to form a passive of a formally intransitive verbal phrase.

However, it is much more common for the analytic construction with future tenses to express a future resultative or stative meaning.[220] Contrastive analysis of synthetic and analytic future forms, when possible, points to the opposition between a punctual event and the resultant state of its non-agentive argument ('to get fulfilled' vs. 'to stay fulfilled', 'to sit down' vs. 'to remain seated'). The presence of this semantic trait in periphrastic predicates is formally proven by their compatibility with adverbial expansions denoting time intervals, such as ⲛⲛⲉϩⲟⲟⲩ ⲧⲏⲣⲟⲩ 'all days' or ϣⲁ- 'until'. Since the adverbs expand the predicate as a whole, and not just the subordinate clause, the property of durativity must also be taken as pertaining to the predicate as a whole, as in:

(130) Num 6:8

ⲛⲛⲉϩⲟⲟⲩ ⲧⲏⲣⲟⲩ ⲛⲧⲉ ⲡⲉϥⲉⲣⲏⲧ ⲉϥⲉϣⲱⲡⲉ ⲉϥⲟⲩⲁⲁⲃ ⲙⲡϫⲟⲉⲓⲥ

πάσας τὰς ἡμέρας τῆς εὐχῆς αὐτοῦ **ἅγιος ἔσται** κυρίῳ

'All the days of his vow **he is holy** to the Lord'[221]

(131) Luke 1:20

ⲉⲓⲥ ϩⲏⲏⲧⲉ **ⲉⲕⲉϣⲱⲡⲉ ⲉⲕⲕⲱ ⲣⲱⲕ** ⲉⲙⲙⲛϭⲟⲙ ⲙⲙⲟⲕ ⲉϣⲁϫⲉ **ϣⲁⲡⲉϩⲟⲟⲩ** ⲉⲧⲉⲣⲉⲛⲁⲓ ⲛⲁϣⲱⲡⲉ

καὶ ἰδοὺ **ἔσῃ σιωπῶν** καὶ μὴ δυνάμενος λαλῆσαι **ἄχρι ἧς ἡμέρας** γένηται ταῦτα

*'And behold, **you will be silent** and unable to speak **until the day** that these things take place'*

(132) O.Crum 22

ⲁⲩⲱ ⲁⲓⲇⲓⲥⲥⲁ ⲧⲉⲕⲡⲟⲗⲓⲥ **ⲛⲁϣⲱⲡⲉ ⲉⲥⲥⲙⲁⲙⲁⲁⲧ ϣⲁ ⲉⲛⲉϩ**

*'and Edessa your city **shall be blessed for all time**'*

(133) Lev 11:24

ⲁⲩⲱ ⲉⲧⲉⲧⲛⲁϫⲱϩⲙ ϩⲛ ⲛⲁⲓ ⲟⲩⲟⲛ ⲛⲓⲙ ⲉⲧⲛⲁϫⲱϩ ⲉⲛⲉⲧⲙⲟⲟⲩⲧ ⲛϩⲏⲧⲟⲩ **ϥⲛⲁϣⲱⲡⲉ ⲉϥϫⲁϩⲙ ϣⲁ ⲡⲛⲁⲩ** ⲛⲣⲟⲩϩⲉ

καὶ ἐν τούτοις μιανθήσεσθε πᾶς ὁ ἁπτόμενος τῶν θνησιμαίων αὐτῶν **ἀκάθαρτος ἔσται ἕως ἑσπέρας**

*'By these you will make yourselves unclean, whoever touches their carcasses **will be unclean till evening**'*

---

220 My definition coincides with Lambdin's "durative or continuous process or state in the future".
221 Translation mine – N.S.

The two tokens of ⲭⲱⲣⲙ 'be(come) unclean, polluted' in the last quotation constitute a minimal syntactic pair not only with respect to their tense, but also with respect to their diathesis. The use of the periphrastic construction cannot, therefore, be attributed to the passive genus of the verb, but reflects the aspectual difference between the two predicates. I could not find in the biblical corpus a single instance of the infinitive ⲭⲱⲣⲙ with a non-punctual meaning; my guess is that the clause *ϥⲛⲁⲭⲱⲣⲙ ϣⲁ ⲡⲛⲁⲩ ⲛⲣⲟⲩϩⲉ 'he will become unclean till evening' would be ungrammatical.

The case of ⲭⲱⲣⲙ does not, however, rule out the possibility of a synthetic form with the future stative meaning:

(134) Num 35:28

ⲙⲁⲣⲉϥⲟⲩⲱϩ ϩⲛ ⲧⲡⲟⲗⲓⲥ ⲙⲡⲙⲁ ⲙⲡⲱⲧ ϣⲁⲛⲧⲉϥⲙⲟⲩ ⲛϭⲓ ⲡⲛⲟϭ ⲛⲟⲩⲏⲏⲃ

ἐν γὰρ τῇ πόλει τῆς καταφυγῆς **κατοικείτω**, ἕως ἂν ἀποθάνῃ ὁ ἱερεὺς ὁ μέγας

'*For he **must remain** in his city of refuge until the death of the high priest*'

(135) Deut 28:24

ⲉⲣⲉⲡϫⲟⲉⲓⲥ ϯ ⲛⲟⲩϣⲟⲉⲓϣ ⲙⲡⲉⲕⲕⲁϩ ⲛⲧⲉ ⲟⲩⲕⲁϩ ϣⲟⲩⲟ ⲉϫⲱⲕ ⲉⲃⲟⲗ ϩⲛ ⲧⲡⲉ ϣⲁⲛⲧϥⲧⲁⲕⲟⲕ

ⲁⲩⲱ ϣⲁⲛⲧϥϥⲟⲧⲕ ⲉⲃⲟⲗ

δῴη κύριος τὸν ὑετὸν τῇ γῇ σου κονιορτόν, καὶ χοῦς ἐκ τοῦ οὐρανοῦ **καταβήσεται** ἐπὶ σέ, ἕως ἂν ἐκτρίψῃ σε καὶ ἕως ἂν ἀπολέσῃ σε

'*The Lord will make the rain of your land powder. From heaven dust **shall come down** on you until you are destroyed* (lit.: *until it destroys you and until it wipes you out*')

Evidently, the degree of obligatoriness of the periphrastic construction varies with different verbal lexemes. This variation does not come at random but is regulated by the lexical aspect of the verb. The main operative distinction is the distinction between telic and atelic / durative verbs. Telic or terminative verbs are defined in Nedjalkov & Jaxontov (1988) as the verbs that denote a transition from one state to another or acquiring a quality ('sit down', 'fall', 'forget', etc.), while durative verbs do not imply a definite purpose ('sing', 'run', 'look') or else they express a state (sit, know).[222] For the Coptic periphrasis, the crucial distinction seems to be the following: with telic verbs, the resultant state comes at the final point of the event, whereas for an atelic verb, the 'result', or the eventive facet, basically coincides with the entry into the state denoted by the verb. An extreme case of the telic class are strong transitive verbs;[223] statal verbs and the verbs of motion constitute the opposite extreme. In a most general form, the rule sounds as follows: telicity of the verb correlates with the obligatoriness of the periphrastic construction as a future atelic non-causative form. The scheme below gives a graphic representation of the semantic/syntactic/lexical range of the periphrastic pattern with future tenses / modi:

---

222 Nedjalkov (1988:5). This semantic category and its application to Coptic verbal system is also discussed in 1.3.4.6.

223 See the definition in 1.3.4.6.

Meaning of periphrasis	Passive (?)		Resultative	Stative		Iterative (?)	
Paradigmatic function	Suppletive			Contrastive		Facultative	
Verb classes	Strong transitive		Labile telic	Atelic / Statal		Motion	
Examples	ca̅ẓoy 'curse'		ϫⲱⲕ 'fulfil'	ⲙⲟⲩϩ 'burn'	ϩⲗⲟϭ 'be sweet'		ⲙⲟⲟϣⲉ 'walk'

The following two examples illustrate the facultativity of the analytic construction with the verbs of motion:

(136) Genesis 3:14

ⲉⲕⲉⲙⲟⲟϣⲉ ⲉϫⲛ ⲧⲉⲕⲙⲉⲥⲑⲏⲧ ⲁⲩⲱ ⲉϫⲛ ϩⲏⲧⲕ

ἐπὶ τῷ στήθει σου καὶ τῇ κοιλίᾳ πορεύσῃ

'*on your belly (*lit.*: on your breast and your belly) you shall go*'

(137) Abbaton (Budge 1914:238, 19-21)

ⲉⲕⲉϣⲱⲡⲉ ⲉⲕⲙⲟⲟϣⲉ ⲉϫⲛ̅ ϩⲏⲧⲕ̅ • ⲛ̅ⲛⲉϩⲟⲟⲩ ⲧⲏⲣⲟⲩ ⲙ̅ⲡⲉⲕⲱⲛϩ̅ •

'*You shall be walking upon your belly all the days of your life*'

The difference between the two expressions marked in bold lies on the margin of grammar, since it cannot be represented in terms of binary opposition of any grammatical feature, aspect included. Both predicates denoting identical events, the adverbial expansion ⲛ̅ⲛⲉϩⲟⲟⲩ ⲧⲏⲣⲟⲩ ⲙ̅ⲡⲉⲕⲱⲛϩ̅ 'all the days of your life' is the only overt distinction between them, and it would be reasonable to suppose that this expansion has triggered or at least motivated the change in the form of the verb. In such cases, as this, the grammatical opposition is not that of punctual synthetic vs. durative analytic form, but rather that of an aspectually unmarked synthetic vs. marked durative analytic form. The periphrastic pattern in the last example supposedly might have iterative, rather than durative reading. However, this is a matter of interpretation and cannot be directly proven.

Periphrasis occurs more frequently with the class of durative and statal verbs. However, I could not find a context that would help to detect the semantic difference between the simple and the complex form in such cases. Extrapolating the previous findings onto these cases, we might suspect that the longer form stresses the stative aspect of the verb, but it is difficult to determine, whether a native speaker would find a significant difference in sense between

(138) Ps 103:34

ⲡⲁϣⲁϫⲉ **ⲛⲁϣⲱⲡⲉ ⲉϥϩⲟⲗϭ** ⲛⲁϥ

ἡδυνθείη αὐτῷ ἡ διαλογή μου

'*May my meditation be pleasing to him*'

and

(139) Sir 49:2

ϥⲛⲁϩⲗⲟϭ ⲛⲧϩⲉ ⲛⲟⲩⲉⲃⲓⲱ ϩⲛ ⲧⲧⲁⲡⲣⲟ ⲧⲏⲣⲥ

ἐν παντὶ στόματι ὡς μέλι γλυκανθήσεται

'*it is (*lit*.: will be) as sweet as honey to every mouth*'[224]

This non-obligatory kind of periphrasis cannot be accounted for by any theory that treats it as a strictly suppletive structure. It does not fill any paradigmatic void, either as a passive / intransitive, or as a stative form. Rather, it constitutes a device of categorial refinement, which would be quite common for such structures, as pointed out in Bybee (1994).[225] Structurally, it seems to be a secondary development; one can imagine that the pattern has been initially used as a suppletive form with various classes of telic verbs, and then, having become associated with the stative meaning, has spread to the durative class.

In quantitative terms, at least, telic verbs constitute the nucleus of the lexical repertory of periphrasis. This class consists of two subgroups, specified above as the labile (e.g., ϫⲱⲕ 'fulfil / be fulfilled', ϫⲱϩⲙ 'make (yourself) unclean') and the strong transitive (ⲥⲁϩⲟⲩ 'curse', etc.) verbs. With the verbs of the first group, the opposition <infinitive : periphrastic form> is the opposition of aspects, punctual vs. stative:

(140) John 15:25

ⲁⲗⲗⲁ ϫⲉⲕⲁⲥ **ⲉϥⲉϫⲱⲕ ⲉⲃⲟⲗ** ⲛϭⲓ ⲡϣⲁϫⲉ ⲉⲧⲥⲏϩ ϩⲙ ⲡⲉⲩⲛⲟⲙⲟⲥ

ἀλλ' ἵνα πληρωθῇ ὁ λόγος ὁ ἐν τῷ νόμῳ αὐτῶν γεγραμμένος

'*But the word that is written in their Law must be fulfilled*'

(141) John 16:24

ϫⲉⲕⲁⲥ ⲉⲣⲉⲡⲉⲧⲛⲣⲁϣⲉ **ϣⲱⲡⲉ ⲉϥϫⲏⲕ ⲉⲃⲟⲗ**

ἵνα ἡ χαρὰ ὑμῶν ᾖ πεπληρωμένη

'*that your joy may be full*'

(142) 1Cor. 14:25

ⲛⲉⲧϩⲏⲡ ⲙⲡⲉϥϩⲏⲧ **ⲛⲁⲟⲩⲱⲛϩ ⲉⲃⲟⲗ**

τὰ κρυπτὰ τῆς καρδίας αὐτοῦ φανερὰ γίνεται

'*the secrets of his heart are disclosed*'

(143) Isa 2:2

ⲡⲧⲟⲟⲩ ⲙⲡϫⲟⲉⲓⲥ **ⲛⲁϣⲱⲡⲉ ⲉϥⲟⲩⲟⲛϩ ⲉⲃⲟⲗ** ϩⲛ ⲧϩⲁⲏ ⲛⲛⲉϩⲟⲟⲩ

ἔσται ἐν ταῖς ἐσχάταις ἡμέραις ἐμφανὲς τὸ ὄρος κυρίου

'*The mountain of the Lord will be visible in the latter days*'[226]

Here the periphrastic structure obviously supplies the stative future.

---

224 English translation: New Revised Standard Version.

225 "New periphrases develop to express meanings that are more specific than the meanings already expressed grammatically in the language at the time." Bybee et al. (1994:133).

226 Translation – N.S. The ESV translation ("It shall come to pass in the latter days that the mountain of the house of the Lord shall be established as the highest of the mountains") deviates strongly from the Coptic text.

The verbs belonging to the second group have an animate agent, are active and mono-diathetic: their infinitive has a causative reading only. Here, the opposition <infinitive : periphrastic form> is the opposition of both aspect and diathesis. This group constitutes the biggest source of periphrastic constructions in Sahidic. Here belong, e.g., ⲥⲁϩⲟⲩ 'curse', ⲱⲡ 'count', ⲥⲟⲃⲧⲉ 'prepare'[227], ϭⲱⲡⲉ 'seize, take', ⲧⲟⲛⲧⲛ̄ 'make alike', ⲧⲁⲉⲓⲟ 'honor', as well as ⲥⲙⲟⲩ 'bless', which has developed a stative form, despite not being historically a transitive verb.

(144) Pierpont Morgan Library M.593 (Installation of Gabriel), 77:25
ⲧⲉⲛⲟⲩ ϭⲉ ⲛⲉⲥⲛⲏⲩ **ϣⲱⲡⲉ ⲉ̄ⲧⲉⲧⲛ̄ⲥⲃ̄ⲧⲱⲧ** ⲛ̄ⲧⲉⲧⲛ̄ϣⲉⲣⲉⲡⲧⲏⲩⲧⲛ̄ ⲉⲛⲥⲩⲛⲁⲍⲓ̈ⲥ ⲛ̄ⲛⲉⲕⲕⲗⲏⲥⲓ̈ⲁ ⲉ̄ⲧⲟⲩⲁ̄ⲁⲃ
'*Now then, brethen, be prepared and go early to the services of the holy churches*'

(145) Shen.Can. 8, XO 78:57-60
ⲙⲁⲣⲟⲩϣⲱⲡⲉ ⲉⲩⲥϩⲟⲩⲟⲣⲧ̄ ⲛ̄ⲛⲁϩⲣⲛ̄ⲡⲛⲟⲩⲧⲉ
'*Let them be cursed before God*'

(146) Shen.Can. 3, YA 309-10
ⲉⲩⲉϣⲱⲡⲉ ⲉⲩⲙⲏⲣ ⲉϩⲟⲩⲛ ⲉⲛⲕⲁⲛⲱⲛ ⲉⲧⲕⲏ ⲉϩⲣⲁⲓ ⲛⲛⲉⲥⲛⲏⲩ ⲧⲏⲣⲟⲩ
'(And all who dwell next to us) *shall be bound by the canons that are laid down for all the siblings*'[228]

(147) Shen.Can. 1, 6, XC 13-14
ⲉⲩⲉϣⲱⲡⲉ ⲉⲩϣⲏⲡ ⲉϩⲣⲁⲓ ⲉϫⲙ ⲡⲉⲑⲩⲥⲓⲁⲥⲧⲏⲣⲓⲟⲛ ⲛⲧⲉⲕⲕⲗⲏⲥⲓⲁ
'*Sie sind am Altar der Gemeinde der Erstgeborenen, die in den Himmeln angeschrieben sind, empfangen*' (lit.: '*they shall be received at the altar of the church*')

Of course, the above schema of verbal classes represents only the most basic correlations between forms and grammatical categories. Individual lexemes may develop an idiosyncratic behavior which would lie beyond the scope of this rough approximation. So, for example, the grammatical marking of the aspectual split by periphrasis may overlap with a lexical and semantic split. Such is, e.g., the case of the verb ⲟⲩⲟⲡ 'be(come) clean, holy'. Whereas its periphrastic stative is used 13 times in the Bible to translate ἅγιος ἔσται, the corresponding punctual mediopassive ἁγιάζομαι 'become holy' is usually rendered by ⲧⲃⲃⲟ (e.g., 1Cor. 6:11, 1Cor. 7:14, 1Tim. 4:5, Heb. 10:29) and only twice by the infinitive ⲟⲩⲟⲡ, in the identical phrases of Matt. 6:9 and Luke 11:2 (ⲙⲁⲣⲉⲡⲉⲕⲣⲁⲛ ⲟⲩⲟⲡ 'hallowed be your name'). In other cases, ⲟⲩⲟⲡ conveys the sense of 'become pure, unblemished' (Psalms 118:80, Job11:15, Sirach 16:12). So, periphrastic predicates with ⲟⲩⲁⲁⲃ, seemingly, do not have any synthetic counterpart of the same root.

---

227 Crum (1939) treats ⲥⲟⲃⲧⲉ as a labile verb. However, most attestations marked as intransitive are in Bohairic, or else have the causative reading 'prepare (something)' with an omitted DO. Although Luke 10:10 proves that sporadic anticausative/passive use was not altogether excluded, it still seems rather a marginal option in Sahidic.
228 Text according to Leipoldt (1954: 120). Translation according to Layton (2014:118-119).

In much the same way, the infinitive of ϣⲟⲩⲟ 'pour down, empty' is used mainly or, perhaps, exclusively with the meaning 'pour down', while the stative form ϣⲟⲩⲉⲓⲧ means 'empty'; thus, for ϣⲟⲩⲟ, the synthetic form cannot under any conditions serve as a syntactic alternative for the analytic construction:

(148) 1Cor. 1:17

ϫⲉⲕⲁⲥ **ⲉⲛⲛⲉϥϣⲱⲡⲉ ⲉϥϣⲟⲩⲉⲓⲧ** ⲛ̅ϭⲓ ⲡⲉⲥⲧⲁⲩⲣⲟⲥ ⲙ̅ⲡⲉⲭⲥ

ἵνα μὴ κενωθῇ ὁ σταυρὸς τοῦ Χριστοῦ

'*lest the cross of Christ be emptied of its power*'

Finally, periphrasis can supply missing tenses or modi for stative verbs incompatible with the eventive conjugation. In my opinion, this can explain the use of periphrastic constructions with the verb ⲉⲓⲛⲉ 'be like' whose infinitive is not attested in the Tripartite. The periphrastic construction is employed, when there is a need to express the idea of 'being alike' in tenses or modi other than present indicative:

(149) Shen.Can. 4, GI 98:37 (Wessely 1909)

ⲛ̅ⲛⲉⲗⲁⲁⲩ ϩⲣⲁⲓ̈ ⲛ̅ϩⲏⲧⲛ̅ ⲉⲓⲧⲉ ϩⲟⲟⲩⲧ ⲉⲓⲧⲉ ⲥϩⲓⲙⲉ **ϣⲱⲡⲉ ⲉⲩⲉⲓⲛⲉ** ⲛ̅ⲛⲓⲣⲉϥⲣ̅ⲛⲟⲃⲉ ⲧⲏⲣⲟⲩ
ⲉⲧⲙ̅ⲙⲁⲩ

"*so that none of you, man or woman, would resemble all those sinners*"

(150) 1John 3:2

ⲧⲉⲧⲛ̅ⲥⲟⲟⲩⲛ ϫⲉ ⲉϥϣⲁⲛⲟⲩⲱⲛϩ ⲉⲃⲟⲗ **ⲧⲉⲛⲛⲁϣⲱⲡⲉ ⲉⲛⲉⲓⲛⲉ** ⲙ̅ⲙⲟϥ

οἴδαμεν ὅτι ἐὰν φανερωθῇ, ὅμοιοι αὐτῷ ἐσόμεθα

'*but we know that when he appears, we shall be like him*'

A less rigorous, but similar behavior is demonstrated by the verb ϭⲱϣⲧ 'look, watch', whose infinitive is not, strictly speaking, incompatible with the non-durative tenses, but strongly prefers the durative pattern.

Cases, as these, provide an ideal illustration to Funk's concept of periphrasis as a medium for combining the stative aspect with the non-present tenses. One should, however, keep in mind that the variable here is not the aspect, which is an inherent part of the lexeme, but the tense. Periphrastic forms of these verbs complete the paradigm not only in future tenses, but in perfect, as well:

(151) Shen.Can. 9 DF 261:24, Funk (unpublished)

ⲉⲁⲩϣⲱⲡⲉ ⲉⲩⲉⲓⲛⲉ ⲙ̅ⲙⲟϥ

'*It was him they started to resemble*'

(152) Exodus 2:4

ⲁⲧⲉϥⲥⲱⲛⲉ ϣⲱⲡⲉ ⲉⲥϭⲱϣⲧ ⲙ̅ⲡⲟⲩⲉ ⲉⲉⲓⲙⲉ ⲉⲛⲉⲧⲛⲁϣⲱⲡⲉ ⲙ̅ⲙⲟϥ[229]

καὶ κατεσκόπευεν ἡ ἀδελφὴ αὐτοῦ μακρόθεν μαθεῖν, τί τὸ ἀποβησόμενον αὐτῷ

'*His sister was looking from afar to know what would happen to him*'

---

229 Translation – N.S.

2.5 Periphrasis: perfect

The difference between the synthetic and the analytic form is much less obvious with perfect, than it is with future tenses. As will be shown in 2.7, the periphrastic perfect in most cases conveys the meaning of the change of state. At the same time, as also with future tenses, it clearly serves to represent the predicated event as interminate. This leads to one of the two possible ways of interpretation: 1) the event is represented as begun in the past but taking place at the time of speech or for an indefinite length of time; 2) the event as such pertains to the past, but its result is valid at the time of speech or for an indefinite length of time. As far as my examples go, the first interpretation is associated with the absolute and the second one with the stative form of the subordinate predicate.

(153)   Shenoute, Canon 6

ⲘⲠⲒⲉϢϬⲘϬⲟⲘ Ⲏ ⲦⲚⲀϢϬⲘϬⲟⲘ ⲀⲚ ⲉϬⲱ Ϫⲉ ⲦϨⲚⲱ Ϩⲱ ⲉⲘⲚⲢⲰⲘⲉ ⲤⲟⲟⲨⲚ ⲉⲂⲟⲗ Ϫⲉ **ⲀϤϢⲰⲠⲉ ⲉϤϪⲉⲢⲟ** ϨⲢⲀⲒ ϨⲘ ⲠⲀϨⲎⲦ ⲚϬⲒ ⲠϢⲰⲚⲉ ⲉⲦⲘⲘⲀⲨ ⲚⲖⲟⲒⲘⲟⲤ ⲚⲐⲉ ⲚⲟⲨⲔⲰϨⲦ ϨⲒⲦⲚ ⲚⲉⲦⲚⲒϤⲉ ⲚⲤⲰϤ ⲚⲐⲉ ⲚϨⲉⲚϪ̄ⲂⲂⲉⲤ ⲉⲨϪⲉⲢⲟ ϨⲚ ⲞⲨⲢⲰ ϨⲒⲦⲚ ⲚⲉⲦⲚⲒϤⲉ ⲉⲢⲟⲞⲨ ⲀⲨⲱ **ⲀϤϢⲰⲠⲉ ⲉϤⲂⲢⲂⲢ** ϨⲢⲀⲒ ϨⲘ ⲠⲀⲤⲰⲘⲀ ⲚⲐⲉ ⲚⲞⲨⲘⲟⲞⲨ ⲉⲨⲤⲀϨⲦⲉ ϨⲀⲢⲟϤ ⲚϬⲒ ⲚⲉⲦⲚⲉϪϢⲉ ϨⲒ ⲤⲀⲀⲤⲉ ⲉⲠⲔⲰϨⲦ ⲉⲦⲘⲘⲀⲨ

'*I could not and will not be able to stay, for I am hurt, and no one knows it, because this filthy illness **has come to burn** in my heart, like a fire under (the breath of) those who breath on it, like the coals that burn in the oven, when one fans them. And it **has become boiling** in my body, like water being heated by those who throw wood and logs to the fire (underneath it).*'

A frequent Greek equivalent of the first type of this pattern is the phrase: γίγνομαι εἰς + Acc., as in

(154)   Ruth 4:16

ⲀⲨⲱ ⲚⲞⲉⲘⲒⲚ ⲀⲤϪⲒ ⲘⲠϢⲎⲢⲉ ⲔⲞⲨⲒ ⲀⲤⲔⲀⲀϤ ϨⲚ ⲔⲞⲨⲚⲤ **ⲀⲤϢⲰⲠⲉ ⲉⲤϨⲖⲟⲞⲖⲉ** ⲘⲘⲟϤ

καὶ ἔλαβεν Νωεμιν τὸ παιδίον καὶ ἔθηκεν εἰς τὸν κόλπον αὐτῆς καὶ **ἐγενήθη** αὐτῷ **εἰς τιθηνόν**.

'*Then Naomi took the child and laid him on her lap and **became** his **nurse**.*'

(155)   Shen.Can. 6, MONB.XV, 98, Amel. 1, 37

ⲠⲦⲞⲞⲨ ⲉⲚⲦⲀⲠⲚⲞⲨⲦⲉ ⲤϨⲞⲨⲰⲢϤ **ⲀϤϢⲰⲠⲉ ⲉϤⲢⲟⲔϨ ⲉϤⲞ ⲚⲔⲀⲔⲉ ⲉϤⲦⲀⲔⲎⲨ** ⲦⲎⲢϤ ⲘⲚ ⲚⲉϤⲰⲚⲉ

'*the mountain that God has cursed **became burnt out, dark and destroyed**, all of it with its stones*'

(156)   Apocr. John 29:18-19

ⲀϤϨⲦⲎⲦⲘ̄ ⲠⲞⲨⲟⲉⲒⲚ ⲀⲨⲱ ⲘⲠϤϢⲰⲠⲉ Ⲛ̄ⲞⲨⲞⲉⲒⲚ ⲞⲨⲦⲉ Ⲛ̄ⲔⲀⲔⲉ ⲀⲖⲖⲀ **ⲀϤϢⲰⲠⲉ ⲉϤϢⲟⲚⲉ**

'*it darkened the light. So, it did not become light, nor darkness, but rather **it became weak***'

The above examples show that periphrastic perfect constructions denote events consisting of two parts, the change of state and the new state, of which the second has no tense value of its own, but is assigned a tense depending on the context. Thus, the present reading is appropriate for (153), but not for (154)-(156), which refer to narrative past.

The first type of perfect periphrasis may be termed 'antiperfect' based on its time schema: essentially, it denotes an event that is NOT completed at any known reference time-point. On the other hand, the second type has the same two facets, as the usual perfect: a prior event and a resultant state. Hence, no great semantic change would possibly ensue, if we rephrase (155) in the following way:

ⲡⲧⲟⲟⲩ ⲉⲛⲧⲁⲡⲛⲟⲩⲧⲉ ⲥⲉⲟⲩⲱⲣϥ **ⲁϥⲣⲱⲕⲉ ⲁϥⲣ ⲕⲁⲕⲉ ⲁϥⲧⲁⲕⲟ**

However, the use of the analytic construction clearly shifts the accent from the event itself to the resulting state. Taking this shift to be the main function of periphrasis, we can extend this idea to cases where such semantic nuances cannot be obtained from the context, such as:

(157) Shen.Can. 1, 17.5

ⲁⲩⲕⲁⲁⲥ ⲉⲥⲁⲥⲭⲏⲙⲟⲛⲉⲓ ⲁⲩⲱ **ⲁⲥϣⲱⲡⲉ ⲉⲥϭⲟⲗⲡ̄ ⲉⲃⲟⲗ** ⲛ̄ϭⲓ ⲧⲁⲥⲭⲏⲙⲟⲥⲩⲛⲏ ⲛ̄ⲧⲉⲥⲡⲟⲣⲛⲉⲓⲁ
'*indem man sie entkleidete und beschämte und die Schamlosigkeit ihrer Unzucht wurde aufgedeckt*'

The biblical passage quoted by Shenoute uses a synthetic form, a non-causative infinitive, to render the same meaning (the difference in tenses does not seem to play any role here):

(158) Ezek 23:29

ⲛⲥϭⲱⲗⲡ ⲉⲃⲟⲗ ⲛ̄ϭⲓ ⲧⲁⲥⲭⲏⲙⲟⲥⲩⲛⲏ ⲛⲧⲟⲩⲡⲟⲣⲛⲓⲁ
καὶ ἀποκαλυφθήσεται αἰσχύνη πορνείας σου
'*and the nakedness of your whoring shall be uncovered*'

2.6 Types of periphrastic predicates and the lexical inventory of the pattern

Seemingly at variance with the definition of periphrasis as resultative-stative form is the fact that the periphrastic predicate is not confined to formally intransitive forms, i.e., statives and intransitive infinitives, but includes verbs with direct objects, as well, as, for instance, in

(159) Gen 3:14

ⲉⲕⲉϣⲱⲡⲉ ⲉⲕⲟⲩⲉⲙ ⲕⲁϩ ⲛⲛⲉϩⲟⲟⲩ ⲧⲏⲣⲟⲩ ⲙⲡⲉⲕⲱⲛϩ
γῆν φάγῃ πάσας τὰς ἡμέρας τῆς ζωῆς σου
'*dust you shall eat all the days of your life*'

However, examples such as this last one show that 'staging' the event as atelic involves a change in the agentivity properties of its subject, such as volitionality and non-affectedness. Indeed, here, as also in the example from Luke 1:20 (ⲉⲕⲉϣⲱⲡⲉ ⲉⲕⲕⲱ ⲣⲣⲱⲕ 'you will be silent'), the core event of the predicate is forced on the subject referent as a punishment. Another detransitivizing feature of such constructions is the low individuation of the object. Thus, generally, even if the actant A performs an action on the actant B, the imperfective aspect of periphrasis represents this event as the state of A, and not of B. In Vendler's schema, this corresponds to states and activities, but not achievements or accomplishments. This semantic content may appear in three different syntactic shapes:

(a) intransitive infinitive (e.g., ⲙⲟⲟϣⲉ 'walk') or – mostly – stative predicate:

(160) Shen.Can. 6, Amel. 2 (299:6)
ϣⲁⲛⲧⲟⲩⲛⲧϥ ⲉⲡⲥⲁ ⲛⲃⲟⲗ **ⲛϥϣⲱⲡⲉ ⲉϥⲥⲕⲣⲕⲱⲣ** ⲉϥⲣⲓⲙⲉ ⲟⲛ ⲛⲟⲩϩⲓⲣ ⲙⲙⲟⲟϣⲉ
'*till they bring him outside and **he turns over** (or perhaps: **lies upside down)** crying in the street*'

(b) transitive infinitive with a non-specific (most often, zero-articled) object:

(161) Shen.Can. 3 YA 552:39
ⲛⲧⲛϣⲱⲡⲉ ⲉⲛϯⲥⲃⲱ ⲛⲛⲉⲛⲉⲣⲏⲩ
'*And **we shall teach** each other*' (lit: '*we shall give learning to each other*')

(162) Deut 19:11
ⲉⲣⲉϣⲁⲛⲟⲩⲣⲱⲙⲉ ⲇⲉ **ϣⲱⲡⲉ ⲉϥⲙⲟⲥⲧⲉ ⲙⲡⲉⲧϩⲓⲧⲟⲩⲱϥ**
ἐὰν δὲ γένηται ἄνθρωπος **μισῶν τὸν πλησίον**
'*if anyone **hates his neighbor**'*

(c) 'impersonal passive' construction; in this case, the deep structure patient corresponds to two surface-syntactic actants: the object of the core verb and the subject of the auxiliary. At the semantic level, it manifests the split between its status as the topic of the speech (corresponding to syntactic subject) and its non-agentivity (corresponding to syntactic object). At the syntactic level, it is obviously a mechanism for expressing intransitive imperfective future / perfect with such verbs that do not have intransitive forms (i.e., with stative-less verbs), in this sense an allotagm of (a):

(163) Nag Hammadi Codex V, The Apocalypse of Adam, f.85
ⲙⲁⲣⲉⲡⲉⲩⲟⲩⲧⲁϩ ⲗⲱⲱⲙ• ⲁⲗⲗⲁ **ⲥⲉⲛⲁϣⲱⲡⲉ ⲉⲩⲥⲟⲟⲩⲛ ⲙⲙⲟⲟⲩ** ϣⲁ ⲛⲓⲛⲟϭ ⲛⲛⲉⲱⲛ•
'*Their fruit does not wither. But they will be known up to the great aeons*'

(164) On the Punishment of Sinners, 77,26-78,2, Kuhn (1956:8, 28-30)
ⲡⲉⲩϥⲛⲧ ⲛⲁⲙⲟⲩ ⲁⲛ ⲁⲩⲱ ⲡⲉⲩⲕⲱϩⲧ / ⲛⲁϫⲉⲛⲁ ⲁⲛ. **ⲛⲥⲉϣⲱⲡⲉ ⲉⲣⲉⲥⲁⲣⲝ ⲛⲓⲙ ⲛⲁⲩ ⲉⲣⲟⲟⲩ**:
'*Their worm shall not die, and their fire shall not be quenched and they shall be for all flesh to see them*'

Each of the three constructions is available for the Greek loan verbs:

a) Periphrasis with intransitive infinitive:

(165) NHC II Gospel of Thomas, 70, Layton (1989)
ⲡⲉϫⲉ ⲓ̅ⲥ̅ ϫⲉ **ϣⲱⲡⲉ ⲉⲧⲉⲧⲛⲣ̅ⲡⲁⲣⲁⲅⲉ**
'*Jesus said, "Become such who pass by."*'

(166) Pepper Receipt (Crum 1925:106-7)
ⲉⲥⲛⲁϣⲱⲡⲉ ⲉⲥⲟⲣⲝ ⲁⲩⲱ **ⲉⲥⲃⲉⲃⲁⲓⲟⲩ** ϩⲙ ⲙⲁ ⲛⲓⲙ
'*It shall be valid and guaranteed wherever it may be produced*'

b)   Periphrasis with transitive infinitive and non-specific object

(167) Abbaton (Budge 1914:241,32-33).

ⲉⲣⲉⲛⲉⲕⲃⲁⲗ ⲛⲁϣⲱⲡⲉ ⲉⲩⲑⲉⲱⲣⲉⲓ ⲛ̅ⲛⲉⲧⲥⲁⲡⲉⲥⲏⲧ ⲙ̅ⲡⲕⲁϩ ϣⲁϩⲣⲁⲓ̈ ⲉⲛⲉⲧϩⲛ̅ ⲙ̅ⲙⲟⲩⲛⲉⲓⲟⲟⲩⲉ •
'*Your eyes shall be looking at the things below the earth, up to (and including) the things that are in the waters*'

c)   Periphrasis with 'impersonal passive' structure:

(168) Nag Hammadi Cod. VI, Asclepius 21-29

ⲛ̅ⲧⲟϥ ⲇⲉ ϥⲛⲁϣⲱⲡⲉ ⲉⲩⲣ̅ ⲁⲡⲟⲥⲧⲉⲣⲓ ⲙ̅ⲙⲟϥ ⲛ̅ⲧⲉϥϩⲉⲗⲡⲓⲥ ⲉϥϣⲟⲟⲡ` ϩⲛ̅ ⲟⲩⲛⲟϭ ⲛ̅ⲗⲩⲡⲏ•
'*And he will be deprived of his hope, since he will be in great pain*'

(169) Nag Hammadi Cod. VI, The Concept of our great power

ⲧⲟⲧⲉ ϥⲛⲏⲟⲩ ⲉϥⲟⲧⲟⲩ ⲧⲏⲣⲟⲩ ⲉⲃⲟⲗ• ⲁⲩⲱ ⲥⲉⲛⲁϣⲱⲡⲉ ⲉⲩⲣ̅ⲕⲟⲗⲁⲍⲉ ⲙ̅ⲙⲟⲟⲩ ϣⲁⲛⲧⲟⲩⲧ̅ⲃⲃⲟ•
'*Then he shall come to destroy them all, and they shall be punished until they become pure*'

Inside the class of verbs used in the periphrastic pattern, there appears to be a striking percentage of synonymy, both among the native vocabulary and between the native and the loaned Greek lexemes. The noteworthy micro-groups are: 'remain' (ⲙⲟⲩⲛ ⲉⲃⲟⲗ, ⲡⲣⲟⲥⲕⲁⲣⲧⲏⲣⲉⲓ), 'watch' (ⲛⲁⲩ, ϭⲱϣⲧ, ⲑⲉⲱⲣⲉⲓ), 'believe' (ⲛⲁϩⲧⲉ, ⲡⲓⲥⲧⲉⲩⲉ), 'walk, be engaged in the act of walking' (ⲙⲟⲟϣⲉ, ⲉⲓ, ⲡⲁⲣⲁⲅⲉ), 'govern' (ⲁⲙⲁϩⲧⲉ ⲉϫⲛ, ⲁⲣⲭⲉⲥⲑⲁⲓ), 'resemble' (ⲉⲓⲛⲉ, ⲧⲟⲛⲧⲛ), 'be small, empty' (ⲥⲃⲟⲕ, ϣⲱϫⲡ, ⲟⲩⲱⲥϥ), 'be insignificant / despised / distressed' (ϩⲱϣ, ⲥⲁⲱϣ, ⲥⲱⲱϥ, ⲙⲕⲁϩ), 'be/ make firm, strong' (ⲱⲣϫ, ⲧⲁϫⲣⲟ, ⲃⲉⲃⲁⲓⲟⲩ). This can hardly come as a surprise, seeing that all these lexical groups belong to the atelic class and that the use of periphrasis is heavily influenced by the aspectual features of the verbal lexeme.

2.7 The issue of inchoativity

As previously mentioned, periphrasis is now generally understood as a form characterized by both imperfective (atelic) and bounded aspect, which means that the event in question is represented as a temporally unlimited change of a previous state. Moreover, this change-of-state nuance of meaning is thought by some researchers (e.g., Layton) to be the sole trigger of analytic constructions with a subordinate infinitive. However, the very first example used by Layton to illustrate this statement makes one question its veracity.

(170) Luke 7:38

ⲁⲥⲁϩⲉⲣⲁⲧⲥ ϩⲓⲡⲁϩⲟⲩ ⲙⲙⲟϥ ϩⲁⲣⲁⲧϥ ⲉⲥⲣⲓⲙⲉ ⲁⲥⲁⲣⲭⲓ ⲛϩⲣⲡⲛⲉϥⲟⲩⲉⲣⲏⲧⲉ ⲛⲛⲉⲥⲣⲙⲓⲟⲟⲩⲉ
ⲉⲁⲥϥⲟⲧⲟⲩ ⲙⲡϥⲱ ⲛⲧⲉⲥⲁⲡⲉ ⲁⲥϣⲱⲡⲉ ⲉⲥϯⲡⲓ ⲉⲛⲉϥⲟⲩⲉⲣⲏⲧⲉ ⲉⲥⲧⲱϩⲥ ⲙⲙⲟⲟⲩ ⲙⲡⲥⲟϭⲛ
καὶ στᾶσα ὀπίσω παρὰ τοὺς πόδας αὐτοῦ κλαίουσα, τοῖς δάκρυσιν ἤρξατο βρέχειν τοὺς πόδας αὐτοῦ, καὶ ταῖς θριξὶν τῆς κεφαλῆς αὐτῆς ἐξέμασσεν, καὶ **κατεφίλει** τοὺς πόδας αὐτοῦ καὶ ἤλειφεν τῷ μύρῳ.
'*And standing behind him at his feet, weeping, she began to wet his feet with her tears and wiped them with the hair of her head and **kissed his feet** and anointed them with the ointment.*'

For the periphrastic phrase ⲁⲥϣⲱⲡⲉ ⲉⲥϯⲡⲓ ⲉⲛⲉϥⲟⲩⲉⲣⲏⲧⲉ, Layton suggests a translation containing the marker of inchoativity ('she began kissing his feet'), based on his word-for-word reading of the phrase as "she-became she kissing". The Greek original, however, does not warrant such reading. The inchoative meaning in this verse is associated with another verb (βρέχειν - ϩⲱⲣⲡ 'wet'). Following the original, the Coptic translator marks it by ⲁⲣⲭⲓ. On the contrary, the event of kissing is coded by the simple narrative imperfect. The text gives no reason for a change-of-state interpretation in this case ("she stopped whatever she was doing and began kissing his feet"). Thus, paradoxically, Layton attempts to prove his point with one of the very few instances of perfect periphrasis that does not hold with the inchoativity hypothesis.

However, most occurrences of perfect periphrasis in the biblical corpus, with very few exceptions, entail the change-of-state meaning, being the usual translation equivalent of Greek γίγνομαι -phrases, as in:

(171) Joshua 9:18 (9:12)
ⲧⲉⲛⲟⲩ ϭⲉ ⲁⲩϣⲟⲟⲩⲉ ⲁⲩⲱ ⲁⲩϣⲱⲡⲉ ⲉⲩϣⲏϥ ⲉⲃⲟⲗ ⲙⲡⲱⲥⲕ ⲛⲧⲉϩⲓⲏ
νῦν δὲ ἐξηράνθησαν καὶ γεγόνασιν βεβρωμένοι·
'but now, behold, it is dry and crumbly (lit.: has become dry and crumbly)'

(172) Lamentations 1:16
ⲁⲛⲁϣⲏⲣⲉ ϣⲱⲡⲉ ⲉⲩⲧⲁⲕⲏⲩ
ἐγένοντο οἱ υἱοί μου ἠφανισμένοι
'my children are desolate (lit.: 'have become desolate')'

(173) Joel 2:2
ⲙⲡⲉ ⲟⲩⲟⲛ ⲛⲓⲙ ϣⲱⲡⲉ ⲉϥⲉⲓⲛⲉ ⲙⲙⲟϥ ϫⲓⲛ ⲛϣⲟⲣⲡ ⲁⲩⲱ ⲙⲛⲛⲥⲁ ⲛⲁⲓ
ὅμοιος αὐτῷ οὐ γέγονεν ἀπὸ τοῦ αἰῶνος καὶ μετ᾽ αὐτὸν
'their like has never been before, nor will be again after them'

If the inchoative sense can hardly be termed the main trigger of periphrasis in these cases, it is at least not altogether excluded from the semantics of the phrase. The situation is different with future tenses. Here, the Coptic analytic pattern almost always corresponds to Greek < εἰμί + participle>:

(174) Deut 28:34
ⲛⲅϣⲱⲡⲉ ⲉⲕⲥⲟϣⲙ ϩⲛ ⲛⲉⲧⲉⲣⲉⲛⲉⲕⲃⲁⲗ ⲛⲁⲩ ⲉⲣⲟⲟⲩ
ἔσῃ παράπληκτος διὰ τὰ ὁράματα τῶν ὀφθαλμῶν σου
'so that you are driven mad by the sights that your eyes see'

(175) Mark 13:13
ⲛⲧⲉⲧⲛϣⲱⲡⲉ ⲉⲣⲉⲟⲩⲟⲛ ⲛⲓⲙ ⲙⲟⲥⲧⲉ ⲙⲙⲱⲧⲛ ⲉⲧⲃⲉ ⲡⲁⲣⲁⲛ
ἔσεσθε μισούμενοι ὑπὸ πάντων διὰ τὸ ὄνομά μου
'And you will be hated by all for my name's sake'

Interestingly, the observable neutralization of the change-of-state meaning of the auxiliary in future tense is not unparalleled among modern languages. In this connection, one can recall the German change-of-state verb *werden*, which is used as an auxiliary for inchoative past passive, but has no inchoative sense as a future auxiliary.

The syntactic and semantic problem behind these observations is, of course, far too complicated to try to treat it in the present work, but the first naive explanation could be as follows: the meaning of change does not require a specific morphological marker in future tenses, because it immanently pertains to the future tense as such. For Coptic, this means that the periphrastic construction generally depicts the event as a change from some previous state, though this component of meaning is never the central or the single one.

The absence of periphrastic predicates in temporal subordinate clauses can be sufficiently well explained and comprehended, if one takes into account that the temporal pattern ⲛⲧⲉⲣⲉ-ϥ-ⲥⲱⲧⲙ 'after he heard' denotes a point of time understood as the starting point of the event denoted by the main clause, hence it is bound to contain a terminative verb; the interminativity of periphrasis must be what makes it incompatible with this conjugation pattern. Slightly less intuitive seems the fact that the limitative clause, as well as the temporal one, requires its predicate to be terminative-punctual and not just start-punctual, in which case periphrasis would have a chance to occur with that pattern.

2.8 The issue of iterativity

An open question is the interrelationship between periphrasis and the semantic category of iterativity. As shown in Khrakovsky (1989), this category pertains to the domain of quantifiability of events. Since punctual events are singular, iterative (multiple) events tend to take a morphological shape that expresses non-punctuality. As a consequence, iterativity is often expressed by the same means as imperfectivity; not infrequently, inside the class of verbal markers used to express imperfectivity, there may be a subclass "specializing" on iterative Aktionsart. Thus, there would be nothing strange about one and the same periphrastic structure employed as a marker of both durativity and iterativity.

However, the evidence of an iterative use of periphrasis is scarce and remains dubious to me. I have managed to find no more than four or five instances of iterative periphrastic predicate, one of them being the above cited example from Luke 7:38. In three further instances, the core verb is a verb of movement (ⲉⲓ 'come', ⲡⲱⲧ 'run', ⲃⲱⲕ 'go'); iteration is overtly expressed by temporal or spatial adverbials (ϩⲁϩ ⲛⲥⲟⲡ 'many times', ⲉⲡⲓⲥⲁ ⲙⲛ ⲡⲁⲓ 'here and there, to this and other side') or implicitly suggested by the context.

(176) Besa On Theft, frag. 23: II,3 (Kuhn 1956:63)
       ⲉⲧⲃⲉ ⲡⲁⲓ ⲟⲩⲟⲓ ⲛⲏⲧⲛ ϫⲉ ⲁⲟⲩⲕⲣⲓⲧⲏⲥ ⲉϥⲣϩⲟⲧⲉ ⲁⲛ ϩⲏⲧϥ ⲙⲡⲛⲟⲩⲧⲉ, ⲁⲩⲱ ⲉⲛϥϣⲓⲡⲉ ⲁⲛ
       ϩⲏⲧϥ ⲛⲣⲱⲙⲉ ⲣ ⲡϩⲁⲡ ⲛⲟⲩⲭⲏⲣⲁ ϫⲉ **ⲛⲛⲉⲥϣⲱⲡⲉ ⲉⲥⲛⲏⲩ** ϣⲁⲣⲟϥ ⲛϩⲁϩ ⲛⲥⲟⲡ• ⲉⲥϯ ϩⲓⲥⲉ ⲛⲁϥ•
       'Therefore, woe to you, because a judge who neither feared God nor respected man, gave judgment for a widow that she should not be coming to him so often and troubling him.'[230]

---

230 (This instance is an almost exact quotation of Luke 18:5 with a different time adverb, but an identical sense: ϯⲛⲁⲣ ⲡⲉⲥϩⲁⲡ ϫⲉ ⲛⲛⲉⲥϣⲱⲡⲉ ⲉⲥⲛⲏⲟⲩ ϣⲁⲃⲟⲗ ⲛⲥϯ ϩⲓⲥⲉ ⲛⲁⲓ / ἐκδικήσω αὐτήν, ἵνα μὴ εἰς τέλος ἐρχομένη ὑπωπιάζῃ με / "…I will give her justice, so that she will not beat me down

(177) Hochzeit zu Kana, 248:3-5

ογο2 ⲁϥϣⲱⲡⲓ ⲉϤ϶ⲏⲧ ⲉⲡⲁⲓⲥⲁ ⲛⲉⲙ ⳨ⲁⲓ ⲉϥϣⲑⲉⲣⲑⲱⲣ

'Und er begann zu fliehen nach dieser und jener Seite, indem er in Erregung geriet'[231]

(178) Shen.Can. 1 17.7

ⲙⲡⲣⲟϣⲡⲉ ⲉⲣⲉⲃⲏⲕ ⲉ2ογⲛ ⲉⲡⲙⲁ ⲉⲧⲉⲥγⲛⲁⲅⲉ ⲛ2ⲏⲧϥ ⲉⲣⲉϣⲟⲟⲡ 2ⲛογⲕⲣⲟϥ

'Gehe nicht hinein zu dem Ort, an dem du dich zum Gottesdienst versammelst wenn du etwas Schlimmes planst'

The iterative perfect in (179) and (180) proves that, even if the analytic form bears any relation to the iterative meaning whatsoever, it is, at least, not obligatory in perfect:

(179) Pistis Sophia, Book 1 23b 24,19-22

ⲛⲧⲉⲣⲟγⲛⲁγ ⲉⲡⲛⲟϭ ⲛογⲟⲉⲓⲛ ⲉⲛⲉϥϣⲟⲟⲡ ⲙⲙⲟï· ⲁγϣⲧⲟⲣⲧⲣ̄ ⲧⲏⲣⲟγ ⲉⲭⲛ̄ ⲛⲉγⲉⲣⲏγ ⲁγⲱ ⲁγⲡⲱⲧ ⲉⲡⲓⲥⲁ ⲙⲛ̄ ⲡⲁï 2ⲣⲁï ⲍ̄ⲛ ⲛⲁⲓⲱⲛ

'when all those saw the great light which I had, they were all together (lit.: over each other) troubled and flew from side to side in the aeons'

(180) Ps 77:40

2ⲁ2 ⲛⲥⲟⲡ ⲁγ† ϭⲱⲛⲧ ⲛⲁϥ 2ⲓ ⲡⲭⲁⲓⲉ

ποσάκις παρεπίκραναν αὐτὸν ἐν τῇ ἐρήμῳ

'How often they rebelled against him in the wilderness'

Yet, the periphrasis of the unspecific-object infinitive might arguably highlight the iterative semantics in:

(181) Nag Hammadi Codex VII, Teachings of Silvanus f. 87 (Peel 1996:286)

ⲁγⲱ ⲉγϣⲁⲛⲡⲁⲓⲇⲉγⲉ ⲙⲙⲟⲕ 2ⲛ 2ⲱⲃ ⲛⲓⲙ ϣⲱⲡⲉ ⲉⲕⲣ̄ ⲡⲉⲧⲛⲁⲛⲟγϥ

'And should you be educated in any matter, be doing what is good.'

2.9 Conclusion

The Coptic circumstantial periphrasis is compatible with the tenses and modes of future meaning (future, optative, imperative, future conjunctive, jussive and future conditional) and with perfect. Occurrences with aorist are extremely infrequent, periphrastic subordinate clauses, if they exist, seem to be very rare.

Depending on the form of the core verb, the predicate in the circumstantial clause most often belongs to one of the three formal types: a stative or an intransitive infinitive (mostly with Greek verbs); transitive infinitive with a non-specific object; two-argument infinitive with a non-specific subject, i.e. the 'impersonal passive' construction. The impersonal

---

by her continual coming." Here, of course, the parallel with the Greek participle suggests itself as another possible trigger of the periphrastic construction in Coptic. However, such structural nuances would not be supported in quotations.)

231 Mueller (Heidelberg 1968:248). Though aware of committing a methodological transgression in using instances from a non-related corpus and, still worse, from a different dialect, I cannot give up on this token of iterative periphrasis: the instances are altogether so rare, that losing a single one, you are in danger of missing a grammatical nuance.

passive type serves as an equivalent of the stative predicate for stative-lacking verbs. Predicates consisting of an infinitive with a specific subject and a specific object, such as Ruth 4:16 ⲁⲥϣⲱⲡⲉ ⲉⲥ̅ⲣⲟⲟⲗⲉ ⲙⲙⲟϥ ἐγενήθη αὐτῷ εἰς τιθηνόν '(she) became his nurse', are rather an exception.

The specific semantic interpretation of a periphrastic construction depends on the employed form and the lexical aspect of the core verb. With the statives of telic verbs, including strong transitives, perihprastic pattern denotes, respectively, future or past objective resultative. The periphrastic resultative past theoretically could be opposed to the stative past expressed by the imperfect converter with stative, as, e.g., in Luke 9:45 ⲛⲉϥⲅ̅ⲟⲃⲥ ⲉⲣⲟⲟⲩ / ἦν παρακεκαλυμμένον ἀπ' αὐτῶν 'it was concealed from them'; however, I was not able to find any actual minimal pair of periphrastic perfect vs. stative imperfect with the same core verb. Further on, with the statives or infinitives of atelic / statal verbs, the periphrastic form has the respective reading as future stative or past interminate ("anti-perfect"). Finally, with unspecific-object infinitives and with statives of motion verbs, it presumably can also denote a multiple, iterating situation.

As to the structural place of the pattern, with telic verbs it is a suppletive, i.e., paradigme-filling form. With atelic / statal / motion verbs, it seems to be facultative, highlighting the durative, or possibly sometimes iterative aspect.

Interestingly, whereas the past resultative periphrasis has the semantic component of inchoativity (hence the parallelism with the Greek copular pattern γίγνομαι + noun / adjective / participle), the same construction referring to future does not usually denote a change of state. Possibly, this shade of meaning is neutralized in future tenses by the general sense of future as a change of the preceding state.

2.10 Appendix: periphrasis in Demotic

The tokens of the periphrastic *ḫpr(=f) jw(=f)* pattern in the Demotic corpus of the Thesaurus Linguae Aegyptiae are very few, hardly more than 10. All the more remarkable is that most of them occur within the tense bases that can be largely defined as future-type tenses. Among them are:

a)   ***Future and negative future***

(182) TM47388, P.Rylands 9, X, 18
       mtw =f p3 ntj-jw =f r ḫpr tw =f sḫn n.im =n ꜥn[232]
       "It is him who will be responsible for us"

(183) TM54058, P.Harkness, II, line 2, Smith (2005)[233]
       ...dd bn-tw-n3.w t3j t̯ꜥm ḫpr tw =s d̯sj D.t
       "...saying: This little girl should not be in want of anything"

---

232 The verb 'sHn' in this example can be understood as either transitive ("he will command us") or
     intransitive. In my interpretation of this clause as intransitive, I follow G.Vittmann's translation.
233 Translation mine, based on the translation in the Thesaurus Linguae Aegyptiae data base.

b)   *Conjunctive with future meaning*

(184) TM6378, Canopus decree, CG 22186 /18, Simpson (1996:238-239)
       [*mtw*] [*p3*] [*sd*] [*n*] [*t3j*] [*ʿrʿ*][*j*]*,t ḫpr iw =f grmrm r.r =f*
       "[and the tail of the Uraeus-snake] should be twined round it (i.e., papyrus stalk)"

(185) TM6378, Canopus decree, CG 22186 / 61, Simpson (1996:238-239)
       p3 sḥn n nb ntj-iw =w dj,t ḥʿ p3j =s sṭm-(n-)nṯr n.im =f mtw =f ḫpr iw =f šb{,t} r p3
       ntj-iw =w dj,t ḥʿ t3 rpj.t n [t3] pr-ʿ3,t brng3 ʿnḥ-wd3-snb t3j =s mw,t n.im =f
       "…the gold diadem with which her cult image is crowned should be different from
       the one with which is crowned the statue of Queen Berenice her mother."

(186) TM55955, P. London-Leiden III, line 10, Griffith-Thompson (1921:34-35)
       mtw =k dj,t <st> r t3 bʿtʿne,t ḥm sp-2 n-wš-n dj,t ḥpr ḥʿjse mtw =f ḫpr iw =f stf m-šs
       sp-2
       "... and (you should) add (it) to the dish gradually without producing perturbance,
       so that it becomes clear exceedingly…"

c)   *Optative*

(187) TM55955, P. London-Leiden X, line 3, Griffith-Thompson (1921:74)[234]
       mj-ir =w ḫpr jw =w šs sp-2 jw =w smn D.ḥ jw =w swtn iw =w pḫr
       "Let them be proved (bis), established, correct, enchanted…"

All the examples above share three grammatical characteristics: they refer to **future**
events from the speaker's time perspective, they have **imperfective** aspect and they are
all univalent clauses with the verbal lexeme used in an **intransitive** structure, whatever
guess we could make regarding its actual morphological shape. However, the aspectual
characteristics may vary, as can be seen from the following perfective example:

(188) TM46443, P.Berlin P 13548[235]
       iw=f-ḫpr iw rḫ p3-šr-p3-mr-iḥ p3 (r.)ḳd r ij r-ḥrj mtw =f ir p3 hrw 2 ḳd mj iw =f mtw
       =<¿f?> ḫpr iw =f ij r-ḥrj p3 hrw tḥb r dj,t wʿb n ḥ,t-nṯr
       "If the architect Psenpelaias can come and make 2 days of building job, let him
       come. And **let him come** on the day of watering, so that he cleans the temple."

As for the tense characteristics, it is unclear, whether the few occurrences of the seemingly
identical construction in non-future tenses (exx. 10 and 11) can be interpreted as periphrasis,
at all:

234   My translation is based on that of Griffith-Thompson who however translate the periphrasis
       analytically ("let them come into being, proved").
235 My translation is based on that in the Thesaurus Linguae Aegyptiae data base.

(189) TM56179, P.Carlsberg 302(8), frag. 13, II, lines 2-3[236]

ḫpr pꜣ mwt tw =f ḥl r [m]ꜣ nb ntj [ḥr] tꜣ p,t tw =f šnb irm pꜣ [ꜥnḫ] [¿i.ir?] pr n pꜣ nwn

"The Death flew (flew out? was flying?) to every place which is under the sky uniting
with the [life which] came forth from the Primaeval Ocean"

(or: "There appeared the Death, flying in every place under the sky…" etc.)

(190) P. Insinger XX, 18, TM55918

ḫpr ḥr tw =f kpe ḥꜣ pꜣ ḏwf ir =f ḥrj {r} <n> pꜣ tꜣ m wḥmꜣ

"Though Horus hid himself (was hidden?) behind the papyrus, he ruled the land
again."

The Demotic data at our disposal are really too scarce to safely determine what grammatical
factors (imperfective aspect? intransitive diathesis?) were the primary triggers of the
periphrastic construction. One can easily imagine that in some cases the pattern was used
to avoid an agent-preserving intransitive interpretation:

* *mj-ir =w smn mj-ir =w swtn mj-ir =w pḫr*

"Let them establish, let them set upright, let them charm (?)…" (cf. example (8)).

In any case, imperfectivity and intransitivity are just complementary ways of atelic representation of an event. Thus, we can claim that the Demotic periphrasis, in all probability,
served as an atelic future construction.

---

236 My translation is based on that by M.Smith, with the altered periphrastic phrase. Smith's translation
goes as follows: "Death came into existence, flying…" etc.

3 Greek loan verbs in Coptic: diathesis and grammatical voice marking

3.1 Defining research object and research objectives

As the substrate language in the bilingual society of the Ptolemaic, Roman and Byzantine Egypt, Egyptian language was subjected to a heavy influence of Greek which has replaced Demotic as the language of administration. The extent of the interaction between the two cultures and the two languages in the everyday life of different social strata is as yet difficult to measure, as can be seen, e.g., from the careful evaluation of the bilingual situation in the Ptolemaic Egypt in Bagnall and Cribiore (2006):

> "The last two decades have gradually made it clear that Greek and Egyptian documen-
> tation does not correspond in any simple fashion to underlying realities. The same in-
> dividuals in some cases operated in both spheres for different purposes: Greek in royal
> service, often Egyptian in religion, but much more mixed in law and private relations.
> Long before the end of the Ptolemaic period, Greek was overtaking Egyptian as a means
> of communication in practically every sphere except the religious, and yet, at least until
> the late second century BC, private legal instruments in Demotic remained common.
> What seems clear is that society contained a considerable spectrum of individual posi-
> tions in the use of language, ranging from Greek settlers whose Egyptian was limited
> to a few words for talking to servants or tradesmen, to numerous Egyptian peasants
> who encountered Greek almost exclusively in the person of bureaucrats and even there
> used intermediaries as far as possible. Between these extremes were many more or less
> bilingual persons… <Moreover,> generation of Greek documentation <…> extended
> by proxy much farther in society than did actual competence in Greek."[237]

The linguistic influence originating in multiple social contacts between the Hellenic and the gradually hellenized native community certainly could not be unilateral. However, it is obvious that the mutual impact of Greek and Egyptian was asymmetrical, mostly taking the form of linguistic borrowing from Greek as a dominant language to Coptic as a socially subordinate one.[238] Now, according to Sakel (2007), the character of borrowing tends to correlate with the type of the sociolinguistic contact between the donor and the recipient languages; the borrowing of grammatical patterns / categories often results from the influence of a substrate language, whereas a dominant language provokes code switching with the ensuing borrowing of the 'physical' linguistic matter, mostly vocabulary[239]. It is, therefore, not surprising that in case of Greek borrowings into Coptic, the borrowed stuff consisted mainly or exclusively of what Muysken calls the 'fabric' of language, namely, of lexical items, whereas the borrowing of grammatical patterns or categories, if any

---

237 Bagnall & Cribiore 2006:58.
238 See Muysken (2017:6). For the reverse side, namely, the impact of Coptic on Greek, see Torallas Tovar (2017).
239 See Sakel (2007:15-16).

such occurred, has yet to be demonstrated.[240] Among these borrowings, according to the estimates of the DDGLC project, roughly 50% are represented by nouns and about 20% more by verbs. The ratio of actual occurrences of nouns and verbs is different: here, verbs account only for some 10% (or less) of all the loans. At present, the data base includes ca. 600 Greek loan verbs. This number may slightly change with the arrival of new documents and new attestations, but hardly significantly.

A substantial part of studies treating the accommodation of Greek verbs in Coptic concentrate on verb integration strategies. This issue comprises two questions: what exactly was the form loaned, infinitive, imperative or the bare verbal stem; and what strategy, — a direct insertion of the verbal lexeme or the light verb construction, — had the temporal and the structural priority. The first topic has been investigated by Böhlig (1995), Funk (2017); the second one is treated, inter alia, in Reintges (2001), Egedi (2017), Grossman & Richter (2017). The 'input' part of the borrowing process has thus attracted a sufficient amount of attention among the linguists of Coptic.

Compared to that, the 'output' part, namely, the diathesis and valency of a newly minted Graeco-Coptic verb, is as yet a rather uncharted territory. The studies in this field include Zakrzewska (2017a, 2017b) and Grossman (2019). Following Reintges (2001) in his interpretation of the absolute infinitive as a morphosyntactic noun introduced by a covert or overt light verb[241], Zakrzewska (2017a) suggests a number of questions as the desiderata for future investigations, among them: what is the valency of the verbs obtained by the light verb derivation; are there regularities in the number and morphological marking of arguments of the derived verbs; is the valency pattern of a derived verb influenced by the valency of the incorporated Greek form, or in other words, are there correspondences between the valency of the original lexeme in Greek and its replica in Coptic; and how precisely occurred the phonetic attrition of the light verb to reach its final stage of zero representation in Sahidic. The question of a possible correspondence between the valency patterns employed by a lexeme in Greek and in Coptic is addressed in Zakrzewska (2017b), with the conclusion that the verbs of Greek origin in Coptic pattern rather with the semantically close native verbs, than with their Greek prototypes, although both languages use a case-marking system, i.a., to mark the patient's non-prototypical affectedness.[242]

Whereas the main point of Zakzewska's research lies in various non-default (i.e., non-transitive) valency patterns, Grossman (2019) focuses on the integration of Greek-origin loan verbs into the Coptic transitivity patterns. Under a somewhat narrow definition of transitivity as the property of a two-argument construction with A- and P-arguments, Grossman concludes that Greek origin verbs have properties similar to those of native

---

240 Zakrzewska (2017a). Still, the grammatical influence of Greek is immediately evident in the domain of discourse structuring, cf. Zakrzewska (2017b:218): "As for grammatical borrowings, the strongest degree of Greek influence can be observed in the adoption of discourse strategies and clause combining strategies, including the use of function words such as conjunctions and discourse markers."

241 Reintges (2001:184).

242 Zakrzewska (2017b:230-231).

verbs in the domain of A/S-coding, but differ from them in the coding of P in that the Greek morphs do not allow P-incorporation or indexing of P on the verb. According to Grossman, this deficiency cannot be explained by mere phonological reasons[243], since both indexing and incorporation of an object are possible for native verbs with the same final segments (e.g., 'krine' and 'Cine', 'staurou' and 'čoou'). Without pronouncing any final judgement on the matter, Grossman admits that the inability of Greek-origin verbs to incorporate a nominal or a pronominal object might be related to diachronic factors, assuming that Greek verbs entered the Coptic language system after the mechanism of argument incorporation and indexing had stopped being productive.

The present study continues exploring the accommodation of Greek loan verbs into the Coptic valency and diathesis patterns, with a special focus on causativity alternations. In the most general way, the problem can be phrased as follows: is the category of voice marked on loaned Greek verbs in Coptic? And if yes, what grammatical mechanisms participate in this marking?

The topic being vast, an exhaustive description would take far more than a single study. My intention is therefore to delineate the observable tendencies. Even this modest task stumbles upon many methodological difficulties which heavily impact the validity of any conclusions and which I would like to register here as 'limited liability' signs.

The first of these impediments consists in the definition of the object of research. One has to bear in mind that the original Greek lexeme and its Coptic reflection cannot be equated for the simple reason that the Graeco-Coptic morph is a member of a totally different system of signs. This idea is advocated by Shisha-Halevy who stresses the importance of "viewing Greek-origin elements as special 'Graecitas Coptica' linguistic signs, with all this implies, and mainly Listener's Model decoding analytical function". He argues that once a Greek morph starts its career in Coptic, it becomes "rather a special Coptic sign, and as such is caught in an oppositive tension within C(optic), between C(optic)-G(reek) and C(optic)-E(gyptian) signs... Any "memories" or rhetorical aura it might have of its Greek career are in principle only marginally, if at all, relevant for the Coptic *état de langue*, and for us in practice rather elusive and subjective."[244] The distance between a Greco-Coptic morph and its Greek origin is immediately expressed through semantic differences between them which can sometimes go so far, as to make the question of grammatical similarity irrelevant. Thus, ⲁⲗⲗⲁⲥⲥⲉ 'exchange', as it seems, has preserved only one specific facet of the meaning of ἀλλάσσω 'change' and therefore cannot denote a spontaneous process; if the Greek verb in the Hellenistic period acquires an anticausative usage based on this semantic trait of spontaneity, we obviously cannot expect the Coptic replica to demonstrate the same behavior. A certain degree of discrepancy between the source lexeme and the loaned one is also observable in such cases where a Coptic translator uses one 'Greek' word to translate another, as, e.g., in

---

243 Grossman (2019:106).
244 Shisha-Halevy (2017:442).

(191) Acts 28:26

Ἀκοῇ ἀκούσετε καὶ οὐ μὴ **συνῆτε**

ϩⲛ ⲟⲩⲥⲱⲧⲙ ⲧⲉⲧⲛⲁⲥⲱⲧⲙ ⲛⲧⲉⲧⲛⲧⲙⲛⲟⲓ

'*You will indeed hear but never understand*'

(192) Acts 18:17

καὶ οὐδὲν τούτων τῷ Γαλλίωνι **ἔμελεν**

ⲁⲩⲱ ⲙⲡⲉⲅⲁⲗⲗⲓⲱⲛ **ⲡⲣⲟⲥⲉⲭⲉ** ⲉⲣⲟⲟⲩ

'*But Gallio paid no attention to any of this*'

These considerations do not compromise the idea of comparison between the grammatical properties of the borrowed item and those of its replica in the source language but call for greater exactitude in our treatment of the compared items.

Another limitation encountered in the present type of research is so self-evident to any linguist of a dead language that it makes almost no sense to mention it anew. This is the limitation in the number and the quality of accessible attestations. In terms of statistics, the situation is as follows: At present, the medium number of attestations per verb in the DDGLC database is approximately 31. However, they are very unequally distributed between such giants as ⲃⲁⲡⲧⲓⲍⲉ 'baptize' (117 attestations), ⲗⲩⲡⲉⲓ 'be sad, grieve' (161 attestations), on the one hand, and far less frequent, and therefore all the more interesting, ⲕⲟⲛⲓⲁ 'whitewash' (2 attestations), ⲧⲁⲣⲁⲥⲥⲉ 'bother' (6 attestations), ϩⲁⲣⲙⲟⲍⲉ 'join together' (7 attestations). In some cases, a diathetic variant of a verb is attested only once, or else the context is so unclear, as to put any conclusive interpretation beyond our reach. Furthermore, the data may vary across the dialects, but the poor numbers in all the dialects do not prove anything about the actual use of the lexeme in question. And, needless to say, some usages or morphological shapes seem to be an idiosyncratic property of a specific corpus of texts. This is often the case with the corpus of Nag Hammadi which accounts for a large part of middle-passive forms in Sahidic. Therefore, in this study, a meticulous description merits much more than a hasty conclusion. But even this target is barely attainable, where the data is so scarce, that it is often impossible to distinguish between accidental usage occurrences, and regular, but underrepresented phenomena.

3.2 Koine: summary of changes to verbal system (after Lavidas 2009)

The variety of Greek to be used for the comparison of a source lemma with its Coptic offshoot presents an additional problem. At the first glance, the most natural candidate for this comparison seems to be the language of the New Testament, a strain of post-Classical Greek best described in grammars and dictionaries. E.g., in Zakrzewska (2017b), the author advocates her choice of a source idiom as follows:

"...As information about the valency patterns of the Greek verbs quoted is not included in Crum's dictionary, I excerpted the necessary data from Bauer's 1988 [1979]) dictionary of New Testament Greek, the standard dictionary of the variety of Greek with which the Coptic writers were most likely to be familiar."[245]

According to Bortone, the choice of the Biblical Greek as the source of information on the grammar of Hellenistic Greek in general is warranted by the following factors:

i) Septuagint and the New Testament together constitute the longest extant text written in Koine;

ii) Uninfluenced by the literary conventions of the Atticist prose[246], the language of the Greek Bible must be closer to the vernacular Koine, than the contemporary literary works.[247]

However, the choice of New Testament Greek as the best representative of Koine is not unproblematic for several reasons. For one, it is not uniform in itself: some gospels reveal more archaic linguistic traits, than the others, the gospel of Mark appearing as the most innovative one.[248] More importantly, even if the influence of Semitic original, and possibly Semitic mother tongue of the writers has been overestimated by the earlier scholars of the Biblical language[249], it was nevertheless significant enough to not embrace this idiom as the purest sample of Hellenistic Greek. What is still more relevant for the Graeco-Coptic contact research, the idea that "the Greek spoken from the south of Italy through Asia Minor, Syria, Egypt, and the erstwhile Persian Empire and as far as the plains of the Punjab, was basically uniform"[250] and that the variety documented in the Bible may as well stand for the one spoken in Egypt looks highly improbable. On the contrary, though the New Testament (as also the Septuagint) Greek could possibly serve as a literary standard for Coptic writers, we can hardly be sure that this was the source language of Coptic borrowings, at least not in the areas other than Christian theology. Certainly, in their everyday life, Egyptian population was rather exposed to the Greek vernacular whose closest approximation we find in non-literary papyri. The language of papyri is known to be significantly different from the language of New Testament, especially in its syntactical mechanisms.[251]

Moreover, even the papyri do not do full justice to the linguistic reality of the vernacular Koine, since writing as medium calls for a certain degree of formalizing and 'smoothing out' of speech and thereby gives a distorted representation of the living language.[252]

---

245 Zakrzewska (2017b:230).

246 Cf. Bortone (2010:172): "A bigger problem is the prestige that Classical Attic had, and the influence it therefore exerted on Hellenistic Greek prose as represented, for example, by the works of Polybius, Diodorus Siculus, Epictetus, or Strabo. Most literary authors wrote in a language that appears to differ from Attic only on close inspection <...>, although the effects of Atticism at this stage are not as far-reaching as in the following centuries."

247 Bortone (2010:172).

248 Ibid.

249 Bortone (2010:174-175).

250 Bortone (2010:172).

251 Cf. Wallace, D.B. (1996:23).

252 Cf., e.g., Torallas Tovar (2010:254), Koester (2012/I:107), Brixhe (2010:231).

Not only official documents written in Egyptian Koine, but also private letters often use technical language with fixed formulaic expressions[253] that tend to ignore or hide grammatical changes. All that does not make the comparative work desperate, but yields it a certain degree of approximation.

Finally, tracking down the changes occurring to a borrowed lexeme suggests that the source language is a pure idiom, untainted by any previous contact with the target language. Would this approach prove accurate in case of Koine, in particular with regard to its verbal system? On the one hand, the Egyptian influence on Greek in the area of verb grammar has never yet, to my knowledge, been a topic of discussion among the researchers of either Coptic, or Koine Greek.[254] Multiple changes in the morphology and syntax of Koine verbs are attributed to internal Greek factors.[255] On the other hand, it is hard to imagine that such crucial part of language usage, as the tense-aspect-modus-voice system, remained intact for the linguistical habits of many non-Greek speakers. And indeed, there is an indirect evidence suggesting that the speech of Egyptian Greek-speaking community deviated from the classical canon, i.a., in the way they applied the Greek voice morphology:

> "[Den aktiv-transitiven Verben] sind nicht gleich die Verba ζῶ, ὑπάρχω, εἰμί, πνέω, φρονῶ und ähnliche. Von diesen wird keine analoge Passivbildung vorhanden sein, weil sie nicht einmal im Indikativ Personen darstellen können, die von der Handlung affiziert werden, so dass sie von sich ein leidendes Verhalten aussagen könnten... Daher müssen **diejenigen, welche solche Wörter durch das ganze Passiv durchflektieren** (emphasis mine – N.S.), eingestehen müssen, dass sie solches bloss um der formellen Übung willen thun, nicht aber dass eine solche Flexion naturgemäss oder auch nur denkbar wäre. Es ist gerade so, wie wenn jemand eine Maskulinform verzeichnen wollte von Wörtern wie γαλουχέσασα ('breastfeeding'), ἐκτρώσασα ('having a miscarriage')"[256] [Apollonius Dyscolus, Syntax, A.D. II]

' 'aito:' and 'aitoumai' are different; as the first one means that I ask for something in order to take it once and not to give it back, the other I ask for something to use it and return it' (Ammonius, 7; A.D. V).[257]

In these explanations, one can distinctly hear an irritated note of a language expert observing the decline of a former linguistic norm. Both authors being the citizens of Alexandria, though with an interval of some 300 years, their descriptions must refer to the same geographical variety of Koine, the Egyptian one, and might theoretically point to some interaction between Greek and its Egyptian substrate.

---

253 Torallas Tovar (2010:254).

254 E.g., Torallas Tovar, in her brief review of Egyptian grammatical traits in Egyptian Greek, points out several phenomena connected with the use of prepositions (ὑπό and ἐν as analogous to Egyptian ḥn), adverbs (ἐπάνω as a possible equivalent of ⲉⲝⲛ), conjunctions (ὅτι in front of a direct speech in the manner of the Egyptian ϫⲉ), with the reference system in relative clauses, but does not mention any phenomenon in the domain of the verb. (Torallas Tovar 2010:262-264).

255 See Lavidas 2009:119-120.

256 A. Buttmann (1877:227).

257 Quoted from Lavidas (2009:109).

In short, a comparative study of Greek and Coptic grammatical categories has to recur to several gross approximations: it has to take the relationship between Koine and Coptic as a unilateral <donor – recipient> one; further on, it has to assume that Koine of the written sources renders the spoken language with sufficient accuracy; finally, different written sources, such as documentary papyri, private letters and literary and sacral texts, must be regarded as largely representing one and the same language variety.

With this in mind, let us review the basic grammatical innovations of Koine in the domain of the voice system, as they are represented in the exhaustive study by Lavidas (Lavidas 2009).

1) Causativisation and Transitivisation of intransitive verbs

- *New causative interpretation of formerly intransitive verbs*

(Septuagint; II-I BC) βασιλεύω 'to cause someone to rule', ἐξαμαρτάνω 'to cause someone to make a mistake'; (New Testament; AD I) ἀνατέλλω 'to make someone stand up', ἀναφαίνω 'to make someone appear', μαθητεύω 'to make someone a pupil elsewhere', κατακληρονομῶ 'to cause someone to inherit.ACT', etc.

- *Emergence of active forms with causative meaning corresponding to the existing anticausative medio-passive forms*

Classical Greek: ἥδομαι 'to enjoy oneself/take one's-pleasure → Koine: ἥδω 'give pleasure'
Classical Greek: μαίνομαι 'to rage/be furious' → Koine: (ἐκ)μαίνω 'drive mad'

- *Innovative causative use of former active and middle anticausatives*

Classical Greek: λευκαίνω, λευκαίνομαι 'become white' → Koine: λευκαίνω 'make white / become white', λευκαίνομαι 'become white'

- *Addition of a direct object to former intransitives with the ensuing specification of meaning*

New Testament Koine: ἱερουργῶ: 'to sacrifice/minister the gospel'
ὑβρίζω: 'to run riot (in the use of superior strength or power)'
ἐνεδρεύω: 'to lie in wait for/lay snares for'
μένω: 'to stay/wait for'

2) Changes towards the expansion of active morphology

- *Loss of non-active morphology in marking of benefactive meaning and increase in the use of reflexive pronouns*

ψηφίζει τὴν δαπάνην 'he counts the cost' (New Testament, Luke, 14, 28, with the meaning of the Classical Greek transitive ψηφίζομαι)

- *Decline of medio-passive future forms and leveling of the verbal paradigm towards active morphology*

  ἀκούσω: hear.ACT.FUT [instead of ἀκούσομαι hear.MED-PASS.FUT]
  ἁμαρτήσω: fail.ACT.FUT (Matthew, 18, 21)
  ἁρπάσω: snatch-away.ACT.FUT (John, 10, 28)
  βλέψω: see.ACT.FUT (Matthew, 13, 14)
  ἐμπαίξω: mock.ACT.FUT (Mark, 10, 34)

- *Extension of active forms to the majority of the anticausative class*

  ἀλλάσσω: 'to undergo a change'
  ἐκτοπίζω: 'to take oneself from a place/go abroad'
  ἀναζευγνύω: 'to yoke or harness again/withdraw'
  κινῶ: 'to move forward'

The use of medio-passive morphology with active verbs implied by the above quotations from Apollonius and Ammonius does not belong to the main grammatical phenomena of Koine; on the contrary, it rather goes against the mainstream. Lavidas attributes its very occurrence to the instability of the voice system,[258] but this anomaly is also worth discussing in the context of intra-Coptic grammatical innovations.

3.3 Borrowing of grammar: theoretical preliminaries

Focusing this study on voice and voice marking of the loaned Greek-origin verbs in Coptic means examining a set of related issues: the function of the Greek voice morphology in Coptic, alternative mechanisms of voice marking for Greek verbs in Coptic, and the extent of semantic field covered by all these mechanisms. Obviously, to clarify the first issue, the study should consider not the verbal lexeme as a whole, but rather the distribution of the voice markers. This part of the study has to define, whether these markers are borrowed into Coptic 'wholesale' with the marked lexeme, or function as autonomous morphemes. That being the objective, I shall first sketch the typological perspective of borrowing, so that very diversified facts of Coptic borrowing from Greek could be categorized and compared to other cross-linguistic data.

   Borrowing as a result of language contact has attracted much attention on the side of historical linguists and typologists, since it is regarded, along with phonematic change and analogical re-analysis, one of the major factors of linguistic change. Yet, whereas the borrowing of lexical material is clearly observable and statistically quantifiable and thereby gives an immediate 'feel' of the degree of language contact, the borrowing of grammatical entities was until relatively recently denied by many linguists even as a possibility. The first work to systematically treat the question of non-lexical borrowing was provided by

---

258 Lavidas (2009:109): "In many instances, active voice instead of non-active was used, but also vice versa. These changes comprise evidence of changes in the voice system of the Hellenistic period, resulting in instability in the voice system (as we can see from the tendencies observed in the ongoing changes)."

Weinreich (1953). Since then, the topic was discussed and elaborated on in many treatises, such as Sakel (2007), Heine and Kuteva (2003, 2005), Gardani (2018, 2020), Seifart (2015), Gardani, Arkadiev and Amiridze (2015), Muysken (2000, 2010), Matras and Sakel (2007), Matras (2011), Mithun (2012), Wichmann & Wohlgemuth (2008), Wohlgemuth (2009), to name just the most cited ones. So, by now it is well established that, in terms of M. Mithun, structure can be borrowed as well, as substance. This basic distinction between the lexical and the grammatical borrowed material is captured in the terminology proposed in Matras and Sakel (2007). The authors use the term 'MAT borrowing' to denote morphological material and its phonological shape from a donor language replicated in a recipient language. The contrasted term 'PAT borrowing' is defined in Sakel (2007) in the following way:

> "PAT describes the case where only the patterns of the other language are replicated, i.e. the organisation, distribution and mapping of grammatical or semantic meaning, while the form itself is not borrowed."

The terms MAT and PAT thus refer to the most specific (lexical and morphological) and most abstract (syntactic and semantic) language elements, respectively. Obviously, the diverse material of interlingual borrowing cannot be divided dichotomously into MAT and PAT; rather, these terms denote the two extremities of what can migrate from one language to another. Heine & Kuteva (2005) propose the following classification of transferrable linguistic material:

a. Form, that is, sounds or combinations of sounds
b. Meanings (including grammatical meanings or functions) or combinations of meanings
c. Form–meaning units or combinations of form–meaning units
d. Syntactic relations, that is, the order of meaningful elements
e. Any combination of (a) through (d)[259]

Now, this list is the result of a typological work aiming at the generalization of very diverse data gathered from the description of individual languages. In the present study, I would like to do the reverse and to try to apply typological generalizations to the description of Greek-Coptic contact phenomena, namely, to classify the Greek loans in Coptic as loans of forms, or meanings, or else of combinations of forms and meanings. To this end, I had to devise my own scale, a kind of 'borrowing thermometer', matching the grammatical depth, or the level of abstraction, of a borrowed element with a specific kind of transfer. Theoretical and descriptive studies on contact borrowing, most importantly Gardani (2018) and Gardani (2020), suggest the following scale of the elements of linguistic transfer:

Borrowing classification scale

(1) "content words": a specific combination of phonetic material and meaning is transferred from the source language (SL) to the recipient language (RL)

---

259 Heine & Kuteva (2005:2).

(2)   morpheme of the SL transferred as a 'frozen', non-analyzable part of a borrowed
       lexeme (e.g., English plural morpheme -s in Russian English-loaned nouns *chips-y*
       'chips', *baks-y* 'bucks', where *-y* is the Russian plural morpheme)

(3)   morpheme of the SL retaining or modifying its grammatical meaning in the RL,
       but used only on the stock of loaned lexemes, thus establishing a paradigm parallel
       to an existing native paradigm, e.g., the parallel native and Arabic-loaned verbal
       paradigms in Ghomara Berber[260]. This phenomenon is labelled *parallel system
       borrowing* (PSB) in Kossman (2010);

(4)   morpheme borrowed from the SL replacing a native morpheme in an existing
       paradigm, e.g., Spanish plural morpheme replacing native plural in Quechua[261];

(5)   morpheme borrowed from the SL spreads to the native vocabulary giving rise to a
       previously absent category or categorial paradigm;

(6)   a new dimension for an already existing paradigm, which is copied from the SL; the
       morphological material filling out the new paradigmatic dimension is supplied by
       the RL, e.g., 'hot news perfect' in Irish English tense paradigm[262], or development of
       dual number in Tayo possibly after the model of Melanesian languages Drubéa and
       Cèmuhi[263];

(7)   the RL develops a grammatical category attested in the SL, but totally new in the RL,
       e.g., the rise of category of noun-adjective agreement in Yucatec possibly due to the
       contact with Indo-European languages[264], or 'nominal past' category in Mawayana
       (used to express former possession, deceased persons, etc.) born from the contact
       with Cariban languages[265]. In that case, one can speak of complete linguistic
       subsystems transferred as a result of language contact.

(1) to (5) represent MAT-borrowing or a combination of MAT and PAT; (6) and (7)
illustrates pure instances of PAT-borrowing.

The differentiation between (6) and (7) is somewhat alien to the concepts and
terminology used in authoritative studies on PAT-borrowing, such as Heine & Kuteva
(2005) who regard borrowing, or replication from the perspective of the types of changes
produced in the original system of the recipient language. Thus, Heine and Kuteva treat
the rise of the category of evidentiality in Portuguese used by native speakers of Tariana[266]
similarly to the development of dual number in Tayo or the reflexive use of the possessive
pronoun *oma* in Estonian[267], since all these developments "fill a categorial gap", in other
words, are signs of a newly acquired linguistic subsystem previously absent from the
recipient language. For the sake of the present work, however, it seemed important to be
more precise about the nature of grammatical entities presumably replicated from Greek to

---

260 Gardani (2020).
261 Gardani (2018).
262 Gast & van der Auwera (2012:8).
263 Heine & Kuteva (2005:125).
264 Stolz (2015:286-288).
265 Gardani, Arkadiev, Amiridze (2015:3)
266 Aikhenvald (2002: 315–16), Heine & Kuteva (2005:74).
267 See Heine & Kuteva (2005: 124 ff).

Coptic. Let us define a category as a basic semantic property whose various manifestations have grammatical relevance, and a categorial facet as one such individual manifestation of a category.[268] From this point of view, 'dual' is a facet of the category of number, whereas evidentiality is a basic category, whose facets are, e.g., 'visual', 'non-visual', 'inferred', 'reported'.[269]

Clearly, the above borrowing classification scale is very rough and cannot claim to be in any way exhaustive. It may only serve for an approximate orientation, when a specific borrowing phenomenon is to be evaluated with respect to its place in the target grammatical system. Importantly, it suggests that borrowing a morpheme from the source language does not automatically import the category originally marked by that morpheme into the recipient language. This idea sounds trivial on the theoretical level, but in practical research, it is not always easy to realize how exactly a borrowed sign changes its signifié to become accommodated to the new system.

As follows from the above principle, the **degree of matching** between an original element of the SL and its replica in the RL is an essential property of a borrowed morpheme. This degree is known to vary greatly depending on the complexity of functions the morpheme has in the source language. As stated in Gardani et al.(2015),

> "There is... no reason to assume that mat-borrowed grammatical morphemes in a RL take over the full gamut of functions of their sources, as is implied, e.g., in <the> notion of global copying. As has been repeatedly shown by different scholars... if interlinguistic transfer of morphemes occurs at all, it is the morphemes with a higher degree of functional transparency that are borrowed more frequently. From this, it follows that morphemes that are polyfunctional in the SL, are borrowed into the RL primarily with their more concrete and transparent functions."[270]

The most general claim to this sense made in Heine (2012) states that, "in contact-induced grammaticalization, the replica element or construction in the RL almost invariably occupies a less advanced stage of functional-semantic development than its model in the SL."[271] Thus, borrowing of inflectional morphemes does not warrant their membership in

---

268 The notion of 'category' applied here is strictly defined in Mel'čuk (1993:5-6): "An inflectional category of class {K_i} of signs of language L is a set of mutually exclusive significations {'σ_1', 'σ_2', ... , 'σ_n'} such that:
1. with any K_i, one of 'σ_j' is obligatorily expressed and every σ_j' is obligatorily expressed at least with some K_i;
2. All 'σ_j'-s are expressed regularly, i.e.:
(a) an 'σ_j' is strictly compositional—in the sense that it is joined to the meaning 'K_i' without any unpredictable effect;
(b) an 'σ_j' has a small set of markers distributed according to general rules of L;
(c) an 'σ_j' is applicable to (nearly) all K_i -s."
What is here called a facet, is Mel'čuk's grammeme defined as follows: "A grammeme is an element of an inflectional category. Thus, a specific voice (e.g., the passive) is a grammeme."
269 Heine & Kuteva (2005:74).
270 Gardani, Arkadiev, Amiridze (2015:6).
271 Gardani, Arkadiev, Amiridze (2015:6).

a full-fledged inflectional paradigm in the target language. For instance, Greek feminine adjective endings in Coptic are subject to several constraints: occurring solely on loaned adjectives, they also restrict the set of possible syntactic heads to loaned feminine nouns. This led Böhlig to regard respective nominal phrases as "gelehrte Überreste", frozen and obsolete expressions, which might not be quite true, since sporadic exceptions are possible: e.g., in the late text of Commentary to the gospel of Matthew, written by Rufus of Shotep, a Greek feminine adjective modifies a Coptic feminine noun: ⲧⲉⲓⲥⲁⲅⲱⲅⲓⲕⲏ ⲛ̄ⲥⲃⲱ[272]; a few further isolated examples can be found in the Bible. Such examples prove that the feminine ending morpheme probably remained analyzable within the tenets of Coptic grammar, but constituted a small subsystem in the general Coptic system of adnominal modification. From typological point of view, it constitutes an instance of *parallel system borrowing*.

Another pivotal trait of a borrowed morpheme is the **degree of its integration** in the target language, as specified in (2) through (4). The stage (4), where a borrowed formative applies to the native vocabulary of the recipient language, marking a class of elements with some common semantic property, and becomes productive there is termed 'borrowing proper' in Gardani (2020)[273]. However, the same author recurs to a weaker version of this so-called 'nativization constraint', admitting that if a borrowed morpheme applies to (and possibly becomes productive on) the loan vocabulary, this is enough to consider the phenomenon as morphemic borrowing. Different kinds of morphemes are claimed to have different degrees of propensity for borrowing. Supposedly, derivational morphemes have greater chances to be transferred to a language-in-contact, compared to inflectional morphemes. This claim has been first made in Weinreich (1953) and is mostly corroborated by later studies. For example, on Thomason and Kaufman's borrowability scale, adpositions and derivational affixes are situated one level higher than inflectional morphology. Neither is the class of inflectional morphemes uniform with respect to borrowability. Gardani (2008, 2012) claims that the borrowing potential of an inflectional morpheme correlates with its appurtenance to either 'inherent', or 'contextual' morphemes, in Booij's terminology[274]. The borrowing of inherent morphemes statistically largely outweighs that of agreement and structural case markers.

The way morphological borrowing is influenced by the respective types of languages involved, is an issue still in need of a thorough investigation. On the one hand, typological changes are not altogether excluded, as shown by multiple examples, e.g., case syncretism, transformation of goal adverbials into direct objects etc., in Heine & Kuteva (2005:148 ff.). On the other hand, situations of a contact between two languages belonging to completely different structural types were never, to my knowledge, systematically stud-

---

272 Sheridan (1998:92). Rufus of Shotep Homilies on Luke and Matthew.
273 Gardani (2020:4.3)
274 Booij (1994, 1996 Inherent versus contextual inflection and the split morphology hypothesis) distinguishes two types of inflection; inherent inflection does not depend on syntactic content, though it may define it. Basically, it is a set of morphemes with pragmatic semantics, such as plural endings, or TAM morphemes, negation, mood, evidentiality morphemes. On the other hand, contextual morphemes are syntactically dependent; here belong, in the first line, all morphemes that mark agreement or structural case.

ied. In particular, there seems to be no proof that a language of an analytic type is likely to loan morphemic paradigms or develop a system of affixes replicating that of a synthetic donor. As stated in Haspelmath (2008), "structural incompatibility has often been invoked as explaining resistance to borrowing, although in recent years it has come under attack. For grammatical borrowing, it seems undeniable that it plays a role (e.g. it seems very unlikely that an isolating language like Vietnamese would borrow a case suffix)..."[275]

To sum up, the diagnostics of morphological borrowing consists basically in two procedures: a) defining whether a morpheme X' in the recipient language has a function, at least, partly identical to that of the original morpheme X in the source language; b) defining whether it is confined to the loan vocabulary or it can form regular combinations with native elements. Presumably, the second option is naturally confined to contact between languages of the same typological class, although no definitive data on that issue is currently available.

Now, a borrowed morpheme participating in regular alternations in the recipient language necessarily denotes some grammatical category. The thing to be assessed is, whether the category marked in this way has formerly been present in the recipient language, or else it is innovative, and then possibly loaned as PAT. In the first case, the change consists in loaned markers replacing the native ones, as it happens with Spanish-origin plural marker in Quechua (see borrowing classification scale (4)). The second type of change, the rise of a new category or categorial facet loaned together with its markers, represents "a type of morphological transfer that lies in between" MAT- and PAT-borrowing[276] and seems to occur even less frequently. However, it is not altogether unattested. Such process, for instance, is taking place in Western Neo-Aramaic where, according to Coghill, Arabic-origin passive derivation has spread to the native lexicon forming a new passive.[277]

Whereas the presence of the non-native lexical material usually makes it relatively easy to establish that a combination of MAT- and PAT-borrowing has taken place, there is no secure way to trace down the possible transfer of a pure grammatical meaning.[278] In any case, it seems relatively clear that a new (or, in Heine & Kuteva's terms, "incipient") grammatical category is not "installed" in the recipient language in its entirety, but rather evolves gradually from recurrent patterns of discourse that bear some structural-semantic likeness to the category markers in the source language.[279] The resulting incipient category has a few cross-linguistically recurrent properties, the most salient of which are:

---

275 Haspelmath, M. (2008:53). For the opposite view, see Thomason & Kaufman (1988:53).
276 Gardani et al. (2015:7).
277 Coghill (2014:100): "The morphology, which first appeared in WNA as an integral part of the Arabic verbs with which it had been borrowed, has since taken on a life of its own: the borrowed derivations are now used productively to form passives of derivation I verbs, including inherited ones."
278 For the detailed discussion on the matter see Heine & Kuteva (2015:21ff.).
279 Cf. Heine & Kuteva (2005:70): "Grammatical change in general and grammaticalization in particular start out with pragmatically motivated patterns of discourse that may crystallize in new, conventionalized forms of grammatical structure. Use patterns are discourse pragmatic units that need not, and frequently do not, affect the structure of grammatical categorization. However, once language contact gives rise to major use patterns, this may lead to a transition from pragmatically

a. Incipient categories are ambiguous between their earlier (= source) and their present (= target) meanings, that is, an interpretation in terms of the source meaning is generally possible.

b. Their use is optional in that they may but need not be used. This means that the grammatical meaning expressed by the category is not obligatorily marked.

c. They are phonetically and morphosyntactically largely indistinguishable from the source category and their use is confined to the context in which they arose.[280]

This brief survey will enable us to consider the Coptic borrowing data in the wide typological context and to match them with a specific type of linguistic matter transfer. But such comparison needs correct 'settings' that will be discussed in the next chapter.

3.4 Voice in Greek and in Coptic: categorial clash

There is an illusory ease in tracing down the ways of linguistic transfer from a synthetic to an analytic language. The only simple task, it would seem, is to investigate, if the morphs $c_1, c_2 \ldots c_n$ of a grammatical category C of the source language comply with the same rules of alternation / distribution in the recipient language. If they do, this may result in a parallel system borrowing (if only the loan part of the vocabulary is affected), or else in the rise of a new grammatical category (if the new morph / morphs extend onto the native vocabulary and on the condition that the category C was not a functional grammatical category of the RL before the contact). An intermediary borrowing situation of a loan morpheme replacing a native morpheme in an existing paradigm is less probable, when the recipient language in question is an analytic one, with few or no bound morphemes to express syntactic meanings. If, however, the distribution of c_1, c_2 etc. differs from that of the source language, one states that the category C has not been borrowed and that the c-morphs are to be regarded simply as phonetic strings, borrowed as "frozen" parts of lexemes that contain them.

Whereas the positive results yielded by this approach must be quite reliable, there appears to exist not a little probability of a 'false negative', since it reduces C to its morphological markers in the source language and by doing that, disregards the possible interference of the native grammatical system.

The analysis of the Graeco-Coptic verbal morphology borrowing in Funk (2017) follows the logic I have briefly sketched above. Since valency-reducing morphology in Coptic is confined to the present tense,[281] the category of voice is generally understood to be unmarked for native Coptic verbs; Greek verbs, on the other hand, have overt voice morphology, partly borrowed into Coptic, albeit attested mostly in Bohairic and Fayumic dialects. Thus, the question to answer appears to be relatively simple: given a pair of alter-

---

motivated to morphosyntactic templates, in particular to the emergence of new grammatical (functional) categories. <...> transition is gradual. There is no straightforward replacement of major use patterns by full-fledged grammatical categories; rather, use patterns gradually acquire properties of grammatical categories".

280 Heine & Kuteva (2005:71).

281 Cf. Stern (1880), Funk (1978a), Layton (2011), Grossman (2019).

nating (causative / non-causative) verbs, does the Greek medio-passive morph regularly mark the non-causative member, and the absence of this morph, the causative member of the pair, at least, in these dialects? Funk answers this question in the negative:

> "The frequent usage of verb forms ending in –cⲟⲉ (= Greek -σθαι) in Bohairic clearly suggests a certain degree of functioning of the Greek category of "voice" with the verbs borrowed into Coptic, and yet this functioning is rather limited or fragmented. At best, it can be seen to be "lexicalized" in some verbs at the time of the borrowing process itself. This may be largely the case of the deponent verbs: some of the more common ones, such as ⲁⲛⲉⲭⲉⲥⲑⲉ, appear to be firmly established in their long form. But if we look at transitive Greek verbs with a variable active vs. passive usage, the forms we find to be used in the most carefully edited Bohairic manuscripts are not too often the ones we would expect."[282]

So, even Bohairic, of all Coptic dialects the one most conservative with regard to the Greek verbal morphology[283], does not unambiguously display the morpheme-category 'package borrowing'. For all the dialects that did not borrow the Greek passive morph, in other words, for all the dialects other than Bohairic and Fayyumic, Funk suggests a perfect congruence between the borrowed verbal form and the native *status absolutus*:

> "All other dialects – that is, those that import most verbs in an almost "naked stem", imperative-like form – use these forms in the same way as many "transitive" native verbs are used in their *status absolutus*. This is to say, whether they are meant to cover an active or a medio-passive meaning in a given case is determined not by their form but by the syntactic and semantic context".[284]

The above diagnosis is generally accepted in today's Coptic linguistics and can be supported by numerous examples, such as those cited in Grossman (2019):

ešče pek-bal=de n-ounam skandalize mmo-k
'If your right eye offends you…' (Sahidic, Matthew 5:29)

(The Pharisees who heard this word) a-u-skandalize
'They were offended' (Sahidic, Matthew 15:12)[285]

or the even more extreme case where the causative and the non-causative meaning can be distinguished neither by form, nor by construction, to make one wonder if they were discerned, at all, by the Coptic audience:

---

282 Funk (2017:378).
283 This concerns both the mediopassive and the active infinitive suffix / ending.
284 Funk (2017:378).
285 Grossman (2019:109).

(193) James 1:13

ⲡⲛⲟⲩⲧⲉ ⲅⲁⲣ **ⲙⲉϥⲡⲉⲓⲣⲁⲍⲉ** ⲛⲗⲁⲁⲩ ⲉⲡⲡⲉⲑⲟⲟⲩ **ⲙⲉϥⲡⲉⲓⲣⲁⲍⲉ** ⲛⲧⲟϥ ⲛⲗⲁⲁⲩ

ὁ γὰρ Θεὸς **ἀπείραστός ἐστιν** κακῶν, **πειράζει** δὲ αὐτὸς οὐδένα.

'for God cannot **be tempted** with evil, and he himself **tempts** no one.'

Yet, such description does not cover all the phenomena pertaining to the loan verb voice and possibly does not do justice to the essential ones: e.g., the data of the DDGLC database demonstrate that the property of lability ascribed to all Greek-origin verbs by default is manifested in only about 10% of such verbs (some 60-65 out of ~600). Moreover, the free infinitive of native transitive verbs is not used as freely, as can be deduced from the above description. As shown in chapter 1 of the present work, for many, if not most Egyptian verbal roots, the infinitival form does not have a non-causative reading in present. An intransitive present infinitive of a loan verb is, therefore, a structural equivalent of a native Egyptian stative. Besides, the correlation between the Greek active / mediopassive form and causative / non-causative meaning can be described with more precision. While there certainly is no universally valid formula for assessing the form / meaning distribution of all Greek loan verbs, some tendencies of this distribution can be detected. The prerequisite for the more detailed view is the analysis that would take into account the native voice grammar and semantics. In what follows, I discuss the respective features of Coptic and Greek voice categories that might influence the loan verb accommodation in Coptic.

As explained above in chapter 1, the Coptic system of voice is inherently connected to that of aspect: eventive anticausative / passive (*status absolutus*) is morphologically different from stative anticausative / passive (*qualitative / stative*) and, as follows from the dichotomy of the Coptic TAM system, is incompatible with the TAM pattern of the stative. In short, each Coptic verb form codes two categories simultaneously: aspect AND voice.[286]

Interestingly, the Greek three-voice morphological system largely based on the affectedness of the subject actant was not an 'inborn' trait of the language, but the result of a historical development. In the older stages of Greek, semantics of affectedness must have interacted with aspect, Aktionsart and tense semantics, in a way somewhat recalling the Egyptian tense-aspect-patterns system. Thus, at least, in Homeric Greek, a verbal paradigm often comprised two stems differing both in aspect and in diathesis. The imperfective stem served as a transitive base, the perfective one as an intransitive. Such is, e.g., the case of the verb ἀραρίσκω / ἤραρα 'join, fit together':

a. αὐτὸς δ' ἀμφὶ πόδεσσιν ἑοῖς ἀράρισκε πέδιλα
    'but he himself was fitting sandals about his feet' (Homer, Odyssey, 14, 23; 8 BC)

---

286 More precisely, stative is marked for aspect and diathesis, while *status absolutus* has a default anticausative meaning in eventive tenses and a default causative meaning in the durative tenses. The important thing is, however, that aspectual and diathetic meanings of Coptic verb forms are coordinated.

b. ὃ δὴ καὶ πᾶσιν ἐνὶ φρεσὶν ἤραρεν ἥμιν
   '(our decision) that suited all of us just now in our minds' (Homer, Odyssey, 4, 777; 8 BC)[287]

However, this aspect-diathesis split was hardly systematic and, at any rate, non-productive by the time of Koine where different tense forms became eventually aligned with respect to their voice morphology.[288] Besides, seeing that the overwhelming majority of Greek-origin verbs in Coptic were borrowed in their imperfective stem[289], this split could not possibly influence the use of the verbs in any way.

In short, the contact of Greek and Coptic voice systems was the contact of one-dimensional (voice) and multi-dimensional (voice-aspect/tense) categories, similar in that respect, e.g., to the contact between the category of number in Spanish (number) and Nahuatl (number-animacy).[290] This means that the migration of Greek verbs into Coptic was bound to raise a certain tension, especially in such contexts where the semantic field of the two categories did not overlap, e.g., with a non-eventive anticausative/ passive, which by the Coptic criteria corresponded to a stative / passive form, whereas a stative Greek verb could well be morphologically active. The seemingly chaotic distribution of morphological passive markings observed by Funk in various Bohairic corpora[291] might have roots in that tension.

One should add that in contrast to the regularity of the plural morpheme with Spanish inanimate nouns that has triggered the change in Nahuatl number marking, the mediopassive morphology of Koine was far from being semantically consistent, due to multiple changes to the verbal morphology (see 3.2 above for details). Besides the group of verbs with the regular morphological alternation, there were also lexemes displaying mediopassive morphology with an active sense (deponents) and labile verbs where the active morphology could denote both the causative and the anticausative meaning. The complexity of the source system may be responsible for the diversity of the response observable in the way Coptic treats the voice of loaned verbs. Indeed, even within Sahidic alone, Greek-origin verbs can function as labile or monodiathetic, may have or have not the mediopassive suffix which, in its turn, usually, but not always, corresponds to an anticausative meaning; further on, these verbs may prefer one certain tense base or be freely used in both.

---

287 These examples are taken from Lavidas (2009:56-57). For the discussion of 'split causativity' phenomenon in Ancient Greek, see Kulikov (1999).

288 Lavidas (2009:111).

289 About 10 aorist forms are attested in the DDGLC database. No perfect stem seems to have been borrowed into Coptic. The rest (~590 verbal lexemes) are represented by their imperfective stems.

290 Canger & Jensen (2007:404).

291 Commenting on the distribution of morphologically marked verbs in Bohairic and Fayyumic, Funk remarks that the active and medial forms, "instead of being used in a clear-cut way as members of oppositional pairs (active vs. passive voice) are chosen at random or according to a scribe's inexplicable personal preference". Of course, an alternative explanation is always possible, which would attribute the random usage of forms to their actual obsolescence at the time of writing / copying / editing of a specific text.

To find, quoting Polonius, if there is a method to this madness, I thought it useful to regard the grammar of Greek loan verbs in Coptic as a multi-dimensional system built on some interplay of one formal and two semantic oppositions:

1) active vs. non-active (medio-passive) verb morphology
2) causative vs. anticausative meaning
3) eventive vs. durative aspect

Between the members of these oppositions there can theoretically exist multiple dependencies. Greek medio-passive morphology may reflect the difference in causativity or may do so, e.g., with stative aspect, but not with the eventive one. It is also not unthinkable that stative aspect is marked by non-active morphology regardless of whether or not the form is anticausative. The morphologically unmarked (=active) forms may be labile in any environment, as suggested by Funk, or may be influenced by the same syntactic mechanisms (tense-aspect alternation) that define the diathesis of native verbs, imitating the syntactic behavior of the native marked forms, i.e., stative and transitive eventive infinitive. Finally, there might be no difference whatsoever in the functioning of both active and medio-passive forms, the latter being used as a kind of stylistic ornament or a vague allusion to a never really acquired norm.

To systematically examine these interdependencies, I divide all the loaned verbs into classes defined by: a) voice morphology, b) diathesis. Four classes obtained in such way are:

A) 2 forms, 2 diatheses: verbs with attested active and middle-passive forms and two diathetic variants, causative and anticausative.
B) 2 forms, 1 diathesis: verbs with attested active and middle-passive forms, both corresponding to a single diathesis, whether causative or anticausative; it seemed proper to include here also such verbs that are attested only in their middle-passive form, because retaining this form is a marked feature in Sahidic.
C) 1 form, 2 diatheses: labile verbs with active morphology denoting both causative and anticausative meaning; this class is used in the way similar to the native *status absolutus* of transitive verbs and therefore displays what Funk regards as a typical behavior of a loaned verbal lexeme.
D) 1 form, 1 diathesis: verbs with active morphology corresponding to either causative, or anticausative meaning.

This classification is made for utilitarian purposes only. The appurtenance to one or another class is seemingly not directly conditioned by any semantic or morphological properties of the verb in the source language; moreover, it is not permanent, but depends, i.a., on the actual attestations of the verb found in Sahidic documents. Thus, each class represents nothing more than an observable array of verbs with similar overt parameters used to track down repeating patterns of morphosyntactic behavior. The investigation has to find: 1) the relation between the Greek voice morphology and the causative / non-causative meaning; 2) the relation between the Greek voice morphology and the tense / aspect meaning; 3) the correlation of tense / aspect values and the causative / non-causative diathesis (if there is any) in Sahidic.

However scarce and valuable all the attestations of alternative morphology or meaning throughout the dialects are, I thought it necessary to limit this study to those belonging to Sahidic dialect, so that our notion of the interplay between different grammatical factors would not be distorted by peculiar usages in different dialects. On the other hand, the research makes use of every Sahidic text found in the DDGLC database, without exceptions. The consequence of such formal approach is that Sahidic texts bearing the marks of heavy influence on the part of other dialects, e.g. Bohairic or Akhmimic (such as some texts from the Nag Hammadi corpus), are necessarily subsumed in the overall analysis. However, excluding the influenced forms from consideration would, in my opinion, be even less justified than taking the risk of ascribing them to the dialect where they were not deeply rooted.

3.5 Analysis of morphological-diathetic classes of verbs

3.5.1 Class A: two forms, two diatheses

3.5.1.1   Class A: overview

At present, the group of bidiathetic verbs with attested suffixed forms comprises the following Graeco-Sahidic lexemes:[292] ⲁⲛⲁⲡⲁⲩⲉ 'give rest / have rest', ⲃⲁⲣⲉⲓ 'weigh down, oppress / be heavy', ⲃⲗⲁⲡⲧⲉⲓ 'harm / be harmed', ⲕⲟⲗⲁⲍⲉ 'punish, torture / be punished', ⲡⲁⲣⲁⲕⲁⲗⲉⲓ 'beseech, entreat / be urged', ⲡⲉⲓⲑⲉ 'convince / be convinced', ⲡⲗⲁⲛⲁ 'mislead / err', ⲡⲗⲏⲣⲟⲫⲟⲣⲉⲓ 'satisfy / be satisfied', ⲧⲣⲉⲫⲉ 'feed, nourish / be fed', ⲱⲫⲉⲗⲉⲓ 'help / profit'. ⲃⲁⲣⲉⲓ and ⲱⲫⲉⲗⲉⲓ deviate from the canonical causative alternation scheme, one member of each pair being a stative;[293] nevertheless, since each pair stands for two mean-

---

292 Here and below, the Greek prototypes are cited in the form they appear in the DDGLC database. The Coptic variants have a standardized form following the corresponding Greek morphology. This form must not, and indeed often does not, match those actually attested. This list, needless to say, is not closed or final, since new attestations might show new forms or new diathesis variants for these and other verbal lexemes. It is best regarded as a representative group exhibiting some observable tendencies.

293 Causative ⲃⲁⲣⲉⲓ:'weigh down' is opposed to stative 'be heavy'. In the pair ⲱⲫⲉⲗⲉⲓ: 'be helpful, profitable for : profit', the second member of the pair codes the core event, whereas the state expressed by the first member is interpreted as its causative counterpart; the semantic role of the core actant, the 'profittee', is not unambiguous: it can be interpreted as the entity most affected by the event, i.e., the patient, or the 'receiver' or goal of the event, i.e., the recipient. This ambiguity is resolved in the causative predication where the 'profittee' can be coded as a direct or an oblique object (the first option being evidently preferable):
ⲉⲕⲣⲱⲫⲉⲗⲉⲓ ⲙ̄ⲙⲟⲕ ⲟⲩⲁⲁⲕ '... helping yourself only' (Nag Hammadi, Teachings of Silvanus, 117, 22-23)
ⲁⲩⲱ ⲉⲓⲧⲥⲃⲱ ⲛ̄ⲓⲁ[ⲕⲱⲃ (...)]ⲉⲧⲱⲫⲉⲗⲉⲓ ⲛⲁϥ 'teaching Ja[cob ...] that will profit him' (P.Mon. Epiph. 140, 25)
Moreover, the causative tokens of this verb in Sahidic never code the eventive ('to help') meaning which is expressed by another lexeme (ⲃⲟⲏⲑⲉⲓ). The causative ⲱⲫⲉⲗⲉⲓ, therefore, has only the stative ('to be helpful, profitable') interpretation.

ings roughly correlating as cause and result, it seemed convenient to consider them together with the cases of the usual causative alternation.

Table 7 | Form-meaning distribution of the verbs of class A[294]

Verb	Short form		Long form	
	Causal reading	Non-causal reading	Causal reading	Non-causal reading
ⲁⲛⲁⲡⲁⲩⲉ	6	4	-	3
ⲃⲁⲣⲉⲓ	12	1	1(?)	2
ⲃⲗⲁⲡⲧⲉⲓ	31	2	-	1
ⲕⲟⲗⲁⲍⲉ	79	1	-	1
ⲡⲁⲣⲁⲕⲁⲗⲉⲓ	490	-	-	1
ⲡⲉⲓⲑⲉ	101	138	-	3
ⲡⲗⲁⲛⲁ	65	56	-	11
ⲡⲗⲏⲣⲟⲫⲟⲣⲉⲓ	21	5	-	6
ⲧⲣⲉⲫⲉ	1	-	-	1
ⲱⲫⲉⲗⲉⲓ	26	34	-	7

The short forms of ⲁⲛⲁⲡⲁⲩⲉ, ⲡⲗⲁⲛⲁ, ⲡⲉⲓⲑⲉ and ⲱⲫⲉⲗⲉⲓ are just about equally represented in both diatheses, i.e., they display labile valency alternation with occasional vestiges of a morphological passive. On the other hand, ⲃⲁⲣⲉⲓ, ⲃⲗⲁⲡⲧⲉⲓ, ⲕⲟⲗⲁⲍⲉ, ⲡⲁⲣⲁⲕⲁⲗⲉⲓ, ⲡⲗⲏⲣⲟⲫⲟⲣⲉⲓ are predominantly causative verbs. For some of them (ⲃⲁⲣⲉⲓ, ⲃⲗⲁⲡⲧⲉⲓ, ⲕⲟⲗⲁⲍⲉ, ⲡⲁⲣⲁⲕⲁⲗⲉⲓ), the non-causative reading is attested only or almost only in the suffixed form. The tokens of ⲧⲣⲉⲫⲉ are extremely scarce (one occurrence in the Codex Tchacos, and one in NHC II); the short form is transitive, whereas the long form stands for passive. Importantly, there is hardly any token of a long form of any verb in a causative reading, except for one rather dubious attestation of ⲃⲁⲣⲉⲓⲥⲑⲁⲓ as 'weigh down' in NHC VII.

For a grammatical opposition to be established between the two forms of a verb, they have, at minimum, to be found inside one and the same corpus. Such instances, although rare, are not unavailable. Both ⲡⲗⲁⲛⲁ and ⲡⲗⲁⲛⲁⲥⲑⲁⲓ are attested in the Gospel of Philipp (NHC II,3), On the Origin of the World (NHC II,5) and the Paraphrase of Shem (NHC VII,1). ⲡⲁⲣⲁⲕⲁⲗⲉⲓ / ⲡⲁⲣⲁⲕⲁⲗⲉⲓⲥⲑⲁⲓ and ⲡⲗⲏⲣⲟⲫⲟⲣⲉⲓ / ⲡⲗⲏⲣⲟⲫⲟⲣⲉⲓⲥⲑⲁⲓ occur in P. Budge. Both ⲱⲫⲉⲗⲉⲓ and ⲱⲫⲉⲗⲉⲓⲥⲑⲁⲓ are attested within the documentary corpus of P.Kru. Yet, the co-occurrence of two different forms in one corpus does not necessarily amount to a voice opposition. Thus, ⲱⲫⲉⲗⲉⲓ and ⲱⲫⲉⲗⲉⲓⲥⲑⲁⲓ are both used for 'get profit' in the documentary texts; NHC II employs ⲡⲗⲁⲛⲁ and ⲡⲗⲁⲛⲁⲥⲑⲁⲓ indifferently for 'err, be misled'. The cases where the morphological voice opposition seems to function (ⲡⲁⲣⲁⲕⲁⲗⲉⲓ, ⲡⲗⲏⲣⲟⲫⲟⲣⲉⲓ in P.Budge and ⲡⲗⲁⲛⲁ in the Paraphrase of Shem) are isolated. Thus, no systematic voice distinction is realized through the use of the suffix morpheme.

Besides, since the main (albeit not the only) source of the suffixed forms for these verbs are the Nag Hammadi manuscripts, one cannot claim with certainty, whether the suffixed forms used there belong to Sahidic, or are vestiges of other Southern dialects.[295]

---

294 The statistics is calculated based on the data in the DDGLC data base, as of 12.12.2020.

295 The discussed forms are attested in the central corpus of Codex II and in Codex VII, described in Funk (1995: 129 ff.) as 'distinctly southern' and not bearing any traces of northern Coptic.

The mere suggestion that suffixed forms could have Sahidic 'citizenship', may appear unlikely to anyone familiar with the classical Sahidic literature. Yet, it must not be refuted too rapidly. The sporadic occurrence of the suffixed forms in later Sahidic texts could mean that these forms were not always alien to this dialect, even more so since their use does not appear to be random: they are consistently used to denote non-causative meanings. The semantic functions of the middle-passive voice morpheme in class A verbs are discussed in the next section.

3.5.1.2 Functions of the middle-passive voice morpheme

Whether constituting the sole attested form of a verb, or standing in an opposition to the short form, the suffixed form almost invariably has a non-causative meaning. The present work cannot aim at precisely determining the genesis of this regularity. It might well be, and indeed it would be only logical, that the suffixed form of a verb was borrowed coupled to its non-causative meaning. Alternatively, what we find in the manuscripts could be the result of an erudite editorial work. Finally, there is a chance that the use of the middle-passive suffix was an intra-Coptic development. This suggests not a little degree of linguistic competence in Greek on the side of Coptic speakers, but such competence is not at all improbable, seeing that, at least, in order to omit the suffix and to obtain the short form, the 'borrower' ought to recognize it as a separate morpheme. Whatever its origin, in most cases, the suffixed form co-occurs with the promotion of a patient actant to the subject position, as in:

(194) P.Budge, 243-244, Schiller (1968:106)

ⲁⲩⲱ ⲧⲁⲣⲉⲧⲉⲧⲛ̄**ⲡⲁⲣⲁⲕⲁⲗⲉⲓⲥⲑⲁⲓ** ⲛ̄ⲧⲉⲧⲛ̄ⲁⲁⲥ ϩⲁ ⲡⲛⲟⲩⲧⲉ ⲛ̄ⲧⲉⲧⲛ̄ⲉⲗⲉⲅⲭⲉˋ ⲙ̄ⲙⲟⲟⲩ ⲛ̄⟦ⲗ⟧ ⲥⲉⲗⲟˋ ⲉⲩⲙⲏⲛ ⲉⲃⲟⲗ ϩⲛ̄ ⲧⲉⲩⲙⲛ̄⟦ⲧ⟧ⲁⲭⲣⲟⲙⲱⲥ

*'and so that you (the arbiters) **may be urged** to act for God's sake and examine them, so that they cease persevering in their shamelessness...'*

(195) Exegesis on the Soul, 137, 9

ⲧⲟⲧⲉ ⲥⲛⲁⲣ̄**ⲃⲗⲁⲡⲧⲉⲥⲑⲁⲓ**

*'she then will **be hurt**'*

(196) BL Pap 82, P.KRU 83, 12-15

ⲡⲣⲟⲧ[ⲟⲛ] ⲙⲉⲛ ⲛⲛⲉϥⲟⲫⲩⲗⲓⲥⲑⲁⲓ ⲛⲗⲁⲁⲩ ⲇⲉⲩⲧⲉⲣⲟⲛ ⲇⲉ ⲉϥⲛⲁⲥⲱⲕ ⲉϩⲣⲁⲓ ϩⲁ ⲡⲉⲕⲣⲓⲙⲁ ⲙ̄ⲡⲛⲟⲩⲧⲉ ⲛ̄ϥϣⲱⲡⲉ ⲉϥ**ⲕⲟⲗⲁⲥⲉⲥⲑⲁⲓ** ⲛ̄ⲛⲁϩⲣⲛ̄ ⲡⲃⲏⲙⲁ ⲉⲧϩⲁϩⲟⲧⲉ

*'first of all, he shall not benefit at all, and second, he shall draw upon himself the judgment of God, and he **shall be punished** before the fearful tribunal'*

Interestingly, in this last example the **suffixed** form is used in a periphrastic conjunctive with a future meaning, i.e., in the environment where a native verb would be expected to appear in its **stative** form.

According to Funk, "the large number of peculiarities that distinguish the language of each tractate from the standard Sahidic are all found to be in agreement with one or several known southern dialects", presumably either Akhmimic or L6. It is not improbable that the suffixed passive forms of several Greek loan verbs belong to the non-Sahidic traits of the language of the codices.

The obscurity of the text in the Paraphrase of Shem turns it nearly impossible to determine the precise functional load of the suffixed form (ⲣ-)ⲃⲁⲣⲉⲓⲥⲑⲁⲓ which is consistently used there in intransitive present clauses. In two out of three occurrences, the translators render this form as (objectless) causative stative:

(197)   NHC VII, ParShem 7, 24-27:

ⲁⲩⲱ ⲛⲉⲧⲛⲟⲩⲛⲉ ⲛ̅ⲧⲫⲩⲥⲓⲥ ⲉⲧⲏⲙⲡⲥⲁ ⲙⲡⲓⲧⲛ̅ ⲟⲟⲟⲩϭ• ⲉⲥⲣ̅ⲃⲁⲣⲉⲓⲥⲑⲁⲓ ⲁⲩⲱ ⲉⲥⲣ̅ⲃⲗⲁⲡⲧⲉⲓ
*'And the root of Nature, which was below, was crooked, since it is **burdensome** and harmful.'*

(198)   NHC VII, ParShem, 48, 8-11

ϩⲉⲛⲙⲁⲕⲁⲣⲓⲟⲥ ⲛⲉ ⲛⲉⲧⲁⲣⲉϩ ⲉⲣⲟⲟⲩ ⲉⲧⲡⲁⲣⲁⲑⲏⲕⲏ ⲙ̅ⲡⲙⲟⲩ• ⲉⲧⲉ ⲡⲁⲓ̈ ⲡⲉ ⲡⲙⲟⲟⲩ ⲛ̅ⲕⲁⲕⲉ ⲉⲧⲣ̅ⲃⲁⲣⲉⲓⲥⲑⲁⲓ•
*'Blessed are they who guard themselves against the heritage of death, which is the **burdensome** water of darkness'*

Yet, the same form is translated with the non-causative stative expression in ParShem 15, 32:

(199)   ⲉⲧⲣⲁⲃⲱⲕ ⲉⲡⲓⲧⲛ̅ ⲉⲡⲧⲁⲣⲧⲁⲣⲟⲛ ϣⲁ ⲡⲟⲩⲟⲉⲓⲛ ⲙ̅ⲡⲡ̅ⲛ̅ⲁ̅ ⲉⲧⲣ̅ⲃⲁⲣⲓⲥⲑⲁⲓ ϣⲓⲛⲁ ⲉⲓ̈ⲛⲁϩⲁⲣⲉϩ ⲉⲣⲟϥ ⲉⲧⲕⲁⲕⲓⲁ ⲙ̅ⲡⲃⲁⲣⲟⲥ•
*'...that I might get an opportunity to go down to the nether world, to the light of the Spirit which **was burdened**, that I might protect him from the evil of the burden.'*

Assuming that one and the same form could acquire diathetically opposed meanings, one has to arrive at the conclusion that in that case the suffix signals the stative aspect, with the voice distinction neutralized. However, such an assumption does not look convincing. It seems more plausible that in each of these cases, the form has the non-causative sense 'be heavy' (as opposed to 'burden, be cumbersome'), otherwise regularly expressed in Coptic with the stative ϩⲟⲣϣ. Since only two verbs of class A, ⲃⲁⲣⲉⲓ and ⲡⲗⲁⲛⲁ, consistently use -ⲥⲑⲁⲓ in present tense predicates, it is unlikely that the suffixed form is in any way associated with the stative aspect.

Excursus. Middle-passive suffix in P.Budge (P.Col.600)

The so-called Papyrus Budge containing a transcript of a court hearing that took place in Apollonopolis Magna (Edfu, Upper Egypt) in the 7th century CE, provides unique tokens of the suffixed form for two verbs of class A (ⲡⲁⲣⲁⲕⲁⲗⲉⲓⲥⲑⲁⲓ, ⲡⲗⲏⲣⲟⲫⲟⲣⲉⲓⲥⲑⲁⲓ). Both forms accurately render the respective non-causative meaning ("be urged", "be satisfied").

(200)   P.Budge, 235-236, Schiller (1968:104)

ⲉⲩⲡⲣⲟⲥⲇⲟⲕⲉⲓ̈ ⲛⲁⲩ ϫⲉ ⲉⲩϣⲁⲛϭⲱ ⲉⲩⲥⲭⲟⲗⲁⲍⲉ [[ⲛ̅]]ⲉ ⲛⲓϣⲁϫⲉ ⲛ̅ϯⲙⲓⲛⲉ ϣⲁⲥⲁⲡⲁⲛⲧⲁ ⲛⲁⲩ ⲉⲣ̅ ⲡⲉⲧⲉⲡⲱⲛ ⲙ̅[ϣ]ⲡϣⲟⲩ ⲟⲡⲉⲣ ⲁⲕⲣⲓⲃⲱⲥ ⲧⲛ̅ⲡⲗⲏⲣⲟⲫ<ⲟⲣ>ⲉⲓⲥⲑⲁⲓ ⲉ[[. ̄]]ⲡⲁⲓ̈ ϫⲉ ⲙⲁⲥⲁⲡⲁⲛⲧⲁ ⲛⲁⲩ
*'...whereas they expect that if they continue busying themselves with these aforesaid words, it would be of avail for them to make what is ours theirs, which——**we are completely convinced** that it will be of no avail to them...'*

Taken for granted that Sahidic borrowed verbal lexemes in their abridged form and that the sporadic occurrences of the suffix are due to the influence of other dialects in such early and abstruse corpora as the one of Nag Hammadi, the fact that the long forms surface in a relatively late Sahidic text is surprising. Not less surprising is the fact that these forms pertain to the discourse of a peasant (Philemon) and are hardly a result of a post-factum editorial work, since Philemon's language in all other respects seems to bear the marks of an unpolished oral speech, such as a very fuzzy syntax. Could it be possible that in its treatment of Greek verbal morphology, the spoken Sahidic differed from the literary norm familiar to us from the Biblical translations and the Shenoute corpus? If the lack of documents recording the spoken language will never allow us to clear up this question, we can nevertheless venture an explanation as to why these forms do appear in Philemon's speech. As can be seen in the example of the verb ⲱⲫⲉⲗⲉⲓ(ⲥⲉⲁⲓ) 'get profit', and moreover in several instances of the verbs of class B that will be discussed below, the use of the suffixed form can often be a mark of the legal language in Sahidic. Philemon delivers his speech in the trial; moreover, he endeavors to make it sound as competent as possible by an informed use of specific legal terms, like ⲕⲟⲙⲡⲗⲉⲩⲥⲓⲥ ⲛⲛⲟⲙⲓⲕⲟⲥ 'notarial completion' (P.Budge 86 & 105) etc. Perhaps, the unexpected suffixed forms of the above-named verbs are but an additional sign of the imitation of the learned 'legal' language.

Excursus. The middle-passive suffix of ⲛⲓⲕⲉⲥⲉⲁⲓ

The sole attestation of the verb ⲛⲓⲕⲉⲥⲉⲁⲓ 'win' merits a separate discussion, not only because being a *hapax legomenon*, it cannot be properly assigned to any class of loan verbs, but also because the use of the middle suffix in this one attestation is quite peculiar in that it occurs on a causative member of the pair 'win / lose, be vanquished':

(201) Evod.rossi, Homily on the Passion f.27v b, 86
ⲉⲣϣⲁⲛⲡⲣⲣⲟ **ⲛⲓⲕⲉⲥⲉⲁⲓ** ϣⲁⲣⲉⲙⲙⲁⲧⲟⲓ̈ ⲫⲟⲣⲉⲓ̈ ⲛ[ⲛ]ⲉⲩⲉⲛⲧⲅⲓ̈ⲙⲁ ⲉⲧⲡⲣⲉⲓ̈ϣⲟⲩ
'*When the king **is victorious**, (his) soldiers wear their radiant white garments.*'

It is not necessary, however, to resort to the explanation by 'random usage' to account for such morphology. True, according to the data in Liddell-Scott dictionary, the Greek νικάω has two diatheses, the active and the passive one, and the form used in Sahidic could read only in the sense of 'be vanquished, lose'. Yet, it is not implausible that the Coptic writer in this case consciously uses the middle-passive morphology in some sense that would be closer to the Greek middle voice, even though such usage deviates from the way this verb is used in the source language. The parallel place in another version of the same text, pMorgan M595, lends credence to this conjecture. Here, instead of the verb 'to win', the compound 'to take victory' (ϫⲓ-ⲛⲓⲕⲏ) is used:

(202) Hom. Pass. Res. (M.595), 48r b,34-48v a,3, 86, Chapman (1993:103)
ⲉⲣϣⲁⲛ ⲡⲣⲣⲟ ⲅⲁⲣ **ϫⲓ ⲛⲧⲛⲓⲕⲏ** ϣⲁⲣⲉⲙⲙⲁⲧⲟⲓ ⲫⲱⲣⲉⲓ ⲛⲛⲉⲩⲉⲛⲧⲏⲙⲁ ⲉⲧⲡⲣⲓϣⲟⲩ
'*So, if the king is victorious (lit.: **takes victory**), the soldiers wear their radiant garments.*'

According to the observation made by L.Stern, ϫⲓ 'take' is often found in compounds that constitute the passive counterpart to the compounds with ϯ 'give' and the same core verb[296]. Obviously, the semantics of 'winning' in Coptic lacks some components that make up for agentivity, perhaps such as volitionality. The victory is 'taken', not 'realized'. In the verbal lexeme of Evod.rossi, this might trigger the use of the formative that is usually associated with involitionality and affectedness of the passive, quite like the native formative of the same function in pMorgan M595.

3.5.1.3 Class A: syntactic properties of short forms

In 3.4, we surmised that Greek-origin verbs might theoretically display some kind of correlation between their diathesis / voice and the tense-aspect base they are used with, in analogy to native verbs. The combination of intransitive non-causative use with durative conjugation would align Greek infinitives with Egyptian statives. The attestations of the class A verbs collected in the DDGLC database suggest no such correlation, with active, as well as with middle-passive morphology. For the four verbs whose short forms are unmarked for voice, this dissociation between aspect and causativity signifies the degree of lability surpassing anything available for native verbs. Thus, 'ofelei' can mean 'get profit' and 'bring profit' both in the present and in the optative tense, 'peithe' as 'be persuaded, agree' is employed in the formulae ⲁⲛⲡⲉⲓⲑⲉ [PST] 'we have agreed' and ϯⲡⲉⲓⲑⲉ [PRES] 'I agree'.

> (203) P.Mon. Epiph. 253, 8-10
>
> ⲉϣⲱⲡⲉ **ϥⲡⲉⲓⲑⲉ** ⲛ̄ⲧⲛ̄ⲧⲁⲁⲩ ⲉϫⲛ̄ ⲡϣⲁⲣ, ⲉⲧⲛⲏⲩ ⲉⲧⲛⲁⲡⲱⲣϫ̄ ⲕⲁⲛ ϩⲓⲧⲟⲟⲧϥ̄ ⲕⲁⲛ ϩⲓⲧⲟⲟⲧϥ̄ ⲛ̄ⲕⲉⲟⲩⲁ ⲛ̄ⲧⲛ̄ⲧⲁⲁⲩ•
>
> *'If he **agrees**, and we sell them at the value that is going to be fixed, whether by him or by someone else, and we (then) sell them...'*

> (204) BL Pap 104, P.KRU 39, 18-21
>
> ⲛⲧⲟϥ ⲕⲟⲙⲉⲥ ⲡⲇⲓⲟⲓⲕ(ⲏⲧⲏⲥ) ⲁϥⲕⲉⲗⲉⲩⲉ ⲛⲁⲛ ⲡⲣⲟⲥ ⲑⲉ ⲛ̄ⲧⲁⲛⲡⲉⲓⲑⲉ
>
> *'Komes the administrator, he commanded us in the way to which we **agreed**'*

In many cases, the voice distinction is marked by different valency patterns. So, '*a=s-peithe na=f*' means 'she obeyed / listened to him', whereas '*a=s-peithe mmo=f*' means 'she convinced him'. However, in case of a zero or nominal object, any possible syntactic difference is neutralized, in the same way as we have seen in (193) above. So, probably, the context was the only means to retrieve the meaning of the subordinate clause in the following sentence:

> (205) Abraham of Farshut, 104, 24
>
> ⲉⲧⲃⲉ ⲟⲩ ⲙ̄ⲡⲉⲕⲡⲓⲑⲉ ⲙ̄ⲡⲁⲣⲭⲏⲙⲁⲛⲇⲣⲓ̈ⲧⲏⲥ **ⲉⲧⲣⲉϥⲡⲓⲑⲉ** ⲙ̄ⲡⲣ̄ⲣⲟ
>
> *'Why did you not **convince** the archimandrite to **agree** with the emperor?'*

---

296 Stern (1880:316).

This subsystem of 'total lability' is peculiar in two respects. First, it is difficult to understand how a system of signs with identical forms, but mutually opposite content could ever be functional, which is an old objection to the very idea of lability.[297] Admitting, however, that due to the factor of linguistic adaptability it probably worked in Coptic, it is yet to be grasped how such subsystem has developed alongside the somewhat different native one, whether it happened by direct indiscriminate insertion of the short form, or else gradually, through the decline of the suffixed form as a marker of non-causativity.

One of the verbs in class A, ⲁⲛⲁⲡⲁⲩⲉ, displays an alternative mechanism of decausativization by means of an object pronoun coreferential with the subject.

(206) Coptic Museum EG-c Ms 3811, Panegyric on Macarios of Tkow, VIII, 11
       ⲧⲱⲟⲩⲛ ⲁ̄ⲙⲏⲓⲧⲛ̄ ⲛ̄ⲧⲉⲧⲛ̄ϭⲱⲡⲉ ⲛ̄ⲛⲉϩⲓ̈ⲟⲙⲉ **ⲛ̄ⲧⲉⲧⲛ̄ⲁ̄ⲛⲁⲡⲉⲩⲉ̄ ⲙ̄ⲙⲱⲧⲛ̄** ⲛ̄ⲙⲙⲁⲩ
       '*Arise, come and seize the women and rest with them.*'

Formally, this construction is reflexive, but it cannot be interpreted as a self-directed causative action, since the causative meaning of this verb, 'give rest in the afterlife', is meaningful only with one specific actor, God, and cannot denote a self-directed action. Thus, reflexivization in this case must be understood as a purely grammatical device which was for some reason preferred to the non-causative use of the short form. Except for the two reflexive attestations of ⲁⲛⲁⲡⲁⲩⲉ, this type of non-causative derivation is not attested among the class A verbs.

3.5.1.4 Class A: Summary

The class consists of 4 labile and 6 transitive verbs with the vestiges of a middle-passive form attested for each of them. Almost every middle-passive form (every form, if we accept ⲃⲁⲣⲉⲓⲥⲑⲁⲓ as a non-causative predicate) corresponds to the non-causative meaning of the respective alternation pair. Thus, the distribution of the suffix in this class can by no means be called random or accidental.

Most of the suffixed forms belong to the Nag Hammadi codices II (the so-called "central corpus") and VII (Paraphrase of Shem), the tractates that, according to Funk, display several "distinctly southern" features. The sporadic tokens of the middle-passive morphology may, therefore, be traces of the influence of some other southern dialect, such as Akhmimic. Yet, the occurrence of such forms in later Sahidic texts, such as P.KRU 83 (8th century C.E.) or P.Budge, suggests that these forms could be employed in Sahidic proper, in non-literary texts. That these late tokens are found in the texts of the legal genre can be accidental, seeing that besides literary texts, the documentary Sahidic is the only register

---

297 See, e.g., the quotation from V.Henry in Kulikov (2014:1141). Obviously, one has to undertake a more sober approach to the functionality of languages, agreeing with Labov that though "...it is often asserted that speakers take the information state of their addressee into account as they speak, and that given a choice of two alternatives, they favor the one that will put across their meaning in the most efficient and effective way, <...> quantitative studies of the use of language fail to confirm this assertion." (Labov:1994:549).

sufficiently well documented for any linguistical analysis. Otherwise, these forms could be a mark of legal discourse.

Neither the long, nor the short forms of the verbs belonging to class A display any link between the tense-aspect features of the predicate and its causative / non-causative semantics. In contrast to native verbs, the category of voice for this class is separated from aspect. On the other hand, since the suffix morpheme does not seem to be linked to the durative conjugation, clearly it had not been reinterpreted as an aspect marker. The way this morpheme is employed in the discussed verb class can be tentatively described as the vestiges of parallel system borrowing.

3.5.2 Class B: two forms, one diathesis

3.5.2.1 Class B: overview

In Sahidic, the inventory of this class includes the following verbs:

a) Verbs with both active and middle-passive morphology attested (22 lexemes):

ⲁⲓⲥⲑⲁⲛⲉ / ⲁⲓⲥⲑⲁⲛⲉⲥⲑⲁⲓ	αἰσθάνομαι	'feel'
ⲁⲛϩⲏⲕⲉⲓ / ⲁⲛϩⲏⲕⲉⲥⲑⲁⲓ	ἀνήκω	'belong'
ⲁⲛⲉⲭⲉ / ⲁⲛⲉⲭⲉⲥⲑⲁⲓ	ἀνέχω	'endure, put up with'
ⲁⲡⲟⲗⲁⲩⲉ / ⲁⲡⲟⲗⲁⲩⲉⲥⲑⲁⲓ	ἀπολαύω	'enjoy, partake of'
ⲁⲣⲛⲁ / ⲁⲣⲛⲉⲓⲥⲑⲁⲓ	ἀρνέομαι	'reject, deny'
ⲇⲓⲁⲗⲉⲅⲉⲓ / ⲇⲓⲁⲗⲉⲅⲉⲓⲥⲑⲁⲓ	διαλέγω	'discourse, preach'
ⲇⲓⲁⲥⲧⲉⲗⲗⲉ / ⲇⲓⲁⲥⲧⲉⲗⲗⲉⲥⲑⲁⲓ	διαστέλλω	'specify'
ⲇⲓⲁⲫⲉⲣⲉⲓ / ⲇⲓⲁⲫⲉⲣⲉⲓⲥⲑⲁⲓ	διαφέρω	'pertain, belong'
ⲉⲝⲏⲅⲓ / ⲉⲝⲏⲅⲓⲥⲑⲉ	ἐξηγέομαι	'expound, preach'
ⲉⲙⲫⲁⲛⲓⲍⲉ / ⲉⲙⲫⲁⲛⲓⲥⲑⲁⲓ	ἐμφανίζω	'show, produce (a document)'
ⲉⲡⲓⲭⲉⲓⲣⲉⲓ / ⲉⲡⲉⲭⲉⲓⲣⲉⲓⲥⲑⲁⲓ	ἐπιχειρέω	'attempt, try'
ⲕⲩⲣⲓⲉⲩⲉ / ⲕⲩⲣⲓⲉⲩⲉⲥⲑⲁⲓ	κυριεύω	'be the owner of, possess'
ⲙⲁⲣⲧⲩⲣⲉⲓ / ⲙⲁⲣⲧⲩⲣⲉⲓⲥⲑⲁⲓ	μαρτυρέω	'be witness, testify to'
ⲛⲉⲙⲉⲓ / ⲛⲉⲙⲉⲥⲑⲁⲓ	νέμω	'hold sway over, manage'
ⲡⲟⲗⲓⲧⲉⲩⲉ / ⲡⲟⲗⲓⲧⲉⲩⲉⲥⲑⲁⲓ	πολιτεύω	'conduct one's life'
ⲡⲣⲁⲅⲙⲁⲧⲉⲩⲉ / ⲡⲣⲁⲅⲙⲁⲧⲉⲩⲉⲥⲑⲁⲓ	πραγματεύομαι	'do business, trade in'
ⲡⲣⲁⲥⲥⲉ / ⲡⲣⲁⲧⲧⲉⲥⲑⲁⲓ	πράσσω	'act'
ⲡⲣⲟⲥⲉⲩⲭⲉ / ⲡⲣⲟⲥⲉⲩⲭⲉⲥⲑⲁⲓ	προσεύχομαι	'pray'
ⲥⲓⲭⲁⲛⲉ / ⲥⲓⲭⲁⲛⲉⲥⲑⲁⲓ	σικχαίνω	'loathe, despise /be nauseated'
ⲥⲕⲉⲡⲧⲉⲓ / ⲥⲕⲉⲡⲧⲓⲥⲑⲁⲓ	σκέπτομαι	'consider, examine'
ⲧⲉⲣⲡⲉ / ⲧⲉⲣⲡⲉⲥⲑⲁⲓ	τέρπω	'enjoy, delight in'
ϩⲩⲡⲟⲩⲣⲅⲉⲓ / ϩⲩⲡⲟⲩⲣⲅⲉⲓⲥⲑⲁⲓ	ὑπουργέω	'assist, serve'

b) Verbs attested only in middle-passive form (9 lexemes):

ⲁⲛϯⲡⲟⲓⲉⲓⲥⲑⲁⲓ	ἀντιποιέω	'oppose to'
ⲁⲣⲁⲥⲑⲁⲓ	ἀράομαι	'pray to'
ⲇⲓⲁⲧⲓⲑⲉⲥⲑⲁⲓ	διατίθημι	'dispose by will'
ⲉⲡⲉⲣⲉⲓⲇⲉⲥⲑⲁⲓ	ἐπερείδω	'lean, rest on'
ⲕⲧⲁⲥⲑⲁⲓ	κτάομαι	'acquire'
ⲟⲓⲕⲉⲓⲟⲩⲥⲑⲁⲓ	οἰκειόω	'claim as one's own, appropriate'
ⲥⲉⲃⲉⲥⲑⲁⲓ	σέβομαι	'worship'
ⲅⲩⲡⲟⲕⲉⲓⲥⲑⲁⲓ	ὑπόκειμαι	'be liable, subjected, available'
ⲫⲁⲓⲛⲉⲥⲑⲁⲓ	φαίνω	'be clear, obvious'

Semantically, most of these verbs belong to the class of unergatives. The large share of deponents among the Greek prototypes (10 of 31 lexemes) is obvious even in this primary synopsis. This share appears to be even more significant, if one checks the borrowed lexemes against the data in Greek papyri of comparable time period, i.e., first centuries C.E. The necessary adjustments concern the following verbs:

ἀνέχω: Between the active and the medium form of this verb in Greek, there is a significant semantic difference: ἀνέχω means 'hold up, raise, maintain', while the medium ἀνέχομαι means 'hold oneself up, be patient, suffer'.[298] The semantics of the lexeme adopted in Coptic suggests that in this case, as in several others discussed below, the middle form served as a prototype for the borrowing.

(207) P.Cair. Masp. 3 67290, TM 18422 (VI C.E.)

[οὐδὲν γὰρ] **ἀνέχομαι** τῷ κυρίῳ Εὐδοξίῳ περὶ τούτου
'*I will not **tolerate** lord Eudoxios with regard to this matter*'

(208) HGV SB 20 14241, TM 23699 (VI C.E.)

τὰ νῦν καταξιούτω μὴ **ἀνέχεσθαι** συναρπαγῆναι παρά τινος
'*please do not **suffer** them to be snatched away by somebody*'

ἀντιποιέω: again, the divergence of senses between the active 'do in return' and the middle 'oppose, resist' in Greek qualifies the middle form as the predecessor of the Coptic lexeme. Multiple examples from documentary papyri support this conclusion:

(209) P.Bodl. 1 45, TM 22584 (~ VII C.E.)

καὶ βεβαιώσομεν ὑμῖν τήνδε τὴν πρᾶσιν καὶ τὴν νομὴν πάσῃ βεβαιώσει διὰ παντὸς ἀπὸ παντὸς τοῦ ἐπελευσομένου ἢ ἀντιποιησομένου, τὸν δὲ ἐπελευσόμενον ἢ ἀντιποιησόμενον παραχρῆμα ἡμεῖς οἱ πεπρακότες ἐκστήσομε[ν] καὶ ἐκδικήσομεν
'*And we confirm this sale and the possession with every warranty through everything and against everything that will happen or befall, and everything that will come or befall, we the sellers will immediately replace and repay.*'[299]

---

298 Liddell-Scott.
299 Here and below, the translation of the quotations from papyri is mine. – N.S.

διαλέγω: Whereas the active form of this verb has the meaning 'pick out, choose', the medium form διαλέγομαι has developed the meaning "converse, discourse", which is the meaning adopted by Coptic. This statement from LSJ is supported by the data from papyri, e.g.:

(210) P.Ant. 2 92, TM 32722

ὥστε **διαλέγ[ε]σθαι** καὶ τῷ κυρίῳ Θεοφείλῳ περεὶ τοῦ Λείλο[υ] καὶ παρα[δοῦν]αι αὐτῷ τὰ δ νομίσματα

'*in order to **talk** with the lord Theophilos concerning Lilos and to give him 4 solidi*'

διατίθημι: The rare tokens of this verb in the preserved papyri display the middle form διατίθεμαι (HGV P.Heid. 6 376, TM 3073 ὅπως κομισάμενοι τὸ φορτίον διατιθώμεθα 'so that having received the load, we distribute it').

ἐμφανίζω: the active form is found in the earlier papyri,[300]the middle-passive ἐμφανίζομαι in the later ones:

(211) P.Cair. Masp. 1 67032, TM 18996 (VI C.E.)

παρακ[λήσ]εις ... λαβεῖν τὴν εἰρημένην θείαν κέλευσιν ... καὶ **ἐμφανίσασθαι** τοῖς κατὰ χώραν δικαστηρίοις

'*demand... to take the above-mentioned divine order ... and **produce** it before the local courts*'

(212) P.Cair. Masp. 2 67151, TM 18905 (VI C.E.)

...ἐξεῖναι δὲ μόνον αὐτῇ τὰ ἑαυτῆς γονικὰ πράγματ[α] συλλαβεῖν ἐξερχομένη τοῦ οἴκου μου, ἅπερ ἐναποδείκτω[ς] **ἐμφανήσεται** ὡς ἦσαν ἐκεῖνα συνεισηνεγμένά μοι παρ' αὐτῆς γονικόθεν

'*She is only allowed, when leaving my home, to take the things she inherited from her parents, which she can ostensibly **prove** to be brought by her to me by inheritance.*'

ἐπερείδω: the meaning 'lean on' is rendered by the middle form (LSJ); in Greek papyri, the lexeme occurs very infrequently, always in the form of present passive participle, as in:

(213) HGV PSI 5 452, TM 33127 (IV C.E.)

οἱ δὲ οἰκέται **ἐπεριδόμενοι** τῇ δεξιᾷ αὐτοῦ, ὥς φα[σι, ἀπαρνοῦνται(?)] τὴν ἡμετέραν ὑπηρεσίαν

'*and the house slaves **guided** by his promise, as they say, refuse to serve us*'

(214) P.Cair. Masp. 1 67087, TM 19016 (VI C.E.)

ἀπῆλθεν τυραννίδι **ἐπερειδόμενος**

'*he went forth **supporting himself** by the tyranny*'

οἰκειόω: in Coptic documents this lexeme is used in the meaning 'dispose of, claim as one's own' which in Greek is rendered by the middle form (LSJ). This form is found in Antinoopolis VI C.E. papyri, e.g.:

---

300 E.g., in HGV P.Eleph. 8 TM 5842 (III B.C.), HGV P.Köln 5 216 TM 2482 (III B.C.), BGU 4 1209 TM 18659 (I B.C.).

(215) P.Cair. Masp. 2 67167, TM 18923

...προσήγεγές μοι τὰ εἰρημένα ἐνέχυρα ἀντὶ τοῦ προσημανθέντος χρέους καὶ τῆς αὐτοῦ παραμυθείας ἔχειν καὶ κατέχειν καὶ **οἰκειοῦσθαι** ἐμαυτῷ δεσποτικῷ δικαίῳ

'*You have brought me the afore-said pledges in lieu of the above-mentioned debt and its interest, to own, to possess and to **dispose of** by my own exclusive right*'

The active form of this verb seems to be attested in earlier texts only, such as Thucydides (IV B.C.), or Herculanum papyri of III-I B.C. containing philosophical texts attributed to Philodemus and Epicurus.

πολιτεύω: Classical Attic prose (Thucydides, Xenophon etc.) makes use of the active form, whereas the IV-VI C.E. Greek papyri from Egypt invariably use the middle-passive participle to designate the residence of persons involved, e.g.:

(216) P.Flor. 1 43, TM 23558 (Hermopolis, 370 C.E.)

Αὐρήλιος Κῦρος Ἑρμείου **πολιτευόμενος** Ἑρμοῦ πόλεως

'*Aurelius Kyros, son of Hermias, **citizen** of Hermopolis*'

σικχαίνω: Though this verb is used in active form in late Greek prose (Polybios, Marcus Aurelius etc.), a case can be made for medium σικχαίνομαι as a competing form. This is, e.g., the form Aquila, a Jewish translator of the Old Testament, uses in Exodus 1:12 as a gloss to the LXX βδελύσσομαι 'feel a loathing': καὶ ἐσικχαίνοντο τοὺς υἱοὺς Ισραηλ[301] and καὶ ἐβδελύσσοντο (οἱ Αἰγύπτιοι) ἀπὸ τῶν υἱῶν Ισραηλ, respectively. The lexeme is too poorly documented to make confident claims about the form it could be loaned in, but the possibility of a deponent (medium equivalent to active) usage cannot be excluded.

τέρπω: According to Liddell-Scott (1996), this verb whose active form meant 'make glad, joyful' was more frequently used in the middle-passive form τέρπομαι corresponding to the anticausative meaning 'enjoy, be glad'. Coptic seems to have adopted only the anticausative facet. Unfortunately, I could not find this lexeme attested in any of the published Greek documentary papyri. It is possible, though, that the use of the middle-passive morphology in Coptic is triggered by the frequency of the anticausative usage in the spoken or, more probably, the literary Greek.

Thus, not being deponents *stricto sensu*, the above 9 verbs probably functioned as ones in Koine, namely, their medium form had no active counterpart with a corresponding causative meaning. If we consider them as deponents, the total number of deponent prototypes in class B will amount to 19 out of 31. In the next section, I shall discuss some properties of this subgroup in a broader context of the marking of Greek deponents in Sahidic. In section 3.5.2.3, I shall return to the rest of the members of this class and try to account for their occurrence.

---

301 Origenis Hexaplorum quae supersunt (1875:81, fn.25), where also a gloss from Cod.85: "σικχαίνομαι τοῦτον τὸν ἄνθρωπον taedet me huius hominis".

3.5.2.2 Treatment of Greek deponents in Sahidic

Since Greek deponents make up about two thirds of the class, it seems reasonable to expect that the split into two forms is a standard development for a borrowed deponent verb. This assumption proves to be wrong. In the course of their transfer to Sahidic, the majority of monodiathetic middle verbs lose the middle-passive morphology and receive the stem-like form common for most borrowed lexemes. The switch from middle-passive to active morphology occurs with:

a) λογίζομαι   λοгιze⁺   *'consider, recite'* and its derivates:
    ἀπολογίζομαι   απολοгιze⁺   *'pay back, reimburse'*
    συλλογίζομαι   cγνλοгιze   *'make sense, discuss'*

b) δέχομαι   ⳉεxι⁺   *'receive'* and its derivates:
    διαδέχομαι   ⲇιⲁⳉεxe⁺   *'follow someone as a successor'*
    ἀποδέχομαι   αποⳉεxe⁺   *'accept, welcome'*
    παραδέχομαι   παραⳉεxe⁺   *'receive'*

c) χαρίζομαι   xαριze⁺   *'give, grant'* and its derivates:
    ἀποχαρίζομαι   αποxαριze⁺   *'give as a gift'*
    προσχαρίζομαι   προcxαριze   *'gratify'*

and many other deponents, such as:
ἀγωνίζομαι αгⲱνιze 'fight', ἀπαρνέομαι απαρνα⁺ 'deny', ἀσπάζομαι αcπαze⁺ 'embrace, greet', δαιμονίζομαι ⲇⲁιⲙονιze 'be possessed by a demon', ἐγκρατεύομαι εгκρατεγε 'practice self-control', ἐνθυμέομαι ενθγⲙει 'meditate, contemplate', εὐαγγελίζομαι εγαггελιze 'proclaim', καθηγέομαι καθηгει⁺ 'instruct, teach', μέμφομαι ⲙεⲙфει⁺ 'reproach, blame', ὀρχέομαι ορxει⁺ 'dance', παρρησιάζομαι παρρнcιαze 'speak freely', ὑπισχνέομαι ⳉγπιcxογ⁺ 'promise'.

The derivates of the verb ἔρχομαι 'come, go, walk' (the base verb itself has obviously not been borrowed) constitute a special case in that only their suppletive (active) aorist is borrowed in Coptic:

    παρέρχομαι   παρελθε   'pass over'
    προσέρχομαι   προcελθε   'approach'
    συνέρχομαι   cγνηλθαι   'join, work together'

The noteworthy feature of the truncated group of deponents is that most of them are transitive (these are marked by ⁺).[302] Conversely, relatively few deponents of class B (ⲁⲛεxε, εⲙфⲁⲛιze, επερειⳉεcⲑⲁι, κταcⲑⲁι, οικειογcⲑⲁι) are confined to the transitive valency pattern. Most other verbs either have a single argument (πολιτεγε, τερπε), or employ a non-transitive valency pattern, e.g., the PP with ε– (ⲁιcⲑⲁⲛε, cεβεcⲑⲁι), ⲛ– (ⲁⲣⲁcⲑⲁι, ⳉγποκειcⲑⲁι) etc. It may be inferred that Sahidic tends to treat the middle passive suffix and the transitive valency pattern as mutually exclusive morphosyntactic patterns. This

---

302 One should also notice that this group includes verbs of movement (compounds of ελθε and ορxει), i.e., active non-ergative verbs.

idea gains further support from the fact that in a subclass of B, the use of valency patterns may vary in accordance with the morphological shape of the verb, as is illustrated by the table below.

Table 8 | Middle-passive morpheme in the detransitivized predicate[303]

Meaning	Active form	Valency pattern	Meaning	Middle form	Valency pattern
'reject, deny'	ⲁⲣⲛⲁ	ⲛ-/ⲙⲙⲟ=	'reject, deny'	ⲁⲣⲛⲓⲥⲑⲉ	ⲛ-/ⲙⲙⲟ= ⲛ-/ⲛⲁ=
'exactly describe, specify'	ⲇⲓⲁⲥⲧⲉⲗⲗⲉ	ⲛ-/ⲙⲙⲟ=	'dispose of, see about'	ⲇⲓⲁⲥⲧⲉⲗⲗⲉⲥⲑⲁⲓ	ⲉⲧⲃⲉ
'partake in, enjoy'	ⲁⲡⲟⲗⲁⲩⲉ	ⲛ-/ⲙⲙⲟ=	'partake in, enjoy'	ⲁⲡⲟⲗⲁⲩⲉⲥⲑⲁⲓ	ⲉⲃⲟⲗ ϩⲛ̄
'bear witness'	ⲙⲁⲣⲧⲩⲣⲉⲓ	ⲛ-/ⲙⲙⲟ= Ø	'testify to, bear witness'	ⲙⲁⲣⲧⲩⲣⲉⲥⲑⲁⲓ	ⲉ-/ⲉⲣⲟ= ϩⲁ- / ϩⲁⲣⲟ=
'enact, carry out; be in charge'	ⲡⲣⲁⲥⲥⲉ	ⲛ-/ⲙⲙⲟ= Ø	'be in charge'	ⲡⲣⲁⲧⲧⲉⲥⲑⲁⲓ	Ø
'feel loathing towards'	ⲥⲓⲭⲁⲛⲉ	ⲙⲙⲟ= ⲉⲣⲟ=	'be indisposed'	ⲥⲓⲭⲁⲛⲉⲥⲑⲁⲓ	Ø

While omitting the Greek middle-passive morphology, Coptic may sometimes recur to the native mechanism of reflexivization to mark the affectedness of the subject in the borrowed intransitive deponents. In section 3.5.1.3, we have already seen an instance of the reflexive morpheme used to mark valency reduction of the verb ⲁⲛⲁⲡⲁⲩⲉ 'lay to rest / take repose'. There, the semantic affinity of the reflexive construction with the non-causative alternant justified regarding it as a voice-changing grammatical device: replacing the reflexive object pronoun by any other nominal object would radically change the meaning of the predicate. The syntax of the deponent verbs is different. Here, as it seems, both replacing of the pronominal object by any other noun and omitting it altogether would make the sentence ungrammatical. In Geniušienė's terms, such constructions are called '*reflexive tantum*'.[304] Thus, ⲡⲁⲣⲣⲏⲥⲓⲁⲍⲉ (παρρησιάζομαι) 'speak boldly, act boldly, encourage oneself to act / speak' invariably appears with a direct object coreferential with the subject of the clause:

(217) Cyprianus, f. 73r b,1-8

ⲉⲧⲃⲉ ⲡⲁⲓ ⲙⲛ̄ⲧⲁⲓ ⲡⲣⲟⲥⲟⲡⲟⲛ ⲙ̄ⲙ̄ⲁⲩ· ⲉⲡⲁⲣϩⲩⲥⲓⲁⲍⲉ ⲙ̄ⲙⲟⲓ̈ ⲛϩⲏⲧⲟⲩ

'*because of that I do not have the countenance to speak freely with them.*'

(218) Festal Letter 16, DS 191 b 26-DS 192 a 10

ⲁⲗⲗⲁ ⲙⲁⲣⲉⲡϣⲁϫⲉ ⲙ̄ⲡⲉⲡⲣⲟⲫⲏⲧⲏⲥ ⲉⲓ ⲉⲧⲙⲏⲧⲉ ⲉϥⲡⲁⲣⲣⲏⲥⲓⲁⲍⲉ ⲙ̄ⲙⲟϥ

'*But may the word of the prophet come forth in the middle, speaking freely*'

---

303 For examples, see Appendix 1.
304 Geniušienė (1987).

The same analysis may be proposed for ⲁⲛⲁⲕⲧⲁ (ἀνακτάομαι) 'refresh oneself', ⲁⲛⲉⲭⲉ (ἀνέχομαι) 'wait'[305], ⲉⲅⲕⲣⲁⲧⲉⲩⲉ (ἐγκρατεύομαι) 'control oneself', ⲥⲕⲩⲗⲗⲉⲓ (σκύλλομαι) 'take the trouble', ⲥⲧⲣⲁⲧⲉⲩⲉ (στρατεύομαι) 'serve in someone's army, be a soldier for someone':

(219) Pistis Sophia, Book 2, 231b-232a

ⲁⲩⲱ ⲙ̄ⲡⲣ̄ⲁⲛⲁⲕⲧⲉ ⲙ̄ⲙⲱⲧⲛ̄ \ ϣⲁⲛⲧⲉⲧⲛ̄ϭⲓⲛⲉ ⲛ̄ⲙ̄ⲙⲩⲥⲧⲏⲣⲓⲟⲛ ⲛ̄ⲣⲉϥⲥⲱⲧϥ̄

'*And do not refresh yourselves until you find the purifying mysteries*'

(220) Epima, f. 26v

ⲁⲩⲱ ⲧⲁⲕⲉⲥϩⲓⲙⲉ. ⲉⲓⲥ ⲥⲁϣϥⲉ \ ⲛ̄ⲣⲟⲙⲡⲉ. ϫⲓⲛⲧⲁⲓⲕⲁⲁⲥ ⲛ̄ⲥⲱⲓ. **ⲉⲓⲉⲛⲅⲣⲁⲧⲉⲩⲉ ⲙ̄ⲙⲟⲓ** ⲉⲧⲃⲉ ⲡⲉⲕⲣⲁⲛ ⲉⲧⲟⲩⲁⲁⲃ.

'*And my wife, too, it has been seven years since I have left her behind, exercising self-control because of your holy name.*'

(221) Colluthus, f. 94r-121v Chapman / Depuydt (1993:47)

ⲁⲡⲉⲕⲉⲓⲱⲧ ⲙⲉⲛ **ⲥⲧⲣⲁⲧⲉⲩⲉ ⲙ̄ⲙⲟϥ** ⲙ̄ⲡⲣⲣⲟ ⲙ̄ⲡⲕⲁϩ ⲙⲛ̄ⲛⲥⲱⲥ ⲁϥⲣ̄ ⲡⲟⲩⲱϣ ⲙ̄ⲡⲣⲣⲟ ⲛ̄ⲧⲡⲉ ⲙⲛ̄ ⲡⲕⲁϩ ⲓ̅ⲥ̅ ⲡⲉⲭ̅ⲥ̅

'*For your father has served as a soldier for the king of the earth. Afterwards he did the will of the king of heaven and earth, Jesus Christ.*'

Thus, the borrowed middle suffix and the native reflexive direct object constitute two alternative ways for marking anticausative or durative (e.g., in the case of ⲥⲧⲣⲁⲧⲉⲩⲉ) meaning. Both morphs may alternate with one and the same lexeme, as in the case of ⲁⲡⲟⲗⲁⲩⲉ 'take pleasure, partake of, enjoy':

(222) Spiteful Monk, 55

ⲛ̄ⲧⲟⲕ ⲇⲉ, ⲱ ⲡⲁϣⲏⲣⲉ, ⲡⲱⲧ ⲉⲃⲟⲗ ⲛ̄ⲧⲙⲟⲧⲛⲉⲥ ⲙ̄ⲡⲉⲓ̈ⲁⲓ̈ⲱⲛ ϫⲉ **ⲉⲕⲉⲁⲡⲟⲗⲁⲩⲉ ⲙ̄ⲙⲟⲕ** ϩⲙ̄ ⲡⲉⲓ̈ⲁⲓ̈ⲱⲛ ⲉⲧⲛⲏⲩ.

'*But you, O my son, flee the satisfaction of this era, so that **you will enjoy yourself** in the future era.*'[306]

(223) BL Pap 78, P. KRU 65

ⲉⲩ(ⲟⲩ)ⲟⲛϩ ⲉⲃⲟⲗ ⲛ̄ⲥⲡⲟⲩⲇⲏ ⲛⲓⲙ ⲉϩⲛⲉ` ⲉⲟⲩϭⲁϫⲙⲉⲥ ⲛ̄ⲛⲁ` ⲙⲛ ⲟⲩⲉⲓⲱⲧⲉ ⲙ̄ⲙⲟⲟⲩ̄ ⲉⲉϣⲙ̄ ⲡⲉⲩⲉⲓⲃⲉ ⲁⲩⲱ **ⲉⲩⲁⲡⲟⲗⲁⲩⲉⲥⲑⲁⲓ** ⲉⲃⲟⲗ ϩⲛ̄ ⲛ̄ⲁⲅⲁⲑⲟ[ⲛ] ⲛ̄ⲁⲧϣⲁϫⲉ ⲉⲣⲟⲟⲩ

'*they exhibit every zeal to find a handful of mercy and a drop of water to quench their thirst and **enjoy** the good things which words cannot describe.*'

Quite exceptionally, the middle suffix and the reflexive object overlap, as can be illustrated by ⲥⲕⲉⲡⲧⲉⲓ / ⲥⲕⲉⲡⲧⲓⲥⲑⲁⲓ 'consider': in most cases, this verb is used with the pronominal object ⲙⲙⲟ= co-referential with the subject:

---

305 Strictly speaking, this meaning is not registered for the Greek verb and must have developed inside Coptic, but possibly on the basis of the medial form with the sense of 'suffer, endure'.
306 Translation: A.Grons.

(224) Colluthus, f. 89v b, Schenke (2013:45)

ⲙⲏⲡⲱⲥ ⲕ̄ⲟⲩⲱϣ ⲉⲥⲕⲏⲡⲧⲉⲓ ⲙ̄ⲙⲟⲕ

'*Perhaps you want to think it over*'

(225) Ms. Gr. fol. 21, P.KRU 74, 42-44

ⲗⲟⲓⲡⲟⲛ ⲁⲓⲥⲕⲉⲡⲧⲉⲓ ⲙⲙⲟ[ⲓ] ϩⲛ ⲟⲩⲗⲟⲅⲓⲥⲙⲟⲥ ⲉϥⲥⲟⲩⲧⲱⲛ ⲋⲉ ⲟⲩⲇⲓⲕⲁⲓⲟⲛ ⲡⲉ ⲁⲩⲱ
ⲟⲩⲡⲉⲧⲉϣϣⲉ ⲡⲉ

'*Furthermore, I considered in straight reasoning that it is just and fitting*'

The combination of both detransitivizing devices in one verbal phrase is a sign of the decreased functionality of one or both of them in the later period:

(226) Hom. Pass. Res. (M.595), 39v b, 27-33, Chapman (1993:93); 9th C.E.

ⲡⲛⲟⲩⲧⲉ ⲅⲁⲣ ⲁϩⲉⲣⲁⲧϥ ϩⲁ ⲧⲕⲁⲧⲁⲇⲓⲕⲏ ⲉⲣⲉ ⲛⲣⲱⲙⲉ ϩⲱⲱϥ ⲛⲕⲁϩ ϩⲓⲕⲉⲣⲙⲉⲥ ϩⲙⲟⲟⲥ
ⲉⲧⲣⲉⲩⲥⲕⲉⲡⲧⲓⲥⲑⲁⲓ ⲙⲙⲟⲟⲩ

'*Verily, God is standing to be sentenced, while people of earth and dust sit to give judgement*'

The reflexivization by means of the PP with ⲙⲙⲟ= tends to occur fairly regularly with one and the same lexeme, as it does with native lexemes like ⲕⲱⲧⲉ. Conversely, the occurrences of the Greek middle suffix are sporadic and mostly look like lexicalized relics of the borrowed form.

Thus, in Sahidic, Greek intransitive deponents can appear in three different shapes: in a short stem-like form, bearing no marking altogether (ἀγωνίζομαι ⲁⲅⲱⲛⲓⲍⲉ 'fight', δαιμονίζομαι ⲇⲁⲓⲙⲟⲛⲓⲍⲉ 'be possessed by a demon' and a few other verbs), with a reflexive object PP and with the Greek middle-passive suffix morpheme. We could expect that the morphological variant which is closest to the morphology of the source language would also have temporal precedence. However, the chronological evidence does not unequivocally prove the mediopassive form to be the most ancient one. Moreover, this form can appear in texts as late, as IX C.E. Yet, whether early, or late, its use seems to be corpus-specific. The table below displays comparative attestation dates for a set of verbs mainly attested in literary sources (ⲁⲓⲥⲑⲁⲛⲉ 'feel', ⲁⲛⲉⲭⲉ 'endure', ⲁⲡⲟⲗⲁⲩⲉ 'take pleasure, partake of', ⲁⲣⲁⲥⲑⲉ and ⲡⲣⲟⲥⲉⲩⲭⲉ 'pray', ⲁⲣⲛⲁ 'deny', ⲇⲓⲁⲗⲉⲅⲓ 'converse', ⲉϩⲏⲅⲓ 'preach', ⲡⲟⲗⲓⲧⲉⲩⲉ 'conduct one's life', ⲡⲣⲁⲅⲙⲁⲧⲉⲩⲉ 'trade in', ⲥⲉⲃⲉⲥⲑⲁⲓ 'worship', ⲥⲓⲭⲁⲛⲉ 'feel loathing against', ⲥⲕⲉⲡⲧⲉⲓ 'consider', ⲧⲉⲣⲡⲉ 'enjoy', ⲫⲁⲓⲛⲉⲥⲑⲁⲓ 'seem').

Table 9 | Deponent morphology dating

Long form	Short form
ⲁⲛⲉⲭⲉⲥⲑⲉ: Nag Hammadi Codex IX (**4 C.E.**), O.Crum 171 (**6-8 C.E.**)	ⲁⲛⲉⲭⲉ: multiple attestations (**4 C.E. to 10 C.E.**), inter alia Nag Hammadi Codex II, VII
ⲁⲣⲛⲓⲥⲑⲉ: Nag Hammadi Codex V, VII (**4 C.E.**); P.Mich. 3520 (**4 C.E.**)	ⲁⲣⲛⲁ: multiple attestations (**3- 11 C.E.**)
ⲁⲣⲁⲥⲑⲉ: Nag Hammadi Codex V (**4 C.E.**)	

Long form	Short form
ⲇⲓⲁⲗⲉⲅⲓⲥⲑⲁⲓ: Pierpont Morgan M.595 and GIOV.AM (**9 C.E.**)	ⲇⲓⲁⲗⲉⲅⲉⲓ: Historia Ecclesiastica Coptica (**date unknown**)
ⲉⲍⲏⲅⲓⲥⲑⲉ: Pierpont Morgan Library M.580 (**9 C.E.**), Pierpont Morgan Library M.583 (**9 C.E.**), Bibl. Nat. Copte 129.16.76 (**9 C.E.**), Bodleian Library 42b.4.1 (**?**)	ⲉⲍⲏⲅⲓ: Coptic Museum EG-c Ms 3811 (**early 10 C.E.**)
ⲡⲟⲗⲓⲧⲉⲩⲉⲥⲑⲁⲓ: Nag Hammadi Codex II, VI (**4 C.E.**); Pierpont Morgan M.595 and GIOV.AM Homily on the Passion (**9 C.E.**)	ⲡⲟⲗⲓⲧⲉⲩⲉ: different mss. ranging from **4 to 11** C.E.
ⲡⲣⲁⲅⲙⲁⲧⲉⲩⲉⲥⲑⲁⲓ: Nag Hammadi Codex VI (**4 C.E.**)	ⲡⲣⲁⲅⲙⲁⲧⲉⲩⲉ: Pierpont Morgan Library M.583, M.591 (**9 C.E.**)
ⲡⲣⲟⲥⲉⲩⲭⲉⲥⲑⲁⲓ: Nag Hammadi Codex II (**4 C.E.**)	ⲡⲣⲟⲥⲉⲩⲭⲉ: BL Add MS 5114 Pistis Sophia (**4-5 C.E.**)
ⲥⲉⲃⲉⲥⲑⲁⲓ: Nag Hammadi Codex II, VI, VII (**4 C.E.**)	
ⲥⲓⲭⲁⲛⲉⲥⲑⲁⲓ: Nag Hammadi Codex VII (**4 C.E.**)	ⲥⲓⲭⲁⲛⲉ: Nag Hammadi Codex II, VII (**4 C.E.**)
ⲥⲕⲉⲡⲧⲓⲥⲑⲁⲓ: Pierpont Morgan M.595 and GIOV. AM Homily on the Passion (**9 C.E.**)	ⲥⲕⲉⲡⲧⲉⲓ: various sources of **6-11** C.E., inter alia in Pierpont Morgan M.595 and GIOV.AM Homily on the Passion
ⲧⲉⲣⲡⲉⲥⲑⲁⲓ: Nag Hammadi Codex III (**4 C.E.**)	ⲧⲉⲣⲡⲉ: BG 8502 (**4 C.E.**)
ⲫⲉⲛⲉⲥⲑⲁⲓ: Nag Hammadi Codex VI (**4 C.E.**)	

Most of the longer forms occur in the corpus of Nag Hammadi codices. Still, some pre-sumably later texts can contain the suffixed forms, too. In that case, one could surmise the existence of an earlier text variant, although it is also possible that the longer form, hardly of everyday use, served to create a patina of antiquity. A text particularly prominent in this respect is the "Homily on the Passion and the Resurrection Attributed to Evodius of Rome", both in the p.Morgan M595 and Giov.AM manuscripts dating from ca. IX C.E.[307] Some lexemes may be represented in both forms inside one and the same corpus (ⲥⲓⲭⲁⲛⲉ 'feel loathing' in NHC VII, ⲥⲕⲉⲡⲧⲉⲓ 'consider, examine' in both mss. of the Homily of the Passion), though such situation is evidently extremely unusual. One possible explanation can be found in the beginning of this section.

---

307 M.Sheridan suggests VI-VII C.E., the time of an increased pressure exercised on the Egyptian church, as the most likely period for the composition of this homily (Sheridan 2012:146). Thus, the text could stem from much earlier epoche, than the manuscript. Its attribution, however, goes even further back, ascribing the authorship to a certain Evodius, traditionally held to be Peter's successor in the See of Rome. It is, therefore, unclear whether the linguistical trait referred to here genuinely reflects the contemporal usage, or is to be taken as an imitation of the more sober antiquated style.

3.5.2.3 Class B: Intra-Sahidic deponentialization

The phenomenon of the productive middle-passive suffix in Sahidic, unwarranted by the morphological properties of the source verbs, has hitherto attracted little attention. This is quite understandable considering the altogether negligible number of such tokens. Almost all the verbs with the unexpected middle form are found in the corpus of Sahidic legal papyri dating from 8th C.E.[308] The idiosyncrasy of this corpus merits a separate discussion and must probably be ascribed to conservativeness of legal idiom, in general, an inevitable consequence of the idea of immutability and continuity of the law. In the language of legal documents, formulae obtain the force of validating the content allowing to trace down a unique occurrence to its model event or historic precedent. That is why people mastering this specific language register are taught to escape linguistic innovations.[309] This policy might occasionally result in intentional archaization and hypercorrection, in pursuit of a linguistic standard that had either long ago become obsolete or else never really existed. It is hard to think of any other explanation for the sudden occurrence of the suffix morpheme in a dialect notorious for omitting it.

Yet, if we want to account for the unexpected morphological changes, it is not enough to refer to a specific register that prompted them to happen. These novel forms are not random monstrosities, but appear to be to a certain degree grammatically rooted, even by virtue of their regular use with the verbs in question, namely, ⲁⲛϩⲏⲕⲉⲓ / ⲁⲛϩⲏⲕⲉⲥⲑⲁⲓ, ⲇⲓⲁⲥⲧⲉⲗⲗⲉ / ⲇⲓⲁⲥⲧⲉⲗⲗⲉⲥⲑⲁⲓ, ⲇⲓⲁⲫⲉⲣⲉⲓ / ⲇⲓⲁⲫⲉⲣⲉⲓⲥⲑⲁⲓ, ⲕⲩⲣⲓⲉⲩⲉ / ⲕⲩⲣⲓⲉⲩⲉⲥⲑⲁⲓ, ⲙⲁⲣⲧⲩⲣⲉⲓ / ⲙⲁⲣⲧⲩⲣⲉⲓⲥⲑⲁⲓ, ⲡⲣⲁⲥⲥⲉ / ⲡⲣⲁⲧⲧⲉⲥⲑⲁⲓ. As to my knowledge, the first and only researcher to take a notice of this phenomenon was P.V. Jernstedt. In his opinion, the emergence of these forms is due to an incorrectly applied analogy to the true deponents:

"ⲁⲛϩⲏⲕⲉⲓⲥⲑⲁⲓ is based on ἀνήκειν 'belong to'. The medium form of an indefinite mood can in no way compel us to hypothesize that a corresponding form was used in Greek. Other Greek transitive verbs may likewise exhibit a medium voice indefinite mood form in Coptic. So, BM 1703 ⲡⲉⲧⲇⲓⲁⲫⲉⲣⲉⲥ[θ] ⲉⲣⲟⲕ undoubtedly reproduces τὸ διαφέρον σοι … ϩⲩⲡⲟⲕⲉⲓⲥⲑⲁⲓ and other medium forms, such as ⲉⲛⲉⲭⲉⲥⲑⲁⲓ, have probably served as a source for the use of the medium ending in the verbs that have originally had an active form."[310]

Now, linguistic analogy works as regularization of forms under the assumption of some grammatical or semantic relation common for the compared entities.[311] Therefore, even if we accept the explanation by analogy proposed in Jernstedt (1959), it would still need a clarification: why exactly did the analogy work towards lengthening the form in those rather anomalous cases? Is it possible to single out a specific syntactic or semantic parameter responsible for what looks like a redundant marking of the verb? Interestingly, there seems to be not one, but three or four such parameters, not all of them coinciding in each case.

---

308 This, of course, may be a sheer coincidence caused by the unequal representation of various genres in surviving Sahidic corpus, as explained in 3.5.1.4.

309 Cf., e.g., Abramova (2019).

310 Jernstedt (1959:13). Translation mine – N.S.

311 In Dinneen (1968), this is termed "the positive side of analogy".

a) Stative aspect of an unaccusative verb

obviously triggers the use of the middle-passive suffix with ⲁⲛⲏⲕⲉⲓ and ⲇⲓⲁⲫⲉⲣⲉⲓ, both of them meaning 'belong'.

> (227) BL Pap 100 - P. KRU 36
>
> ⲁⲩⲱ ⲧⲛ̄ϩⲟⲙⲟⲗⲟⲅⲉⲓ ⲉⲧⲙⲉⲓ ⲉⲃⲟⲗ ⲉⲣⲱⲧⲛ ⲧⲟⲩ ⲗⲟⲓⲡⲟⲩ ϩⲁ ϭⲉⲗⲁⲁⲩ ⲛ̄ϩⲱⲃ ⲉϥⲁⲛⲏⲕⲉⲓⲥⲑⲁⲓ ⲉⲧⲉⲓⲕⲗⲏⲣⲟⲛⲟⲙⲓⲁ ⲛ̄ⲙⲙⲁⲕⲁⲣⲓⲟⲥ ⲉⲡⲓⲫⲁⲛⲉⲓⲟⲥ ⲙⲛ ⲙⲁⲣⲓⲁ
>
> '...and we declare that we shall not henceforth sue you on account of anything **pertaining** to this inheritance of the late Epiphanius and Mary...'

> (228) BL Or. 4868 - P.KRU 14
>
> ⲁⲩⲱ ⲛ̄ⲅⲕⲩⲣⲓⲉⲩⲉⲥⲑⲁⲓ ⲁⲩⲱ ⲛ̄ⲅⲣ̄ ⲡⲭⲟⲉⲓⲥ ⲙ̄ⲡⲏⲓ ⲧⲏⲣϥ ϩⲓ ⲧⲡⲁⲓⲗⲁⲕⲓⲛⲏ ⲡⲣⲟⲥ ⲛ̄ϥⲧⲟϣ ⲛ̄ⲧⲁⲓⲟⲩⲟⲛϩⲟⲩ ⲛⲁⲕ ⲉⲡⲏⲓ ⲧⲏⲣϥ ⲉⲕ ⲧⲉⲧⲣⲁⲅⲱⲛⲟⲛ ϫⲓⲛ ⲛϥ̄ⲥⲛⲧⲉ ϣⲁ ⲣⲁⲧⲏⲩ ⲙⲛ ⲛⲕⲉⲭⲣⲏⲥⲧⲏⲣⲓⲟⲛ ⲉⲧⲁⲛϩⲏⲕⲉⲓⲥⲑⲁⲓ ⲉⲣⲟϥ
>
> 'and you may become lord and take possession of the entire house on Pailakine street according to its borders which I have indicated to you for the entire house on four sides from its foundations to the air, along with the furniture that **belongs** to it'

This form has a free alternant ⲁⲛϩⲏⲕⲉⲓ attested about two times less frequently:

> (229) BL Or. 4881 - P.KRU 8
>
> ⲛ̄ⲧⲟϣ ⲧⲉ ⲛⲁⲓ ⲙ̄ⲡⲉⲛⲙⲉⲣⲟⲥ <ⲙ̄>ⲡⲁⲛϩ ⲧⲏⲣϥ ϫⲓⲛ ⲛⲉϥⲥⲛⲧⲉ ϣⲁ ⲣⲁⲧⲏⲩ ⲙⲛ ⲛⲉϥⲭⲣⲏⲥⲧⲏⲣⲓⲟⲛ ⲧⲏⲣⲟⲩ ⲉⲧⲁⲛϩⲏⲕⲉⲓ ⲉⲣⲟϥ
>
> 'These are the boundaries of our entire share of (the) courtyard, from its foundations to the airspace, together with all the utensils **belonging** to it'

ⲇⲓⲁⲫⲉⲣⲉⲓⲥⲑⲁⲓ, in turn, is attested only in the suffixed form.

> (230) Vienna Nationalbibliothek K 10993 - P.KRU 23
>
> ⲟⲩⲇⲉ ⲉⲣⲟⲕ ⲙⲛ ⲛⲉⲕϣⲏⲣⲉ ⲙⲛ ⲛ̄ϣⲏⲣⲉ ⲛ̄ⲛⲉⲕϣⲏⲣⲉ ⲟⲩⲇⲉ ⲥⲟⲛ ⲟⲩⲇⲉ ⲥⲱⲛⲉ ⲟⲩⲇⲉ ϣⲛⲟⲩⲁ ⲟⲩⲇⲉ ϣⲛ̄ⲥⲛⲁⲩ ⲟⲩⲇⲉ ⲛⲉⲕϫⲱϩ ⲟⲩⲇⲉ ⲛⲉⲕϫⲱϩ ⲛ̄ϫⲱϩ ⲟⲩⲇⲉ ⲗⲁⲁⲩ ⲛ̄ⲣⲱⲙⲉ ⲉϥⲇⲓⲁⲫⲉⲣⲓⲥⲑⲁⲓ ⲉⲣⲟⲕ ⲕⲁⲧⲁ ⲗⲁⲁⲩ ⲛ̄ⲥⲙⲟⲧ ⲁⲡⲗⲱⲥ
>
> 'neither against you, your children, or your children's children, nor a brother or sister, nor a first- or second-degree relative, nor your kin or your kin of kin, nor anyone **belonging** to you in any way at all'

> (231) BL Or. 4884 - P. KRU 44
>
> ϫⲓⲛ ⲧⲉⲛⲟⲩ ⲉⲛⲉⲓⲉϣ ϭⲙϭⲟⲙ ⲉⲉⲓ ⲉⲃⲟⲗ ⲉⲣⲱⲧⲛ (...) ⲟⲩⲇⲉ ϩⲁ ⲗⲁⲁⲩ ⲛ̄ϩⲱⲃ ⲉϥⲇⲓⲁⲫⲉⲣⲓⲥⲑⲁⲓ ⲉⲡⲙⲁⲕ/ ⲑⲉⲟⲇⲱⲣⲟⲥ ⲟⲩⲇⲉ ϩⲁ ⲛⲛⲟⲩⲃ ⲟⲩⲇⲉ ϩⲁ ϩⲁⲁⲧ ⲟⲩⲇⲉ ϩⲁ ⲥⲭⲁⲁⲧ ⲟⲩⲇⲉ ϩⲁ ϣⲉⲗⲉⲉⲧ ⲟⲩⲇⲉ ϩⲁ ⲣⲟⲙⲡⲉ ⲛⲟⲩⲱⲙ
>
> 'From now on, I shall not be able to proceed against you, (...) neither for anything **pertaining** to the late Theodore, nor for gold, nor for silver, nor for dower, nor for dowry, nor for year's eating'

b) Detransitivized stative predicate

Detransitivization is here defined as a diathetic shift that preserves the agent, but lowers the syntactic status of the non-agential actant or suppresses this actant altogether. The combination of this shift with the stative aspect of the verb ⲡⲣⲁⲥⲥⲉ 'act' is also often marked with the middle-passive suffix in the documentary Sahidic:

(232) BL Or. 4871 - P.KRU 15

ⲛϥⲧⲓ ⲉⲡⲗⲟⲅⲟ[ⲥ ⲙⲡ]ⲣⲟⲥⲧⲓⲙⲟⲛ ⲙⲙⲁⲁⲃⲧⲁⲥⲉ ⲛⲹⲟⲗⲟⲕ/ ⲛⲛⲟⲩⲃ ⲛⲧⲉⲋⲟⲩⲥⲓⲁ ⲉⲧⲡⲣⲁⲧⲧⲉⲥⲑⲁⲓ
ⲋⲙ ⲡ{ⲉⲓ}ⲟⲩⲟⲉⲓⲱ ⲉⲧⲙⲙⲁⲩ

'...and he shall pay as the sum of the fine thirty-six gold holokottinoi to the authority which **is in office** at that time'

(233) P. 10607 - P. KRU 45

ⲛϥⲧⲓ ⲉⲡⲗⲟⲅ(ⲟⲥ) ⲙ(ⲡ)ⲡⲣⲟⲥⲧⲓⲙⲟⲛ ⲙⲙⲁⲃⲧⲁⲍⲉ ⲛⲹⲟⲗⲟⲕ/ ⲛⲛⲟⲩⲃ ⲛⲧⲉⲋⲟⲩⲥⲓⲁ ⲉⲧⲡⲣⲁⲧⲧⲉⲥⲑⲁⲓ
ⲉⲋⲱⲛ ⲙⲡⲕⲁⲓⲣⲟⲥ ⲉⲧⲙⲙⲁⲩ

'...and subsequently he shall pay to the account of the fine thirty-six gold holokottinoi to the authority which **is in office** over us at that time'

Among the documents collected in the DDGLC database, two display the short form in the same position (ⲡⲣⲁⲥⲥⲉ in P.Kru 9 and ⲡⲗⲉⲥⲥⲉ in P.Kru 18):

(234) BL Or. 4882 - P.KRU 9

ⲉϥⲛⲁⲋⲩⲡⲟⲕⲩⲥⲑⲁⲓ ⲛ[ⲛⲕⲁ]ⲧⲁⲇⲓⲕⲏ ⲛⲧⲁⲛⲛⲟⲙⲟⲥ ⲛⲁⲓⲕⲁⲓⲟⲛ ⲋⲟⲣⲓⲍⲉ ⲙⲙⲟⲟⲩ ⲉⲧⲉ ⲛⲁⲓ ⲛⲉ
ⲥⲛⲧⲉ ⲛⲟⲛⲅⲓⲁ ⲛⲛⲟⲩⲃ ⲙⲡⲁⲣⲭⲱⲛ ⲉⲧⲡⲣⲁⲥⲥⲉ ⲋⲙ ⲡⲕⲩⲣⲟⲥ ⲉⲧⲙⲙⲁⲩ (...)

'...he shall fall under the fines which the just laws have imposed — which are two ounces of gold — (to be paid) to the official who **is in office** at that time'

The four surviving attestations of transitive ⲡⲣⲁⲥⲥⲉ ('carry out, put in effect') invariably use the short form:

(235) MONB.FY, Historia Ecclesiastica Coptica, FY 49

ⲡⲉⲕⲉⲓⲱⲧ ⲅⲁⲣ ⲡⲣⲣⲟ ⲁϥⲋⲩⲡⲟⲅⲣⲁⲫⲏ ⲉⲧⲉϥⲕⲁⲑⲉⲣⲉⲥⲓⲥ ⲁⲩⲱ ⲁϥⲡ<ⲣ>ⲁⲥⲥⲉ ⲙⲙⲟϥ ⲋⲓ ⲡⲉⲡⲁⲣⲭⲟⲥ
'For your father, the emperor, signed his excommunication and he enacted it through the governor...'

c) Detransitivized predicate

It was already mentioned that in some cases, detransitivization alone seems to suffice to trigger the morphological change in the verb, as shown in Table 8. I shall confine myself here to the single example with ⲡⲣⲁⲧⲧⲉⲥⲑⲁⲓ, since the phenomenon is exemplified in Appendix 1.

(236) CG 8730, P.KRU 75, 89-91

ⲋⲁⲡⲗⲱⲥ ⲛⲅⲡⲣⲁⲧⲧⲉⲥⲑⲁⲓ ⲉⲧⲃⲉ ⲛⲁⲓ ⲧⲏⲣⲟⲩ ⲋⲛ ⲋⲱⲃ ⲛⲓⲙ ⲕⲁⲧⲁ ⲛⲟⲙⲏ ⲛⲓⲙ ⲋⲓ ⲙⲛⲋⲟⲉⲓⲥ ⲛⲓⲙ
ⲋⲓ ⲕⲁⲧⲟⲭⲏ ⲛϣⲁ ⲉⲛⲉⲋ

'...in short: that you may act regarding all these things in every matter, according to all possession, and ownership, and eternal possessorship...'

d) Affected (involved) subject participant

The effect of this factor can be seen in the morphological shape of the term ⲕⲩⲣⲓⲉⲅⲉ(ⲥⲑⲁⲓ) 'be owner' in Sahidic documents[312]. The Coptic lexeme must have acquired its shape quite independently from Greek, since contemporary (in the broad sense) Greek legal documents make use only of the active form (the object is in accusative, if it immediately follows the verb, as follows from BGU 1 241, BGU 3 805, BGU 3 917 and others):

(237) HGV BASP 48, TM 132139 (VI C.E.)

[- ca.5 - μετὰ τὴν] ἐμὴν τελευτὴν κρατεῖν καὶ **κυριεύειν** καὶ δεσπόζειν διὰ παντὸς τοῦ αὐτοῦ τρίτου μέρους μοναστηρίου ὁλοκλήρου
'(I agree ... that after) my death you possess, **have authority** and are master forever over the same third part of the whole monastery'[313]

(238) P.Cair. Masp. 1 67097 V D, TM 19026 (VI C.E.)

εὐδοκῶ καὶ πίθωμαι πρὸς τὼ σὲ ἀπεντεῦθεν κρατεῖν καὶ **κυριεύειν** καὶ δεσπόζειν το(ῦ) προδηλωθέντος ὁλοκλήρου πατρῴου κτήμ[ατος μετὰ πα]ντὸς αὐτο(ῦ) το(ῦ) δικαίου καὶ χρηστηρίων ἁπάντων
'I consent and agree that from now on you possess, **have authority** and are master over the whole above-defined property inherited from (my) father, including all the rights on it and all the utensils'[314]

In Coptic, sporadic tokens of the active form (e.g., in p. CLT 7, p. KRU 28) are by far less frequent than the suffixed form, as in:

(239) Vienna Nationalbibliothek K 10993, P.KRU 23

(...) ⲛⲅⲁⲙⲁϩⲧⲉ ⲁⲩⲱ ⲛⲅⲣ ϫⲟⲉⲓⲥ ⲛⲅ**ⲕⲩⲣⲓⲉⲅⲉⲥⲑⲁⲓ** ⲙⲡⲣⲁϣⲟⲙⲛⲧ ⲙⲡⲏⲓ ⲧⲏⲣϥ ⲉⲧⲙⲙⲁⲁⲩ
'(...) and take possession, and **have authority** and be the master over the third of the whole said house'
(Similar formulae are found in p.KRU 8, 14, 25, 39, 46, 71 etc.)

Remarkably, this 'passive' form can be expanded by a direct object phrase, as in:

(240) P. KRU 77

ⲛⲧⲉⲧⲛⲣ̄ [ϫⲟⲉⲓⲥ] ⲉⲣⲟⲟⲩ ϩⲛ̄ ⲙⲛⲧϫⲟⲉⲓⲥ ⲛⲓⲙ ⲡⲣⲟⲥ ⲑⲉ ⲛ̄ⲧⲁⲓ̈ϩⲟⲣⲓⲍ̄ⲉ ⲙ̄ⲙⲟⲟⲥ ⲛⲏⲧⲛ̄ ⲛ̄ⲧⲡⲉ [ⲛⲧⲉ] ⲧ[ⲛ̄]**ⲕⲩⲣⲓⲉⲅⲉⲥⲑⲁⲓ ⲙ̄ⲙⲟⲟⲩ** ⲛ̄ⲧⲉⲧⲛ̄ϫⲡⲟⲟⲩ ⲛⲏⲧⲛ
'(...) and you shall be their [owners] in all ownership as I have bestowed it on you above, [and] you **have authority over them**, and acquire them for you'

Outside of the possession formula, the long form of ⲕⲩⲣⲓⲉⲅⲉ is attested once in the sense 'be valid, authoritative', in an objectless present clause:

---

312 Often erroneously written as ⲕⲉⲗⲉⲅⲉⲥⲑⲁⲓ (observation of F.Krueger, DDGLC database.) Since, however, the meaning of the verb and the formula it appears in are exactly identical to those of ⲕⲩⲣⲓⲉⲅⲉⲥⲑⲁⲓ, I take 'keleuesthai' to be an orthographic variant and not a form of 'keleue' in need of a special consideration.

313 Translation: J.Combs & J. Miller (2011:85).

314 Translation mine. – N.S.

(241) P.CLT 4, mss 24-25

ⲉϥⲛⲁϣⲱⲡⲉ ⲉϥⲉⲙϭⲟⲙ ⲉϥ**ⲕⲩⲣⲓⲉⲩⲥⲟⲁⲓ̈** ϩⲙ ⲙⲁ ⲛⲓⲙ ⲉⲩⲛⲁⲉⲙⲫⲁⲛⲓⲍⲉ ⲙ̅ⲙⲟϥ ⲛ̅ϩⲏⲧϥ̅ ϩⲓⲧⲛ
ⲑⲩⲡⲟⲅⲣⲁⲫⲏ ⲙ̅ⲫⲩⲡⲟⲅⲣⲁⲫⲟⲥ ⲛ̅ⲧⲁϥⲥϩⲁⲓϥ ⲙ̅ⲛ ⲛⲁⲍⲓⲟⲡⲓⲥⲧⲟⲥ ⲙ̅ⲙⲁⲣⲧⲩⲣⲟⲥ

'*It shall be valid and **authoritative** wherever it may be produced, by the signature
of the subscriber who has written it, as well as the trustworthy witnesses.*'

The shorter form is not attested in this meaning, at all.

Since the legal formula uses conjunctive, i.e. a tense of the eventive paradigm, it is
hardly justified to ascribe to the predicate the stative aspect. The verb must possibly be
interpreted as 'gain, acquire control', rather than 'have control'. Therefore, the affectedness
or the involvement of the subject ('you shall gain for yourself the control') remains the
most plausible candidate for setting off the morphological change.

e) Involved subject participant and detransitivized predicate: the case of ⲙⲁⲣⲧⲩⲣⲉⲓ(ⲥⲟⲁⲓ)

The Liddell-Scott dictionary contains two separate verbal entries based on the stem
μαρτυρ-. One of them, μαρτυρέω 'bear witness to' is inflected in the active in the present
tense, but takes the middle morpheme in the future tense and in the aorist. The other one,
μαρτύρομαι (in later texts μαρτυροῦμαι) means 'call to witness' or 'declare'. The middle
suffix in the present tense obviously functions as a causative or intensifying morpheme.[315]
The active form is far more frequent; it is used either with dative of an entity witnessed
(CPR 1 30 μαρτυρῶ τοῖς αὐτοῖς γαμικοῖς συμβολαίοις 'I bear witness to the wedding
contract', HGV BGU 3 900 μαρτυρῶ τῇ μισθώσι 'I bear witness to the lease', HGV BGU 2
404 μαρτυρῶ τῇδε τῇ ὁμολογίᾳ 'I bear witness to the agreement' etc.), or else in objectless
testimonial statements after a personal name (HGV BGU 2 668 Φλ(άυιος) Δῖος Ἀβραμίου
στρ(ατιώτης) μαρτυρῶ 'I, the soldier Flavius Dios, son of Abramios, bear witness' etc.).

The middle-passive form is usually expanded by an accusative object or by a content
clause:

(242) P.Oxy. 8 1120, TM 31719 (III C.E.)

κατὰ τοῦτο **μαρτύρομαι τὴν βίαν** γυνὴ χήρα καὶ ἀσθενής.
'*I accordingly testify to his violence, being a feeble widow woman*'

(243) P.Oxy. 54 3759, TM 15268 (IV C.E.)

μαρτύρομαι ὅτι κατά τινων ἀνήνεγκεν ἐπὶ τὸν κύριόν μου τὸν ἔπαρχον καὶ κάτ
ἑτέρων εἰσάγει νῦν...
'*...I declare that he has brought forward (a complaint) against some persons to my
lord the eparch and that he is suing the others...*'

To complete the picture, one should mention that in Koine, this stem has produced various more or less synonymous compounds (ἐκμαρτυρέω, διαμαρτυρέω, προμαρτυρέω),

---

315 Such parallelism of valency changing functions in the same morpheme is cross-linguistically not
uncommon. See, e.g., Lyutikova & Bonch-Osmolovskaya (2006) for Balkar data.

which as a rule combine the middle-passive form with the active semantics, i.e. function as deponents.

Interestingly, the Coptic loan verb does not reproduce the form~meaning split observed in Greek. Both ⲙⲁⲣⲧⲩⲣⲉⲓ and ⲙⲁⲣⲧⲩⲣⲉⲓⲥⲑⲁⲓ have the meaning 'bear witness'; the short form is mainly attested in literary sources (Paraphrase of Shem NH VII, Berliner Koptisches Buch), the suffixed form invariably occurs in legal documents. The short / active form is often used with a cognate object:

(244) NHC VII, ParShem, 29,19-22

ⲛ̄ⲥⲟⲇⲟⲙⲓⲧⲏⲥ ⲇⲉ ⲕⲁⲧⲁ ⲡⲟⲩⲱϣ ⲙ̄ⲡⲙⲉⲅⲉⲑⲟⲥ ⲥⲉⲛⲁⲣ̄ⲙⲁⲣⲧⲩⲣⲓ ⲛ̄ⲧ`ⲙⲁⲣⲧⲩⲣⲓⲁ ⲛ̄ⲕⲁⲑⲟⲗⲓⲕⲏ

'...but the Sodomites, according to the will of the Majesty, shall **bear witness** to the universal testimony...'[316]

The long form can be expanded by a prepositional phrase with ⲉ- (seemingly reserved for inanimate objects) and / or ϩⲁ- (mostly for animate objects)[317], both meaning 'for, on account of':

(245) BL Or. 4885 Ro - P. KRU 59

ⲉⲩⲱⲣⲝ ⲛⲁⲕ ⲁⲓⲥⲙⲛ ⲧⲉⲓⲉⲡⲓⲧⲣⲟⲡⲏ ⲉⲥⲟ ⲛⲧⲩⲡⲟⲥ ⲛⲁⲥⲫⲁⲗⲉⲓⲁ ⲁⲩⲱ ⲁⲓⲡⲁⲣⲁⲕⲁⲗⲉⲓ ⲛϩⲉⲛⲣⲱⲙⲉ ⲛⲁⲝⲓⲟⲡⲓⲥⲧⲟⲥ ⲁⲩⲙⲁⲣⲧⲩⲣⲉⲥⲑⲁⲓ ⲉⲣⲟⲥ

'...As a security for you I have drawn up this commissioning in the form of a declaration of indebtedness, and I have asked trustworthy men who have **testified** to it...'

(246) BL Or 1061 C + Or 1062 - P. KRU 68

ⲉⲓⲡⲁⲣⲁⲕⲁⲗⲉ ⲛϩⲉⲛⲙ[ⲁⲣ]ⲧⲩ[ⲣⲟⲥ ⲉⲧⲣ]ⲉⲩⲙⲁⲣⲧⲩⲣⲓⲥⲑ ϩⲁⲣⲁⲓ ⲉⲡⲁⲓⲅⲣⲁⲫⲟⲛ ⲛⲃⲟⲩⲗⲉⲩⲙⲁ ⲛⲇⲓⲁⲑⲏⲕⲏ [ⲛ]ϣⲁϫⲛⲉ ⲛϩⲁⲛ ⲉⲧⲥϩⲏ

'...I beseech w[it]ne[sses that] they might **testify** on my behalf to this document that is a will, testament, [and] written last decision...'

Let us also consider the following. In Coptic documentary texts, ⲙⲁⲣⲧⲩⲣⲉⲓⲥⲑⲁⲓ can alternate with its native equivalent ⲣ ⲙⲛⲧⲣⲉ which takes the stative form ⲟ ⲙⲙⲛⲧⲣⲉ in the present tense formulae "I am the witness" and "I bear witness to...": P.Lond. 4 1494, TM 19924 ⲓⲥⲁⲁⲕ ⲡⲣⲱⲙ ⲧϫⲕⲱⲟⲩ ϯⲟ ⲛⲙⲛⲧⲣⲉ ⲉⲧⲓϩⲟⲙⲟⲗⲟⲅ[ⲓⲁ] 'Isaak of Tjkoou, I **bear witness** to this agreement'; P.Lond. 4 1511, TM 39814 ⲁ[ⲛⲟⲕ -ca.?-] ϯⲟ ⲙⲙⲛⲧⲣⲉ ⲉⲧⲓⲉⲅⲅⲏ ⲡⲣⲟⲥ ⲧⲉⲥϭⲟⲙ 'I... **bear witness** to this contract of pledge in its full force'. Needless to say, only infinitive is compatible with the non-present tenses: P.KRU 67, TM 85968 ⲁⲓⲣ ⲙⲛⲧⲣⲉ ⲉⲧⲉⲇⲓⲁⲑⲏⲕ(ⲏ) ⲡⲣⲟⲥ ⲧⲉϥⲁⲓⲧⲏⲥⲓⲥ 'I have testified to this testament by his request...'; P.KRU 75, TM 85976 ⲙⲛ ⲙⲙⲛⲧⲣⲉ ⲉⲧⲛϩⲟⲧ ⲉⲧⲛⲁⲣ ⲙⲛⲧⲣⲉ ⲕⲁⲧⲁ ⲧⲉⲛⲁⲓⲧⲏⲥⲓⲥ '...and the trustworthy witnesses who shall subsequently testify by our request...'. On the other hand, the Sahidic Bible has multiple tokens of the form ϯⲣ ⲙⲛⲧⲣⲉ 'I witness by something, call to witness, solemnly declare' which almost always translates the Septuagint διαμαρτύρομαι. In the documentary texts, this form is attested just once in HGV O.Frange 188:

---

316 Translation: D.Burns.

317 Due to the limitation in the number of attested tokens, it is impossible to give stricter definitions.

(247) †ⲣ ⲙⲛⲧⲣⲉ ⲛⲁⲕ ⲭⲉⲡⲁϩⲏⲧ· ⲧⲉⲧ ⲉⲭⲱⲕ ⲉⲙⲁⲧⲉ

I profess that my heart is very content with you

Syntactically (it takes sentential actants) and semantically, this second ⲣ ⲙⲛⲧⲣⲉ looks analogous to Greek μαρτύρομαι. The following table summarizes the form / meaning distribution of the original Greek verb, its Egyptian counterpart and the loaned lexeme.

Table 10 | Greek-Coptic correlates for 'witness'

	Greek	Coptic (present)	Graeco-Coptic
'bear witness'	μαρτυρέω	ⲟ ⲙⲙⲛⲧⲣⲉ	ⲙⲁⲣⲧⲩⲣⲉⲓ ⲙⲁⲣⲧⲩⲣⲉⲥⲑⲁⲓ
'call to witness, declare' (intensified)	μαρτύρομαι	ⲣ ⲙⲛⲧⲣⲉ	

The function of the middle-passive morph, as it seems, does not copy the Greek one, but rather follows the Coptic pattern, where the affectedness or involvement of the subject actant is marked by a valency-reduced form of stative.

As a post-scriptum to this complicated story, one should add that in the documentary Sahidic there are actually attested two cognate verbal lexemes with the identical sense of 'bearing witness': ⲙⲁⲣⲧⲩⲣⲉⲓ and ⲙⲁⲣⲧⲩⲣⲓⲍⲉ. Though both of them, at the first sight, look genuinely 'Greek' from the point of view of their morphology, the second one, ⲙⲁⲣⲧⲩⲣⲓⲍⲉ, might well constitute an intra-Coptic derivate: no such lexeme is registered for Greek either in the Liddell-Scott dictionary, or among the documents published on the *papyri. info* online resource.[318] However, as witnessed by the preserved Sahidic documents, this variant was the one more frequently used: it yields approximately 7 times as much attestations in legal texts as the real borrowed verb. This neologism had possibly been coined and accepted by way of standardizing the opaque original lexeme.

Thus, if the loan verb deponentialization found in Sahidic documents is not considered completely incidental, it must originate in semantic (affectedness / involvement of the subject actant, less sure the stative aspect of the predicate) and syntactic (valency reduction, detransitivization) properties of the clause. Importantly, the role of the suffix as the marker of valency reduction and subject affectedness copies its function in the source language.

3.5.2.4 Class B: Summary

Greek deponents make up the bulk of the class of monodiathetic verbs with two forms attested. This does not mean, however, that the middle-passive suffix morpheme was automatically preserved in Sahidic. The attestations show that: 1) with most verbs, the suffixed form occurs far less frequently and is generally corpus-conditioned; 2) an intransitive deponent has much more chances to keep up the suffix, than a transitive deponent, although exceptions, such as ⲕⲧⲁⲥⲑⲁⲓ or ⲉⲙ̄ⲫⲁⲛⲓⲥⲑⲁⲓ, do occur. All in all, a clear correlation exists between the use of the suffix and the intransitive diathesis of the predicate, which

---

318 LBG cites a single instance of μαρτυρίζομαι with the meaning 'zum Zeugen anrufen' ("call to witness") in a 12th century text of Analecta Manassea.

is conspicuous in the cases where the split of forms is associated with the split in valency patterns (Table 8). The majority of Greek deponent verbs with transitive valency were borrowed in their stem form.[319]

A remarkable subgroup of class B consists of those verbs whose middle-passive morphology is at variance with what is attested for their counterparts in the source language. Besides the six verbs discussed in 3.5.2.3, it might also include ϩⲩⲡⲟⲩⲣⲅⲉⲓ 'render service', once found in the suffixed form ϩⲩⲡⲟⲩⲣⲅⲓⲥⲑⲉ which is not warranted by its Greek usage:

(248) Four Creatures, f. 14v a, 7-16 (Wansink 1991: 38, 16-18); 9th century C.E.
ⲁⲗⲏⲑⲱⲥ ⲟⲩⲛⲟϭ ⲡⲉ ⲡⲉⲟⲟⲩ ⲙⲛ ⲡⲧⲁⲓⲟ ⲛⲧⲁ ⲡⲛⲟⲩⲧⲉ ⲭⲁⲣⲓⲍⲉ ⲙⲙⲟϥ ⲛⲛⲉⲓⲁⲥⲱⲙⲁⲧⲟⲥ ⲉⲧⲟⲩⲁⲁⲃ ⲉⲩϩⲩⲡⲟⲩⲣⲅⲓⲥⲑⲉ ⲉⲑⲩⲡⲉⲣⲉⲥⲓⲁ ⲙⲡⲉⲩϫⲟⲉⲓⲥ ⲕⲁⲗⲟⲥ ⲁϫⲛ ϩⲓⲥⲉ
'truly, great is the honor and the glory which God has granted to these holy incorporeal ones; they perform the service of their lord well, without weariness'

Even if this subgroup constitutes not more than one percent of all the borrowed Graeco-Coptic verbs, the described morphological re-shaping points to a certain productivity of the Greek bound morph inside Coptic, albeit only on the stock of borrowed lexemes. Its grammatical functions mainly mirror those in the source language since it is used to mark intransitive constructions with an affected subject. This type of grammatical behavior of a borrowed element is defined as *parallel system borrowing* in 3.3.

The productivity of a borrowed morpheme is a phenomenon not yet, to my knowledge, described for Coptic. (By way of comparison, the productivity of the Coptic plural ending on borrowed nouns, e.g., ⲯⲩⲭⲟⲟⲩⲉ 'souls', is a well-established Coptic grammatical trait[320]). However, the Greek middle-passive suffix is not the only Greek-origin morph to be used in Coptic word-formation. A set of Graeco-Coptic verbal lexemes display combinations of stem and suffix that do not have prototypes in genuine Greek texts. In such cases, the derivation must probably have taken place inside Coptic itself. The suffixes most frequently found in such derivations are *-eue* and *-ize*. Thus, the stem of σκοτόω 'become dizzy' in Coptic is represented by ⲥⲕⲟⲑⲟⲩ and ⲥⲕⲟⲧⲉⲩⲉ, φθονέω 'envy' has cognates ⲫⲑⲟⲛⲉⲓ and ⲫⲑⲟⲛⲉⲩⲉ, for δαπανάω 'spend' there are attested the variants ⲇⲁⲡⲁⲛⲏ, ⲇⲁⲡⲁⲛⲉⲩⲉ, ⲇⲁⲡⲁⲛⲓⲍⲉ, the Greek deponent verb δωρέομαι 'grant, give as a gift' is entirely replaced by ⲇⲱⲣⲓⲍⲉ which is not attested in genuine Greek texts, etc. We encountered an additional instance of the same phenomenon in our discussion of ⲙⲁⲣⲧⲩⲣⲉⲓ, with its cognate ⲙⲁⲣⲧⲩⲣⲓⲍⲉ, seemingly also an intra-Coptic development.

Almost all the tokens of the newly-coined suffixed forms occur in the corpus of documentary texts.

The 'true' deponents with preserved middle suffixes occur mainly in the Nag Hammadi codices II, III, V, VI, VII and IX. However, some late texts, such as pMorgan 595, also show sporadic use of the deponent forms.

---

319 The difference between the stem and the middle imperative form suggests that, in case of deponentia, at least, it was stem that was borrowed.

320 See, e.g., Egedi (2015:1339).

3.5.3 Class C: one form, two diatheses (labile verbs)

3.5.3.1 Class C: general remarks

The mechanism of morphological voice marking by means of the Greek middle-passive suffix morpheme discussed in sections 3.5.1 and 3.5.2 was clearly very limited in terms of its lexemic distribution; it is attested in marginal corpora, and its use appears to be irregular and ambiguous. Conversely, a sufficient number of verbs in standard literary Sahidic display regular labile alternation. Thus, contrasted to the rudimentary morphological voice marking, lability appears to be the default valency alternation device for loan verbs in Sahidic and is treated as such in Funk (2017) and Grossman (2019)[321]. Accordingly, there seems to be no need in specifying the verbal classes it applies to. Meanwhile, the notion that every Graeco-Coptic verb allowing for valency alternation can be used in both senses indiscriminately is not correct. True, lability must have been productive, seeing that apart from the core of ~8-9 verbs that demonstrate lability throughout the whole Sahidic corpus, there are about 40 more lexemes which occasionally display an unmarked valency switch in specific texts. Yet, generally, lability of Graeco-Coptic verbs is lexically conditioned, whereas two other mechanisms of valency alternation, the valency increasing prefix тре- and the detransitivizing 'impersonal passive' construction, do not seem to be confined to any specific set of lexemes. Semantic and grammatical properties of the labile class must therefore be weighed out against the majority of Graeco-Coptic verbal lexemes that either do not form causal pairs, or form them by means of the above mentioned morphosyntactic devices.

It was already said that the number and the inventory of labile verbs is fluctuating depending on the corpus in the question. Apart from the occasional absence of a certain verb in the corpus (e.g., the corpus of Shenoute's Canons seemingly does not contain a single token of вапτιζε 'baptize'), this is often due to many verbal lexemes being used asymmetrically, with one (causative or non-causative) facet far more frequent than the other. As a rule, some alternative marking of valency change is preferred with these verbs. Such is the case of the predominantly intransitive ҫγποτᴀссᴇ 'be subdued' which for the most part demonstrates causative alternation by means of suppletion or morphological causativization. Both suppletion (by means of the native verb кω 'put') and morphological causativization (by means of the causative infix тре-) are illustrated in the following example:

---

(249) 1Cor. 15:27

πάντα γὰρ **ὑπέταξεν** ὑπὸ τοὺς πόδας αὐτοῦ. ὅταν δὲ εἴπῃ ὅτι πάντα **ὑποτέτακται**, δῆλον ὅτι ἐκτὸς τοῦ **ὑποτάξαντος** αὐτῷ τὰ πάντα.

ⲁϥⲕⲁ ⲛⲕⲁ ⲅⲁⲣ ⲛⲓⲙ ϩⲁ ⲛⲉϥⲟⲩⲉⲣⲏⲧⲉ ϩⲟⲧⲁⲛ ⲇⲉ ⲉϥϣⲁⲛϫⲟⲟⲥ ϫⲉ ⲛⲕⲁ ⲛⲓⲙ ⲁⲩϩⲩⲡⲟⲧⲁⲥⲥⲉ ⲛⲁϥ ⲉⲓⲉ ⲡⲃⲟⲗ ⲙⲡⲉⲛⲧⲁϥⲧⲣⲉ ⲛⲕⲁ ⲛⲓⲙ ϩⲩⲡⲟⲧⲁⲥⲥⲉ ⲛⲁϥ

'For "God has **put** all things **in subjection** under his feet." But when it says, "all things **are put in subjection**," it is plain that he is excepted who **put** all things **in subjection** under him.'

At times, the decision on the lability of a specific verb must be made on the basis of a single contrastive usage, as, for instance, in the case of ⲁⲛⲁⲅⲕⲁⲍⲉ 'compel' that is once attested in the sense 'be compelled, urged' (pMoscow Copt 69). The verbs with strongly unequal frequency of transitive and intransitive tokens are called 'partially labile' in Letuchiy (online). The partially labile lexemes differ significantly from lexemes like ⲁⲩⲝⲁⲛⲉ 'make grow / grow' which has an almost equal proportion of causative and non-causative tokens. Certain lexemes are monodiathetic in one corpus, but behave as labile in another one. For instance, the NT knows only transitive use of ⲑⲗⲓⲃⲉ, whereas Shenoute understands it as both 'suffer, be distressed' and 'make suffer, torture':

(250) Shen.Can. 6, Amel. 2 (322:10)

ϯⲑⲗⲓⲃⲉ ⲁⲩⲱ ϯⲣⲉⲭϩⲱϫ ⲛϩⲟⲩⲟ ⲡⲁⲣⲁ ⲧⲁϭⲟⲙ ⲉⲃⲟⲗ ϫⲉ ϯϣⲁⲁⲧ ⲙⲡⲟⲉⲓⲕ ⲉⲟⲩⲟⲙϥ ⲛⲧⲟⲟⲧⲟⲩ ⲛⲛⲁⲥⲛⲏⲩ

'I suffer and I am distressed much over my endurance, for I lack the bread to eat from the hands of my brothers'

(251) Shen.Can. 6, Amel. 1 (70:7)

ⲉⲛⲑⲗⲓⲃⲉ ⲛⲛⲉⲛⲉⲣⲏⲩ ⲉⲡϫⲓⲛϫⲏ

'Whereas we torture each other in vain'

The New Testament, on the other hand, treats ⲃⲁⲥⲁⲛⲓⲍⲉ as both a transitive (252) and an intransitive (253) verb:

(252) Mark 5:7

ϯⲱⲣⲕ ⲉⲣⲟⲕ ⲙⲡⲛⲟⲩⲧⲉ ϫⲉ ⲛⲛⲉⲕⲃⲁⲥⲁⲛⲓⲍⲉ ⲙⲙⲟⲓ

ὁρκίζω σε τὸν Θεόν, μή με βασανίσῃς.

'I adjure you by God, do not torment me.'

(253) Matthew 8:6

ⲡⲁϣⲏⲣⲉ ⲛⲏϫ ϩⲣⲁⲓ ϩⲙ ⲡⲁⲏⲓ ⲉϥϭⲟ ⲁⲩⲱ ⲉϥⲃⲁⲥⲁⲛⲓⲍⲉ ⲉⲙⲁⲧⲉ

ὁ παῖς μου βέβληται ἐν τῇ οἰκίᾳ παραλυτικός, δεινῶς βασανιζόμενος.

'...my servant is lying paralyzed at home, suffering terribly'

The complementary distribution of the two verbs for 'suffering' between the corpora signals a variation, worth further study, between the idiom of the New Testament translation and the original literary Sahidic.

In view of the above considerations, the list of Greek labile lexemes in Sahidic cannot claim to represent the ultimate reference base. Rather, it must be regarded as a broad enough sample serving analytical purposes. At present, it includes 51 verbal lexemes: ⲁⲛⲍⲁⲗⲓⲥⲕⲉ 'be consumed / consume', ⲁⲛⲁⲅⲕⲁⲍⲉ 'be compelled / compel', ⲁⲡⲟⲣⲉⲓ 'be in doubt, confused / confuse', ⲁⲩⲍⲁⲛⲉ 'grow / make grow', ⲃⲁⲡⲧⲓⲍⲉ 'be baptized / baptize', ⲃⲁⲥⲁⲛⲓⲍⲉ 'be tormented / torment', ⲃⲉⲃⲁⲓⲟⲩ 'be confirmed / confirm', ⲅⲩⲙⲛⲁⲍⲉ 'be trained / train (someone)', ⲇⲟⲅⲙⲁⲧⲓⲍⲉ 'subject oneself / teach someone, affirm something', ⲉⲛⲉⲣⲅⲉⲓ 'be active / put to action', ⲉⲩⲫⲣⲁⲛⲉ 'rejoice, be glad / please', ⲍⲱⲅⲣⲁⲫⲉⲓ 'be painted / depict', ⲑⲉⲱⲣⲉⲓ 'look, be like / watch, behold', ⲑⲗⲓⲃⲉ 'be afflicted, oppressed / oppress', ⲕⲁⲑⲁⲣⲓ, ⲕⲁⲑⲁⲣⲓⲍⲉ 'be purified, cleansed / purify', ⲕⲁⲑⲓⲥⲧⲁ 'be appointed / appoint', ⲕⲁⲗⲱⲡⲓⲍⲉ 'be beautiful/ perform, make beautiful', ⲕⲁⲧⲁⲍⲓⲟⲩ 'be deemed worthy / deem worthy', ⲕⲁⲧⲁⲣⲅⲉⲓ 'be abolished / abolish', ⲕⲁⲧⲁⲫⲣⲟⲛⲉⲓ 'be neglected / despise, neglect', ⲕⲁⲧⲉⲭⲉ 'be delayed, wait / delay', ⲕⲁⲧⲟⲣⲑⲟⲩ 'be erect / rectify', ⲕⲉⲣⲁ 'be mixed / mix', ⲕⲟⲗⲗⲁ 'cling, stick to / join (something together)', ⲕⲟⲥⲙⲉⲓ 'be put in order, adorned / adorn', ⲕⲟⲩⲫⲓⲍⲉ 'be diminished / relieve, lessen', ⲗⲩⲡⲉⲓ 'suffer / cause suffer', ⲙⲁⲑⲏⲧⲉⲩⲉ 'be a disciple / make a disciple', ⲛⲏⲫⲉ 'be sober / make sober', ⲡⲁⲓⲇⲉⲩⲉ 'learn / educate', ⲡⲁⲣⲁⲃⲁ 'transgress / mislead', ⲡⲁⲣⲁⲅⲉ 'pass by / lead astray, pervert', ⲡⲁⲣⲁⲙⲩⲑⲓⲍⲉ 'enjoy / comfort, console', ⲡⲉⲓⲣⲁⲍⲉ 'be tempted / tempt', ⲡⲗⲏⲣⲟⲩ 'be full / fulfill, satisfy', ⲥⲁⲗⲉⲩⲉ 'be shaken / shake', ⲥⲕⲁⲛⲇⲁⲗⲓⲍⲉ 'be offended / offend', ⲥⲕⲩⲗⲗⲉⲓ 'take the trouble / give the trouble', ⲥⲧⲉⲫⲁⲛⲟⲩ 'be crowned / crown', ⲥⲧⲟⲗⲓⲍⲉ 'be dressed / dress', ⲥⲩⲛⲁⲅⲉ 'receive communion / give communion', ⲥⲩⲛⲁⲗⲗⲁⲥⲥⲉ 'be changed / change', ⲥⲩⲛⲍⲓⲥⲧⲁ 'consist / assemble', ⲥⲩⲣⲉ 'crawl, drag', ⲥⲭⲏⲙⲁⲧⲓⲍⲉ 'be arranged / arrange', ⲧⲁⲣⲁⲥⲥⲉ 'be troubled / upset, trouble', ⲧⲁⲥⲥⲉ 'be assigned / assign', ⲧⲣⲩⲫⲁ 'delight in / put at ease, make delight', ⲫⲁⲛⲉⲣⲟⲩ 'appear / reveal', ⲍⲁⲣⲙⲟⲍⲉ 'be put together / join', ⲣⲛⲇⲁⲛⲏ 'be pleased / please'[322].

This extensive list gathered from multiple corpora of various ages, genres and authors represents the maximum number of presently known Graeco-Sahidic labile verbs. To assess the number of invariably labile verbs, we can consider two specific corpora, that of Shenoute's Canons and the Sahidic New Testament. As far as could be ascertained, Shenoute's Canons contain only nine labile verbs: ⲁⲩⲍⲁⲛⲉ, ⲑⲗⲓⲃⲉ, ⲕⲟⲥⲙⲉⲓ, ⲗⲩⲡⲉⲓ, ⲡⲁⲓⲇⲉⲩⲉ, ⲡⲁⲣⲁⲅⲉ, ⲡⲉⲓⲑⲉ, ⲡⲗⲁⲛⲁ, ⲥⲕⲁⲛⲇⲁⲗⲓⲍⲉ. The labile set of the New Testament is somewhat more extensive: it includes 16 verbs (ⲁⲩⲍⲁⲛⲉ, ⲃⲁⲡⲧⲓⲍⲉ, ⲃⲁⲥⲁⲛⲓⲍⲉ, ⲅⲩⲙⲛⲁⲍⲉ, ⲉⲛⲉⲣⲅⲉⲓ, ⲉⲩⲫⲣⲁⲛⲉ, ⲑⲗⲓⲃⲉ, ⲕⲁⲧⲁⲣⲅⲉⲓ, ⲕⲁⲧⲉⲭⲉ, ⲕⲉⲣⲁ, ⲕⲟⲥⲙⲉⲓ, ⲗⲩⲡⲉⲓ, ⲡⲁⲣⲁⲅⲉ, ⲡⲉⲓⲑⲉ, ⲡⲗⲁⲛⲁ, ⲥⲕⲁⲛⲇⲁⲗⲓⲍⲉ, ⲥⲕⲩⲗⲗⲉⲓ). The intersection of the two sets consists of 8 verbs and must, in all probability, represent the core of the labile class used similarly in all Sahidic texts.

Further on, let us remember that verbs in Classical Greek and (to a lesser degree) in Koine are diathetically flexible by which I mean that they are generally capable of promoting any argument to the subject position.[323] In other words, passive constructions

---

322 Labile interpretation is somewhat dubious with ⲉⲡⲓⲅⲉ 'be urged, hasten / press, urge (?)', ⲗⲁⲛⲑⲁⲛⲉ 'be confused, ignore / confuse, let ignore', ⲥⲧⲁⲥⲓⲁⲍⲉ 'rise up, rebel / make rebellious (?).

323 "Bei der Umwandlung des Aktivs mit einem Objekte in das Passiv geht nicht nur, wie in anderen Sprachen, der Objekts-Akkusativ in den Subjekts-Nominativ über, z. B. Ἕκτωρ ὑπ᾽ Ἀχιλλέως ἐφονεύθη (akt. Ἀχιλλεὺς ἐφόνευσεν Ἕκτορα), sondern auch Verba mit Objekts-Genetiv oder Dativ können ein persönliches Passiv bilden, so dass also der Genetiv oder Dativ in den NSubjektsnominativ übergeht. So sagt der Grieche: φθονοῦμαι, ἐφθονήθην, φθονήσομαι ὑπό τινος (v. φθονεῖν τινι, invidere alicui), d. h. ich empfange, empfing, werde empfangen Neid von einem, der Lateiner

are not restricted to transitive verbs, but can be formed with intransitive verbs having more than one argument, such as διακονέω or πιστεύω:

(254) Matthew 8:15

καὶ ἠγέρθη καὶ διηκόνει αὐτῷ.

'and she rose and began to serve him'

Matthew 20:28

ὥσπερ ὁ Υἱὸς τοῦ ἀνθρώπου οὐκ ἦλθεν διακονηθῆναι, ἀλλὰ διακονῆσαι καὶ δοῦναι τὴν ψυχὴν αὐτοῦ λύτρον ἀντὶ πολλῶν.

'... even as the Son of Man came not to be served but to serve, and to give his life as a ransom for many.'

(255) John 5:46

εἰ γὰρ ἐπιστεύετε Μωϋσεῖ, ἐπιστεύετε ἂν ἐμοί·

'For if you believed Moses, you would believe me'

2 Thessalonians 1:10

...ὅτι ἐπιστεύθη τὸ μαρτύριον ἡμῶν ἐφ' ὑμᾶς ἐν τῇ ἡμέρᾳ ἐκείνῃ.

'... because our testimony to you was believed.'

Thus, we might expect that labile alternation in Graeco-Sahidic verbal system would not be restricted to transitive verbs but would also include at least some verbs with other valency patterns. As it is, no verbs with non-transitive valency are attested in labile alternation, with one possible exception of ⲕⲟⲓⲛⲱⲛⲉⲓ 'be shared / share, partake in':

(256) Shen.Can. 8, XO 167a, Boud'hors (2013:217)

ϫⲉ ⲁⲧⲉⲧⲛ̄ⲕⲟⲓⲛⲱⲛⲉⲓ̄ ⲉⲛⲉϩⲃⲏⲩⲉ ⲉⲧⲉⲙⲉϣϣⲉ ·

'...because you **have participated in** forbidden actions'

(257) NHC VIII, Zostrianos, 22

ⲁⲩⲱ ϣⲁϥⲕⲟⲓⲛⲱⲛⲓ ⲛ̄ϭⲓ ⲡⲛⲟⲉⲣⲟⲥ ⲛ̄ⲕⲁⲑⲟⲗⲓⲕⲟⲛ· ⲉϣⲁϥϫⲱⲕ ⲉⲃⲟⲗ ⲛ̄ϭⲓ ⲡⲓⲙⲟⲟⲩ ⲛ̄ⲁⲩⲧⲟⲅⲉⲛⲏⲥ·

'The universal intelligence **is shared** when the self-begotten water is completed'

However, the only non-causal attestation of this verb belongs to an obscure text and must be received with caution. Generally, Graeco-Coptic intransitive verbs use other devices of valency alternation, most often the 'impersonal passive' construction:

(258) Matt. 20:28 ⲛ̄ⲑⲉ ⲙ̄ⲡϣⲏⲣⲉ ⲙ̄ⲡⲣⲱⲙⲉ ⲛ̄ⲧⲁϥⲉⲓ ⲁⲛ ⲉⲧⲣⲉⲩⲇⲓⲁⲕⲟⲛⲉⲓ ⲛⲁϥ ⲁⲗⲗⲁ ⲉⲇⲓⲁⲕⲟⲛⲉⲓ ⲁⲩⲱ ⲉϯ ⲛ̄ⲧⲉϥ ⲯⲩⲭⲏ ⲛⲥⲱⲧⲉ ϩⲁϩⲁϩ (cf. the example 254).

Thus, lability of Graeco-Sahidic verbs is of the patient-prominent type and in that respect resembles rather the valency alternation system of target language (Sahidic), than that of the source language (Greek).

---

dagegen: invidetur mihi ab aliquo; πιστεύομαι u. ἀπιστοῦμαι ὑπό τινος (v. πιστεύειν u. ἀπιστεῖν τινι), ich empfange Glauben, keinen Glauben." (Raphael Kühner, Bernhard Gerth, Ausführliche Grammatik der griechischen Sprache, §378). See also Luraghi (2010).

Even the most cursory comparison of Sahidic and Bohairic data suggests that labile alternation has been far less productive in Bohairic. Only a small part of the Bohairic counterparts of the labile set can be found in the digitalized and searchable corpora. It seems that in many cases, Bohairic prefers the native equivalents (ⲁϣⲁⲓ / ⲧⲣⲉ-ⲁϣⲁⲓ for ⲁⲩⲝⲁⲛⲉ 'grow', ϫⲓ / ϯ ωⲙⲥ for ⲃⲁⲡⲧⲓⲍⲉ 'baptize'). As is well known, loan verbs in Bohairic bear Greek morphological markers of voice. Interestingly (and somewhat at variance with the observations published in Funk 2017), those marked with the active infinitive morpheme -ⲓⲛ (e.g., ⲁⲛⲁⲅⲕⲁⲍⲓⲛ, ⲃⲁⲥⲁⲛⲓⲍⲓⲛ, ⲡⲁⲓⲇⲉⲩⲓⲛ, ⲡⲉⲓⲣⲁⲍⲓⲛ, ⲥⲕⲁⲛⲇⲁⲗⲓⲍⲓⲛ) appear to function almost invariably as monodiathetic causatives. If confirmed by further research, this lack of flexibility in the active form might correlate with the more rigorous preservation of the middle-passive form in Bohairic. Presumably, the reduced use of labile alternation in Bohairic is compensated for by other valency changing strategies. E.g., the causative ⲑⲣⲉ- will possibly occur in Bohairic with far greater frequency than in Sahidic.

3.5.3.2 Looking for lability triggers: frequency, semantics, diathesis in the source language

The small percentage of labile verbs indicates that lability was not the dominant strategy of voice alternation for loan verbs in Sahidic, or else that loan verbs were generally less liable to valency alternations than the native vocabulary. If this strategy was nevertheless preferred in some cases, this could theoretically result from multiple reasons, such as the influence of the source language or certain semantic properties of the verbs in the labile set. Alternatively, one could assume that lability as a less marked and more versatile alternation model resulted from equally frequent use of a lexeme in both causative and non-causative senses.[324] Let us examine the respective influence of each factor on the choice of labile type of alternation.

1) 'Spin' frequency

The choice of a lighter pattern of valency change marking may correlate with the frequency of this change or can even be triggered by this frequency. The following procedure has been devised in order to test this conjecture. For 15 randomly picked verbs of the labile class, we count the ratio of non-causative tokens to the overall number of tokens.[325] For 15 randomly picked transitive verbs of the non-labile class, we count the ratio of the impersonal passive tokens to the overall number of tokens.[326] This ratio which may

324 On the relation between frequency and markedness, see Haspelmath (2008b), Greenberg (1966).

325 All the numbers correspond to the DDGLC data, as of 11.11.2020.

326 Thus, we ignore the impersonal passive tokens of the labile verbs. However, this does not influence the results, since adding these tokens could only strengthen our conjecture. We also do not examine the non-labile verbs with non-transitive valency patterns, since it has been observed that the labile class does not include verbs with non-transitive valency of the causal alternant. Finally, labile verbs are not juxtaposed to non-labile intransitive verbs that use the morpheme ⲧⲣⲉ- as a causativization marker. This procedure is considered superfluous for our purposes and is left for some further study.

be dubbed 'spin frequency' will show the average inclination of each group to passive
diathesis. We predict that this ratio will be significantly higher in the labile group. The
table below displays the labile and the non-labile verbs with their respective number of
occurrences and of non-causative tokens.

Table 11 | Non-causative token ratio for labile and non-labile Greek loan verbs

Class of verbs	Verbal lexeme	Non-causative / impersonal passive tokens	Overall occurrences
Labile	ⲁⲩⲍⲁⲛⲉ	38	65
	ⲃⲁⲡⲧⲓⲍⲉ	10	88
	ⲃⲁⲥⲁⲛⲓⲍⲉ	16	67
	ⲉⲩⲫⲣⲁⲛⲉ	80	98
	ⲍⲱⲅⲣⲁⲫⲉⲓ	5	20
	ⲑⲗⲓⲃⲉ	32	90
	ⲕⲉⲣⲁ	7	22
	ⲕⲟⲗⲗⲁ	4	11
	ⲕⲟⲥⲙⲉⲓ	19	60
	ⲕⲟⲩⲫⲓⲍⲉ	2	7
	ⲛⲏⲫⲉ	73	84
	ⲡⲗⲏⲣⲟⲩ	9	26
	ⲥⲁⲗⲉⲩⲉ	2	5
	ⲧⲁⲥⲥⲉ	2	15
	ⲋⲁⲣⲙⲟⲍⲉ	5	6
Non-labile	ⲁⲑⲉⲧⲉⲓ	2	49
	ⲉⲡⲁⲓⲛⲟⲩ	1	30
	ⲑⲁⲗⲡⲉⲓ	1	8
	ⲑⲩⲥⲓⲁⲍⲉ	0	119
	ⲕⲁⲧⲁⲗⲁⲗⲉⲓ	2	45
	ⲕⲱⲗⲩⲉ	8	131
	ⲟⲓⲕⲟⲛⲟⲙⲉⲓ	1	64
	ⲡⲁⲣⲁⲇⲓⲇⲟⲩ	8	68
	ⲡⲁⲧⲁⲥⲥⲉ	0	58
	ⲥⲕⲉⲡⲁⲍⲉ	5	52
	ⲥⲧⲁⲩⲣⲟⲩ	39	142
	ⲥⲫⲣⲁⲅⲓⲍⲉ	3	171
	ⲫⲟⲣⲉⲓ	1	191
	ⲋⲉⲣⲙⲏⲛⲉⲩⲉ	19	43
	ⲋⲩⲡⲟⲙⲛⲓⲍⲉ	0	3

The average ratio of the labile group is ~0.415. The average ratio of the non-labile group is ~0.085. The number of passive occurrences for labile verbs is thus about 5 times as great as that for the non-labile sample which confirms our initial suggestion. However, the sheer frequency of diathetic switches does not guarantee that the verb in question becomes labile. Labile usage is not attested, e.g., for ⲥⲧⲁⲩⲣⲟⲩ 'crucify' and ϩⲉⲣⲙⲏⲛⲉⲩⲉ 'interpret' (19 non-causal to 43 overall attestations and 39 to 142 attestations, respectively). The fact that both of them belong to the literary variety of Sahidic suggests that the spoken language might have been more prone to introduce labile usages.

2) Source diathesis pattern

Now, let us check the assumption that the diathetic properties of a Graeco-Coptic verb are derived from or, at least, influenced by its Greek correlate. Broadly taken, this hypothesis predicts that the prototypes of the labile group will generally have more diathetic flexibility, than those of the Graeco-Coptic monodiathetic class. A necessary prerequisite for testing this idea would be a full diathetic chart of all Greek verbs that were borrowed into Coptic. The chart, moreover, should be tailored to include all voice alterations that were attested in the era of Koine, and only such alternations. At present, such reference base is but a desideratum. The data in the dictionaries, such as Liddell-Scott (1996), cannot be relied upon, first because morphological variants are not time-classified, and secondly, because the presence of a morphological variant in the dictionary does not tell anything about its mode of use. The most exhaustive study of diachronic voice alternations in Greek, Lavidas (2009), marks important tendencies, but does not offer any sort of 'voice vocabulary' our test requires. The following analysis is therefore confined to very uncertain preliminary observations that can at best propose some questions to be answered by future studies. For each prototype of the labile group and for a random sample of the prototypes of the monodiathetic class, we provide a form-diathesis distribution pattern based on the data from the Strong's New Testament Concordance and the digitalized documentary papyri. The two lists, the 'labile' and the 'monodiathetic' one, are then compared to each other and to their Coptic parallels, respectively.

Table 12 | Diathetic patterns of Koine verbs

Pattern number	Morphological shape	Diathetic pattern	Examples
1	active / active and middle ~ passive	causative ~ non-causative	κατέχω delay – wait, be delayed
2	mostly active	causative	καταφρονέω despise, neglect
3	active	non-causative	διστάζω hesitate
4	active ~ active and middle-passive	causative ~ non-causative	παράγω lead astray – pass by
5	active and middle-passive	non-causative	αὐξάνω grow

One thing that leaps to the eye is the absence of the purely labile model where the active form would correspond to both causative and non-causative diatheses. Labile usage is 'embedded' in model 4, where the active form stands for both meanings, but even here the middle-passive can regularly express the non-causative meaning. Thus, the assumption that lability of a verb in Coptic is caused by the lability of its prototype in Greek must be rejected.

Of the verbs belonging to the labile class in Sahidic, pattern 1 adequately describes 32 lexemes (ἀναλίσκω, ἀναγκάζω, ἁρμόζω, βαπτίζω, βασανίζω, βεβαιόω, δογματίζω, εὐφραίνω, θλίβω, καθαιρέω + καθαρίζω, καθίστημι, καταξιόω, καταργέω, κατέχω, κολλάω, κοσμέω, κουφίζω, λυπέω, μαθητεύω[327], παιδεύω, πειράζω, πληρόω, σαλεύω, σκανδαλίζω, σκύλλω, στεφανόω, στολίζω, συναλλάσσω, συνίστημι, ταράσσω, φανερόω, ὑποτάσσω), pattern 2 describes 3 lexemes (καταφρονέω, κοινωνέω, τάσσω), pattern 3 describes 3-4 lexemes (νήφω, παραβαίνω, τρυφάω, less certainly σχηματίζω[328]), pattern 4 describes παράγω, pattern 5 describes αὐξάνω. Four verbs, γυμνάζω, ζωγραφέω, κατορθόω and κεράννυμι, by and large seem to follow pattern 1, but mostly with finite active and non-finite (participle) passive forms. Finally, for two verbs, ἡδάνω and παραμυθίζω, no unambiguous Greek equivalents were found.[329] Consequently, the verbs of pattern 1 constitute about 68% of the labile group. I hypothesize that the share of this type of verbs in the non-labile class may be significantly smaller, as opposed to the pattern 2 and pattern 3 verbs (causative and non-causative verbs with active morphology). A random sample of the prototypes of the Sahidic monodiathetic class, indeed, yields a much larger percentage (50% or more) of these two types of verbs. A full statistical analysis of the non-labile prototypes lies beyond the scope of the present paper. Still, it is evident that this class also contains many pattern-1 verbs which means that Greek bidiathetic verbs were often borrowed in one diathesis only.

Interestingly, however, the set of labile prototypes proves that the reverse situation was also possible, and Greek monodiathetic verbs could acquire a second diathesis in Coptic. It cannot be claimed with certainty regarding the pattern 2 verbs: after all, the visible absence of the non-causative diathesis in Greek may well be an observer-based fault. But for νήφω 'be sober', παραβαίνω 'pass beside / over, transgress' and τρυφάω 'live luxuriously, be licentious', no causative meaning is attested in the whole corpus of the Greek language. Their causative interpretation illustrated in (259-261) must, therefore, have developed within Coptic itself.

---

327 Κουφίζω and μαθητεύω are represented as labile verbs in Liddell-Scott (1996).

328 Due to very poor attestation in our sources, the diathetic model can be only hypothesized. Moreover, it might well be that any association with the Coptic ⲥⲭⲏⲙⲁⲧⲓⲍⲉ is erroneous, since in Coptic, this verb allegedly has a quite different semantics ("bind as a prisoner" according to DDGLC database, as of 26.10.2020).

329 Lefort (1950) derives ⲣϩⲏⲇⲁⲛⲏ from ἀνδάνω 'be pleased / please, gratify'. However, ἀνδάνω seems to be attested only in the Classical Ionian prose and poetry (Homerus, Euripides, Hipponax, Herodotus); it is absent from LBG. It is, therefore, an open question if ἀνδάνω can be taken as the source form for ⲣϩⲏⲇⲁⲛⲏ. The Greek New Testament correlate of ⲣϩⲏⲇⲁⲛⲏ is συνήδομαι (Romans, 7:22). In its turn, ⲡⲁⲣⲁⲙⲅⲟⲓⲍⲉ seems to be an intra-Coptic formation based on the stem of the Greek παραμυθέομαι, which is not attested in Coptic.

(259) Pistis Sophia, Book 1, 49b

ⲁⲩⲱ **ⲁϥⲛⲏϥⲉ ⲙ̅ⲙⲟ**ï ⲛ̅ϭⲓ ⲡⲉⲕⲡⲛ̅(ⲉⲩⲙ)ⲁ̅ ⲉⲧⲛ̅ⲙ̅ⲙⲁï

'*And as for your spirit which is with me, it made me sober*'

(260) White Mon. - Unknown Anaphora 3, part 1, 115, 2-3

ⲁⲥϫ̈ⲓ ⲉⲃⲟⲗ ϩⲙ ⲡϣⲏⲛ ⲁⲥⲟⲩⲱⲙ **ⲁⲥⲡⲁⲣⲁⲃⲁ ⲙ̅ⲡⲕⲉⲁⲇⲁⲙ** ⲛ̅ⲙⲙⲁⲥ

'*She took from the tree, she ate, she made Adam too transgress with her.*'

(261) Hom. Pass. Res. (M.595), 36v b, 30-37r a, 1, Chapman (1993:89)

ⲉϣⲁⲩⲙⲁⲕⲁⲣⲓⲍⲉ ⲁⲛ ⲙ̅ⲡⲣⲱⲙⲉ ⲉⲧϣⲟⲟⲡ ϩⲛ ⲧⲁⲣⲭⲏ ⲙ̅ⲡⲁⲣⲓⲥⲧⲟⲛ ϫⲉ ⲁϥ**ⲧⲣⲩⲫⲁ**
ⲛ̅ⲛⲉⲛⲧⲁϥⲧⲁϩⲙⲟⲩ

'*Someone who is at the beginning of the banquet-speech is not praised because he has delighted his guests.*'

The potential ability of a borrowed Greek verb to develop a causative reading in Coptic must probably be considered also for cases outside Sahidic. Thus, it is tempting to give causative interpretation to the otherwise syntactically quite confusing instances of the verb ⲁⲛⲉⲭⲉ 'endure, suffer' in the Mesokemic dialect, such as:

(262) Matthew / Scheide 11:22, ms. 145,13-146,4

ⲡⲗⲏⲛ ϯϫⲱ ⲙ̅ⲙⲁⲥ ⲛⲏⲧⲛ· ϫⲉ ⲥⲉⲛⲉⲁⲛⲉⲭⲉ ⲛ̅ⲧⲧⲩⲣⲟⲥ ⲙⲛ ⲧⲥⲓⲇⲱⲛ ϩⲙ̅ ⲡⲉϩⲁⲩ ⲛ̅ⲧⲉⲕⲣⲓⲥⲓⲥ
ⲛ̅ϩⲟⲩⲁ̈ⲉⲓⲥⲧⲉ ⲉⲣⲟⲧⲛ·

πλὴν λέγω ὑμῖν, Τύρῳ καὶ Σιδῶνι ἀνεκτότερον ἔσται ἐν ἡμέρᾳ κρίσεως ἢ ὑμῖν.

'*But I tell you, it will be more bearable on the day of judgment for Tyre and Sidon than for you.*'

Under the usual (non-causative) interpretation of the predicate, the two cities are represented as the stimulus, and not as the patient, in other words, as the thing to be endured rather than the entity that endures. The causative reading of the verb ("they will make Tyre and Sidon endure... rather than you") would better correspond to the original sense.

The above analysis leads to the following conclusions: since Greek monodiathetic verbs constitute, at best, less than 15% of the Graeco-Sahidic labile class, there is an evident correlation between lability in Sahidic and the double, causative and non-causative, diathesis of the source verb. However, there is no evidence that lability in Greek triggered lability in Sahidic. Moreover, there is the principal possibility that a monodiathetic (at least, a non-causative) Greek verb can be reinterpreted as a bidiathetic verb in Sahidic which results in its labile usage.

3) Semantic classes of labile verbs

The previous sections have established that lability of the loan verbs is linked to the frequency of the valency change, but presumably is not directly connected to the diathesis of the source verb. Both phenomena are in themselves not decisive and must therefore be side-effects of some semantic selection that defines the grammar of valency increase / reduction for a specific verb. Here I shall try to find the underlying principle of this selection. Undoubtedly, labile use correlates with ***affectedness of the patient*** which is manifest in the following groups of labile verbs:

a) Verbs of feeling or causing an emotion (ⲁⲡⲟⲣⲉⲓ 'be at a loss, confused / confuse', ⲃⲁⲥⲁⲛⲓⳅⲉ 'be tormented / torment', ⲉⲩⲫⲣⲁⲛⲉ 'be / make glad', ⲑⲗⲓⲃⲉ 'suffer / make suffer', ⲗⲩⲡⲉⲓ 'be / make sad', ⲡⲁⲣⲁⲙⲩⲑⲓⳅⲉ 'enjoy / comfort, console', ⲧⲁⲣⲁⲥⲥⲉ 'be disturbed, worried / disturb', ⲧⲣⲩⲫⲁ 'delight in / put at ease, make delight', ⳉⲛⲇⲁⲛⲏ 'be pleased / please');

b) Verbs denoting some change in physical parameters (ⲁⲩⳅⲁⲛⲉ 'grow (intr.) / grow (trans.)', ⲁⲛⳉⲁⲗⲓⲥⲕⲉ 'be consumed, destroyed / consume', ⲥⲩⲛⲁⲗⲗⲁⲥⲥⲉ 'be changed / change'); here also belong the Greek deadjectival verbs ⲃⲉⲃⲁⲓⲟⲩ 'be confirmed / confirm', ⲕⲁⲑⲁⲣⲓ / ⲕⲁⲑⲁⲣⲓⳅⲉ 'be clean / clean, purify', ⲕⲟⲩⲫⲓⳅⲉ 'be lightened, reduced / reduce', ⲡⲗⲏⲣⲟⲩ 'be fulfilled, satisfied / fill, satisfy');

c) Verbs denoting change in external properties (ⲕⲟⲛⲓⲁ 'be whitewashed / whitewash', ⲕⲟⲥⲙⲉⲓ 'be decorated / ornate', ⲥⲧⲟⲗⲓⳅⲉ 'be dressed / dress', ⲥⲧⲉⲫⲁⲛⲟⲩ 'be crowned / crown');

d) Verbs with the general meaning of joining or uniting different elements: ⲕⲟⲗⲗⲁ 'glue', ⳉⲁⲣⲙⲟⳅⲉ 'unite, join', ⲥⲩⲛⳉⲓⲥⲧⲁ 'be assembled / assemble', ⲕⲉⲣⲁ 'mix'.

Affectedness of the patient, however, cannot be the decisive criterion, since among the verbs that are not attested in the labile use, there are transitives with affected patient, such as ⲡⲁⲣⲁⲇⲓⲇⲟⲩ 'betray', ⲡⲁⲧⲁⲥⲥⲉ 'smite', ⲥⲧⲁⲩⲣⲟⲩ 'crucify', ⲁⲣⲛⲁ 'reject, deny', ⲇⲓⲱⲕⲉⲓ 'pursue, chase', ⲇⲟⲕⲓⲙⲁⳅⲉ 'examine, test, ⲑⲁⲗⲡⲉⲓ 'care for', ⲑⲉⲣⲁⲡⲉⲩⲉ 'heal', ⲕⲁⲧⲁⲗⲁⲗⲉⲓ and ⲇⲓⲁⲃⲁⲗⲗⲉ 'slander', ⲕⲁⲧⲏⲅⲟⲣⲉⲓ 'accuse', ⲕⲣⲓⲛⲉ 'judge', ⲕⲁⲧⲁⲕⲣⲓⲛⲉ 'condemn' ⲕⲱⲗⲩⲉ 'hinder', ⲁⲓⲭⲙⲁⲗⲱⲧⲓⳅⲉ 'take captive', ⲉⳉⲱⲣⲓⳅⲉ 'banish, exile', ⲭⲉⲓⲣⲟⲧⲟⲛⲉⲓ 'ordain, elect', ⳉⲟⲙⲟⲗⲟⲅⲉⲓ 'acknowledge, confess', and many others. Neither does **animacy / inanimacy of the patient** directly determine the mechanism of valency reduction, although a random sample taken from the non-labile group shows that the ratio of the verbs with an inanimate patient to those with an animate one is higher in the labile group (~0.6 in the labile group vs. ~0.3 in the non-labile).[330] A far more essential semantic factor seems to be the necessary presence of an **animate actor** in the semantics of the event, as opposed to a possible spontaneous interpretation. By way of illustration, let us compare two sets of the non-causative correlates of verbs with inanimate patients. The first set consists of verbs attested in the labile alternation; the verbs of the second set belong to the monodiathetic group.

Labile verbs with inanimate patients: ⲁⲛⳉⲁⲗⲓⲥⲕⲉ 'vanish, be consumed', ⲁⲩⳅⲁⲛⲉ 'grow', ⲃⲉⲃⲁⲓⲟⲩ 'be confirmed', ⲕⲟⲗⲗⲁ 'glue together', ⲕⲟⲩⲫⲓⳅⲉ 'become light', ⲥⲁⲗⲉⲩⲉ 'shake', ⲥⲩⲛⳉⲓⲥⲧⲁ 'combine', ⲕⲉⲣⲁ 'mix', ⳅⲱⲅⲣⲁⲫⲉⲓ 'be painted', ⲥⲭⲏⲙⲁⲧⲓⳅⲉ 'be arranged, bound';

---

330 All in all, the verbs with animate, or more precisely human, referents of the second argument constitute the majority in the loan Greek verbal vocabulary, which is indeed a remarkable sociolinguistic fact. One can hypothesize that the restructuring of social relations in the Late Antique Egypt triggered a significant renewal in the corresponding part of the vocabulary.

<u>Monodiathetic verbs with inanimate patients</u>: ⲣⲁⲅⲓⲁⲍⲉ 'consecrate', ⲁⲡⲟⲇⲓⲇⲟⲩ 'give away', ⲁⲡⲟⲥⲉⲑⲧⲓⲍⲉ 'learn by heart', ⲙⲓⲥⲑⲟⲩ 'give in lease', ⲇⲓⲟⲓⲕⲉⲓ 'manage', ⲉⲙⲫⲁⲛⲓⲍⲉ 'show, produce', ⲅⲉⲣⲙⲏⲛⲉⲩⲉ 'translate', ⲉⲩⲡⲟⲣⲉⲓ 'supply, provide'.

With a few exceptions, the verbs of the first set have two possibilities of interpretation, namely, as a result of a volitional action (of an animate actor) or a spontaneously occurring event. The second interpretation is not available for the verbs of the monodiathetic group. Consequently, spontaneity must be singled out as a factor setting off labile alternation.

In some cases, spontaneity is gained as a result of a specific 'staging' of an otherwise agentful verb; this untypical use is the source of the partial lability we mentioned above in 3.5.3.1.

(263) P.MoscowCopt. 55, TM 87164

ⲁⲣⲓ ⲧⲁⲅⲁⲡⲏ ⲛ̄ϭⲃⲱⲕ ⲡⲉⲥⲕⲩⲗⲙⲟⲥ ⲛ̄ⲧⲉⲧⲛ̄ⲉⲓ ⲉⲣⲏⲥ ϫⲉ ⲛ̄ⲉⲕⲕⲗⲏⲥⲓⲁ **ⲕⲁⲧⲁⲫⲣⲟⲛⲏ**

'*Please take the trouble to come south, because the churches **are neglected**.*'

(264) White Mon. - Bread-breaking prayer of Patriarch Severus, 182, 12-15

ⲡⲉⲓⲛⲉ ⲁⲩⲱ ⲡⲉⲭⲁⲣⲁⲕⲧⲏⲣ ⲛ̄ⲧⲉ ⲡⲛ̄ⲟⲩⲧⲉ ⲡⲓⲱ̄ⲧ ⲡ̄ⲣⲏⲛⲉ ⲛⲧⲁϥϯ ⲙⲁⲧⲉ ⲁⲩⲱ **ⲁϥⲣ{ⲁ}ⲕⲁⲧⲁⲍ̈ⲓⲟⲩ**

'*The image and the representation of God, the Father, incense that has pleased and **has proved itself worthy**…*'

The link between lability and spontaneity forms a remarkable contrast in the way Graeco-Sahidic verbs are marked for voice compared to their Koine prototypes. Greek passive form can mark the non-active voice, whether the verb has a non-causative (spontaneous) meaning, as in (265), or a volitional actor is implied, as in (266). Sahidic prefers a labile form in the first case, and an impersonal passive construction in the second.

(265) Matt. 26:33

Εἰ καὶ πάντες σκανδαλισθήσονται ἐν σοί ἐγὼ οὐδέποτε σκανδαλισθήσομαι

ⲉϣϫⲉ ⲥⲉⲛⲁⲥⲕⲁⲛⲇⲁⲗⲓⲍⲉ ⲛ̄ⲣⲏⲧⲕ ⲧⲏⲣⲟⲩ ⲁⲛⲟⲕ ⲇⲉ ⲛ̄ⲧⲛⲁⲥⲕⲁⲛⲇⲁⲗⲓⲍⲉ (sic!) ⲁⲛ ⲉⲛⲉϩ

'*Though they all fall away because of you, I will never fall away.*'

(266) 2Cor. 4:9

διωκόμενοι ἀλλ᾽ οὐκ ἐγκαταλειπόμενοι

ⲉⲩⲇⲓⲱⲕⲉ ⲙⲙⲟⲛ ⲁⲗⲗⲁ ⲉⲛϥⲕⲱ ⲙⲙⲟⲛ ⲁⲛ ⲛⲥⲱϥ

'*(We are…) persecuted, but not forsaken*'

Now, the majority of native lexemes form labile pairs of causative and anticausative counterparts (see 1.3.4.2, 1.3.4.6). In that respect, the valency alternation model of loan verbs aligns with that of the native vocabulary.

The feature of spontaneity has some implications on the aspectual distribution of labile verbs. These implications will be discussed at some length in the next section.

3.5.3.3 Aspect and causativity

Whereas the native Egyptian verbal system displays the morphologically marked opposition between the (non-causative) stative / resultative, the causative eventive, and the non-causative eventive form, the body of loaned labile verbs does not bear any morphological marking of either aspect, or diathesis. That does not rule out the possibility that the subsystem of loan verbs is sensitive to the interplay of the two categories, but this dependence, if it exists, can only be manifested at the syntactic level. Whether or not a given verb shows the link between aspect and diathesis, can be measured by the respective number of the non-causal tokens of this verb in the durative and the eventive tense patterns. In particular, a high incidence of non-causal tokens of a specific lexeme in durative environment and the absence of such tokens in the eventive pattern would signal aspectual-diathetic patterning similar to the one observed with native verbs.

When applied to the class of labile Greek loan verbs, the above test shows that the verbs of the labile class can be divided in two groups. Slightly more than a half of these verbs (25 lexemes) prove to be aspect- and voice-neutral, similarly to the verbs of class A discussed in 3.5.1.3. This group includes: ⲁⲛϩⲁⲗⲓⲥⲕⲉ, ⲁⲛⲁⲅⲕⲁⲍⲉ, ⲁⲩⲝⲁⲛⲉ, ⲃⲁⲡⲧⲓⲍⲉ, ⲕⲁⲑⲁⲣⲓ(ⲍⲉ), ⲕⲁⲑⲓⲥⲧⲁ, ⲕⲁⲧⲁⲝⲓⲟⲩ, ⲕⲁⲧⲁⲣⲅⲉⲓ, ⲕⲁⲧⲉⲭⲉ, ⲕⲁⲧⲟⲣⲑⲟⲩ, ⲕⲟⲗⲗⲁ, ⲕⲟⲩⲫⲓⲍⲉ, ⲗⲩⲡⲉⲓ, ⲛⲏⲫⲉ, ⲡⲁⲓⲇⲉⲩⲉ, ⲡⲁⲣⲁⲃⲁ, ⲡⲁⲣⲁⲅⲉ, ⲡⲉⲓⲣⲁⲍⲉ, ⲡⲗⲏⲣⲟⲩ, ⲥⲁⲗⲉⲩⲉ, ⲥⲕⲁⲛⲇⲁⲗⲓⲍⲉ, ⲧⲁⲣⲁⲥⲥⲉ, ⲫⲁⲛⲉⲣⲟⲩ, ϩⲁⲣⲙⲟⲍⲉ, ϩⲏⲇⲁⲛⲏ. In the other group, there are verbs that have very few or no attestations of eventive non-causal usage (ⲃⲁⲥⲁⲛⲓⲍⲉ, ⲃⲉⲃⲁⲓⲟⲩ, ⲍⲱⲅⲣⲁⲫⲉⲓ, ⲕⲉⲣⲁ, ⲕⲟⲥⲙⲉⲓ, ⲥⲧⲉⲫⲁⲛⲟⲩ, ⲥⲭⲏⲙⲁⲧⲓⲍⲉ) or seem to strongly prefer durative non-causal use over the eventive non-causal one (ⲁⲡⲟⲣⲉⲓ, ⲅⲩⲙⲛⲁⲍⲉ, ⲇⲟⲅⲙⲁⲧⲓⲍⲉ, ⲉⲛⲉⲣⲅⲉⲓ, ⲉⲩⲫⲣⲁⲛⲉ, ⲑⲗⲓⲃⲉ, ⲕⲁⲧⲁⲫⲣⲟⲛⲉⲓ, ⲙⲁⲑⲏⲧⲉⲩⲉ, ⲡⲁⲣⲁⲙⲩⲑⲓⲍⲉ, ⲥⲕⲩⲗⲗⲉⲓ, ⲥⲧⲟⲗⲓⲍⲉ, ⲥⲩⲛϩⲓⲥⲧⲁ, ⲧⲁⲥⲥⲉ, ⲧⲣⲩⲫⲁ).

The observed divergence seems to correlate with two semantic features: the possibility of a spontaneous interpretation for the core event and the lexical (a)telicity of the verb. The aspect-neutral non-causatives are telic unergatives (e.g., ⲡⲁⲓⲇⲉⲩⲉ, ⲡⲁⲣⲁⲃⲁ, ⲡⲁⲣⲁⲅⲉ) and unaccusatives (e.g., ⲕⲟⲗⲗⲁ, ⲕⲟⲩⲫⲓⲍⲉ, ⲗⲩⲡⲉⲓ, ⲛⲏⲫⲉ). Contrastingly, atelic (ⲁⲡⲟⲣⲉⲓ, ⲃⲁⲥⲁⲛⲓⲍⲉ, ⲉⲛⲉⲣⲅⲉⲓ) and agentful (ⲍⲱⲅⲣⲁⲫⲉⲓ, ⲕⲟⲥⲙⲉⲓ, ⲥⲧⲉⲫⲁⲛⲟⲩ) non-causatives show strong preference for durative use. The last type of constraint is far from being self-evident and needs a brief grammatical commentary.

For the purposes of the present research, agentful verbs are non-causative verbs with a necessary volitional, i.e., agentive component in their semantics, although this component may be (and, in the existing attestations, is) never overtly marked. The assessment whether or not a specific verb is agentful, is based solely on its general lexical meaning and is accordingly very rough.[331] However, it proves effective for the ensuing analysis. The notion of agentful verbs is based on the following definition provided in Haspelmath (2016):

> "*AGENTFUL* is an ad hoc term used here for (potential) verb meanings that refer to processes such as 'be cut', 'be washed', 'be beaten', 'be thrown' which are quite difficult to construe as occurring on their own, without an agent, because of agent-oriented manner components in their meaning (i.e. they seem to require reference to an agent in their definition). In this regard, these verb meanings are quite different from unaccusatives such as 'melt', 'sink', 'break (intr.)' and 'change (intr.)'. We can easily

---

331 The precise distinction between non-causative and passive predicates is notoriously difficult. See, e.g., the discussion in Kulikov (1998:140 ff.).

talk about wax melting, a boat sinking, a stick breaking, and a person changing without
thinking of an agent, but when we talk about cutting, washing and throwing, we seem
to necessarily have an agent in mind".[332]

According to this definition, the absence of the feature of spontaneity in their semantics
distinguishes agentful verbs from unaccusatives and may have a bearing on their respective
coding.[333] If, for instance, a language employs a morphological marking for passive
predicates, this marking is more likely to appear on agentful verbs, than on spontaneous
non-causatives, although the differences in marking are seldom or never clear-cut in any
known language.[334] Perhaps, it would be wrong even to regard spontaneity or its absence
as a permanent property of a verbal lexeme; to a greater or lesser degree it is a matter of
the overt realization of syntactic arguments and, as a consequence, of a specific reading
in every single occurrence. Thus, in Russian, (267) has a spontaneous predicate and
is perfectly grammatical, while (268) with the same verb forming a passive predicate
violates the norm.

(267) kniga napisala-s' sama soboj
       book (NOM)   write. PFV:PAST-PASS / ANTICAUS by itself
       'The book was written all by itself'

(268) *kniga napisala-s' Pushkinym
       book (NOM)   write. PFV:PAST-PASS / ANTICAUS Pushkin (INS)
       'The book has been written by Pushkin'

The last example shows that telic past is incompatible with a passive meaning in Russian.
However, the sentence turns perfectly grammatical in either of two cases: 1) the finite
verbal form is replaced by a **resultative** passive participle with the past auxiliary:

(269) kniga byla napisana Pushkinym
       book be:PAST write.PASS.PRT Pushkin (INS)
       'The book has been written by Pushkin'

or 2) the perfective verb is replaced by its **imperfective** (i.e., atelic) counterpart:

(270) kniga pisala-s' Pushkinym shest' let
       book (NOM) write.IPFV:PAST-PASS / ANTICAUS Pushkin (INS) six years
       'Pushkin has been writing this book for six years' (lit.: 'The book was being
       written by Pushkin for six years')

As can be seen from the above examples, Russian verbal grammar makes a link between
two semantic parameters, aspect and 'aspontaneity' (this last one amounting possibly to
the necessary presence of an animate agent in the sememe of the verb). At least, in the
past tense, agentful verbs, or agentful-passive counterparts of transitive verbs can be either
atelic, or resultative, but never eventive telic (in the common terminology of Russian

---

332 Haspelmath (2016:36).
333 Haspelmath (2016:40).
334 See Kulikov (1998) for a thorough discussion.

linguistics, *perfective*). Such constellation of features does not look accidental.[335] Indeed, as indicated in Hopper and Thompson (1980), punctuality and telicity of the verb are associated with transitivity and may resist passive interpretation.

If the Graeco-Coptic agentful verbs avoid the eventive conjugation, this may be ascribed to similar reasons. Like Coptic statives, they have the **passive-resultative** reading in the durative conjugation, as in (271-273):

(271) Great Mysterious, B28, 23-25 (Crégheur 2013:256)

ⲓⲥ ⲇⲉ ⲁϥⲉⲓⲣⲉ ⲙ̄ⲡⲉⲓ̈ⲣ̄(ⲩⲥⲧⲏⲣⲓⲟⲛ) ⲉⲣⲉⲛⲉϥⲙⲁⲑⲏⲧⲏ<ⲥ ⲧⲏ>ⲣⲟⲩ ϭⲟⲟⲗⲉ ⲛ̄ϩⲉ<ⲛ>ϩⲃⲟⲟⲥ ⲛ̄ⲉⲓⲁⲁⲩ **ⲉⲩⲥⲧⲉⲫⲁⲛⲟⲩ** ⲙ̄ⲙⲟⲣⲥⲩⲛⲏ

'*But Jesus performed this mystery while all his disciples were clothed in linen garments and* **crowned** *with myrtle*'

(272) Theodore, f. 68v a, 13-16 (Müller/Uljas 2019:231)

ⲁⲩⲱ ⲛⲉⲣⲉⲡⲇⲓⲁⲃⲟⲗⲟⲥ ϩⲓⲡⲉⲥⲏⲧ ⲛ̄ⲧⲡⲉⲛⲛⲏ **ⲉϥⲥⲭⲏⲙⲁⲧⲓⲍⲉ** ⲛⲑⲉ ⲛⲟⲩⲉⲭⲙⲁⲗⲱⲧⲟⲥ·

'*And the devil was underneath the step,* **bound** *like a prisoner.*'

(273) BL Or. 4868, P.Kru 14

ⲕⲁⲧⲁ ⲧⲉⲓⲡⲣⲁⲥⲓⲥ ⲧⲁⲓ ⲉⲧⲥⲏϩ ⲉⲧ**ⲃⲉⲃⲁⲓⲟⲩ** ⲉⲧϣⲏϣ ϩⲛ ⲟⲩϩⲱⲃ ⲛⲟⲩⲱⲧ ϩⲓⲧⲟⲟⲧⲛ

'*...according to this deed of sale, this one, which is written,* **confirmed,** *and evened in every single matter by us*'

In the eventive conjugation, the same verbs invariably have the causative reading:

(274) Four Creatures, f. 11v a, 29 - b, 3 (Wansink 1991: 35)

ⲁⲡⲉⲛϫⲟⲉⲓⲥ ⲕⲉⲗⲉⲩⲉ ⲛⲁⲛ ⲉⲧⲣⲉⲛϯ ⲛⲧⲟⲟⲧⲕ ⲁⲩⲱ ⲁⲛ**ⲥⲧⲉⲫⲁⲛⲟⲩ** ⲙⲙⲟⲕ

'*Our lord commanded us that we should help you and we* **crowned** *you...*'

(275) Theodore, f. 64v a, 6-9 (Müller/Uljas 2019:226)

ⲑⲉⲱⲇⲱⲣⲟⲥ ⲇⲉ ⲙⲛ ⲡⲉϥⲕⲉϣⲃⲏⲣ ⲗⲉⲟⲛⲧⲓⲟⲥ ⲁⲩ**ⲥⲭⲏⲙⲁⲧⲓⲍⲉ** ⲙⲙⲟϥ·

'*Then Theodore and his friend Leontios* **arranged** *him*'

(276) P.Mon.Epiph., Appendix I 7

ⲁⲛ**ⲃⲉⲃⲁⲓⲟⲩ** ⲇⲉ ⲛ̄ⲧⲉⲡⲣⲁϫⲓⲥ ⲛ̄ⲧⲁⲡⲉⲛⲉⲓⲱⲧ ⲛ̄ⲁⲣⲭⲓⲉⲡⲓⲥⲕⲟⲡⲟⲥ ⲇⲓⲟⲥⲕⲟⲣⲟⲥ ⲧⲁϩⲟ[ⲥ ⲉ]ⲣⲁⲧⲥ̄

'*...we* **confirmed** *the act that our father, the archbishop Dioscorus, upheld.*'

---

335 In Latin, as well as in Russian, morphological passives are only compatible with imperfective aspect ('dicitur'), whereas perfective stems build passives based on resultative participles ('dictum est'). Spontaneous non-causatives, on the other hand, form regular morphological perfect (*cado – cecidi* 'fall'). Of course, such data are too scarce to build theories on. Moreover, they get various explanations in terms of each separate language. So, Gerritsen (1988: 132-136, 163-168) argues that the discussed aspectual constraint in Russian is due to that only 'non-actual' readings are possible with passives in -*sja*, which cannot cover the peculiarity of Latin verbal paradigm. Interestingly, the cognate Bulgarian *se*-passive form is not aspectually constrained, as opposed to invariably telic periphrastic passive with a resultative participle (see Dimitrova-Vulchanova 2012:950). Clearly, the issue of passive-telicity link is in need of further research; the present parallel of Russian and Graeco-Coptic systems is intended as an illustration only and in itself does not explain the complex phenomenon in question.

On the other hand, the non-causal verbs compatible with eventive conjugation mainly denote spontaneous occurrences.

(277) Amazed, MONB. HB 28 b:24-29 (Cristea 2011:150)
ⲙⲏ ⲉⲣϣⲁⲛ ⲡⲣⲱⲙⲉ ⲉ̄ⲓ ⲁⲛ ⲉⲃⲟⲗ ϩⲙ ⲑⲏ ⲛ̄ϥⲁⲩϫⲁⲛⲉ ϩⲙ̄ ⲡⲉⲓⲙⲁ ⲛ̄ϣⲱⲡⲉ · ⲏ̄ ⲛϥⲣ̄ ⲉⲩⲥⲉⲃⲏⲥ ⲏ̄ ⲛ̄ϥⲣ̄ ⲁⲥⲉⲃⲏⲥ *'Pray tell, if the person were not to exit the womb and **grow up** in this dwelling place, would he be acting piously or impiously?'*

(278) CG 8737 - P.KRU 97, 7-10
ⲁⲡⲇⲓⲁⲃⲟⲗⲟⲥ ⲡⲉϩⲧ ⲡⲛϣⲏⲣⲉ ⲉⲧⲙⲙⲁⲩ ⲉϩⲟⲩⲛ ⲉⲡⲕⲱϩⲧ ⲁϥⲣⲱⲕϩ ⲛⲥⲁⲃⲏⲗ ϫⲉ ⲁⲛⲣ ⲡⲙⲉⲩⲉ ⲛ̄ⲡⲙⲁ ⲉⲧⲟⲩⲁⲁⲃ ⲁⲛⲥⲡⲥⲱⲡϥ ⲛⲙⲟⲛ **ⲁϥⲁⲛϩⲁⲗⲓⲥⲕⲉ** *'The devil cast our son into the fire, and he would have burned up, had we not remembered the holy place, we beseeched him, lest **he would have perished**.'*

(279) NHC VII, ParShem 6,23-29
ⲡⲑⲁⲩⲙⲁ ⲇⲉ ⲙ̄ⲡ{ⲑⲁⲩⲙⲁ}ⲟⲩⲟⲉⲓⲛ ⲁϥⲛⲟⲩⲟⲩϩ ⲙ̄ⲡⲃⲁⲣⲟⲥ **ⲁϥⲣ̄ⲕⲟⲗⲗⲁ** ⲉⲧⲕⲗⲟⲟⲗⲉ ⲙ̄ⲫⲩⲙⲏⲛ *'And the Astonishment (of the) light cast off the burden. It **stuck** to the cloud of the Hymen.'*

(280) Pistis Sophia, Book 1, 96b
ⲁⲩϥⲓ ⲡⲁⲟⲩⲟⲓ̈ⲛ ⲙ̄ⲛ ⲧⲁϭⲟⲙ · ⲁⲩⲱ ⲁⲧⲁϭⲟⲙ **ⲥⲁⲗⲉⲩⲉ** ϩⲓϩⲟⲩⲛ ⲙ̄ⲙⲟⲓ̈ · *'They took my light and my power. My power **was shaken** inside me.'*

The only two exceptions seem to be ⲃⲁⲡⲧⲓⲍⲉ 'be baptized' and ⲡⲗⲏⲣⲟⲩ 'be satisfied', both of them agentul verbs.

(281) Antiphonary, 6, 24-25
ⲛⲉⲛⲧⲁⲩⲃⲁⲡⲧⲓ̈ⲍⲉ ⲉⲡⲉⲭⲥ̄ · ⲁⲩⲧ̄ ⲙ̄ⲡⲉⲭⲥ̄ ϩⲓ̈ⲱⲟⲩ · *'Those who **have been baptized** to Christ, they have taken Christ upon them.'*

(282) Pushkin Museum I.1.b.682, P.MoscowCopt. 1
ⲁⲓ̈ϫⲓ **ⲁⲓ̈ⲡⲗⲏⲣⲟⲩ ⲛ̄ⲧⲟⲟⲧⲕ̄** ϩⲁ ⲡⲉϥⲟ[ⲣ]ⲟⲥ ⲛ̄ⲧⲥⲉ[ⲧⲉⲓⲱϩⲉ] *'I have received and I **have been satisfied by you** for the rent of the aroura of land...'*

If a verb allows for both a passive and a spontaneous interpretation, these may eventually become quite dissimilar, as in the case of ⲥⲩⲛϩⲓⲥⲧⲁ which means 'be constituted' as a (non-spontaneous) resultative and 'thicken' as (spontaneous) eventive verb:

(283) Berliner "Koptisches Buch", 69 (Schenke Robinson 2004:139)
ⲉϥⲥⲩ[ⲛ]ϩⲓⲥⲧⲁ ⲉⲃⲟⲗ [ϩⲙ̄ ⲡⲉⲥⲛ]ⲁⲩ ⲧⲉⲯⲩⲭ[ⲏ] ⲛⲙ̄ ⲡⲥⲱⲙⲁ *'...**being constituted** out of both the soul and the body...'*

(284) P.Méd.Copt. IFAO, 246-247, Chassinat (1921:238)
ⲟⲩⲛ̄ⲡⲗⲁⲥⲧⲣⲟⲛ ⲉⲧⲃⲉ ⲛⲉϣⲱ ⲁⲗⲟⲥ ⲁⲙⲙⲟⲛⲓⲁⲕⲟⲩ (ⲇⲣⲁⲭⲙⲏ) ⲏ̄ ⲗⲩⲑⲁⲗⲅⲩⲣⲟⲛ (ⲇⲣⲁⲭⲙⲏ) ⲇ̄ ⲥⲧⲉⲡⲧⲉⲣⲓⲁⲥ (ⲇⲣⲁⲭⲙⲏ) ⲓ̄ⲉ ⲟⲩⲗⲁⲕ ⲛ̄ⲛⲉϩ (ⲙ)ⲙⲉ ⲡⲉⲥⲧⲟⲩ ⲕⲁⲗⲱⲥ **ϣⲁⲛⲧⲉⲩⲥⲏⲛϩⲓⲥⲧⲁ** *'A plaster against psora: desert salt: (drachm) 8, litharge: (drachm) 4, alum: (drachm) 15, a small bowl of olive oil: Boil them well, until they **thicken**.'*

The second category of aspect-sensitive labiles are the verbs whose non-causative counterpart is atelic. Depending on the lexeme, this feature can be less or more persistent.
Thus, rather unpredictably, ⲁⲡⲟⲣⲉⲓ 'be confused' may at times read as 'become confused',
whereas ⲃⲁⲥⲁⲛⲓⲍⲉ 'be in pains' is attested in the atelic reading only.

(285) Hom. Pass. Res. (M.595), 34v a,21-25, Chapman (1993:87)
ⲛⲧⲉⲣⲉⲡⲓⲗⲁⲧⲟⲥ ⲇⲉ ⲁⲡⲟⲣⲉⲓ ⲛϥⲧⲙϭⲛ ⲁⲡⲟⲗⲟⲅⲓⲁ ⲉϫⲱ ⲁϥⲛⲉϫ ⲧⲗⲟⲓϭⲉ ⲉϫⲛ ⲛⲓⲟⲩⲇⲁⲓ
'And when Pilate **was dumbstruck** and was unable to find any response to speak,
he cast blame on the Jews...'

(286) NHC XIII, Protennoia, 43, 27-29
ⲧⲟⲧⲉ ⲁⲩⲟⲩⲱϣⲃ ⲛϭⲓ ⲛⲇⲩⲛⲁⲙⲓⲥ ⲉⲩϫⲱ ⲙⲙⲟⲥ ϫⲉ ⲁⲛⲟⲛ ϩⲱⲱⲛ ⲧⲛ̄ⲣ̄ⲁⲡⲟⲣⲓ ⲉⲧⲃⲏⲧϥ` ϫⲉ
ⲙⲡⲛ̄ⲙ̄ⲙⲉ ϫⲉ ⲡⲁ ⲛⲓⲙ ⲡⲉ
'Then, the powers responded, saying, "we, too, **are puzzled** about this, for we did
not know to whom it belongs.'

(287) P.Méd.Copt. IFAO 362, Chassinat (1921:297)
ⲟⲩⲃⲁⲗ ⲉϥⲃⲁⲥⲁⲛⲓⲍⲉ ⲕⲁⲗⲟⲥ ⲉϥⲟ ⲛ̄ϩⲣⲉⲩⲙⲁ
'An eye that **hurts** very much while it suffers from flux...'

The causatives of atelic labiles are not aspectually restricted and occur in both eventive
and durative conjugations.

The constraints on the conjugation pattern apply not only to atelic labile verbs, but
also to several atelic monodiathetics, such as ⲕⲓⲛⲇⲩⲛⲉⲩⲉ 'be in danger, be liable', ⲛⲏⲥⲧⲉⲩⲉ
'fast', ⲕⲁⲧⲟⲓⲕⲓ 'dwell', ⲭⲣⲉⲱⲥⲧⲉⲓ 'be indebted, owe' and some others. Being compatible
with durative pattern only, these verbs are structurally equivalent to Egyptian stative verbs,
e.g., ⲡⲣⲉⲥⲣⲁⲥⲧ 'be stiff', ⲗⲟⲟϭⲉ 'be prone to fall, decadent'.

(288) Hom. Pass. Res. (M.595), 28v a,32-28v b,2, Chapman (1993:80)
ⲧⲡⲟⲗⲓⲥ ⲉⲧⲉⲙⲛ ⲣⲱⲙⲉ ⲛϩⲏⲧⲥ ⲡⲣⲣⲟ ⲉⲧⲁⲣⲭⲉⲓ ⲉϫⲱⲥ ⲕⲩⲛⲇⲩⲛⲉⲩⲉ ϫⲉ ⲛⲛⲉⲛⲃⲁⲣⲃⲁⲣⲟⲥ
ⲧⲟⲣⲡⲥ ⲛⲧⲟⲟⲧϥ
'The king who rules over the city with nobody in it **is in danger**, lest the barbarians
capture it from him.'

(289) Encomium on John the Baptist, Budge (1913:131)
ⲉϣⲱⲡⲉ ⲉⲩϣⲁⲛⲃⲱⲕ ⲛⲁⲩ ⲉⲩⲛⲏⲥⲧⲉⲩⲉ ⲛⲧⲉⲓϩⲉ • ⲥⲉⲛⲁⲥⲱϣⲙ̄ ϩⲓ ⲧⲉϩⲓⲏ •
'If they go while **fasting** like this, they shall faint on the road'

(290) Pistis Sophia, Book 2, 233b[336]
ⲁⲩⲱ ⲛⲉⲧⲙ̄ⲡϣⲁ ⲛ̄ⲛⲙⲩⲥⲧⲏⲣⲓⲟⲛ ⲉⲧⲕⲁⲧⲟⲓⲕⲓ ϩⲙ̄ ⲡⲁⲧϣⲁϫⲉ ⲉⲣⲟϥ • ⲉⲧⲉⲛⲧⲟⲟⲩ <ⲛ>ⲉ
ⲉⲧⲉⲙ̄ⲡⲟⲩⲡⲣⲟⲉⲗⲑⲉ ⲉⲃⲟⲗ •
'And those who are worthy of mysteries which **dwell** in the Ineffable which did not
come forth'

---

336 The verb 'dwell' is attested from one source only, Pistis Sophia; the aspectual restrictions on this
lexeme are in need of further clarification.

(291) BL Or. 4879 - P.KRU 16

ⲁⲕⲛ ⲅⲉⲛⲁⲥⲫⲁⲗⲓⲁ ⲁⲃⲟⲗ ⲉⲣⲟⲓ ⲉⲣⲉⲅⲣⲁⲭⲏⲗ ⲧⲁⲥⲅⲓⲙⲉ **ⲭⲣⲉⲟⲥⲧⲉ** ⲛⲏⲕ ⲛ̄ⲱ̄ⲙⲟⲩⲛ ⲛ̄ⲧⲣⲙⲏⲥⲓⲟⲛ

'You have brought forth certain declarations of indebtedness against me (showing)
*that Rachel my wife **owes** you eight trimesia.'*

We can now summarize the aspectual properties of Greek-origin verbs and compare them
with those of native verbs. As we remember, Coptic has one labile verb form, absolute
infinitive, that has three functions:

intransitive eventive infinitive	ⲁ-ϥ-ⲟⲩⲱⲛ	'he / it opened' (anticausative)
transitive eventive infinitive	ⲁ-ϥ-ⲟⲩⲱⲛ ⲙ-ⲡ-ⲣⲟ	'he opened the door'
transitive durative infinitive	ϥ-ⲟⲩⲱⲛ ⲙ-ⲡ-ⲣⲟ	'he opens the door'

This form can never function as resultative.

The distribution of Graeco-Coptic labiles looks different. Depending on whether the
verb is interpreted as spontaneous or agentive, it includes the following functions.

Spontaneous verbs:

intransitive eventive infinitive	ⲁ-ϥ-ⲁⲛⲅⲁⲗⲓⲥⲕⲉ	'he / it was consumed'
transitive eventive infinitive	ⲁ-ϥ-ⲁⲛⲅⲁⲗⲓⲥⲕⲉ ⲙⲙⲟ=ϥ	'he consumed it'
intransitive durative infinitive (often with resultative reading)	ϥ-ⲁⲛⲅⲁⲗⲓⲥⲕⲉ	'he is (being) consumed'
transitive durative infinitive	ϥ-ⲁⲛⲅⲁⲗⲓⲥⲕⲉ ⲙⲙⲟ=ϥ	'he consumes it'

Agentive verbs:

transitive eventive infinitive	ⲁ-ϥ-ⲥⲧⲉⲫⲁⲛⲟⲩ ⲙⲙⲟ=ϥ	'he crowned him'
intransitive durative infinitive (resultative)	ϥ-ⲥⲧⲉⲫⲁⲛⲟⲩ	'he is crowned'
transitive durative infinitive	ϥ-ⲥⲧⲉⲫⲁⲛⲟⲩ ⲙⲙⲟ=ϥ	'he crowns him'

The functional patterns of native Egyptian and Greek forms do not coincide. Rather,
Coptic conjugation patterns function as derivational templates that modify the general
meaning of a Greek lexeme, as they do with native stems. Whether a certain lexeme is
compatible with either conjugation pattern, is defined by the semantic properties of the
lexeme, namely, agentivity / spontaneity and telicity / atelicity.

3.5.3.4 Class C: Summary

Loan verb lability: general parameters

The class of labile verbs constitutes a minority among all attested Greek verbal lexemes in
Sahidic. The core of this class are some 8-9 verbs that are equally often used as causatives
and non-causatives, irrespective of the corpus. The rest are mostly partially labile verbs,

i.e., causatives with sporadic non-causative usages in specific corpora, or vice versa. At present, there are altogether 54 lexemes attested in labile use in Sahidic. However, new data might expand this list, since the very irregularity of labile usages proves the mechanism of lability to be productive in this dialect.

The non-active alternants in the labile pairs belong to two diathetic classes: non-causatives and passives. Passive lability is not unusual in African languages[337], occasional labile pairs of active-passive meaning are also attested in the native vocabulary of Coptic. Yet, the majority of the labile class, for loan verbs, as well as for native ones, consists of causative-anticausative pairs.

Only syntactically transitive verbs (with one possible exception of ⲕⲟⲓⲛⲱⲛⲉⲓ 'be shared / partake in') participate in labile alternation. The rest of bi- and trivalent verbs employ morphosyntactic instruments of valency change. These alternative instruments are the so-called 'impersonal passive construction' and the causative prefix ⲧⲣⲉ-. The first one is used to demote the agent by inserting an impersonal 3rd person plural pronoun in subject position. Thus, it does not reduce the syntactic valency of the verb, but effectively reduces the semantic one, yielding a passive reading. The causative prefix increases the valency adding a causer. Any of the two mechanisms can be used alternatively to lability, as can possibly also suppletion, which is however rather difficult to trace down. Some lexemes allow for several valency-changing tools. Such is the case of ϩⲩⲡⲟⲧⲁⲥⲥⲉ 'submit to'.

There is no evident correlation between the membership in the labile class and the morphosyntactic properties of the prototype lexeme in the source language. Rather, lability correlates with the possibility of spontaneous interpretation of the event coded by the verbal lexeme. In other words, for a loan verb to be labile, the core event must be construable with, as well as without an animate actor. The animacy of the second actant does not seem to play any role, although primary tests show that inanimate patients are more likely to form labile pairs, than monodiathetic ones. In some cases, such as ⲛⲏⲫⲉ 'to make / become sober', Sahidic creates a causative doublet to an originally monodiathetic non-causative Greek verb. One side effect of lability is an approximately equal number of causative and non-causative tokens of the same lexeme.

Semantic classes of labile verbs

Some of labile verbs can be sorted into various semantic classes, such as verbs of causing / experiencing an emotion, verbs of change in physical parameters or external properties, verbs with general meaning of joining. This classification must be considered tentative, due to semantic diversity of the class; yet, it has cross-linguistic parallels. So, according to Gianollo (2014), verbs meaning 'to join' and its opposite, and verbs meaning 'to change', 'to become different', among them deadjectival verbs, constitute a large part of the labile inventory in Late Latin[338]. There are also some intersections with the semantic classes of labiles listed in Letuchiy (2010:248). On the other hand, the absence of motion and spatial

337 See Cobbinah & Lüpke (2009) for Mande languages, Letuchiy (2006) for typological analysis and some specific examples.

338 Gianollo (2014:971 ff.).

configuration verbs in Graeco-Coptic labile inventory is not very meaningful, since such verbs are generally underrepresented among the loan verbal forms.

ⲁⲣⲭⲉⲓ: issue of phasal verb lability

Similarly, almost no phasal verbs were loaned to Coptic from Greek. The only instance of a phasal verb seems to be ⲁⲣⲭⲉⲓ / ⲁⲣⲭⲉⲥⲑⲁⲓ 'begin'. A unique morphosyntactic behavior of this verb has earned it a separate section in W.-P. Funk's survey of the diathesis of Greek loan verbs in Coptic.[339] According to Funk, the Southern dialects have adopted the form~meaning dichotomy between the active and the passive voice: ἄρχειν 'rule' vs. ἄρχεσθαι 'begin' that had developed in Koine. Later on, however, the suffixed form has eventually been replaced by the shorter one even in the phasal meaning, which, as Funk claims, was rather the result of "scrupulous editing", rather than of a natural linguistic process.

To this account, a few details concerning the diathesis of both verbs must be added. In Sahidic, ⲁⲣⲭⲉⲓ 'rule' and ⲁⲣⲭⲉⲓ / ⲁⲣⲭⲉⲥⲑⲁⲓ 'begin' function as homonyms. ⲁⲣⲭⲉⲓ as 'rule' is monodiathetic active, whereas ⲁⲣⲭⲉⲓ and ⲁⲣⲭⲉⲥⲑⲁⲓ as phasal verbs are bidiathetic, mostly reading as 'start doing something', but also possible in the spontaneous meaning 'have a beginning, start being'.

Spontaneous:

(292) Nag Hammadi Codex V, (Second) Apocalypse of James, 58, 11-13
ⲁⲩⲱ ⲡⲁⲗⲓⲛ ⲉϥⲉϯ [ⲛ̄ⲟⲩ]ϫⲱⲕ ⲉⲃⲟⲗ ⲛ̄ⲧⲉ ⲛⲏ [ⲉⲧ]ⲁⲩⲣ̄ⲁⲣⲭⲉⲓ ⲙ̄ⲛⲛ ⲟⲩⲁⲣⲭⲏ ⲛ̄ⲧⲉ ⲛⲏ ⲉⲧⲛⲁϫⲱⲕ ⲉⲃⲟⲗ•
'*And furthermore, he shall furnish an ending of the things which **have begun**, and a beginning of the things which are to end.*'

(293) Wisdom of Jesus Christ, 96, 5-8, Till/Schenke (1972:232)
ⲉⲃⲟⲗ ⲅⲁⲣ ϩⲙ̄ ⲡⲓⲛⲟⲩⲧⲉ ⲁⲥⲁⲣⲭⲉⲥⲑⲁⲓ ⲛ̄ϭⲓ ⲧⲙ̄ⲛ̄ⲧⲛⲟⲩⲧⲉ ⲙⲛ̄ ⲧⲙ̄ⲛ̄ⲧⲣ̄ⲣⲟ
'*For with this god, the godliness and dominion **began**...*'

Active:

(294) To Herai, 385 (Kuhn 1956:102, 34)
ⲁⲡⲓⲣⲱⲙⲉ ⲁⲣⲭⲉⲓ ⲛ̄ⲕⲱⲧ. ⲙ̄ⲡϥⲉϣϭⲙϭⲟⲙ ⲉϫⲟⲕϥ̄ ⲉⲃⲟⲗ•
'*This man **started** building but was not able to complete it.*'

(295) Apologia de incrudelitate, Crum (195:38)
ⲛ̄ⲧⲉ[ⲣ]ⲉⲡϩⲁⲅⲓⲟⲥ ⲁⲩⲱ ⲡⲕⲩⲛⲏⲅⲟⲥ ⲟⲩⲃⲉ [ⲛ]ⲇⲁⲓⲙⲱⲛ ⲁⲃⲃⲁ ⲉⲩⲁⲅⲣⲓⲟⲥ ⲁⲣ[ⲭ]ⲉⲥⲑⲁⲓ ⲉⲧⲁⲩⲉ ⲛⲉϩⲃⲏⲩⲉ ⲙ̄ⲡⲟⲩⲁ ⲡⲟⲩⲁ ⲛ̄ⲛ̄ⲇⲁⲓⲙⲱⲛ ϩⲛ̄ ⲛⲉϥⲕⲉⲫⲁⲗⲁⲓⲟⲛ ⲁϥϫⲟⲟⲥ ϫⲉ
'*...when the saint and the huntsman of the demons, Abba Evagrius, **began** narrating the works of each and everyone of the demons in his Kephalaia, he said...*'

---

339 Funk (2017:380-381).

(296) Historia Ecclesiastica, Orlandi (1968:42)

ⲁϥⲣⲁϣⲉ ⲁⲩⲱ ⲁϥⲥⲣⲁⲓ ⲉⲁϥⲁⲣⲭⲉⲓ ⲉⲛⲥⲩⲛⲧⲁⲅⲙⲁ ⲉⲧⲟⲩⲁⲁⲃ

*'he rejoiced and wrote, **starting** with holy treatises...'*

(297) Colluthus, f. 96v, Chapman / Depuydt (1993:39)

ⲧⲓⲛⲁⲁⲣⲭⲓⲥⲑⲉ ⲉ·ⲡⲉⲕⲉⲅⲕⲱⲙⲓⲟⲛ ⲕⲁⲧⲁ ⲑⲉ ⲛⲧⲁⲡⲉⲭ̅ⲥ̅ ⲭⲟⲣⲏⲅⲉⲓ ⲛⲁⲓ ⲙⲡⲁⲗⲁⲥ ⲉⲧⲅⲁⲝⲃ

*'...I will **begin** your encomium according as Christ has provided me with my humble tongue.'*

As can be seen from the above examples, the relation between the active and the spontaneous meaning of ⲁⲣⲭⲉⲓ is not the canonical causative one. Letuchiy (2013) shows that agentivity is neither necessarily present in the sememe of the active verb 'to begin (something)', nor necessarily absent from the sememe of the spontaneous 'to start'. Thus, the phrase 'the sermon started' does not mean that the sermon started all by itself, whereas 'the city began its growth by 200 B.C.' or 'the union began to fall apart' lacks an agent. However, in many languages, such as Russian, phasal verbs are coded as transitives, due to a certain semantic affinity between the phasal and the causative type of diathetic variation.[340] Not so in Sahidic. Here, apart from two occurrences, both of them in the Discourse of the Eighth and the Ninth (Nag Hammadi Codex VI), ⲁⲣⲭⲉⲓ / ⲁⲣⲭⲉⲓⲥⲑⲁⲓ is not attested within the transitive valency pattern. It mostly takes ⲉ- with nominal arguments, ⲉ- or ⲛ- with sentencial actants.[341] Consequently, the diathetic variance shown by this verb differs from the labile one.

Aktionsart of loan verbs

The idea that the native Egyptian verbal vocabulary is not uniform with respect to its aspectual properties is advocated in Reintges (2015). Based on the morphological distinctions observed in the *j*-radical stems in the durative and the eventive environment, verbal stems are divided into ***aspect-neutral*** and ***bi-aspectual***.[342] The bi-aspectual verbs have morphologically distinct perfective and imperfective stems, whereas the aspect-neutral verbs use the same stem in various TAM patterns. A similar distinction, with some modifications, applies to Coptic, where the aspect-neutral verbs like ⲅⲁⲣⲉⲅ 'guard' can be used indifferently in both conjugation patterns, whereas the bi-aspectual verbs like ⲟⲩⲱⲛⲅ 'reveal / appear' have restrictions in aspect and diathesis. Thus, morphology has been instrumental in tracing down aspectual distinctions in native verbs. There exists, however, the danger of a logical fallacy that we commit, if we consider morphology to be not an important symptom, but rather the trigger of aspectual asymmetries. In fact, the aspect value of a verb is defined by its specific semantic traits that become manifest, inter alia, through the compatibility properties of the verb. The morphological immutability

---

340 For a profound discussion, see Letuchiy (2013:170 ff.).

341 The choice of a preposition appears to be related to the morphological shape of the verb. ⲁⲣⲭⲉⲓ is more frequent with ⲛ-, and ⲁⲣⲭⲉⲥⲑⲁⲓ, with ⲉ-. In Coptic, ⲛ- typically marks the infinitival part of modal predicates, whereas phasal verbs usually take circumstantial clauses as complements.

342 Reintges (2015:417).

of Greek loan verbs does not mean that they are all aspect-neutral. If a certain lexeme is predominantly used within the durative conjugation, it is a clear enough sign that this lexeme has an inherent atelic aspect / *Aktionsart*.

ⲃⲁⲥⲁⲛⲓⲍⲉ 'suffer, be in pain' is the most transparent instance of an interdependence between the syntactic and the lexical aspect. All the non-causal tokens of this verb attested in the DDGLC data base occur in the durative conjugation which means that the lexeme was strictly atelic in Sahidic. Interestingly, the almost synonymous ⲗⲩⲡⲉⲓ 'grieve' is aspect-neutral. Thus, beside the most general semantic idea, each verb has a specific shade of meaning that must be considered in translation.

Verbs of atelic *Aktionsart* are found among the monodiathetic group, as well as among the labile class. Atelic monodiathetics are identified by the same criterion of compatibility we applied to the labile group. They are mostly confined to the Bipartite conjugation, thus constituting a structural parallel to non-resultative statives of the native vocabulary, such as ⲟⲛ︤ϩ 'live'. Some such instances are ⲛⲏⲥⲧⲉⲩⲉ 'fast', ⲡⲁⲣⲁⲙⲉⲓⲛⲉ 'stay, linger', ⲙⲉⲗⲉⲓ 'be of concern', ⲭⲣⲉⲱⲥⲧⲉⲓ 'owe', ⲥⲡⲁⲧⲁⲗⲁ 'live wantonly', ⲧⲁⲗⲁⲓⲡⲱⲣⲉⲓ 'be unhappy', ϩⲩⲡⲏⲣⲉⲧⲉⲓ 'serve'.

Aspectual constraints on the agentful verbs

Further on, aspectual construals are different for the non-causatives denoting spontaneous events (here belongs the majority of the labile group) and those with an obligatory agent participant in their semantic structure, i.e., agentful or passive verbs. Passive verbs generally seem to avoid eventive conjugation, though exceptions (ⲃⲁⲡⲧⲓⲍⲉ 'be baptized', ⲡⲗⲏⲣⲟⲩ 'be satisfied') are possible. Thus, a causative-passive labile verb will mostly have a causative reading in the Tripartite conjugation, whereas the Bipartite is compatible with both the causative and the passive reading. Causative-anticausative labile verbs, on the contrary, are not liable to any aspectual or diathetic constraints.

The aspectual divergence between spontaneous and passive verbs is not unique to loan verbs in Coptic. One can observe similar developments in Russian and Latin (see Polinsky 2001). Why, despite the semantic affinity between anticausative and passive voice, an anticausative verb has more chances to be coded with the punctual aspect, than an agentful / passive one, is as yet unclear.

In neither case does the distribution of a loan verb form match that of a native one. The functional field of an anticausative labile verb is broader than that of a native absolute infinitive, since it includes also the stative-resultative function. A labile verb with a passive alternant occupies the same paradigmatic slots as the native marked forms, namely, the causative eventive and the non-causative durative slot. However, it also has a causative durative reading which is only possible with the native absolute infinitive.

Similarly to the native verbal subsystem, the lability inside the eventive conjugation is available, as a rule, to causative-anticausative verbs, but not for causative-passive verbs. Thus, aspect-diathesis correlation is ultimately defined by identical semantic principles for both loan and native verbs.

3.6 Greek verbs in Sahidic: voice and aspect system (summary)

Taken together, the results of the present study suggest that the Graeco-Sahidic verbal subsystem represents a near-final stage of transition from morphological to templatic voice marking. Indeed, the Greek middle-passive suffix morpheme in Sahidic is an extremely rare marker occurring in the following cases:

1) It is retained on several verbal lexemes that function as deponents in Koine Greek, mostly co-occurring with non-transitive valency patterns (see 3.5.2.2, Table 8);

2) In the older text corpora (NHC), the suffix marks the non-causative member of a given voice opposition; the shorter form is unmarked for voice, i.e., may usually have a causative, as well as a non-causative / passive reading (see 3.5.1.1, Table 7);

3) It is also occasionally employed in newer texts, mostly in the documentary ones; this use of the suffix morpheme may be completely unwarranted by the morphological properties of the source lexeme (cf., e.g., ⲁⲛⲉⲏⲕⲉⲥⲑⲁⲓ and ἀνήκω 'belong'), but seems to be triggered by (or, at any rate, correlate with) various semantic and syntactic factors, such as the stative aspect of the predicate, agent-preserving valency reduction (alias detransitivization), the component of the agent's affectedness / involvedness in the semantics of the verb.

The above list highlights two important points. Firstly, the sporadic flashings of the middle-suffix in the later texts rather support the idea that, despite being confined to non-standard variants of Sahidic, this form might not, after all, have been the result of an intra-dialectal influence, but might be a vestige of a more archaic state inside Sahidic itself. One could argue that documentary texts occasionally recurred to the suffixed form in order to maintain the conservative character of the legal idiom.[343] Secondly, it should be emphasized that the use of the morpheme does not seem to be as accidental as it is commonly believed. Its permanent association with the non-causal semantics and the intransitive syntax indicates a great degree of affinity with its Greek prototype. It would not, therefore, be too far-fetched to assume that the Greek voice morphology had been initially borrowed into Sahidic by way of *parallel system borrowing* (in the sense that it consequently applied to the loan verbal vocabulary in the meaning close to that of the source language) and then eventually faded and disappeared under the pressure of native valency-changing mechanisms. Such an idea seems to me to provide a better (at least, more economical) explanatory frame for the occurrences of the suffix in Sahidic, than the presently advocated point of view, according to which the voice morpheme was randomly lexicalized in the process of borrowing and did not ever code the oppositions of voice.[344]

---

343 This explanation is, however, rejected by T.S. Richter (p.c.), according to whom it is highly improbable that an archaic form would appear in a corpus so late (VI C.E.) and so closely linked to the Greek legal code.

344 Such an opinion is expressed, e.g., in Grossman & Richter (2017:221). Funk (2017:378) takes this to be true for Bohairic. This would, of course, essentially weaken our hypothesis regarding Sahidic, for it is unlikely that the two dialects should pursue different policies in so crucial a thing.

Labile lexemes with morphological passive alternants (ⲁⲛⲁⲡⲁⲩⲉ, ⲡⲉⲓⲑⲉ, ⲡⲗⲁⲛⲁ, ⲱⲫⲉⲗⲉⲓ) represent, as it were, a battlefield of the two rivalling strategies for valency reduction. The ultimate decline of the morphological strategy might have been connected with the functional fuzziness of the suffix morpheme. Indeed, with some lexemes and corpora, it may mark the combination of a non-causative reading with the stative aspect and the present tense (as is obviously the tendency with ⲡⲗⲁⲛⲁⲥⲑⲁⲓ 'err' in NHC II, VII and IX), yet in other cases it would preferably mark the eventive passive (see ⲡⲉⲓⲑⲉⲥⲑⲁⲓ 'obey, be persuaded' in NHC VI & VII, and in Codex Tchacos). The source of this fuzziness must be the absence of isomorphism between the Coptic and the Greek voice category.[345] In Coptic, the Greek passive voice morpheme may mark the combination of the passive voice with the stative aspect, i.e., the combination that is morphologically distinguished in Coptic, or else it may follow the Greek categorial distinctions and mark the passive voice, irrespectively of the aspect (which seems to be the most frequent situation). Moreover, the case of ⲡⲉⲓⲑⲉⲥⲑⲁⲓ proves that sometimes the passive suffix may be interpreted as an alternative to the native templatic voice marking; here it marks the combination of passive voice and non-stative aspect, i.e., precisely that combination which is unmarked in the native verbal grammar.

Generally, the means of valency alternation for Greek loan verbs comprise templatic lability, the remnants of the morphological marking, and the syntactic tools, i.e., valency increase through the causativizing prefix ⲧⲣⲉ-, and valency reduction through the 'impersonal passive' construction. It is difficult to assess the relative frequency of the templatic vs. the syntactic alternation. It must be noticed, however, that the templatic alternation was applied to a relatively limited number of lexemes, between 60 and 70 in the whole corpus of Sahidic attested in the DDGLC data base. Such solid literary corpora, as Shenoute's Canons or the Sahidic New Testament, make use of 8 to 16 loan labile lemmata, all in all. Many verbs of the labile class display an asymmetric, or partial lability, in other words, they are basically monodiathetic verbs with sporadic valency changes. Thus, in the loan part of the Sahidic verbal vocabulary, the mechanism of lability was productive, but rather irregular.

Lability seems to be the main strategy of voice alternation for such loan verbs whose semantics does not include an obligatory animate / volitional actor. This tendency of Coptic largely corroborates the observation made in Smith (1970) and reiterated in Levin & Rappaport-Hovav (1995):

"The transitive causative verbs that detransitivize are those in which the eventuality can come about spontaneously, without the volitional intervention of an agent."[346]

As shown in 3.5.3.2, the group of labile Graeco-Sahidic verbs comprises also several lexemes with a volitional agent construed in the semantics of the verb, such as ⲍⲱⲅⲣⲁⲫⲉⲓ 'paint', ⲕⲁⲑⲓⲥⲧⲁ 'appoint', ⲕⲟⲥⲙⲉⲓ 'adorn', ⲥⲧⲉⲫⲁⲛⲟⲩ 'crown' etc. These, however, are

---

345 This issue is discussed at length in 3.4.
346 Levin & Rappaport-Hovav (1995:102).

mostly avoided in the eventive conjugation; similarly to Egyptian stative forms, these verbs are employed in the durative conjugation with a resultative meaning.

Besides spontaneous verbs with inanimate patients, the class of labile verbs includes quite a few verbs with animate patients. Their semantics can be subsumed under the notion of spontaneity, if we define spontaneity as the property of an event that does not result from a volitional activity of an agent. A large part of these verbs consists of the verbs denoting an emotion (ⲉⲩⲫⲣⲁⲛⲉ 'enjoy', ⲧⲣⲩⲫⲁ, ⲅⲏⲇⲁⲛⲏ 'delight in', ⲗⲩⲡⲉⲓ 'be sad', ⲃⲁⲥⲁⲛⲓⲍⲉ 'be in pain', ⲥⲕⲩⲗⲗⲉⲓ, ⲧⲁⲣⲁⲥⲥⲉ 'be troubled' etc.) or the verbs with a component of 'unintentional' in their semantics (ⲁⲛⲁⲅⲕⲁⲍⲉ 'be compelled', ⲡⲗⲁⲛⲁ, ⲡⲁⲣⲁⲃⲁ, ⲡⲁⲣⲁⲅⲉ 'err', ⲥⲕⲁⲛⲇⲁⲗⲓⲍⲉ 'stumble, be offended'). If the non-causative reading of an active transitive verb with an animate patient excludes spontaneity, this verb does not, as a rule, form a labile counterpart. Exceptions, such as ⲃⲁⲡⲧⲓⲍⲉ 'baptize', ⲕⲁⲑⲓⲥⲧⲁ 'appoint', ⲡⲗⲏⲣⲟⲩ 'satisfy', are scarce. Labile causativization of these verbs (e.g., *ⲁϥⲁⲡⲁⲧⲁ ⲙⲙⲟⲥ as 'he made her deceive') does not take place, because the core event already has a volitional actor. Yet another category of verbs that are resistant to lability, are the verbs denoting some kind of mental activity, such as ⲇⲓⲥⲧⲁⲍⲉ 'hesitate', ⲙⲉⲧⲁⲛⲟⲉⲓ 'repent', ⲉⲡⲓⲛⲟⲉⲓ 'perceive, conceive' etc. The difference in the treatment of these verbs as opposed to the verbs of emotional change must mean that Coptic conceives the performer of a mental activity as more agent-like compared to a subject of an emotional change. This interpretation is in congruence with the observations made in Tsunoda (1985). According to Tsunoda, verbs of knowledge ('know', 'understand') tend to map onto transitive structures more frequently, than verbs of feeling ('like', 'fear'). One could possibly extend Tsunoda's analysis to all verbs of mental activity, as possessing – to a certain degree – semantics of volition or control.

The absence of aspect-encoding morphology makes syntagmatic features the sole criterion of aspectual constraints on loan verbs. The present study has found two kinds of such constraints, namely, two semantic properties that confine the verb to the durative conjugation pattern, turning it into a structural analogue of stative. The strong preference for the durative conjugation is typical for: 1) monodiathetic intransitive verbs with atelic *aktionsart* , mostly denoting a certain way of life or behavior; 2) non-active members of a labile pair with agentful (i.e., passive proper) meaning. In this last case, the form, as a rule, has resultative reading. Outside these cases, no direct analogy can be established between any of the Coptic verbal forms and the Greek infinitive in terms of their distribution (see 3.5.3.5).Thus, rather than following some formal criteria in the adaptation of loan verbs, Coptic applies to them the same grammatical principles that define the distribution of native forms.

Appendix 1. Morphology ~ diathesis correlation in Greek loan verbs

ⲁⲡⲟⲗⲁⲩⲉ - ⲁⲡⲟⲗⲁⲩⲉⲥⲑⲁⲓ

Besa Codex F - Fr. 40 - Fragment, Paris 130.5,127r, Kuhn (1956:129)

ⲛ̄ⲧⲁϥⲉⲓ ϣⲁⲣⲱⲧⲛ̄ ϫⲉⲕⲁⲥ ⲉϥⲛⲁⲁⲡⲟⲗⲁⲩⲉ ⲛ̄ⲛⲉⲧⲛ̄ⲡⲏⲅⲏ ⲉⲧϣⲟⲩⲟ ⲉⲃⲟⲗ ⲛ̄ⲟⲩϩⲗⲟϭ•

'he came to you in order that he might enjoy your fountains which pour forth sweetness'

BL Pap 78 - P.Mon.Phoib.Test. 4, 25-26, Garel 2020

ⲙⲛ ⲟⲩⲉⲓⲱⲧⲉ ⲙⲙⲟⲟⲩ̄ ⲉⲉϣⲙ̄ ⲡⲉⲩⲉⲓⲃⲉ ⲁⲩⲱ ⲉⲩⲁⲡⲟⲗⲁⲩⲉⲥⲑⲁⲓ ⲉⲃⲟⲗ ϩⲛ̄ ⲛⲛ̄ⲁⲅⲁⲑⲟ[ⲛ] ⲛ̄ⲁⲧϣⲁϫⲉ
ⲉⲣⲟⲟⲩ

'and a drop of water to quench their thirst and enjoy the good things which words cannot
describe'

ⲁⲣⲛⲁ - ⲁⲣⲛⲉⲥⲑⲁⲓ

Paris - Bibliothèque Nationale Copte 78.16-17 - Martyrdom of Apa Colluthus 17r, G.
Schenke (2013:90-91)

ⲡⲉⲧⲛⲁⲁⲣⲛⲁ ⲙⲙⲟⲓ ⲙⲡⲙ̄ⲧⲟ ⲉⲃⲟⲗ ⲛ̄ⲛ̄ⲣⲱⲙⲉ †ⲁⲣⲛⲁ ⲙⲙⲟϥ ϩⲱ ⲙⲡⲙ̄ⲧⲟ ⲉⲃⲟⲗ ⲙⲡⲁⲓⲱⲧ ⲉⲧϩⲛ̄ ⲙⲡⲉⲏⲩⲉ
ⲙⲛ̄ ⲛⲉϥⲁⲅⲅⲉⲗⲟⲥ ⲉⲧⲟⲩⲁⲁⲃ ·

'Whosoever shall deny me before men, him will I also deny before my father which is in
heaven, and His holy angels'

Nag Hammadi Codex VII - Second Treatise of the Great Seth, 52, (Riley 1996:154)
ⲙ̄ⲡⲓ̄ⲁⲣⲛⲉⲥⲑⲁⲓ ⲙⲉⲛ ⲛⲁⲩ• ⲁⲩⲱ ⲉⲧⲣⲁϣⲱⲡⲉ ⲛ̄ⲟⲩⲭⲣ̄ⲥ•
'While, on the one hand, I did not reject them, and so became (the) Messiah…'

ⲇⲓⲁⲥⲧⲉⲗⲗⲉ - ⲇⲓⲁⲥⲧⲉⲗⲗⲉⲥⲑⲁⲓ

P.KRU 48, 15-17

ⲛ̄ⲧⲉⲧⲛⲣ ⲡϫⲟⲉⲓⲥ ⲛⲙⲙⲉⲣⲟⲥ ⲙⲙⲁ ⲛ̄ⲧⲁⲛⲇⲓⲁⲥⲧⲁⲗⲉ ⲙⲙⲟⲩ ⲛⲏⲧⲛ ⲛ̄ⲧⲡⲉ

                        that-PRF-1PL-'specify' DO-3PL

'and become owner of the place-shares which we have specified for you (pl.) above'

Pierpont Morgan M.579, Encomium on St. Antony, f.78v b

ⲛⲁⲓ ⲟⲛ ⲛ̄ⲧⲁϥⲇⲓⲁⲥⲧⲉ<ⲗⲗⲉ>ⲥⲑⲁⲓ ⲉⲧⲃⲏⲏⲧⲟⲩ ⲉϥⲛⲁⲙⲟⲩ ⲁⲩⲱ ⲁϥⲕⲁⲁⲩ ⲛ̄ⲕⲗⲏⲣⲟⲛⲟⲙⲉⲓ<ⲁ>
ⲛ̄ⲛⲉϥⲉⲓⲟⲧⲉ ⲙⲛ ⲛⲉϥϣⲏⲣⲉ

'And about these he gave precise instructions as he was about to die, and he left them as
an inheritance to his fathers and his children'

ⲙⲁⲣⲧⲩⲣⲉⲓ - ⲙⲁⲣⲧⲩⲣⲉⲥⲑⲁⲓ

ParShem, 26, Wisse (1996:78)

ⲉⲥⲣ̄ⲙⲁⲣⲧⲩⲣⲓ ⲛ̄ⲛⲉⲧⲟⲩⲁⲁⲃ ⲛ̄ⲧⲉ ⲧⲙⲛ̄ⲧ`ⲛⲟϭ

'bearing witness to the holy things of the greatness'

Or. 4885 Ro - P.KRU 59, Crum (1912)

ⲁⲓⲡⲁⲣⲁⲕⲁⲗⲉⲓ ⲛ̅ⲅⲉⲛⲣⲱⲙⲉ ⲛⲁ̅ⲍⲓⲟⲡⲓⲥⲧⲟⲥ ⲁⲩⲙⲁⲣⲧⲩⲣⲉⲥⲑⲁⲓ ⲉⲣⲟⲥ

'*I have asked trustworthy men who have testified to it*'

P.KRU 69, Crum (1912)

ⲁⲓⲡⲁⲣⲁⲕⲁⲗⲉ ⲛⲟⲩⲣⲉϥⲥϩⲁⲓ ⲙⲛ ϩⲉⲛⲕⲟⲩⲙⲛ̅ⲧⲣⲉ ⲉⲧⲣⲉ<ⲩ>ⲙⲁⲣⲧⲏⲣⲉⲥⲑⲁⲓ ϩⲁⲣⲟⲓ

'*I have furthermore beseeched a subscriber and witnesses that <they> might testify on my behalf*'

ⲡⲣⲁⲥⲥⲉ - ⲡⲣⲁⲧⲧⲉⲥⲑⲁⲓ

MONB.FY - Historia Ecclesiastica Coptica, Orlandi (1968-70 I,22)

ⲡⲉⲕⲉⲓⲱⲧ ⲅⲁⲣ ⲡⲣ̅ⲣⲟ ⲁϥϩⲩⲡⲟⲅⲣⲁⲫⲏ ⲉⲧⲉϥⲕⲁⲑⲉⲣⲉⲥⲓⲥ ⲁⲩⲱ ⲁϥⲡ<ⲣ>ⲁⲥⲥⲉ ⲙ̅ⲙⲟϥ ϩⲓ ⲡⲉⲡⲁⲣⲭⲟⲥ

'*For your father, the emperor, signed his excommunication and he enacted this through the governor*'

BL Pap 78 - P.Mon.Phoib.Test. 4, 22-26, Garel (2020)

ⲉⲡⲉⲓⲇⲏ ⲙⲁⲩⲕⲟⲧⲟⲩ {ⲙⲁ} ⲉⲃⲟⲗ ⲉⲩⲣ̅ ϩⲱⲃ ⲉⲡⲉⲧⲛⲁⲛⲟⲩ̅ϥ̅ ⲁⲩⲱ ⲉⲩⲡⲣⲁⲧⲉⲥⲑⲁⲓ ⲉⲧⲇⲓⲕⲁⲓⲱⲥⲩⲛⲏ ⲛ̅ⲛⲉϩⲟⲟⲩ ⲧⲏⲣⲟⲩ ⲛ̅ⲡⲉⲩⲱⲛϩ

'*Since they do not turn away from their laboring towards what is good, and their practicing righteousness through all the days of their life*'

ⲥⲓⲭⲁⲛⲉ - ⲥⲓⲭⲁⲛⲉⲥⲑⲁⲓ

ParShem, 45,3, Wisse (1996:116)

ϥⲛⲁⲣ̅ ϩⲁϩ ⲛ̅ϣⲡⲏⲣⲉ• ⲟⲩⲛ̅ ϩⲁϩ ⲛⲁⲣⲥⲓⲭⲁⲛⲉ ⲙ̅ⲙⲟϥ

He will perform many wonders. Many will loathe him

ParShem, 2, 23-24, Wisse (1996:28)

ⲁϥⲛⲁⲩ ⲉⲩⲛⲟϭ ⲙ̅ⲙⲟⲟⲩ ⲛ̅ⲕⲁⲕⲉ• ⲁⲩⲱ ⲁϥⲣ̅ⲥⲓⲭⲁⲛⲉⲥⲑⲁⲓ

And he saw a great, dark water. And he was nauseated

Appendix 2. Non-alternating Greek loan verbs

The table contains active-stem loan verbs that do not display causative alternation in Sahidic. This class is represented by two groups: 1) *hapax legomena* that are *a priori* attested in one diathesis only; 2) well-attested non-labile verbs. The absence of causative alternation in the first group may be accidental. Therefore, keeping the two groups apart seemed to be a more accurate approach. The list does not include uncertain restorations of *hapax legomena* (such as [ⲁⲡⲟ]ⲧⲉⲓⲗ[ⲉ] for ἀποτίλλω 'pull, pluck out'). Omitted are also such verbs that are not attested in a finite form and predicative function. These may appear in Coptic as participles (e.g., <πλύνω> ⲡⲉⲡⲗⲏⲙⲙⲉⲛⲏⲥ 'rinsed'), nominal derivations (e.g., <προσεδρεύω> ⲧ-ϭⲓⲛ-ⲡⲣⲟⲥⲉⲩⲁⲣⲉⲩⲉ), or parts of multi-word expressions and formulae (e.g., <γίγνομαι> ⲙⲏ ⲅⲉⲛⲟⲓⲧⲟ, <χαίρω> ⲭⲁⲓⲣⲉ).

The two rightmost columns supply the argument structure (excluding A- and P-arguments) and the basic diathesis of each verb. Generally, however, the argument structure of a loan verb seems to be less fixed than that of an average native verb. Some verbs can take direct objects, as well as non-transitive prepositional phrases. Such is the case of ⲇⲓⲱⲕⲉⲓ 'pursue, chase' which, if my observations are correct, tends to be transitive in the past tense and intransitive in the present tense. In this and other cases of diathetic non-causative alternation, the diathesis of the verb is marked as '(in)transitive' in the table. The term 'reflexive' is applied to cases where the position of DO can only be occupied by a reflexive pronoun which therefore constitutes a formal marker of the intransitive diathesis.

Notation:

DO : the argument corresponding to the direct object of the English equivalent

dath. eth. : dativus ethicus, here used in the same sense Hebrew grammarians use to describe the construction of the type: "lekh-lekha", lit.: "go to yourself", which is an exact parallel of the Coptic construction in question. Though Muraoka (1978) argues that the term is ill-advised, I employ it here for want of a better one.

pred. compl. : predicative complement, as in: "The court appointed him ***ambassador*** in Spain".

$Ⲛᴰ$: alternation set Ⲛ- / ⲚⲀ=

$Ⲛ^{Acc}$: alternation set Ⲛ- / ⲘⲘⲞ=

Ⲛ : only nominal arguments are attested, therefore impossible to establish the alternation class of the argument.

Hapax legomena

Greek form	Coptic form	Meaning	Non-A/P- actants (if present)	Transitive / Intransitive / Unclear
ἀγγέλλω	ⲁⲅⲅⲉⲗⲓ	'bring a message'		intransitive
ἀκονάω	ⲁⲕⲟⲛⲓ	'become alert'		intransitive
ἀνακεφαλαιογράφω	ⲁⲛⲁⲕⲉⲫⲁⲗⲓⲱⲅⲣⲁⲫⲉⲓ	'summarize'	'for': ⲛᴰ	transitive
ἀναλυτρόω	ⲁⲛⲁⲗⲩⲧⲣⲱⲥⲉ	'resume possession of'		unclear
ἀναλύω	ⲁⲛⲁⲗⲩ	'dissolve, annul'		transitive
ἀνανεύω	ⲁⲛⲁⲛⲉⲩⲥⲉ	'renew'		transitive
ἀναπλάσσω	ⲁⲛⲁⲡⲗⲁⲥⲥⲉ	'form anew'		unclear
ἀναπληρόω	ⲁⲛⲁⲡⲗⲏⲣⲟⲩ	'pay homage to'		unclear
ἀντιγράφω	ⲁⲛⲧⲓⲅⲣⲁⲫⲉ	'write back, respond to'	'to':ⲛᴰ, 'that': ϫⲉ	intransitive
ἀντιφωνέω	ⲁⲛⲧⲓⲫⲱⲛⲏ	'stand surety, vouch'	'to':ⲛᴰ, 'for': ⲉ-	intransitive
ἀπαγοράζω	ⲁⲡⲁⲅⲟⲣⲁⲍⲉ	'redeem'		unclear
ἀπάγω	ⲁⲡⲁⲅⲉ	'be led away' (?)		unclear
ἀποδέχομαι	ⲁⲡⲟⲇⲉⲭⲉ	'accept, welcome'		transitive
ἀποδίδωμι	ⲁⲡⲟⲇⲓⲇⲟⲩ	'hand over'	'to':ⲛᴰ	transitive
ἀποκηρύσσω	ⲁⲡⲟⲕⲏⲣⲩⲥⲥⲉ	'renounce'		transitive
ἀποστατέω	ⲁⲡⲟⲥⲧⲁⲧⲉⲓ	'be unconcerned'		intransitive
ἅπτίζω	ϩⲁⲡⲧⲓⲍⲉ	'put a hand'	'on': ⲉϫⲛ-	intransitive
ἀρκέω	ⲁⲣⲕⲉⲓ	'suffice'	'for': ⲉ-	intransitive
ἀφίστημι	ⲁⲡⲟⲥⲧⲁ	'put away'		transitive
βάπτω	ⲃⲁⲯⲟⲛ	'dip, plunge'		unclear
βασκαίνω	ⲃⲁⲥⲕⲁⲛⲉ	'envy'	'to': ⲉ-	intransitive
βατταλογέω	ⲃⲁⲧⲧⲁⲗⲟⲅⲓ	'babble, stummer'		intransitive
βουλλόω	ⲃⲟⲩⲗⲗⲓⲍⲉ	'seal'	'with': ⲛ-	transitive
γενεαλογέω	ⲅⲉⲛⲉⲁⲗⲟⲅⲉⲓ	'trace a pedigree'		intransitive
γογγύζω	ⲕⲟⲅⲅⲓⲍⲉ	'murmur, grumble'		intransitive
δέχομαι	ⲇⲉⲭⲓ	'receive'		unclear
δημεύω	ⲇⲏⲙⲉⲩⲉ	'seize for public property'		transitive
διαγράφω	ⲇⲓⲁⲅⲣⲁⲫⲏ	'conceive, imagine'		transitive
διαλύω	ⲇⲓⲁⲗⲩⲉ	'resolve, settle'	'with': ⲙⲛ	intransitive
διαμαρτυρέω	ϯⲁⲙⲁⲣⲧⲉⲣⲉ	'protest, object'		unclear
διασῴζω	ⲇⲓⲁⲥⲱⲥⲟⲩ	'send, transfer'	'to':ⲛᴰ	transitive
ἐγκωμιάζω	ⲉⲅⲕⲱⲙⲓⲁⲍⲉ	'praise in speech'		transitive

Greek form	Coptic form	Meaning	Non-A/P- actants (if present)	Transitive / Intransitive / Unclear
ἐκκλίνω	ⲉⲕⲗⲓⲛⲉ	'retire'		intransitive
ἐκφράζω	ⲉⲝⲉⲫⲣⲁⲥⲉ	'express, edit'		transitive
ἐνθυμέομαι	ⲉⲛⲑⲩⲙⲉⲓ	'meditate'		intransitive
ἐντινάσσω	ⲉⲛⲧⲓⲛⲁⲥⲥⲉ	'crash, collide'	'with': ⲉⲣⲟⲩⲛ ⲉϩⲣⲛ-	intransitive
ἐξάγω	ⲉⲝⲁⲅⲉ	'drive away'		transitive
ἐπεξεργάζομαι	ⲉⲡⲉⲝⲁⲣⲅⲁⲍⲉ	'work on'		transitive
ἐπισωρεύω	ⲉⲡⲓⲥⲱⲣⲉⲩⲉ	'accumulate'		transitive
ἐπιτηδεύω	ⲉⲡⲓⲧⲏⲇⲉⲩⲉ	'attempt at'	ⲉ + inf.	intransitive
ἐπιφέρω*	ⲉⲡⲉⲛⲉⲅⲕⲉ	'ascribe'		
θεολογέω	ⲑⲉⲟⲗⲟⲅⲉⲓ	'speak of God'		unclear
θροέω	ⲑⲣⲟⲓ	'cry aloud'		intransitive
ἰατρεύω	ϩⲓⲁⲧⲣⲉⲩⲉ	'heal'		transitive
ἰδιάζω	ⲉⲓⲇⲓⲁⲍⲓⲛ	'make particular'		transitive
κακολογέω	ⲕⲁⲕⲟⲗⲟⲅⲉⲓ	'slander'		transitive
καρπίζω	ⲅⲣⲩⲡⲁⲍⲉ	'be freed' (?)		unclear
κατακενόω	ⲕⲁⲧⲁⲕⲉⲛⲉ	'leave empty, desert'		transitive
καταλλάσσω	ⲕⲁⲧⲁⲗⲗⲁⲥⲥⲉ	'exchange'		transitive
κατάρχω	ⲕⲁⲧⲁⲣⲕⲉⲓ	'begin, start'		intransitive
καταστρέφω	ⲕⲁⲧⲁⲥⲧⲣⲉⲫⲓ	'turn around'		intransitive
καυτηριάζω	ⲕⲁⲩⲧⲏⲣⲓⲍⲉ	'brand'		transitive
κινέω	ⲕⲓⲛⲏⲥⲁⲓ	'take legal action'	'against': ⲕⲁⲧⲁ	intransitive
κρατέω	ⲕⲣⲁⲧⲉⲩⲉ	'grasp, seize' (?)	'at': ϩⲛ	intransitive
κροτέω	ⲕⲣⲟⲧⲉⲩⲉ	'pat'		transitive
κυμαίνω	ⲅⲓⲙⲉⲛ	'swell' (?)		unclear
λαγχάνω	ⲗⲁⲭⲁ	'obtain' (?)	DO : ⲉ-	intransitive
λευκόω	ⲗⲉⲩⲕⲏ	'bleach'		transitive
λογογραφέω	ⲗⲟⲅⲣⲁⲫⲏ	'write down'	DO : ⲉ-	intransitive
μεριμνάω	ⲙⲉⲣⲓⲙⲛⲁ	'be anxious'		intransitive
μεστόω	ⲙⲉⲥⲧⲉ	'be filled' (?)	'with': ∅	unclear
μεταβάλλω	ⲙⲉⲧⲁⲃⲁⲗⲉ	'change the position of'		reflexive
μεταγγίζω	ⲙⲉⲧⲁⲅⲅⲓⲍⲉ	'transfer'		transitive
μεταμορφόω	ⲙⲉⲧⲁⲙⲟⲣⲫⲟⲩ	'transform oneself'		reflexive
μετρέω	ⲙⲛⲧⲣⲉⲩⲉ	'measure'		transitive

Greek form	Coptic form	Meaning	Non-A/P- actants (if present)	Transitive / Intransitive / Unclear
μονάζω	ⲙⲟⲛⲁⲍⲉⲓ	'live in solitude' (?)		unclear
νομίζω	ⲛⲟⲙⲓⲍⲟⲛ	'consider'		intransitive
νουθετέω	ⲛⲟⲩⲑⲉⲧⲉⲓ	'chastise'		transitive
ξενιτεύω	ⲝⲉⲛⲓⲧⲉⲩⲉ	'go abroad'		reflexive
ὀλιγωρέω	ⲟⲗⲓⲅⲱⲣⲉⲓ	'be negligent'		intransitive
παιδαγωγέω	ⲡⲉⲇⲁⲅⲱⲅⲉⲓ	'study' (?)		transitive
παραβάλλω	ⲡⲁⲣⲁⲃⲁⲗⲗⲉⲓ	'submit'		transitive
παροράω	ⲡⲁⲣⲟⲣⲁ	'neglect'		transitive
πατέω	ⲡⲁⲧⲉⲓ	'tread on'		transitive
πειράω	ⲡⲉⲓⲣⲁ	'try, test'		transitive
περάω	ⲡⲏⲣⲁ	'sail across'		transitive
περιάγω	ⲡⲉⲣⲓⲁⲅⲉ	'lead around'		unclear
περιγράφω	ⲡⲉⲣⲓⲅⲣⲁⲫⲉ	'falsify'		transitive
περικακέω	ⲡⲉⲣⲓⲕⲁⲕⲉⲓ	'be exhausted'		intransitive
περιλαμβάνω	ⲡⲉⲣⲓⲗⲁⲙⲃⲁⲛⲉ	'comprehend'		transitive
πιστόω	ⲡⲓⲥⲧⲟⲩ	'prove faithful'	'to': ⲉ-	intransitive
πλεονεκτέω	ⲡⲗⲉⲟⲛⲉⲕⲧⲉⲓ	'claim too much'		intransitive
πολεύω	ⲡⲟⲗⲉⲩⲉ	'go around for' (?)		unclear
πραιδεύω	ⲡⲣⲁⲓⲧⲁ	'rob'		unclear
προκριματίζω	ⲡⲣⲟⲕⲣⲓⲙⲁⲧⲓⲍⲉ	'prejudice'		transitive
προμηνύω	ⲡⲣⲟⲉⲙⲏⲛⲉⲩ	'announce beforehand'		transitive
προξενίζω	ⲡⲣⲟⲝⲉⲛⲓⲍⲉ	'secure'		transitive
προσάγω	ⲡⲣⲟⲥⲁⲅⲉ	'bring forth'		transitive
προσποιέω	ⲡⲣⲟⲥⲡⲟⲓⲉⲓ	'add'		transitive
προσφωνέω	ⲡⲣⲟⲥⲫⲱⲛⲉⲓ	'address, speak to'		transitive
προτάσσω	ⲡⲣⲟⲧⲁⲥⲥⲉ	'be prefixed' (?)		unclear
προτείνω	ⲡⲣⲟⲇⲉⲓⲛⲁ	'put forward'	'to': ⲛ^D	transitive
ῥογεύω	ϩⲣⲟⲕⲟⲩ	'pay out'		unclear
σαββατίζω	ⲥⲁⲃⲃⲁⲧⲓⲍⲉ	'keep Sabbath'	'for' (?): ⲛ	intransitive
σιαίνω	ⲥⲓⲁⲛⲉ	'bother'		transitive
σκορπίζω	(ⲥ)ⲕⲟⲣⲡⲓⲍⲉ	'scatter'		transitive
σοφίζω	ⲥⲟⲫⲓⲍⲉ	'devise, concoct'		transitive
στηρίζω	ⲥⲧⲏⲣⲓⲍⲉ	'be firm, fixed'		intransitive
στίζω	ⲥⲧⲓⲍⲉ	'punctuate'		transitive

Greek form	Coptic form	Meaning	Non-A/P- actants (if present)	Transitive / Intransitive / Unclear
συγκαταβαίνω	ⲥⲩⲛⲕⲁⲧⲁⲃⲁ	'be merciful, lenient'		intransitive
συλλογίζομαι	ⲥⲩⲛⲗⲟⲅⲓⲍⲉ	'consider, discuss'		transitive
συμβοηθέω	ⲥⲩⲛⲃⲟⲏⲑⲉⲓ	'assist'	'to': ⲙⲛ	intransitive
συνέχω	ⲥⲩⲛⲉⲭⲉ	'be kept, contained'	'in': ⲏⲛ	intransitive
συνομιλέω	ⲥⲩⲛⲣⲟⲙⲟⲗⲉⲓⲛ	'converse'	'with': ⲙⲛ	intransitive
συντίθημαι	ⲥⲉⲛⲧⲏⲑⲓ	'consent'	'to' (?):ⲛ	unclear
συστέλλω	ⲥⲩⲥⲧⲓⲗⲉ	'remove, expel'		transitive
συστρέφω	ⲥⲩⲥⲧⲣⲟⲫⲉⲓ	'contract, roll up'		intransitive
σφίγγω	ⲥⲫⲓⲛⲅⲟⲩ	'bind tightly'	'to': ⲉⲣⲟⲩⲛ ⲉ-	transitive
ὑμνολογέω	ⲣⲩⲙⲛⲟⲗⲟⲅⲉⲓ	'sing hymns'		intransitive
ὑπισχνέομαι	ⲣⲩⲡⲓⲥⲭⲟⲩ	'promise'		unclear
ὑποκορίζομαι	ⲣⲩⲡⲟⲕⲟⲣⲉⲩⲉ	'give an endearing name'	'to': ⲣⲁⲣⲁⲧ=	intransitive
ὑπονοέω	ⲣⲩⲡⲟⲓⲛⲉⲓ	'surmise, consider'		transitive
ὑποχωρέω	ⲣⲩⲡⲟⲭⲟⲣⲉⲓ	'withdraw'	dat. eth.: ⲛᴰ	intransitive
φαρμακεύω	ⲫⲁⲣⲙⲁⲕⲉⲩⲉ	'practice witchcraft'		intransitive
φιλονικέω	ⲫⲓⲗⲟⲛⲓⲕⲏ	'be rivals'		intransitive
φιλοπονέω	ⲫⲓⲗⲟⲡⲟⲛⲉⲓ	'love labour'		intransitive
φροντίζω	ⲫⲣⲟⲛⲧⲓⲍⲉ	'consider, think'	'about': ⲉ-	intransitive
χαρακτηρίζω	ⲭⲁⲣⲁⲕⲧⲏⲣⲓⲍⲉ	'characterize, portray'		transitive
χηρεύω	ⲭⲏⲣⲉⲩⲉ	'be widowed'		intransitive
χωνεύω	ⲭⲱⲛⲉⲩⲉ	'pour, cast (metal)'	'to': ⲉ-	transitive
ψέγω	ⲯⲉⲅⲉ	'blame'		transitive

Verbs with more than one attestation

Greek form	Coptic form	Meaning	Non-A/P actants (if present)	Transitive / Intransitive / Unclear
ἀγανακτέω	ⲁⲅⲁⲛⲁⲕⲧⲉⲓ	'be(come) indignant'		intransitive
ἀγαπάω	ⲁⲅⲁⲡⲁ	'love'		transitive
ἁγιάζω	ϩⲁⲅⲓⲁⲍⲉ	'consecrate'		transitive
ἁγνεύω	ϩⲁⲅⲛⲉⲩⲉ	'purify oneself'		reflexive
ἀγνωμονέω	ⲁⲅⲛⲱⲙⲟⲛⲉⲓ	'act / treat unfairly'		(in)transitive
ἀγωνίζομαι	ⲁⲅⲱⲛⲓⲍⲉ	'struggle'	'against': ⲟⲩⲃⲉ	intransitive
ἀδικέω*	ⲁⲇⲓⲕⲉⲓ	'act wrongly'	'towards' (?): ⲛ	unclear
ἀθετέω	ⲁⲑⲉⲧⲉⲓ	'disown, reject'		transitive
ἀθλέω	ⲁⲑⲗⲓ	'fight, compete'	'with': ⲙⲛ	intransitive
αἰτέω	ⲁⲓⲧⲉⲓ	'ask, demand'		two DOs
αἰχμαλωτεύω	ⲁⲓⲭⲙⲁⲗⲱⲧⲉⲩⲉ	'imprison, lock up'		transitive
αἰχμαλωτίζω	ⲁⲓⲭⲙⲁⲗⲱⲧⲓⲍⲉ	'take captive'		transitive
ἀκολουθέω	ⲁⲕⲟⲗⲟⲩⲑⲉⲓ	'follow, accompany'		transitive
ἀκριβάζω	ⲁⲕⲣⲓⲃⲁⲍⲉ	'investigate thoroughly'		transitive
ἀκυρόω	ⲁⲕⲩⲣⲟⲩ	'reject, devaluate'		transitive
ἀλλάσσω	ⲁⲗⲗⲁⲥⲥⲉ	'exchange'		transitive
ἀλληγορέω	ⲁⲗⲗⲏⲅⲟⲣⲉⲓ	'interpret allegorically'		transitive
ἀμελέω*	ⲁⲙⲉⲗⲉⲓ	'be negligent, delay'		intransitive
ἀμφιβάλλω	ⲁⲙⲫⲓⲃⲁⲗⲉ	'be in doubt, dissent'		intransitive
ἀναδίδωμι	ⲁⲛⲁⲇⲓⲇⲟⲩ	'hand over'	'to': ⲛ^D	transitive
ἀναθεματίζω	ⲁⲛⲁⲑⲉⲙⲁⲧⲓⲍⲉ	'pronounce accursed'		transitive
ἀνακαλέω	ⲁⲛⲁⲕⲁⲗⲉⲓ	'call back, summon'		transitive
ἀνακρίνω	ⲁⲛⲁⲕⲣⲓⲛⲉ	'examine, question'		transitive
ἀνακτάομαι	ⲁⲛⲁⲕⲧⲁ	'refresh oneself'		reflexive
ἀναλαμβάνω	ⲁⲛⲁⲗⲁⲙⲃⲁⲛⲉ	'raise, take up'		transitive
ἀναστατόω	ⲁⲛⲁⲥⲧⲁⲧⲟⲩ	'unsettle, upset'		transitive
ἀναστρέφω	ⲁⲛⲁⲥⲧⲣⲉⲫⲉ	'live among'		intransitive
ἀνατρέπω	ⲁⲛⲁⲧⲣⲉⲡⲉ	'upset, overturn'		transitive
ἀναχωρέω	ⲁⲛⲁⲭⲱⲣⲉⲓ	'withdraw, depart'	dat. eth.: ⲛ^D	intransitive

Greek form	Coptic form	Meaning	Non-A/P actants (if present)	Transitive / Intransitive / Unclear
ἀνδραγαθέω	ⲁⲛⲇⲣⲁⲕⲁⲑⲉⲩⲉ	'be brave, behave manly'		intransitive
ἀνομέω	ⲁⲛⲟⲙⲉⲓ	'act lawlessly'		intransitive
ἀντιλέγω	ⲁⲛⲧⲓⲗⲉⲅⲉ	'object, contradict'	'to': ⲛᴰ	intransitive
ἀξιόω	ⲁⲝⲓⲟⲩ	'beg, entreat'		transitive
ἀπαγγέλλω*	ⲁⲡⲁⲅⲅⲉⲓⲗⲉ	'inform, bring a message'	'to': ⲉ- or ⲛᴰ	intransitive
ἀπαιτέω	ⲁⲡⲁⲓⲧⲉⲓ	'require, demand'		transitive
ἀπαντάω	ⲁⲡⲁⲛⲧⲁ	'meet, encounter'	'with': ⲛᴰ	intransitive
ἀπαρνέομαι	ⲁⲡⲁⲣⲛⲁ	'deny'		transitive
ἀπατάω	ⲁⲡⲁⲧⲁ	'mislead, deceive'		transitive
ἀπειλέω	ⲁⲡⲉⲓⲗⲉ	'threaten, admonish'	'to': ⲉ- or ⲛᴰ	intransitive
ἀπελπίζω	ⲁⲫⲉⲗⲡⲓⲍⲉ	'lose hope, despair'	'of': ⲉ-	intransitive
ἀπιστέω	ⲁⲡⲓⲥⲧⲉⲓ	'refuse to believe'	'to': ⲉ- or ⲛᴰ	intransitive
ἀποβάλλω	ⲁⲡⲟⲃⲁⲗⲉ	'throw, cast'		transitive
ἀποδείκνυμι	ⲁⲡⲟⲇⲓⲕⲛⲉⲩⲉ	'demonstrate, prove'	'to':ⲛᴰ; 'that': ϫⲉ	intransitive
ἀποδημέω	ⲁⲡⲟⲇⲏⲙⲉⲓ	'go on a journey'	'to': ⲉ- (place), ϣⲁ- (person)	intransitive
ἀποκαθίστημι	ⲁⲡⲟⲕⲁⲑⲓⲥⲧⲁ	'establish'		transitive
ἀπολογίζομαι	ⲁⲡⲟⲗⲟⲅⲓⲍⲉ	'pay back'	'to':ⲛᴰ	transitive
ἀπολύω	ⲁⲡⲟⲗⲩ	'divorce, release'		transitive
ἀποσοβέω	ⲁⲡⲟⲥⲟⲃⲉ	'reject'		transitive
ἀποστερέω	ⲁⲡⲟⲥⲧⲉⲣⲓ	'deprive'		transitive
ἀποστηθίζω	ⲁⲡⲟⲥⲧⲏⲑⲓⲍⲉ	'learn by heart'		transitive
ἀποτάσσω	ⲁⲡⲟⲧⲁⲥⲥⲉ	'renounce'		transitive
ἀποφαίνω*	ⲁⲡⲟⲫⲁⲛⲉ	'condemn; make an effect'	'on': ⲉϫⲛ-, ϩⲓϫⲛ-	transitive (?)
ἀποχαρίζομαι	ⲁⲡⲟⲭⲁⲣⲓⲍⲉ	'give as a gift'		transitive
ἀρέσκω	ⲁⲣⲉⲥⲕⲉ	'please'	'to':ⲛᴰ	intransitive
ἀριστάω	ⲁⲣⲓⲥⲧⲁ	'have a meal'		intransitive
ἁρπάζω	ϩⲁⲣⲡⲁⲍⲉ	'seize, snatch'		transitive
ἄρχω	ⲁⲣⲭⲉⲓ	'rule'	'over': ⲉϫⲛ-, ⲉ-	intransitive
ἄρχω	ⲁⲣⲭⲉⲓ	'begin'	'DO': ⲉ-	intransitive
ἀσκέω	ⲁⲥⲕⲉⲓ	'train (self or a discipline)'		(in)transitive
ἀσπάζομαι	ⲁⲥⲡⲁⲍⲉ	'kiss, embrace'		transitive

Greek form	Coptic form	Meaning	Non-A/P actants (if present)	Transitive / Intransitive / Unclear
ἀσφαλίζω	ⲁⲥⲫⲁⲗⲓⲍⲉ	'guard, protect'		transitive
ἀσχημονέω	ⲁⲥⲭⲏⲙⲟⲛⲉⲓ	'behave unseemly'		intransitive
ἀτακτέω	ⲁⲧⲁⲕⲧⲓ	'rebel'		intransitive
ἀτονέω	ⲁⲧⲟⲛⲓ	'be exhausted, weakened'		intransitive
αὐτουργέω	ⲁⲩⲧⲟⲩⲣⲅⲉⲓ	'farm'	'on / for' : ⲉ-ϩⲁⲣⲁⲧ=	intransitive
ἀφορίζω	ⲁⲫⲱⲣⲓⲥⲉ	'excommunicate'		transitive
βιάζω	ⲃⲓⲁⲍⲉ	'force, violate'		transitive
βλασφημέω*	ⲃⲗⲁⲥⲫⲏⲙⲓ	'blaspheme'		transitive / ⲉ-
βοηθέω	ⲃⲟⲏⲑⲉⲓ	'help'	'to': ⲉ- or ⲛ^D	intransitive
γράφω	ⲅⲣⲁⲫⲉⲓ	'write'		unclear
δαιμονίζομαι	ⲇⲁⲓⲙⲟⲛⲓⲍⲉ	'be possessed'		intransitive
δαμάζω	ⲇⲁⲙⲁⲍⲉ	'subdue'		transitive
δαπανάω	ⲇⲁⲡⲁⲛⲏ, ⲇⲁⲡⲁⲛⲓⲍⲉ	'spend'		transitive
δεικνεύω	ⲇⲓⲕⲛⲉⲩⲉ	'explain'	'to': ⲛ^D	transitive
δειπνέω	ⲇⲓⲡⲛⲉⲓ	'dine, feast'		intransitive
δηλόω	ⲇⲏⲗⲟⲩ	'specify'	'to': ⲛ^D	transitive
δημιουργέω	ⲇⲏⲙⲓⲟⲩⲣⲅⲉⲓ	'create, make'		unclear
δημοσιόω	ⲇⲏⲙⲟⲥⲓⲟⲩ	'make public'		transitive
δηφεντεύω	ⲇⲏⲫⲉⲛⲧⲉⲩⲉ	'defend'		transitive
διαβάλλω	ⲇⲓⲁⲃⲁⲗⲗⲉ	'slander'		transitive
διαδέχομαι	ⲇⲓⲁⲇⲉⲭⲉ	'succeed'		transitive
διακονέω	ⲇⲓⲁⲕⲟⲛⲉⲓ	'serve, minister'	'to': ⲛ^D	intransitive*
διακρίνω	ⲇⲓⲁⲕⲣⲓⲛⲉ	'discern'		transitive
διανέμω	ⲇⲓⲁⲛⲉⲙⲏ	'distribute'		transitive
διατρέπω	ⲇⲓⲁⲧⲣⲉⲡⲉ	'be confused'		intransitive
διατρίβω	ⲇⲓⲁⲧⲣⲓⲃⲉ	'waste time'		intransitive
διδάσκω	ⲇⲓⲇⲁⲥⲕⲉ	'teach, instruct'		transitive
δικάζω	ⲇⲓⲕⲁⲍⲉ	'judge, litigate'	'to': ⲉ- anim., ⲉϫⲛ- inanim. obj.	intransitive
δικαιολογέομαι	ⲇⲓⲕⲁⲓⲟⲗⲟⲅⲉⲓ	'plead in court'		intransitive
διοικέω	ⲇⲓⲟⲓⲕⲉⲓ	'arrange, take care of'		transitive
διορθόω*	ⲇⲓⲟⲣⲑⲟⲩ	'correct, set straight'	DO: ⲛ^D or ⲛ^{Acc}	transitive (?)
διστάζω	ⲇⲓⲥⲧⲁⲍⲉ	'doubt'	'in': ⲉ-	intransitive

Greek form	Coptic form	Meaning	Non-A/P actants (if present)	Transitive / Intransitive / Unclear
διώκω	ⲇⲓⲱⲕⲉⲓ	'chase, pursue'	DO: ⲛ^Acc or ⲛⲥⲁ-	(in)transitive
δοκέω	ⲇⲟⲕⲉⲓ	'seem'	'to': ⲛ^D	intransitive
δοκιμάζω	ⲇⲟⲕⲓⲙⲁⲍⲉ	'try, test'		transitive
δωρίζω	ⲇⲱⲣⲓⲍⲉ	'donate'	'to': ⲛ^D (person), ⲉϩⲟⲩⲛ ⲉ- (institution)	transitive
ἐγγυάω	ⲉⲅⲅⲩⲁ	'go surety for'	'to': ⲛ^D	transitive
ἐγκακέω	ⲉⲅⲕⲁⲕⲉⲓ	'be discouraged'		intransitive
ἐγκαλέω*	ⲉⲅⲕⲁⲗⲉⲓ	'sue'		intransitive
ἐγκρατεύομαι	ⲉⲅⲕⲣⲁⲧⲉⲩⲉ	'control oneself'		intr. / refl.
ἐκλαμβάνω	ⲉⲅⲗⲁⲃⲉ	'take, pick out'		transitive
ἐλέγχω	ⲉⲗⲉⲅⲭⲉ	'rebuke'		transitive
ἐλευθερόω	ⲉⲗⲉⲩⲑⲉⲣⲟⲩ	'release, set free'		transitive
ἐλπίζω	ϩⲉⲗⲡⲓⲍⲉ	'hope, put one's hope'	'in': ⲉ-	intransitive
ἐμποδίζω	ⲉⲙⲡⲟⲇⲓⲍⲉ	'hinder, delay'		transitive
ἐνάγω	ⲉⲛⲁⲅⲉ	'sue, proceed (against)'	'against': ⲛ^D	intransitive
ἐνοχλέω	ⲉⲛⲟⲭⲗⲉⲓ	'bother, annoy'	DO: ⲛ^D	intransitive
ἐξαπατάω	ⲉⲝⲁⲡⲁⲧⲁ	'deceive, beguile'		transitive
ἐξειλέω	ⲉⲝⲉⲗⲉⲓ	'go free'		intransitive
ἐξετάζω	ⲉⲝⲉⲧⲁⲍⲉ	'scrutinize'		transitive
ἐξομολογέω	ⲉⲝⲟⲙⲟⲗⲟⲅⲉⲓ	'confess, praise'	DO: ⲛ^D or ⲛ^Acc	(in)transitive
ἐξορίζω	ⲉⲝⲱⲣⲓⲍⲉ	'banish'		transitive
ἐπαινέω	ⲉⲡⲁⲓⲛⲟⲩ	'praise, commend'		transitive
ἐπηρεάζω	ⲉⲡⲏⲣⲉⲁⲍⲉ	'insult, threaten'	'to': ⲛ^D	intransitive
ἐπιβουλεύω	ⲉⲡⲓⲃⲟⲩⲗⲉⲩⲉ	'plot, conspire'	'against': ⲉ-	intransitive
ἐπιδίδωμι	ⲉⲡⲓⲇⲓⲇⲟⲩ	'hand over'	'to': ⲛ^D	transitive
ἐπιθυμέω	ⲉⲡⲓⲑⲩⲙⲉⲓ	'desire, want'	DO: ⲉ-	intransitive
ἐπικαλέω	ⲉⲡⲓⲕⲁⲗⲉⲓ	'call, invoke'		transitive
ἐπινοέω*	ⲉⲡⲓⲛⲟⲉⲓ	'conceive, think of'		unclear
ἐπιτάσσω	ⲉⲡⲓⲧⲁⲥⲥⲉ	'order, command'	'to': ⲛ^D	intransitive

Greek form	Coptic form	Meaning	Non-A/P actants (if present)	Transitive / Intransitive / Unclear
ἐπιτελέω*	επιτελει	'celebrate'	DO: ν^Acc / εχν-	(in)transitive
ἐπιτιμάω	επιτιμα	'rebuke, censure'	DO: ν^D	intransitive
ἐπιτρέπω	επιτρεπε	'give commission'	DO: ν^D	intransitive
ἐπιφέρω	επιφερε	'move to and fro'		intransitive
ἐρίζω	εριζε	'quarrel'	'with': μν	intransitive
ἑρμηνεύω	ϩερμηνεγε	'interpret'		transitive
ἐτάζω	ϩεταζε	'test'		transitive
εὐαγγελέω /-ίζομαι	εγαγγελιζε	'proclaim'	'to': ν^D	transitive
εὐδοκέω	εγδοκει	'be content'		intransitive
εὐδοκιμέω	εγδοκιμε	'be famous'		intransitive
εὐλογέω	εγλογει	'praise'		transitive
εὐπορέω	εγπορει	'supply, furnish'		transitive
εὐχαριστέω	εγχαριστει	'give thanks'	'to': ν^D	intransitive
ἡσυχάζω	εσγχαζε	'be silent, at rest'		intransitive
θάλπω	θαλπει	'take care of'		transitive
θαρρέω	θαρρει	'be confident; rely'	'upon': ε-; ν^D; ϩιχν-;	intransitive
θαυμάζω	θαγμαζε	'be amazed at'		transitive
θεραπεύω	θεραπεγε	'heal, restore'		transitive
θεωρέω	θεωρει	'see, look at'		transitive
θυσιάζω	θγσιαζε	'sacrifice'	'to': ν^D	transitive
ἱστορέω	ϩιστορι, ϩιστοριζε	'relate, narrate'	'to': ν^D	transitive
καθαιρέω	καθαιρογ	'remove, expel'		transitive
καθηγέομαι	καθηγει	'teach, instruct'		transitive
καινοτομέω	καινοτομει	'renew'		transitive
καλέω	καλει	'call, summon, invite'		transitive
κανονίζω	κανωνιζε	'prompt, coach'		transitive
καπνίζω	καπνιζε	'fumigate'		transitive
καταβάλλω	καταβαλε	'contribute'		transitive
καταγινώσκω	καταγινωσκε	'condemn, censure'		transitive
καταδικάζω	καταδικαζε	'condemn'	'to': ε-	transitive
κατακρίνω	κατακρινε	'condemn'	'to': ε-	transitive
καταλαλέω	καταλαλει	'slander, malign'		transitive
καταλαμβάνω	καταλαμβανε	'seize, comprehend'		transitive

Greek form	Coptic form	Meaning	Non-A/P actants (if present)	Transitive / Intransitive / Unclear
κατανεύω	ⲕⲁⲧⲁⲛⲉⲩⲉ	'bow, assent'		intransitive
κατανοέω	ⲕⲁⲧⲁⲛⲟⲓ	'contemplate'		transitive
καταντάω	ⲕⲁⲧⲁⲛⲧⲁ	'arrive, attain, reach'	'at': ⲉ-	intransitive
καταπατέω	ⲕⲁⲧⲁⲡⲁⲧⲓ	'trample on, despise'		transitive
καταπλάσσω	ⲕⲁⲧⲁⲡⲗⲁⲥⲥⲉ	'apply as a poultice'		transitive
καταποντίζω	ⲕⲁⲧⲁⲡⲟⲛⲧⲓⲍⲉ	'throw into sea'		transitive
καταστέλλω	ⲕⲁⲧⲁⲥⲧⲉⲓⲗⲉ	'put in order, calm down'		transitive
κατηγορέω	ⲕⲁⲧⲏⲅⲟⲣⲉⲓ	'accuse, reproach'		transitive
κατοικέω	ⲕⲁⲧⲟⲓⲕⲓ	'dwell, take a part'	'in': ⲉ-, ϩⲛ-	intransitive
κελεύω	ⲕⲉⲗⲉⲩⲉ	'order'	'to': ⲛᴰ-	transitive
κερδαίνω	ⲅⲉⲣⲧⲱⲛ	'gain profit' (?)		unclear
κηρύσσω	ⲕⲏⲣⲩⲥⲥⲉ	'preach, proclaim'	'to': ⲛᴰ-	transitive
κιθαρίζω	ⲕⲓⲑⲁⲣⲓⲍⲉ	'play the lyre, play'		transitive
κινδυνεύω	ⲕⲓⲛⲇⲩⲛⲉⲩⲉ	'be in danger; be liable'	'for': ⲛᴬᶜᶜ/ϩⲁ	(in)transitive
κλασματίζω	ⲕⲗⲁⲥⲙⲁⲧⲓⲍⲉ	'break (bread)'		transitive
κληρονομέω	ⲕⲗⲏⲣⲟⲛⲟⲙⲉⲓ	'inherit'		transitive
κληρόω	ⲕⲗⲏⲣⲟⲩ	'inherit, obtain'	DO: ⲉ- or ⲛᴬᶜᶜ	(in)transitive
κολακεύω	ⲕⲟⲗⲁⲕⲉⲩⲉ	'flatter'	'to': ⲉ-	intransitive
κρεμάννυμι	ⲕⲣⲁⲙⲙⲁⲧⲓⲍⲉ	'hang'		transitive
κρίνω	ⲕⲣⲓⲛⲉ	'judge'		transitive
κυβερνάω	ⲕⲓⲃⲉⲣⲛⲁ	'steer, navigate'		transitive
κυρόω	ⲕⲩⲣⲟⲩ	'ordain'		transitive
κωλύω	ⲕⲱⲗⲩⲉ	'prevent, hinder'		transitive
λακτίζω	ⲗⲁⲕⲧⲓⲍⲉ	'kick, hit'		transitive
λάμπω	ⲗⲁⲙⲡⲉⲩⲉ	'shine'		intransitive
[λεαντηριον]	ⲗⲉⲁⲛⲧⲏⲣⲓⲉ	'polish'		transitive
λειτουργέω	ⲗⲓⲧⲟⲩⲣⲅⲉⲓ	'conduct mass; serve'	'to': ⲉ-	intransitive
λεπτύνω	ⲗⲩⲡⲧⲁⲛⲉ	'make thin'		transitive
λευκοφορέω	ⲗⲉⲩⲕⲟⲫⲟⲣⲉⲓ	'dress in white'		intransitive / reflexive
λογίζομαι	ⲗⲟⲅⲓⲍⲉ	'recite'		transitive

Greek form	Coptic form	Meaning	Non-A/P actants (if present)	Transitive / Intransitive / Unclear
λογχίζω	ⲗⲟⲅⲭⲓⲍⲉ	'pierce with a spear'		transitive
μαγεύω	ⲙⲁⲅⲉⲩⲉ	'enchant'		transitive
μακαρίζω	ⲙⲁⲕⲁⲣⲓⲍⲉ	'bless'		transitive
μαλάσσω	ⲙⲁⲗⲁⲥⲥⲉ	'soften'		transitive
μαρτυρίζω	ⲙⲁⲣⲧⲩⲣⲓⲍⲉ	'bear witness'	'to': ⲉ-	intransitive
μαστιγόω	ⲙⲁⲥⲧⲓⲅⲟⲩ	'flog'		transitive
μαυλίζω	ⲙⲁⲩⲗⲓⲍⲉ	'abuse, treat ill'		transitive
μελετάω	ⲙⲉⲗⲉⲧⲁ	'contemplate'		transitive
μέλω	ⲙⲉⲗⲉⲓ	'be of concern'		intransitive
μέμφομαι	ⲙⲉⲙⲫⲉⲓ	'blame, reproach'	DO: ⲉ-	intransitive
μερίζω	ⲙⲉⲣⲓⲍⲉ	'separate, divide'		transitive
μεσάζω	ⲙⲉⲥⲁⲥⲉ	'divide, distribute'		transitive
μετανοέω	ⲙⲉⲧⲁⲛⲟⲉⲓ	'repent'	'of': ⲉⲃⲟⲗ ϩⲛ-, ⲉϫⲛ-, ϩⲁ-	intransitive
μεταστοιχεω	ⲙⲉⲧⲁⲥⲧⲟⲓⲭⲉⲓ	'shape, fashion'		transitive
μετέχω	ⲙⲉⲧⲉⲭⲉ	'partake'	'in': ⲉ- or ⲛᴬᶜᶜ	(in)transitive
μηνύω	ⲙⲉⲛⲉⲩⲉ	'reveal, make known'	'to': ⲛ-	transitive
μυσταγωγέω	ⲙⲩⲥⲧⲁⲅⲱⲅⲓⲛ	'initiate, lead into'		transitive
νηστεύω	ⲛⲏⲥⲧⲉⲩⲉ	'fast'		intransitive
νοέω	ⲛⲟⲉⲓ	'observe, perceive'	DO : ⲉ- or ⲛᴬᶜᶜ	(in)transitive
νομοθετέω	ⲛⲟⲙⲟⲑⲉⲧⲓ	'give laws'	'to': ⲛᴰ	unclear
οἰκονομέω	ⲟⲓⲕⲟⲛⲟⲙⲉⲓ	'manage, take care of'		transitive
ὀκνέω	ⲱⲕⲛⲉⲓ	'hesitate, delay'		intransitive
ὁμιλέω	ϩⲟⲙⲉⲗⲉⲓ	'teach, preach'	'with, to': ⲉ-, ⲙⲛ	intransitive
ὁμοιάζω	ϩⲟⲙⲟⲓⲱⲍⲉ	'be like'	'to': ⲉ-	intransitive
ὁμολογέω	ϩⲟⲙⲟⲗⲟⲅⲉⲓ	'acknowledge, confess'	DO: ⲛᴰ or ⲛᴬᶜᶜ	(in)transitive
ὀνομάζω	ⲟⲛⲟⲙⲁⲍⲉ	'name'		transitive
ὁπλίζω	ϩⲟⲡⲗⲓⲍⲉ	'arm'		transitive
ὁρίζω	ϩⲟⲣⲓⲍⲉ	'appoint, decree'	'to': ⲛᴰ	transitive
ὀρχέομαι	ⲟⲣⲭⲉⲓ	'dance'		intransitive
παραγγέλλω	ⲡⲁⲣⲁⲅⲅⲉⲓⲗⲉ	'command, instruct'	'to': ⲛᴰ	intransitive

Greek form	Coptic form	Meaning	Non-A/P actants (if present)	Transitive / Intransitive / Unclear
παραδειγματίζω	παραδειγματιζε	'put to shame; exemplify'		transitive
παραδείκνυμι	παραδιϭι	'mock, slander'	DO: ν-	unclear
παραδέχομαι	παραδεχε	'accept, take'		transitive
παραδίδωμι	παραδιδου	'give over, betray'	'to': ν^D	transitive
παραιτέομαι	παραιτει	'decline'		transitive
παρακαλέω	παρακαλει	'beseech'		transitive
παραλαμβάνω	παραλαμβανε	'accept, receive'		transitive
παραλλάσσω	παραλλασσε	'change, alter'		transitive
παραμένω	παραμεινε	'stay, wait, serve'	'for/ to': ε-	intransitive
παρανομέω	παρανομει	'transgress, violate'		transitive
παρασκευάζω	παρασκευαζε	'make ready, force'		transitive
παρατηρέω	παρατηρι	'observe. attend'	'to': ε-	intransitive
παραχειμάζω	παραχιμαζε	'be stormy; spend winter'		intransitive
παραχωρέω	παραχωρει	'surrender, give up on'	'to': ν^D	transitive
παρέρχομαι	παρελθε	'pass by, skip, omit'		transitive
παριστάνω	παρϩιστα 'present'	'present'	'to': ν^D	transitive
παρρησιάζομαι	παρρησιαζε	'declare boldly, dare to'		reflexive
πάσχω	παθει	'suffer, endure'		transitive
πατάσσω	πατασσε	'hit, strike'		transitive
πειράζω	πειραζε	'try, tempt'		transitive
πενθέω	πενθει	'grieve'	'for': ε- or ν^D	intransitive
περιεργάζομαι	περιεργαζε	'diligently work'	'on': νϲα-	intransitive
περιχέω	περιχε	'spread, anoint'		transitive
περιχρίω	περιχρε, περιχρια	'anoint'		transitive
πήσσω	πηϲϲε	'fasten, nail down; crucify'		transitive
πιστεύω	πιϲτεγε	trust, believe	'to': ν^D or ε-	intransitive
πλάσσω	πλαϲϲε	'create, form'	pred. compl.: ν-	transitive

Greek form	Coptic form	Meaning	Non-A/P actants (if present)	Transitive / Intransitive / Unclear
πλεαω	ⲡⲗⲉⲁ	'sail'		intransitive
πλήσσω	ⲡⲗⲏⲥⲥⲉ	'be dumbstruck'		intransitive
πολεμέω	ⲡⲟⲗⲉⲙⲉⲓ	'wage war'	'against': ⲙⲛ, ϩⲛ-	intransitive
πονηρεύω	ⲡⲟⲛⲏⲣⲉⲩⲉ	'act maliciously'		intransitive
πορνεύω	ⲡⲟⲣⲛⲉⲩⲉ	'commit adultery'		intransitive
πρέπω	ⲡⲣⲉⲡⲉⲓ	'be fitting'	'to': ⲛᴰ	intransitive
πρεσβεύω	ⲡⲣⲉⲥⲃⲉⲩⲉ	'intercede, help'	'for': ϩⲁ-	intransitive
προβάλλω	ⲡⲣⲟⲃⲁⲗⲉ (ⲉⲃⲟⲗ)	'emanate, produce'		transitive
προδίδωμι	ⲡⲣⲟⲇⲓⲇⲟⲩ	'betray, surrender'		transitive
προέρχομαι	ⲡⲣⲟⲉⲗⲑⲉ	'come forth, emanate'		intransitive
προιστάω	ⲡⲣⲟϩⲓⲥⲧⲁ	'preside'	'over': ⲉ-	intransitive
προκαλέω	ⲡⲣⲟⲕⲁⲗⲉⲓ	'provoke'		transitive
προκόπτω	ⲡⲣⲟⲕⲟⲡⲧⲉ	'advance, progress'		intransitive
προλαμβάνω	ⲡⲣⲟⲗⲁⲙⲃⲁⲛⲉ	'anticipate' (?)		unclear
προνοέω	ⲡⲣⲟⲛⲟⲉⲓ	'foresee'		transitive
προσαγορεύω	ⲡⲣⲟⲥⲁⲅⲟⲣⲉⲩⲉ	'greet'		transitive
προσδοκάω	ⲡⲣⲟⲥⲇⲟⲕⲁ, ⲡⲣⲟⲥⲇⲟⲕⲉⲓ	'hope, expect'	DO: ⲉ-	intransitive
προσέρχομαι	ⲡⲣⲟⲥⲉⲗⲑⲉ	'approach; prosecute'	DO: ⲉ-	intransitive
προσέχω	ⲡⲣⲟⲥⲉⲭⲉ	'care, attend'	'for, to': ⲉ-	intransitive
προσκαρτερέω	ⲡⲣⲟⲥⲕⲁⲣⲧⲉⲣⲉⲓ	'remain, persist, wait'	'for': ⲉ-	intransitive
προσκυνέω	ⲡⲣⲟⲥⲕⲩⲛⲉⲓ	'worship, prostrate before'	'DO': ⲛᴰ or ⲛᴬᶜᶜ	(in)transitive
προσφέρω	ⲡⲣⲟⲥⲫⲉⲣⲉⲓ	'sacrifice'	'to': ⲛᴰ	transitive
προσχαρίζομαι	ⲡⲣⲟⲥⲭⲁⲣⲓⲍⲉ	'gratify, satisfy'	'DO': ⲛᴰ	intransitive
προτρέπω	ⲡⲣⲟⲧⲣⲉⲡⲉ	'urge, exhort'		transitive
προφητεύω	ⲡⲣⲟⲫⲏⲧⲉⲩⲉ	'prophesy'		transitive
πυκτεύω	ⲡⲓⲕⲧⲉⲩⲉ	'fight, box'	'against': ⲟⲩⲃⲉ	intransitive

Greek form	Coptic form	Meaning	Non-A/P actants (if present)	Transitive / Intransitive / Unclear
πυρόω	ⲡⲩⲣⲟⲩ	'set on fire, purify by fire'		transitive
ῥευματίζομαι	ϩⲣⲉⲩⲙⲁⲧⲓⲥⲉ	'suffer from a flux'		intransitive
ῥιπίζω	ϩⲣⲉⲡⲓⲍⲉ	'flap (wings)'		transitive
σαλπίζω	ⲥⲁⲗⲡⲓⲍⲉ	'blow a trumpet'		intransitive
σαφηνίζω	ⲥⲁⲫⲏⲛⲓⲍⲉ	'mention, clarify'		transitive
σεληνιάζομαι	ⲥⲉⲗⲏⲛⲓⲁⲍⲉ	'suffer from epilepsy'		intransitive
σημαίνω	ⲥⲏⲙⲁⲛⲉ	'indicate, suggest, predict'		transitive
σημειόω	ⲥⲩⲙⲓⲟⲩ	'note, write down'		transitive
σκεπάζω	ⲥⲕⲉⲡⲁⲍⲉ	'cover, protect, shelter'		transitive
σκευάζω	ⲥⲕⲉⲩⲁⲍⲉ	'prepare'		transitive
σκιρτάω	ⲥⲕⲓⲣⲧⲁ	'leap, frolic'		intransitive
σκοτόω	ⲥⲕⲟⲑⲟⲩ, ⲥⲕⲟⲧⲉⲩⲉ	'become dizzy, in the dark'		intransitive
σκώπτω	ⲥⲕⲱⲡⲧⲉ	'mock'		transitive
σπαταλάω	ⲥⲡⲁⲧⲁⲗⲁ	'live wantonly'		intransitive
σπουδάζω	ⲥⲡⲟⲩⲇⲁⲍⲉ	'hurry be eager'		intransitive
σταυρόω	ⲥⲧⲁⲩⲣⲟⲩ	'crucify'		transitive
στηλιτεύω	ⲥⲧⲩⲗⲓⲧⲉⲩⲉ	'scorn, ridicule'		transitive
στοιχέω	ⲥⲧⲟⲓⲭⲉⲓ	'agree'	'to': ⲉ-	intransitive
στρατεύω	ⲥⲧⲣⲁⲧⲉⲩⲉ	'wage war; be a soldier'		intransitive / reflexive
στρεβλόω	ⲥⲧⲣⲉⲃⲗⲟⲩ	'be concerned'		intransitive
συγκρίνω	ⲥⲩⲅⲕⲣⲓⲛⲉ	'compare'		transitive
συγχωρέω	ⲥⲩⲛⲭⲱⲣⲉⲓ	'allow, grant'	'to': ⲛᴰ	transitive
συζητέω	ⲥⲩⲛⲍⲏⲧⲉⲓ	'dispute'	'about': ⲉⲧⲃⲉ	intransitive
συλάω	ⲥⲩⲗⲁ	'rob'		transitive
συμβουλεύω	ⲥⲩⲙⲃⲟⲩⲗⲉⲩⲉ	'counsel, advise'	'to': ⲛᴰ, DO: ⲉ-	intransitive
συμπείθω	ⲥⲉⲙⲡⲓⲑⲉ	'make an agreement'	'with': ⲙⲛ	intransitive
συμφανίζω	ⲥⲩⲙⲫⲁⲛⲓⲍⲉ	'mention'		transitive
συμφωνέω	ⲥⲩⲙⲫⲱⲛⲉⲓ	'agree'	to /with': ⲉ-, ⲙⲛ	intransitive
συναινέω	ⲥⲩⲛⲁⲓⲛⲉⲓ	'agree'	to /with': ⲉ-, ⲙⲛ	intransitive

Greek form	Coptic form	Meaning	Non-A/P actants (if present)	Transitive / Intransitive / Unclear
συνακολουθέω	ⲥⲩⲛⲁⲕⲟⲗⲟⲅⲑⲓ	'follow'	'after': ⲛⲥⲁ	intransitive
συναλίζω	ⲥⲩⲛⲁⲗⲓⲍⲉ	'reach an agreement'	'with': ⲙⲛ	intransitive
συναλλάσσω	ⲥⲩⲛⲁⲗⲗⲁⲥⲥⲉ	'exchange'		transitive
συνέρχομαι	ⲥⲩⲛⲏⲗⲑⲁⲓ	'join'	'with /for': ⲙⲛ, ⲉ-	intransitive
συνευδοκέω	ⲥⲩⲛⲉⲩⲇⲟⲕⲉⲓ	'agree, approve'	'with /of': ⲙⲛ, ⲉ-	intransitive
συντάσσω	ⲥⲩⲛⲧⲁⲍⲉ	'agree, instruct, order'		unclear
συντελέω	ⲥⲩⲛⲧⲉⲗⲉⲓ	'contribute'		transitive
συντιμάζω	ⲥⲩⲛⲧⲓⲙⲁⲍⲉ	'value, estimate'	'at': ⲉ-	transitive
συρίζω	ⲥⲩⲣⲓⲍⲉ	'whistle, hiss'		intransitive
σφραγίζω	ⲥⲫⲣⲁⲅⲓⲍⲉ	'seal, cross'		transitive
σχολάζω	ⲥⲭⲟⲗⲁⲍⲉ	'have leisure'	'for': ⲉ-	intransitive
σωματίζω	ⲥⲱⲙⲁⲧⲓⲍⲉ	'draw up (a document)'		transitive
σωφρονέω	ⲥⲟⲫⲣⲟⲛⲓ	'be of a sound mind'		intransitive
ταλαιπωρέω	ⲧⲁⲗⲁⲓⲡⲱⲣⲉⲓ	'be miserable, afflicted'		intransitive
ταχύνω	ⲧⲁⲭⲏ	'make haste'		intransitive
τελειόω, τελέω	ⲧⲉⲗⲓⲟⲩ, ⲧⲉⲗⲉ	'finish, complete'		transitive
τηρέω	ⲧⲏⲣⲉⲓ	'protect, keep'		transitive
τιμάω	ⲧⲓⲙⲁ	'honour'		transitive
τιμωρέω	ⲧⲓⲙⲱⲣⲉⲓ	'punish'		transitive
τολμάω	ⲧⲟⲗⲙⲁ	'dare'		intransitive
τρίβω	ⲧⲣⲓⲃⲉ	'rub, pound'		transitive
τυπόω	ⲧⲩⲡⲟⲩ	'form, mould'		transitive
τυραννεύω	ⲧⲩⲣⲁⲛⲛⲉⲩⲉ	'suppress'		transitive
ὑβρίζω	ϩⲩⲃⲣⲓⲍⲉ	'insult, abuse'		transitive
ὑμνεύω, ὑμνέω	ϩⲩⲙⲛⲓ, ϩⲩⲙⲛⲉⲩⲉ	'sing praises, glorify'	'to, for': ⲉ-	intransitive
ὑπαγορεύω	ϩⲩⲡⲁⲅⲟⲣⲉⲩⲉ	'dictate'		transitive
ὑπηρετέω	ϩⲩⲡⲏⲣⲉⲧⲉⲓ	'serve'	'to': ⲛD or ⲛAcc	(in)transitive
ὑποβάλλω	ϩⲩⲡⲟⲃⲁⲗⲗⲉ	'throw, submit'	'to': ⲛD	transitive
ὑπογράφω	ϩⲩⲡⲟⲅⲣⲁⲫⲉ	'sign'	DO: ⲉ-	intransitive

Greek form	Coptic form	Meaning	Non-A/P actants (if present)	Transitive / Intransitive / Unclear
ὑποδέχομαι	ϩⲩⲡⲟⲇⲉⲭⲉ	'receive (taxes)'		transitive
ὑποκρίνω	ϩⲩⲡⲟⲕⲣⲓⲛⲉ	'counterfeit'		intransitive
ὑπομένω	ϩⲩⲡⲟⲙⲓⲛⲉ	'endure, remain, wait'	'for': ⲉ-	intransitive
ὑπομνήσκω	ϩⲩⲡⲟⲙⲛⲓⲍⲉ	'come back to one's mind; admonish'		trans. / refl.
ὑποτάσσω*	ϩⲩⲡⲟⲧⲁⲥⲥⲉ	'obey, submit oneself'	'to': ⲛᴰ	intransitive
ὑστερέω	ϩⲩⲥⲧⲉⲣⲉⲓ	'lag behind, fail'		transitive
φεύγω	ⲫⲓⲕⲉ	'flee'		intransitive
φθονέω	ⲫⲑⲟⲛⲉⲓ, ⲫⲑⲟⲛⲉⲩⲉ	'envy'	'to': ⲉ-	intransitive
φιλοκαλέω	ⲫⲓⲗⲟⲕⲁⲗⲉⲓ	'tend to, maintain'		transitive
φιλοσοφέω	ⲫⲓⲗⲟⲥⲟⲫⲉⲓ	'study, investigate'		transitive
φλεγμαίνω	ⲫⲗⲉⲕⲙⲁ	'be inflamed'		intransitive
φορέω	ⲫⲟⲣⲉⲓ	'bear, carry'		transitive
φραγελλόω	ⲫⲣⲁⲅⲉⲗⲗⲟⲩ	'flog, scourge'		transitive
φρονέω	ⲫⲣⲟⲛⲉⲓ	'understand'	DO: ⲉ- or ⲛ-	unclear
χαλάω	ⲭⲁⲗⲁ	'let down, lower'		transitive
χαλινόω	ⲭⲁⲗⲓⲛⲟⲩ	'bridle, restrain'		transitive
χαράττω	ⲭⲁⲣⲁⳅⲟⲛ, ⲭⲁⲣⲁⲧⲧⲓⲛ	'engrave'		transitive
χαρίζω	ⲭⲁⲣⲓⲍⲉ	'give, grant'	'to': ⲛᴰ	transitive
χειροτονέω	ⲭⲉⲓⲣⲟⲧⲟⲛⲉⲓ	'ordain'	pred. compl.: ⲛ-	transitive
χλευάζω	ⲭⲗⲉⲩⲁⲍⲉ	'jest, scoff'		transitive
χορεύω	ⲭⲱⲣⲉⲩⲉ	'celebrate'		intransitive
χορηγέω	ⲭⲟⲣⲏⲅⲉⲓ, ⲭⲱⲣⲏⲅⲉⲓ	'supply'	'to': ⲛᴰ	transitive
χρεωστέω	ⲭⲣⲉⲱⲥⲧⲉⲓ	'owe'	'to': ⲛᴰ	transitive
χρηματίζω	ⲭⲣⲏⲙⲁⲧⲓⲍⲉ	'exist; give oracles; act'	'on behalf of': ϩⲁ	intransitive
χρησιμεύω	ⲭⲣⲩⲥⲓⲙⲉⲩⲉ, ⲭⲣⲩⲥⲓⲙⲟⲩ	'be useful'		intransitive
χωρέω	ⲭⲱⲣⲉⲓ	'contain; describe'		transitive
ψάλλω	ϯⲁⲗⲗⲉⲓ	'sing, make music'		intransitive

Bibliography

Abraham, Werner. 2006. 'Introduction: Passivization and typology. Form vs. function – a confined survey into the research status quo', in: W. Abraham, L. Leisiö (eds.), *Passivization and Typology: Form and function* [Typological Studies in Language 68], 1-28. Amsterdam; Philadelphia: John Benjamins.

Abramova. 2019. *"Yuridicheskoe deloproizvodstvo. Posobie dlia bakalavrov"* (Legal paperwork. Bachelor's Guide). Moscow: Prospect.

Aikhenvald, Alexandra Y. 2002. *Language contact in Amazonia*. New York: Oxford University Press.

Allen, James P. 2014. *Middle Egyptian: An Introduction to the Language and Culture of Hieroglyphs* (3rd ed.). Cambridge University Press.

Almond, Mathew 2010. 'Language Change in Greek Loaned Verbs', in: *Lingua Aegyptia* 18, 19-31.

Apresjan, Jurij D. 1974. *"Lexicheskaya semantika. Synonymicheskiye sredstva yazyka"* (Lexical Semantics. Synonymous Means of Language). Moscow: Nauka.

Arkadiev, Peter. 'From resultative to passive: a view from Northwest Caucasian'. Paper presented at the conference "Typology of Morphosyntactic Parameters 2018", Moscow, 22–24 October 2018. (https://inslav.ru/sites/default/files/arkadiev2018_nwcresult_tmp.pdf)

Arkhipov, Ilya, Maxim Kalinin & Sergey Loesov. 2021. 'A Historical Overview of Akkadian Morphosyntax', in: J.-P. Vita (ed.), *History of the Akkadian Language, vol. I: Linguistic Background and Early Periods*. London-Leiden: Brill.

Bagnall, Roger S. & Raffaella Cribiore. 2006. *Women's Letters from Ancient Egypt, 300 BC – AD 800*, Volume I. Ann Arbor: The University of Michigan Press.

Bentein, Klaas. 2011. 'Towards the identification of verbal periphrasis in ancient Greek: A prototype analysis', in: *Acta Classica* 54:1-25.

Böhlig, Alexander. 1953. 'Griechische Deponentien im Koptischen', in: *Aegyptus* 33 *(Raccolta di Scritti in Onore di Girolamo Vitelli IV)*, 91-96, Pubblicazioni dell'Università Cattolica del Sacro Cuore: Vita e Pensiero.

——1955. 'Beiträge zur Form der griechischen Wörter im Koptischen', in: *ZÄS* 80, 90-97.

——1995. 'Die Form der griechischen Verben in den Texten von Nag Hammadi', in: C. Fluck, L. Langener, S. Richter, S. Schaten & G. Wurst (eds.), *Divitiae Aegypti. Koptologische und verwandelte Studien zu Ehren von Martin Krause,* 19-28. Wiesbaden: Reichert.

Booij, Geert. 1996. 'Inherent versus contextual inflection and the split morphology hypothesis', in: *Yearbook of Morphology* 1995, 1-16. (https://geertbooij.files.wordpress.com/2014/02/booij-1996-inherent-and-contextual-inflection-yom.pdf).

Borer, Hagit. 2005. *Structuring sense II: The normal course of events*. Oxford: Oxford University Press.

Bortone, Pietro. 2010. *Greek prepositions from antiquity to the present*. Oxford: Oxford University Press.

Buttmann, Alexander. 1877. *Des Apollonios Dyskolos Vier Bücher über die Syntax, übers. und erläutert von A. Buttmann*, Berlin: Ferd. Dummlers Verlagsbuchhandlung, Harrwitz und Gossmann.

Bybee, Joan L., Revere D. Perkins & William Pagliuca. 1994. *The evolution of grammar: Tense, aspect, and modality in the languages of the world*. Chicago: The University of Chicago Press.

Canger, Una & Anne Jensen. 2007. 'Grammatical borrowing in Nahuatl', in: Y. Matras & J. Sakel (eds.), *Grammatical borrowing in cross-linguistic perspective*, 403–418. Berlin: Mouton de Gruyter.

Černy, Jaroslav. 1976. *Coptic Etymological Dictionary*. Cambridge: Cambridge University Press.

Cobbinah, Alexander & Friederike Lüpke. 2009. 'Not cut to fit – zero coded passives in African languages', in: M. Brenzinger & A.-M. Fehn (eds.), *Proceedings, 6th World Congress of African Linguistics*, 133-144. Cologne: Köppe.

Coghill, Eleanor. 2015. 'Borrowing of Verbal Derivational Morphology between Semitic Languages: the case of Arabic verb derivations in Neo-Aramaic', in: F. Gardani, P. Arkadiev & N. Amiridze (eds.), *Borrowed morphology*, 83-108. Berlin, Boston & Munich: Mouton de Gruyter.

Combs, Jason Robert and Joseph G. Miller. 2011. A Marriage-Gift of Part of a Monastery from Byzantine Egypt, in: *Bulletin of the American Society of Papyrologists* 48 (2011) 79-88.

Comrie, Bernard. 1981. 'Aspect and voice: Some reflections on perfect and passive', in: P. Tedeschi and A. Zaenen (eds.), *Syntax and Semantics, vol. 14: Tense and aspect*. New York: Academic Press.

——1985. 'Causative verb-formation and other verb-deriving morphology', in: Th. Shopen (ed.), *Language typology and syntactic description, Vol. 3: Grammatical categories and the lexicon*, 301-348. Cambridge: Cambridge University Press.

Crum, Walter E. 1939. *Coptic Dictionary*. Oxford: Clarendon Press.

DeLancey, Scott. 1987.'Transitivity in Grammar and Cognition', in: R. Tomlin (ed.), *Coherence and Grounding in Discourse*, 53-68. Amsterdam: John Benjamins.

Depuydt, Leo. 2002. 'Eight Exotic Phenomena of Later Egyptian Explained', in: K. Ryholt (ed.), *Acts of the Seventh International Conference of Demotic Studies, Copenhagen, 23-27 August 1999* ([Carsten Niebuhr Institute Publ 27], 101-129. Copenhagen: Museum Tusculanum Press.

——2009. 'Demotic Script and Demotic Language (IV): Consolidation of a New Rule of Grammar Differentiating Demotic from Coptic', in: G. Widmer & D. Devauchelle (eds.), *Actes du IXe congrès international des études démotiques, Paris, 31 août - 3 septembre 2005* [Bibliothèque d'étude 147], 103-121. Le Caire : Institut Français d'Archéologie Orientale.

Dimitrova-Vulchanova, Mila. 2012. 'Voice', in: R.I. Binnick (ed.), *The Oxford Handbook of Tense and Aspect*, 937-959. Oxford: Oxford University Press.

Dinneen, Francis P. 1968. 'Analogy, Langue and Parole', in: *Lingua* 21 (1968), 98-103.

Dixon, Robert M.W. & Alexandra Y. Aikhenvald. 2000. 'Introduction', in: R.M.W. Dixon & A.Y. Aikhenvald (eds.). *Changing valency. Case studies in transitivity*. Cambridge: Cambridge University Press.

Doron, Edit. 2003. 'Agency and Voice: The Semantics of the Semitic Templates', in: *Natural Language Semantics* 11, 1-67.

Dowty, David R. 1991. 'Thematic Proto-Roles and Argument Selection', in: *Language* 67, 547-619.

Edel, Elmar. 1955. *Altägyptische Grammatik*. Roma: Pontificium Institutum Biblicum.

Egedi, Barbara. 2015. 'Greek Loanwords and Two Grammatical Features of Pre-Coptic Egyptian', in: P. Kousoulis and N.Lazaridis (eds.), *Proceedings of the tenth international congress of egyptologists, University of the Aegean, Rhodes 22-29 May 2008.* [Orientalia Lovaniensia Analecta 241], 1333-1345. Peeters.

——2017. 'Remarks on Loan Verb Integration into Coptic', in: E. Grossman, P. Dils, T.S. Richter & W. Schenkel (eds.), *Greek Influence on Egyptian-Coptic: Contact-Induced Change in an Ancient African Language.* [DDGLC Working Papers 1], 195-206. Hamburg: Widmaier Verlag.

Elanskaya, Alla I. 2010. "*Grammatika koptskogo jazyka: Sahidskij dialekt*" [Grammar of the Coptic Language: Sahidic dialect]. St.Petersburg: Nestor-Istorija.

Emmel, Stephen. 2006. 'Coptic Grammatical Terminology before and after Polotsky: Transitivity and Case (with sōtm "Hear" for an Example)', in: *Lingua Aegyptia* 14, 31-54.

Emmel, Stephen. 2021. *Shenoute, Canon 1* (unpublished preliminary edition, translations: S. Becker).

Engsheden, Åke. 2006. 'Über die Markierung des direkten Objekts im Koptischen', in: *Lingua Aegyptia* 14, 199-222.

——2008. 'Differential object marking in Sahidic Coptic', in: F. Josephson, I. Söhrman (eds.): *Interdependence of diachronic and synchronic analyses*, 323-344. Amsterdam: John Benjamins.

Fillmore, Charles. 1969. 'Types for Lexical Information', in: Kiefer, F. (ed.) *Studies in Syntax and Semantics*. Dordrecht: Reidel.

Funk, Wolf-Peter. 1978a. 'Zur Syntax des koptischen Qualitativs', in: *ZÄS* 105 (1), 94-114.

——1978b. 'Toward a synchronic morphology of Coptic', in: Wilson, R. McL.(ed.), *The future of Coptic studies* [Coptic Studies 1], 104-124. Leiden: Brill.

——1995. 'The Linguistic Aspects of Classifying the Nag Hammadi Codices', in: L. Painchaud, A. Pasquier (eds.), *Les textes de Nag Hammadi et le probleme de leur classification. Actes du colloque tenu à Québec du 15 au 19 septembre 1993.*
[Bibliothèque copte de Nag Hammadi - Études 3], 107-147. Québec: Presses de l'Université Laval.
——2017. 'Differential Loan across the Coptic Literary Dialects', in: E. Grossman, P. Dils, T.S. Richter & W. Schenkel (eds.), *Greek Influence on Egyptian-Coptic: Contact-Induced Change in an Ancient African Language.* [DDGLC Working Papers 1], 368-397. Hamburg: Widmaier Verlag.
——(unpublished) A Work Concordance to Shenoute's Canons.
Gardani, Francesco, Peter Arkadiev & Nino Amiridze (eds.). 2015. *Borrowed morphology.* Berlin, Boston & Munich: Mouton de Gruyter.
Gardani, Francesco. 2018. 'On morphological borrowing', in: *Language and Linguistics Compass* 12(10), 1–17.
——2020. Morphology and contact-induced language change, in: Anthony Grant (ed.), *The Oxford handbook of language contact,* 96–122. Oxford: Oxford University Press.
Gardiner, Alan H. 1957. *Egyptian Grammar; Being an Introduction to the Study of Hieroglyphs.* Oxford: Griffith Institute, Ashmolean Museum.
Gast, Volker, Van der Auwera, Johan. 2012. 'What is 'contact-induced grammaticalization'? Examples from Mayan and Mixe-Zoquean', in: B. Wiemer, B. Wälchli, and B. Hansen (eds.), *Grammatical Replication and Borrowability in Language Contact.* [Trends in Linguistics. Studies and Monographs, 242]. Berlin, New York: Mouton de Gruyter.
Geniušienė, Emma Š. 2006. 'Passives in Lithuanian (in comparison with Russian)', in: W. Abraham and L. Leisiö (eds.), Passivization and Typology: Form and function [Typological Studies in Language 68], 29–61. John Benjamins.
Gerritsen, Nelleke. 1988. 'How passive is 'passive' -sJa?', in: A.A. Barentsen, B.M. Groen & R.Sprenger (eds.) *Dutch studies in Russian linguistics* [Studies in Slavic and general linguistics, 11], 97-179. Amsterdam: Brill Rodopi.
Gianollo, Chiara. 2014. 'Labile verbs in Late Latin', in: *Linguistics* 52 (4), 945–1002.
Girgis, Waheeb A. 1955. *Greek Words in Coptic Usage.* Manchester: University of Manchester, Faculty of Arts.
Givón, Talmy. 1984. *Syntax: A Functional-Typological introduction.* Volume I. Amsterdam, Philadelphia: John Benjamins.
——1995. *Functionalism and Grammar.* Amsterdam: John Benjamins.
Greenberg, Joseph H. 1966. *Language universals: With special reference to feature hierarchies.* The Hague: Mouton de Gruyter.
Grossman, Eitan. 2009. 'Periphrastic Perfects in the Coptic Dialects: A Case Study in Grammaticalization', in: *Lingua Aegyptia* 17 (2009), 81-118.
Grossman, Eitan & Tonio Sebastian Richter. 2015. 'The Egyptian-Coptic language: its setting in space, time and culture', in: E. Grossman, M. Haspelmath & T.S. Richter (eds.), *Egyptian-Coptic Linguistics in Typological perspective,* 69–101. Berlin: Mouton de Gruyter.
——2017. 'Dialectal Variation and Language Change: The Case of Greek Loan-Verb Integration Strategies in Coptic', in: E. Grossman, P. Dils, T.S. Richter & W. Schenkel (eds.), *Greek Influence on Egyptian-Coptic: Contact-Induced Change in an Ancient African Language.* [DDGLC Working Papers 1], 207-236. Hamburg: Widmaier Verlag.
Grossman, Eitan. 2019. 'Language-Specific Transitivities in Contact: The Case of Coptic', in: *Journal of Language Contact,* vol.12 issue 1 2019, 89-115.
Gruber, Jeffrey S. *Studies in Lexical Relations.* PhD Dissertation, MIT 1965.
Haiman, John. 1983. 'Iconic and Economic Motivation', in: *Language* 59, 781−819.
Haspelmath, Martin. 1987. *Transitivity alternations of the anticausative type.* (Arbeitspapiere des Instituts für Sprachwissenschaft N.F. Nr. 4). Cologne: Universität zu Köln.

——1993. 'More on the typology of inchoative/causative verb alternations', in: B. Comrie & M. Polinsky (eds.), *Causatives and Transitivity* [Studies in Language Companion Series 23]. Amsterdam: John Benjamins. 87–120.

——2000. 'Periphrasis', in: G.Booij, C. Lehmann & J.Mugdan (eds.), *Morphology: A Handbook on Inflection and Word Formation.* [Handbücher zur Sprach- und Kommunikationswissenschaft] Vol. 1. Berlin: De Gruyter. 654-64.

——2008a. 'Loanword typology: Steps toward a systematic cross-linguistic study of lexical borrowability', in: T. Stolz, D. Bakker & R. Salas Palomo (eds.), *Aspects of language contact: New theoretical, methodological and empirical findings with special focus on Romancisation processes.* Berlin: Mouton de Gruyter. 43-62.

——2008b. 'Frequency vs. iconicity in explaining grammatical asymmetries', in: *Cognitive Linguistics* 19(1) 2008, 1-33.

——2010. 'Comparative concepts and descriptive categories in crosslinguistic studies', in: *Language* 86 (3), 663-687.

——2011. On S, A, P, T, and R as comparative concepts for alignment typology, in: *Linguistic Typology* 15(3), 535-567.

——2015a. 'Transitivity prominence', in: A. L. Malchukov & B. Comrie (eds.), *Valency classes in the world's languages: A comparative handbook*, vol. 1. Berlin: Mouton de Gruyter, 131–147.

——2015b. 'A grammatical overview of Egyptian and Coptic', in: E. Grossman, M. Haspelmath & T.S. Richter (eds.), *Egyptian-Coptic Linguistics in Typological perspective*. Berlin: Mouton de Gruyter. 103-145.

——2016. 'Universals of causative and anticausative verb formation and the spontaneity scale', in: *Lingua Posnaniensis* 2016, 33-63.

Haspelmath, Martin, Andreea Calude, Michael Spagnol, Heiko Narrog & Elif Bamyacı. 2014. 'Coding causal-noncausal verb alternations: A form-frequency correspondence explanation', in: *Journal of Linguistics* 50(3). 587-625.

Heine, Bernd & Tania Kuteva. 2005. *Language Contact and Grammatical Change.* Cambridge University Press.

Hopper, Paul & Sandra Thompson. 1980. 'Transitivity in Grammar and Discourse', in: *Language*, 56, 251-99.

Jernstedt, Petr V. 1925. 'Zum Gebrauch des koptischen Qualitativs'. *Doklady AN SSSR* 1925, 23-26.

——1959. *Koptskie teksty Gosudarstvennogo Ermitazha.* [Coptic texts of the State Hermitage]. Moscow-Leningrad: AN SSSR.

——1986. *Issledovanija po grammatike koptskogo jazyka.* [Studies in the grammar of Coptic language]. Moscow: Nauka.

Johnson, Janet H. 1976. *The Demotic Verbal System.* Chicago: Oriental Institute of the University of Chicago.

Junge, Friedrich. 2005. *Late Egyptian Grammar: An Introduction.* Transl. David Warburton. Oxford: Griffith Institute.

Khrakovsky, Viktor S. 1989. 'Semanticheskie tipy mnozhestva situacij i ih estestvennaja klassifikacija' [Semantic types of situational multitude and their natural classification], in: Khrakovsky (ed.), *Tipologija iterativnyh konstrukcij [Typology of iterative constructions].* Leningrad: Nauka, 5-53.

Kittilä, Seppo.2002. *Transitivity: Towards a Comprehensive Typology.* [Publications in General Linguistics 5]. University of Turku.

Kossmann, Maarten. 2010. 'Parallel System Borrowing: Parallel morphological systems due to the borrowing of paradigms', in: *Diachronica*, Vol. 27:3 (2010), 459–488.

Kühner, Raphael & Bernhard Gerth. 1898. *Ausführliche Grammatik der Griechischen Sprache von Dr Raphael Kühner.* Zweiter Teil: Satzlehre. Dritte Auflage in zwei Bänden in Neuer Bearbeitung besorgt vom Dr Bernhard Gerth. Erster Band. Hannover und Leipzig. Hahnsche Buchhandlung.

Kulikov, Leonid. 1998. 'Passive, Anticausative and Classification of Verbs: The Case of Vedic', in: *Typology of verbal categories: Papers presented to Vladimir Nedjalkov on the occasion of his 70th birthday* [Linguistische Arbeiten 382], 139-154. Tübingen: Niemeyer.

——1999. 'Split causativity: remarks on correlations between transitivity, aspect, and tense', in: W. Abraham & L. Kulikov (eds.), *Tense-Aspect, Transitivity and Causativity: Essays in honour of Vladimir Nedjalkov*. [Studies in Language Companion Series 50], 21-42. Amsterdam, Philadelphia: John Benjamins.

——2014. 'The decline of labile syntax in Old Indo-Aryan: A diachronic typological perspective', in: *Linguistics* 52(4) [Special issue: Typology of Labile Verbs: Focus on Diachrony], 1139–1165.

Labov, William. 1994. *Principles of Linguistic Change, Vol. 1: Internal factors*. Oxford: Blackwell.

Lambdin, Thomas O. 1983. *Introduction to Sahidic Coptic: New Coptic Grammar*. Macon, GA: Mercer University Press.

Lakoff, George. 1977. 'Linguistic Gestalts', in: W.A. Beach, S.E. Fox, S. Philosoph (eds.), *Papers from the Thirteenth Regional Meeting of the Chicago Linguistics Society*, 236-287. Chicago Linguistic Society.

Lavidas, Nikolaos. 2009. *Transitivity Alternations in Diachrony: Changes in Argument Structure and Voice Morphology*. Newcastle upon Tyne: Cambridge Scholars Publishing.

Layton, Bentley. 2011. *A Coptic Grammar with Chrestomathy and Glossary: Sahidic Dialect*. Wiesbaden: Harrassowitz Verlag. (3rd edition).

Lefort, Louis Théophile. 1950. *Concordance du Nouveau Testament sahidique, I. Les mots d'origine grecque*. Subs. 1. [Corpus Scriptorum Christianorum Orientalium, 124. Subsidia, 1]. Louvain: Imprimerie orientaliste L. Durbecq.

Letuchiy, Alexander. 2010. 'Interpreting the spontaneity scale', in: P. Brandt, M. Garcia García (eds.), *Transitivity: Form, Meaning, Acquisition, and Processing*. Amsterdam, Philadelphia: John Benjamins.

——2013. *"Tipologija labil'nyx glagolov: Semantičeskije i morfosintaksičeskije aspekty"* (Typology of Labile Verbs: Semantic and Morphosyntactic Aspects). Moscow: Jazyki slavianskoj kul'tury.

(online) 'Typology of systems of labile verbs' (http://aletuchiy.narod.ru/handouts_articles/Transitivity/handout_Lancaster_new.pdf).

Levin, Beth, & Malka Rappaport Hovav. 1995. *Unaccusativity*. Cambridge MA: MIT Press.

Liddell, Henry George, Henry Stuart Jones, Robert Scott & Roderick McKenzie. 1996. *Liddell and Scott Greek–English Lexicon* (9th edition, 1940). Clarendon Press: Oxford.

Lincke, Eliese-Sophia. 2018. Sahidic-Coptic prepositions in a typological perspective. PhD Thesis (forthcoming).

Luraghi. Silvia. 2010. 'The extension of the transitive construction in Ancient Greek', in: *Acta Linguistica Hafniensia* 42.1, 60–74.

Lyutikova, Ekaterina & Anastasiya Bonch-Osmolovskaya. 2006. 'A very active passive: Functional similarities between passive and causative in Balkar', in: L. Kulikov, A. Malchukov & P. De Swart (eds.), *Case, Valency and Transitivity* [Studies in Language Companion Series 77]. Amsterdam, Philadelphia: John Benjamins, 393-416.

Malaise, Michel et Jean Winand. 1999. *Grammaire raisonnée de l'égyptien classique* [Aegyptiaca Leodiensia 6]. Liége: C.I.P.L.

Matras, Yaron & Jeannette Sakel (eds.). 2007. *Grammatical borrowing in cross-linguistic perspective*. [Empirical approaches to language typology 38]. Berlin: Mouton de Gruyter.

Matras, Yaron. 2011. 'Universals of structural borrowing', in: P. Siemund (ed.), *Linguistic universals and language variation*. Berlin: Mouton de Gruyter. 200-229.

Mel'čuk, Igor & Alexandr Xolodovič. 1970. "K teorii grammaticheskogo zaloga" [On the theory of grammatical voice], in: *Narody Azii i Afriki*, 1970 (4).

Mel'čuk , Igor. 1993. 'The inflectional category of voice: towards a more rigorous definition', in: B. Comrie & M. Polinsky (eds.), *Causatives and Transitivity* [Studies in Language Companion Series 23]. Amsterdam: John Benjamins. 1-47.

Mithun, Marianne. 2012. 'Morphologies in contact: Form, meaning, and use in the grammar of reference', in: T. Stolz, M. Vanhove, H. Otsuka, and A. Urdzu (eds.) *Morphologies in Contact.* [Studia Typologica 10], 15-36. Berlin: Akademia Verlag.

Muraoka, Takamitsu. 1978. 'On the so-called dativus ethicus in Hebrew', in *The Journal of Theological Studies, New Series*, Vol. 29, No. 2 (October 1978), 495-498.

Muysken, Pieter. 2000. *Bilingual speech. A typology of code-mixing.* Cambridge: Cambridge University Press.

——2010. 'Scenarios for language contact', in: R. Hickey (ed.), *Handbook of language contact,* 265-281. Oxford: Blackwell.

——2017. 'Using Scenarios in Language Contact Studies: Linguistic Borrowing into Coptic', in: E. Grossman, P. Dils, T.S. Richter & W. Schenkel (eds.), *Greek Influence on Egyptian-Coptic: Contact-Induced Change in an Ancient African Language.* [DDGLC Working Papers 1], 3-16. Hamburg: Widmaier Verlag.

Næss, Åshild. 2007. *Prototypical Transitivity* [Typological Studies in Language (TSL) 72]. Amsterdam: John Benjamins.

Nedjalkov, Vladimir P. 1969. "Nekotoryje verojatnostnyje universalii v glagol'nom slovoobrazovanii" (Some probabilistic universals in verbal derivation), in: I.F. Vardul' (ed.), *Jazykovyje universalii i lingvističeskaja tipologija*, 106–114. Moscow: Nauka.

Nedjalkov, Vladimir P. & Georgij G. Sil'nickij. 1969. 'Tipologija morfologiceskogo i leksiceskogo kauzativov' (The typology of morphological and lexical causatives), in: A. Xolodovic (ed.), *Tipologija kauzativnyx konstrukcij: Morfologiceskij kauzativ*, 20-50. Leningrad: Nauka. [Translated: Nedjalkov, V.P. & G.G. Sil'nickij. 1973. 'The Typology of Morphological and Lexical Causatives', in: F. Kiefer (ed.). *Trends in Soviet Theoretical Linguistics.* Dordrecht: D.Reidel.]

Nedjalkov, Vladimir & Sergey Jaxontov. 1988. 'The Typology of Resultative Constructions', in V. Nedjaikov (ed.), *Typology of Resultative Constructions*, 3-62. Amsterdam: John Benjamins.

Paducheva, Elena & Mati Pentus. 2008. 'Formal and informal semantics of telicity', in: Rothstein, Susan (ed.), *Theoretical and Crosslinguistic Approaches to the Semantics of Aspect*, 191-215. Amsterdam: John Benjamins.

Parker, Richard A. 1961. 'The Durative Tenses in P. Rylands IX', in: *JNES*, Vol. 20 (1961), 180–87.

Perlmutter, David M. 1978. 'Impersonal Passives and the Unaccusative Hypothesis', in: *Proceedings of the 4th Annual Meeting of the Berkeley Linguistics Society*, 157-190. University of California Press.

Polinsky, Maria. 2001. 'Grammatical voice', in: N.J. Smelser, P.B.Baltes (eds.), *International Encyclopedia of the Social and Behavioral Sciences*, 6348-6353. New York: Elsevier.

Polotsky, Hans Jakob. 1957. 'Review of W. C. Till, Koptische Grammatik (saïdischerDialekt)', in: *Orientalistische Literaturzeitung* 52, 219–234.

1960. 'The Coptic conjugation system', in: *Orientalia* 29, 4, 392-422. Copy at http://www.tinyurl.com/y2wcnnve.

1987-1990. *Die Grundlagen des koptischen Satzbaus*, Vol.1-2. [American Studies in Papyrology 28-29]. Atlanta / Georgia.

Quack, Joachim Friedrich. 2020. *Demotische Grammatik: Version 2020* (forthcoming).

Reintges, Chris H. 1995. 'Stem allomorphy, verb movement and Case assignment in Coptic Egyptian', in: *Linguistics in the Netherlands*, Volume 12, Issue 1 (1995), 191 – 202.

——2001. 'Aspects of the morphosyntax of subjects and objects in Coptic Egyptian', in: T. van der Wouden and H. Broekhuis (eds.), *Linguistics in the Netherlands* 18, 177-188. Amsterdam: John Benjamins.

——2004. *Coptic Egyptian (Sahidic Dialect): A Learner's Grammar.* Köln: Rüdiger Köppe.

——2013. 'Sapirian 'drift' towards analyticity and long-term morphosyntactic change in Ancient Egyptian', in: R. Kikusawa and L. A. Reid (eds.), *Historical Linguistics 2011: Selected Paper from the 20th International Conference on Historical Linguistics, Osaka, 25–30 July 2011,* 289–328. Amsterdam, Philadelphia: John Benjamins.

——2015. 'Old and Early Middle-Egyptian stative', in: E. Grossman, M. Haspelmath & T.S. Richter (eds.), *Egyptian-Coptic Linguistics in Typological perspective*, 387-455. Berlin: Mouton de Gruyter.

Richter, Tonio Sebastian. 2015. 'Early encounters: Egyptian-Coptic studies and comparative linguistics in the century from Schlegel to Finck', in: E. Grossman, M. Haspelmath & T.S. Richter (eds.), *Egyptian-Coptic Linguistics in Typological perspective,* 3-69. Berlin: Mouton de Gruyter.

Rothstein, Susan. 2008. 'Telicity, atomicity and the Vendler classification of verbs', in:

Rothstein, Susan (ed.), *Theoretical and Crosslinguistic Approaches to the Semantics of Aspect*, 43-77. Amsterdam: John Benjamins.

Sakel, Jeanette. 2007. 'Types of loan: matter and pattern', in Y. Matras & J. Sakel (eds.), *Grammatical borrowing in cross-linguistic perspective*, 15-29. Mouton de Gruyter.

Satzinger, Helmut. 1976. *Neuägyptische Studien. Die Partikel ir – Das Tempussystem.* [Wiener Zeitschrift für die Kunde des Morgenlandes, Beiheft 6.] Wien.

——(online) Late Egyptian, part 2. (https://homepage.univie.ac.at/helmut.satzinger/Texte/LEgn_2.pdf).

Seifart, Frank. 2015. 'Direct and indirect affix borrowing', in: *Language*, Vol. 91/3 (2015), 511-532.

Siewierska, Anna. 1984. *The passive: A comparative linguistic analysis.* London: Croom Helm.

Schenkel, Wolfgang. 1978. 'Infinitiv und Qualitativ des Koptischen als Verbaladverbien, oder die Jernstedtsche Regel und die Satzarten des Koptischen', in: *Enchoria* 8 (1978), 13-15.

Sethe, Karl. 1922. 'Ein Missbrauch des Qualitativs im Koptischen', in: *ZÄS* (1922), 138.

Shibatani, Masayoshi & Prashant Pardeshi. 2002. 'The Causative Continuum', in:

M.Shibatani (ed.), *The Grammar of Causation and Interpersonal Manipulation* [Typological studies in language 48], 85-126. Amsterdam: John Benjamins.

Shisha-Halevy, Ariel. 1981. Bohairic-Late Egyptian Diaglosses: a Contribution to the Typology of Egyptian. In D. W. Young (ed.), *Studies Presented to H.J. Polotsky*. Beacon Hill, 413–438.

——1986. *Coptic Grammatical Categories: Structural Studies in The Syntax of Shenoutean Sahidic.* Analecta Orientalia 53. Roma: Pontificium Institutum Biblicum.

——2017. 'A Structural-Interferential View on Greek Elements in Shenoute', in: E. Grossman, P. Dils, T.S. Richter & W. Schenkel (eds.), *Greek Influence on Egyptian-Coptic: Contact-Induced Change in an Ancient African Language.* [DDGLC Working Papers 1], 441-455. Hamburg: Widmaier Verlag.

Simpson, Robert S. 1996. *Demotic Grammar in the Ptolemaic Sacerdotal Decrees.* Oxford: Griffith Institute, Ashmolean Museum.

Smith, Carlota S. 1970. 'Jespersen's 'Move and Change' Class and Causative Verbs in English', in: M.A. Jazayery, E.C. Polome and W. Winter (eds.), *Linguistic and Literary Studies in Honor of Archibald A. Hill, Vol.2 : Descriptive Linguistics,* 101-109. The Hague: Mouton, 1970.

Steinbach-Eicke, Elisabeth. 2017. 'Experiencing is Tasting. Perception Metaphors of Taste in Ancient Egyptian', in: *Lingua Aegyptia* 25 (2017), 373-390.

Steindorff, Georg. 1951. *Lehrbuch der koptischen Grammatik.* Chicago: University of Chicago Press.

Stern, Ludwig. 1880. *Koptische Grammatik.* Leipzig: T. O. Weigel Verlag.

Stolz, Thomas. 2015. 'Adjective-noun agreement in language contact: loss, realignment and innovation', in: F.Gardani, P. Arkadiev & N. Amiridze (eds.), *Borrowed morphology*, 269-303. Berlin, Boston & Munich: Mouton de Gruyter.

Tenny, Carol. 1987. *Grammaticalizing aspect and affectedness.* Ph.D. dissertation, Massachusetts Institute of Technology, Department of Linguistics and Philosophy.

——1994. *Aspectual roles and the syntax-semantics interface* [Studies in Linguistics and Philosophy 52]. Dordrecht: Kluwer Academic.

Testelec Ya.G. 1998. 'On two parameters of transitivity', in: L. Kulikov & H. Vater (eds.), *Typology of verbal categories: Papers Presented to Vladimir Nedjalkov on the Occasion of his 70th Birthday.* [Linguistische Arbeiten, 382], 29-46. Berlin: Mouton de Gruyter.

Thomason, Sarah Grey & Terrence Kaufman. 1988. *Language Contact, Creolization and Genetic Linguistics.* Berkeley: University of California Press.

Till, Walter C. 1955. *Koptische Grammatik (Saïdischer Dialekt)*. Leipzig: Otto Harassowitz.

Torallas Tovar, Sofia. 2010. 'Greek in Egypt', in: E. J. Bakker (ed.), *A Companion to the Ancient Greek Language*, 253-266. Oxford: Wiley-Blackwell.

——2017. 'The Reverse Case: Egyptian Borrowing in Greek', in: E. Grossman, P. Dils, T.S. Richter & W. Schenkel (eds.), *Greek Influence on Egyptian-Coptic: Contact-Induced Change in an Ancient African Language*. [DDGLC Working Papers 1], 97-113. Hamburg: Widmaier Verlag.

Trapp Erich, Wolfram Hörandner, Johannes Diethart et al. Lexikon zur byzantinischen Gräzität, besonders des 9.–12. Jahrhunderts. (Online edition: http://stephanus.tlg.uci.edu/lbg/).

Tsunoda, Tasaku. 1981. 'Split case-marking in verb types and tense/aspect/mood', in: *Linguistics* 19 (1981), 389-438.

——1985. 'Remarks on Transitivity', in: *Journal of Linguistics* 21 issue 2 (1985), 385-396.

Vendler, Zeno. 1957. 'Verbs and Times', in: *The Philosophical Review*, Vol. 66, No. 2. (Apr., 1957), 143-160.

Verkuyl, Henk J. 1972. *On the compositional nature of the aspects*. Dordrecht: Reidel.

——1993. *A theory of aspectuality: The interaction between temporal and atemporal structure*. [Cambridge Studies in Linguistics 64]. Cambridge: Cambridge University Press.

——1999. *Aspectual issues: Structuring time and quantity*. [CSLI Lecture Notes, 98]. Stanford: Center for the Study of Language and Information.

Wallace, Daniel B. 1996. *Greek Grammar Beyond the Basics: An Exegetical Syntax of New Testament Greek with Scripture, Subject, and Greek Word Indexes*. Grand Rapids MI: Zondervan Publishing House.

Weinreich, Uriel. 1953. *Languages in Contact*. The Hague: Mouton.

Wichmann, Søren & Jan Wohlgemuth. 2008. 'Loan verbs in a typological perspective', in: T. Stolz, D. Bakker, R. Salas Palomo (eds.), *Aspects of Language Contact. New Theoretical, Methodologicaland Empirical Findings with Special Focus on Romancisation Processes*. [EmpiricalApproaches to Language Typology 35], 89-122. Berlin, New York: Mouton de Gruyter.

Winand, Jean. 2015. 'The Oblique Expression of the Object in Ancient Egyptian', in: E. Grossman, M. Haspelmath & T.S. Richter (eds.), *Egyptian-Coptic Linguistics in Typological perspective*, 533-560. Berlin: Mouton de Gruyter.

Winters Margaret E. 1990. 'Toward a theory of syntactic prototypes', in: S. L.Tsohatzidis (ed.), *Meanings and prototypes : Studies in linguistic categorization*, 285-306. London: Routledge.

Wohlgemuth, Jan. 2009. *A typology of verbal borrowings*. [Trends in linguistics: Studies and monographs 211]. Berlin: Mouton de Gruyter.

Wunderlich, Dieter. 2006. 'Towards a structural typology of verb classes', in: D. Wunderlich (ed.), *Advances in the Theory of the Lexicon*, 57–166. Mouton de Gruyter.

Xolodovič, Alexandr A. 1970. "Zalog.l: Opredelenie. Isčislenie". [Voice.1: Definition. Calculus], in: *Kategorija zaloga. Materialy konferencii*, 2-26. Leningrad: Institut jazykoznanija AN SSSR.

Young, Dwight Wayne. 1961. 'On Shenoute's Use of Present I', in: *Journal of Near Eastern Studies* 20 (1961), 115-119.

Zakrzewska, Ewa D. 2017a. "A Bilingual Language Variety" or "the Language of the Pharaohs"? Coptic from the Perspective of Contact Linguistics', in: E. Grossman, P. Dils, T.S. Richter & W. Schenkel (eds.), *Greek Influence on Egyptian-Coptic: Contact-Induced Change in an Ancient African Language*. [DDGLC Working Papers 1], 115 -161. Hamburg: Widmaier Verlag.

——2017b. 'Complex verbs in Bohairic Coptic: Language Contact and Valency', in: B. Nolan, E. Diedrichsen (eds.), *Argument realisation in complex predicates and complex events: Verb-verb constructions at the syntax-semantic interface*, 213-243. Amsterdam: John Benjamins.

Text sources

Allen, James P. 2002.*The Heqanakht Papyri*. [PMMA 27]. New York: The Metropolitan Museum of Art. German translation: I. Hafemann.

Amélineau, Émile. 1914. *Oeuvres de Schenoudi : texte copte et traduction française*. Tome 1, 2. Paris: Ernest Leroux. English translation: N. Speransky.

Barns, John W. B., Henrik Zilliacus. 1960. *The Antinoopolis Papyri, part II. London: Egypt Exploration Society*. English: N. Speransky.

C. Barry et al. (eds.). 2000. *Zostrien*. [BCNH.T 24]. Québec; Leuven: Les presses de l'Université Laval; Peeters. English translation: D. Burns.

Bilabel, Friedrich. 1934. *Griechische, koptische und arabische Texte zur Religion und religiösen Literatur in Ägyptens Spätzeit*. [Veröffentlichungen aus den badischen Papyrus-Sammlungen]. Heidelberg: Verlag der Universitätsbibliothek. English translation: A. Grons.

Boud'hors, Anne. 2013. *Le Canon 8 de Chénouté. Introduction, édition critique*. Le Caire: Institut français d'archéologie orientale. English translation: N. Speransky.

Boud'hors, Anne, Chantal Heurtel. 2016. *Frangué, moine d'Égypte : une correspondance sur terre cuite au VIIIe siècle*. Lis et parle.

Budge, Ernest A.W. 1913. *Coptic Apocrypha in the Dialect of Upper Egypt: Edited, with English Translations*. Oxford: Horace Hart.

Budge, Ernest A. W. 1914. *Coptic Martyrdoms etc. in the Dialect of Upper Egypt*. London: Printed by order of the Trustees.

Bulletin of the American Society of Papyrologists (BASP) 48 (2011), 79-88 (Miller, Joseph G., ed.).

Caminos, Ricardo A. 1954. *Late-Egyptian Miscellanies*. London: Oxford University Press, 497-501. German translation: L.Popko.

Chapman, Paul. 1993. 'Homily on the Passion and Resurrection Attributed to Evodius of Rome', in: L.Depuydt (ed.), *Homiletica From the Pierpont Morgan Library*. [CSCO 524]. Louvain: Peeters.

Chapman, Paul, Leo Depuydt. 1993. *Encomiastica from the Pierpont Morgan Library: 5 Coptic homilies attributed to Anastasius of Euchaita, Epiphanius of Salamis, Isaac of Antiochien, Severian of Gabala, and Theopempus of Antioch.* [CSCO/SC 544/47; 545/48]. Louvain, Paris: Peeters. English translation: A. Grons.

Chassinat, Émile. 1921. *Un papyrus médical copte: Publié et traduit.* [MIFAO 32]. Le Caire: L'Institut Francais d'Archéologie Orientale. English translation: A. Grons.

Coles, Revel A., Herwig Maehler, Peter J. Parsons. 1987. *The Oxyrhynchus Papyri*. London: Egypt Exploration Society.

Cramer, Maria, Martin Krause. 2008. *Das koptische Antiphonar*. Jerusalemer Theologisches Forum 12. Münster: Aschendorff. English translation: A. Grons.

Crégheur, Eric. 2013. *Édition critique, traduction et introduction des "deux Livres de Iéou" (MS Bruce 96),avec des notes philologiques et textuelles*. Québec: Université Laval. English translation: A. Winterberg.

Cristea, Hans-Joachim. 2011. *Schenute von Atripe: Contra Origenistas. Edition des koptischen Textes mit annotierter Übersetzung und Indizes einschließlich einer Übersetzung des 16. Osterfestbriefs des Theophilus in der Fassung des Hieronymus (ep. 96)*. [STAC 60]. Tübingen: Mohr Siebeck. English translation: S. Becker.

Crum, Walter E. 1902. *Coptic Ostraca: From the collections of the Egypt Exploration Fund, the Cairo Museum and Others*. London: The Egypt Exploration Fund.

Crum, Walter E. 1905. *Catalogue of the Coptic manuscripts in the British Museum*. Vol. 1. London: British Museum Dept. of Oriental printed books and manuscripts.

Crum, Walter E. 1910. *Greek papyri in the British Museum. Vol. 4. The Aphrodito Papyri, edited by H. I. Bell, M.A. With an Appendix of Coptic Papyri, edited by W. E. Crum, M.A.* London : The Trustees of the British Museum.

Crum, Walter E. 1915. *Der Papyruscodex Saec. VI - VII der Phillippsbibliothek in Cheltenham. Koptische theologische Schriften: Mit einem Beitr. von A. Ehrhard.* Strasburg: Karl J. Trübner.

Crum, Walter E. 1925. 'Koptische Zünfte und das Pfeffermonopol', in: *ZÄS* 60, 103-111. English translation: A. Grons.

Crum, Walter E., G. Steindorf. 1912. *Koptische Rechtsurkunden des achten Jahrhunderts aus Djême (Theben).* Leipzig: J.C. Hinrichs. English translation: F. Krueger.

Crum, Walter E., H. G. Evelyn White. 1926. *The Monastery of Epiphanius at Thebes.* New York

Dirkse, Peter A., Douglas M. Parrott. 1979. *Nag Hammadi Codices V, 2-5 and VI, with Papyrus Berolinensis 8502, 1 and 4.* [NHS 11]. Leiden: Brill.

Duttenhöfer, Ruth. 1994. Ptolemäische Urkunden aus der Heidelberger Papyrus-Sammlung (P. Heid. VI). Heidelberg : C. Winter. English translation: N. Speransky.

Funk, Wolf-Peter. Unpublished. *A Work Concordance to Shenoute's Canons.* Quebec City. 2007.

Gardiner, A.H. 'Inscriptions from the tomb of Si-renpowet I., prince of Elephantine', in: *ZÄS* 45, 1908-1909, 123-132.

Gardiner, A.H. 1909. Die Erzählung des Sinuhe und die Hirtengeschichte, Hieratische Papyrus aus den Königlichen Museen zu Berlin, vol. V. Leipzig. English translation: N. Speransky.

Garel, Esther. 2020. *Héritage et transmission dans le monachisme égyptien: Les testaments des supérieurs du topos de Saint-Phoibammôn à Thèbes (P.Mon.Phoib.Test.).* [Bibliothèque d'études coptes 27]. Cairo: Institut français d'archéologie orientale.

Garitte, Gérard. 1943. 'Panégyrique de saint Antoine par Jean, évêque d'Hermopolis', in: *Orientalia Christiana Periodica* 9:3, 100-34, 330-65. English translation: F. Krueger.

Goehring, James E. 2012. *Politics, Monasticism, and Miracles in Sixth Century Upper Egypt: A Critical Edition and Translation of the Coptic Texts on Abraham of Farshut.* [Studien und Texte zu Antike und Christentum 69]. Tübingen: Mohr Siebeck.

Grenfell, Bernard P., Hunt, Arthur S. 1898. *The Oxyrhynchus Papyri. Volume VIII (Nos 1073-1165).* London: Egypt Exploration Fund.

Griffith, Francis Ll., Herbert Thompson. 1921. *The Demotic Papyrus London and Leiden.* London.

Hedrick, Charles W., Douglas M. Parrott. 'The (Second) Apocalypse of James', in: *Nag Hammadi Codices V, 2-5 and VI, with Papyrus Berolinensis 8502, 1 and 4.* [NHS 11]. Leiden: Brill.

Jernstedt, Petr V. 1959. Koptskie teksty Gosudarstvennogo muzeia izobrazitel'nykh iskusstv imeni A.S. Pushkina. [Coptic texts of Pushkin State Museum]. Moscow-Leningrad: AN SSSR.

Kuhn, Karl Heinz. 1956. Letters and Sermons of Besa. Corpus Scriptorum Christianorum Orientalium 157/ Scriptores Coptici 21. Louvain: Imprimerie Orientaliste L.Durbecq.

Landgrafova, Renata, Peter Dils. Strukturen und Transformationen des Wortschatzes der ägyptischen Sprache, Sächsische Akademie der Wissenschaften, Leipzig. TLA

Lanne, Emmanuel. 1958. Le Grand Euchologue du Monastère Blanc: Text Copte édité avec traduction française. [Patrologia Orientalis 135]. Paris: Firmin-Didot et Cie.

Lapp, Günther. 1997. *The Papyrus of Nu (BM EA 10477), Catalogue of Books of the Dead in the British Museum,* vol. I. London: British Museum. English translation: N. Speransky.

Layton, Bentley (ed.). 1989. *Nag Hammadi Codex II,2-7 Together With XIII,2*, BRIT. LIB. OR. 4926(1), and P.OXY. 1, 654, 655.* Vol. 1. New York: Brill.

Layton, Bentley. 2014. *The Canons of Our Fathers: Monastic Rules of Shenoute.* Oxford: Oxford University Press.

Lefort, Louis-Théophile. 1956. *Œuvres de S. Pachôme et de ses disciples.* [CSCO / CS 159/23; 160/24] Louvain: Durbecq.

Leipoldt, Iohannes. 1954. *Sinuthii Archimandritae Vita et Opera Omnia iv.* [Scriptores Coptici 5]. Louvain: Imprimerie Orientaliste L.Durbecq.

Leipoldt, Iohannes. 1955. *Sinuthii Archimandritae Vita et Opera Omnia iii.* [Scriptores Coptici 2]. Louvain: Imprimerie Orientaliste L.Durbecq.

Lexa, František. 1926. *Papyrus Insinger: les enseignements moraux d'un scribe égyptien du premier siècle après J.-C.* Paris: Librairie Orientaliste Paul Geuthner. German translation: G. Vittmann.

Lundhaug, Hugo. 2010. *Images of Rebirth: Cognitive Poetics and Transformational Soteriology in the Gospel of Philip and the Exegesis on the Soul.* Leiden, Boston: Brill.

MacRae, George. 1979. *Apocalypse of Adam, in Nag Hammadi Codices V, 2-5 and VI, with Papyrus Berolinensis 8502, 1 and 4*, ed. D.M.Parrott. Nag Hammadi Studies XI. Leiden: Brill.

Maspero, Jean. 1911. *Papyrus grecs d'époque byzantine, Catalogue général des antiquités égyptiennes du Musée du Caire.* Tome 1. Le Caire: Imprimerie de l'IFAO. English translation: N. Speransky.

Maspero, Jean. 1913. Maspero, Jean. 1911. *Papyrus grecs d'époque byzantine, Catalogue général des antiquités égyptiennes du Musée du Caire.* Tome 2. Le Caire: Imprimerie de l'IFAO. English translation: N. Speransky.

Maspero, Jean. 1916. Maspero, Jean. 1911. *Papyrus grecs d'époque byzantine, Catalogue général des antiquités égyptiennes du Musée du Caire.* Tome 3. Le Caire: Imprimerie de l'IFAO. English translation: N. Speransky.

Mina, Togo. 1937. *Le Martyre d'Apa Epima.* Cairo: Imprimerie Nationale. English translation: V. Walter.

Müller, C. Detlef G. 1968. *Die Homilie über die Hochzeit zu Kana und weitere Schriften des Patriarchen Benjamin I. von Alexandrien.* Heidelberg: Carl Winter Universitätsverlag.

Müller, Matthias, Sami Uljas. 2019. *Martyrs and Archangels: Coptic Literary Texts from the Pierpont Morgan Library.* [Studien und Texte zu Antike und Christentum]. Tübingen: Mohr Siebeck.

Munro, Irmtraut. 1994. *Die Totenbuch-Handschriften des 18. Dynastie im Ägyptischen Museum Cairo: Tafelband.* [Ägyptologische Abhandlungen 54]. Harassowitz.

Nestle, Eberhard, Aland, Barbara, Aland, Kurt. 2012. *Novum Testamentum Graece.* 28. Auflage. Stuttgart: Deutsche Bibelgesellschaft.

Orlandi, Tito. 1968. *Storia della chiesa di Allesandria. Vol.II: da Teofilo a Timoteo II. Testo copto, traduzione e commento.* [Studi Copti 2]. Milano, Varese: Istituto Editoriale Cisalpino. English translation: S.Becker.

Peel, Malcolm, Birger A. Pearson. 1996. 'The Teachings of Silvanus', in: *Nag Hammadi Codex VII: Text, Translation, and Notes.* [NHMS 30]. Leiden; New York; Köln: Brill.

Pleyte, W., Boeser, P.A.A. 1897. *Manuscrits coptes du Musée des Pays-Bas à Leide.* Leiden: Brill. English translation: N.Speransky.

Poirier, Paul-Hubert. 2006. *La Pensée Première à la Triple Forme (NH XIII, 1).* [BCNH.T 32]. Québec; Louvain; Paris; Dudley, MA: Les presses de l'Université Laval; Peeters. English translation: D. Burns.

Rahlfs, Alfred, Hanhart, Robert. 2006. *Septuaginta Id est Vetus Testamentum graece.* Stuttgart: Deutsche Bibelgesellschaft.

Rossi, Francesco. 1892. 'Transcrizione con traduzione italiana dal testo copto di un sermone sulla Passione del nostro Signore Gesù Cristo con vari altri frammenti copti del Museo Egizio di Torino', in: *Memorie della Reale Accademia delle Scienze di Torino* 42, 111-143. English translation: N.Speransky.

Rupprecht, Hans-Albert, Joachim Hengstl. 1997. *Sammelbuch griechischer Urkunden aus Ägypten.* Wiesbaden: Harassowitz.

Ryholt, Kim. 1999. *The Carlsberg Papyri 4. The Story of Petese Son of Petetum.* Copenhagen: Museum Tusculanum Press. German translation: L. Popko.

Salomons, Robert P. 1996. *Papyri Bodeleianae I.* [Studia Amstelodamensia ad epigraphicam, ius antiquum et papyrologicam pertinentia 34]. Amsterdam: Gieben. English translation: N. Speransky.

Schenke, Gesa. 2013. *Das koptisch hagiographische Dossier des Heiligen Kolluthos, Arzt, Märtyrer und Wunderheiler: eingeleitet, neu ediert, übersetzt und kommentiert.* [CSCO 650]. Louvain: Peeters.

Schenke Robinson, Gesine. 2004. *Das Berliner "Koptische Buch" (P20915). Eine Wieder Hergestellte Fruhchristlich-theologische Abhandlung.* [CSCO 611]. Louvain: Peeters.

Schenke, Hans-Martin. 1981. *Das Matthäus-Evangelium im mittelägyptischen Dialekt des Koptischen: Codex Scheide*. [Texte und Untersuchungen zur Geschichte der altchristlichen Literatur 127]. Berlin: Akademie Verlag. English translation: V. Walter.

Schiller, Arthur. 1932. *Ten Coptic Legal Texts*. New York: The Metropolitan Museum of Arts.

Schiller, Arthur. 1968. 'The Budge papyrus of Columbia University', in: *Journal of American Research Center in Egypt* 7, 79-118. American Research Center in Egypt.

Schmidt, Carl, Violet MacDermot. 1978. *Pistis Sophia*. [NHS 9]. Leiden: Brill.

Sheridan, J. Mark. 1998. *Rufus of Shotep: Homilies on the Gospels of Matthew and Luke: Introduction, Text, Translation, Commentary*. Rome: Centro Italiano Microfiches.

Sheridan, J. Mark. 2012. *From the Nile to the Rhone and beyond: Studies in Early Monastic Literature and Scriptural Interpretation*. [Studia Anselmiana 156]. Rome: Editions Sankt Ottilien.

Smith, Mark J. 2002. *On the Primaeval Ocean. The Carlsberg Papyri 5*. Copenhagen: Carsten Niebuhr Institute Publications 26.

Smith, Mark J. 2005. *Papyrus Harkness (MMA 31.9.7)*. Oxford: Griffith Institute Publications.

Spiegelberg, William. 1910. *Der Sagenkreis des Königs Petubastis*. Leipzig: J.C.Hinrichs.

Spiegelberg, William. 1917. *Der ägyptische Mythus vom Sonnenauge, der Papyrus der Tierfabeln, Kufi. Nach dem Leidener demotischen Papyrus I 384*. Straßburg: Straßburger Druckerei und Verlagsanstalt.

Steindorf, Georg. 1913. *Das Grab des Ti*. Leipzig: J.C. Hinrichs.

Till, Walter C., Hans-Martin Schenke. 1972. *Die gnostischen Schriften des koptischen Papyrus Berolinensis 8502: Hg. übers. und bearb. von Walter C. Till. 2., erw. Aufl. bearb. v. Hans-Martin Schenke*. [Texte und Untersuchungen zur Geschichte der altchristlichen Literatur 60]. Berlin: Akademie Verlag. English translation: A. Winterberg.

Töpfer, Susanne. 2013. *Eine (Neu-)Edition der Textkomposition "Balsamierungsritual". pBoulaq 3, pLouvre 5158, pDurham 1983.11+pSt.Petersburg 18128*, Diss. Heidelberg.

Vitelli, Girolamo. 1906. *Papiri fiorentini*. Milano: Hoepli. English translation: N.Speransky.

G. Vitelli, M. Norsa et al. (eds.). 1917. *Papiri greci e latini V*. [Publicazioni della Società Italiana per la ricerca dei papiri greci e latini in Egitto]. Firenze: Tipografia Enrico Ariani. English translation: N.Speransky.

Vittmann, Günther. *Der demotische Papyrus Rylands 9:I Text Und Übersetzung*. Wiesbaden: Otto Harrassowitz. English translation: N. Speransky.

Waldstein, Michael, Frederik Wisse 1995. *The Apocryphon of John: Synopsis of Nag Hammadi Codices II,1; III,1; and IV,1 with BG 8502,2*.[NHMS 33]. Leiden: Brill.

Wansink, Craig. 1991. 'Encomium on the Four Bodiless Creatures', in: *Homiletica from the Pierpont Morgan Library: Seven Coptic Homilies Attributed to Basil the Great, John Chrysostom, and Euodius of Rome*. [CSCO /SC 524/43; 525/44]. Louvain: Peeters.

Wessely, Carl. 1909. *Griechische und Koptische Texte Theologischen Inhalts I*. Leipzig: Verlag von Eduard Avenarius.

Wisse, Frederik, Birger A. Pearson. 1996. *Nag Hammadi Codex VII: Text, Translation, and Notes*. [NHMS 30]. Leiden; New York; Köln: Brill.

Wisse, Frederik, Douglas M. Parrott 1979. 'The Concept of Our Great Power', in: *Nag Hammadi Codices V, 2-5 and VI, with Papyrus Berolinensis 8502, 1 and 4*. [NHS 11]. Leiden: Brill.

Zauzich, Karl-Theodor. 1993. *Papyri von der Insel Elephantine (= Dem. Pap. Berlin, Lfg. III)*. Berlin: Akademie-Verlag.

Index of Greek Verbs

Index of Coptic Greek-origin verbs

Index of Coptic native verbs

Lingua Aegyptia – Studia Monographica

Recent Publications and Backlist

ISSN 0946-8641

DOI: 10.37011/studmon

Lingua Aegyptia – Studia Monographica 24

Grammatik des Bohairischen

Matthias Müller

The grammar presents a comprehensive introduction to the Bohairic Coptic dialect. It is divided into 12 chapters covering the major features of the grammar and is augmented by three chapters with short introductions to Bohairic literature, indications of both time reckoning and measurements, as well as an additional chapter introducing patterns specific to the texts of Nitrian monasteries (or better, Sketis). As the grammar is intended for learners, students, and scholars as well as coptologists/egyptologists and linguists, almost all examples are extensively glossed. Furthermore, the book contains extensive annotated texts for reading from the Scripture as well as from literary and even some documentary texts, as well as a glossary to the texts.

Lingua Aegyptia – Studia Monographica 24 Hamburg 2021, paperback, xxiv+936 pages

ISSN: 0946-8641
ISBN: 978-3-943955-24-8

€ 49 (subscribers' price: € 45)
(incl. German VAT, excl. shipping)

Lingua Aegyptia – Studia Monographica 25

Egyptian Root Lexicon

Helmut Satzinger & Danijela Stefanović

The Egyptian Root Lexicon presents the envisaged roots of the Egyptian words, hypothetically established on the basis of attested lexemes on obvious phonetic and semantic resemblance. As the etymological research in the field of Afro-Asiatic is not sufficiently advanced, the lexical roots are not set up on an etymological basis. The main part of the book contains the roots (numerically marked with DRID identifier) in alphabetic arrangement, with their subsequent lexemes marked with an identity number, the "ID," as created by the Thesaurus Linguae Aegyptiae (TLA), of the Berlin Academy of Sciences. The roots section is followed by extensive indexes, including a lexeme index and an index of roots of Semitic origin. A selected bibliography concludes the work.

Lingua Aegyptia – Studia Monographica 25 Hamburg 2021, hardcover, viii+717 pages

ISSN: 0946-8641
ISBN: 978-3-943955-25-5

€ 89 (subscribers' price: € 69)
(incl. German VAT, excl. shipping)

Lingua Aegyptia – Studia Monographica 27

Wer schreibt die Geschichte(n)?

Die 8. bis frühe 12. Dynastie im Licht ägyptologischer und ägyptischer Sinnbildungen

Antonia Giewekemeyer

This study concerns itself with the 8th to early 12th dynasties. A period allegedly interpreted by the Egyptians themselves as a period of change and divided into a time of decline and a time of restoration or renaissance. Antonia Giewekemeyer reconsiders these Egyptological reconstructions by both analysing their scholarly development and by surveying the available contemporaneous Egyptian sources. As a result, she argues that the Egyptian sources emphasise continuation and coherence instead of restauration or renaissance. Furthermore, she demonstrates how the modern experience of change affected and finally misled Egyptological reconstructions.

Lingua Aegyptia –
Studia Monographica 27
Hamburg 2022, cloth,
xxx+530 pages, German text

ISSN: 0946-8641
ISBN: 978-3-943955-27-9

€ 89 (subscribers' price: € 69)
(incl. 7% German VAT, excl. shipping)

Lingua Aegyptia – Studia Monographica

ISSN: 0946-8641

1   Frank Kammerzell, *Panther, Löwe und Sprachentwicklung im Neolithikum.*
    1994 (hardcover, 100 pages), out of print

2   Gerald Moers (ed.), *Definitely: Egyptian Literature: Proceedings of the symposion "Ancient
    Egyptian literature: history and forms", Los Angeles, March 24–26, 1995.*
    1999 (hardcover, X+142 pages), out of print

3   Dörte Borchers, Frank Kammerzell & Stefan Weninger (eds.), *Hieroglyphen – Alphabete –
    Schriftreformen: Studien zu Multiliteralismus, Schriftwechsel und Orthographieneuregelungen.*
    2001 (hardcover, VI+270 pages), €49, now € 30

4   Stephan Jäger, *Altägyptische Berufstypologien.*
    2004 (hardcover, X+340+xlvi+XCIV pages), out of print

5   José M. Galán, *Four Journeys in Ancient Egyptian Literature.*
    2005 (hardcover, V+186 pages), out of print

6   Anthony Spalinger, *Five Views on Egypt.*
    2006 (hardcover, VIII+176 pages), out of print (PDF online)

7   H.J. Polotsky, *Scripta Posteriora on Egyptian and Coptic*,
    edited by Verena M. Lepper & Leo Depuydt.
    2007 (hardcover, VI+230 pages), €49, now € 35

8   Petra Andrássy, Julia Budka & Frank Kammerzell (eds.), *Non-Textual Marking Systems,
    Writing and Pseudo Script from Prehistory to Modern Times.*
    2009 (hardcover, VIII+312 pages), out of print (PDF online)

9   Eitan Grossman, Stéphane Polis & Jean Winand (eds.),
    Lexical Semantics in Ancient Egyptian.
    2012 (hardcover, vi+490 pages), € 69 (subscribers' price: € 59)
    ISBN: 978-3-943955-09-5

10 R.B. Parkinson,
    The Tale of the Eloquent Peasant: A Reader's Commentary.
    2012 (hardcover, xii+384 pages), € 59 (subscribers' price: € 49)
    ISBN: 978-3-943955-10-1

11 Gerald Moers, Kai Widmaier, Antonia Giewekemeyer, Arndt Lümers & Ralf Ernst (eds.),
    Dating Egyptian Literary Texts.
    "Dating Egyptian Literary Texts" Göttingen, 9–12 June 2010, Volume 1
    2013 (hardcover, xiv+653 pages), € 95 (subscribers' price: € 79)
    ISBN: 978-3-943955-11-8

12 Andréas Stauder,
    Linguistic Dating of Middle Egyptian Literary Texts.
    "Dating Egyptian Literary Texts" Göttingen, 9–12 June 2010, Volume 2
    2013 (hardcover, xx+568 pages), € 85 (subscribers' price: € 69)
    ISBN: 978-3-943955-12-5

13   Marc Brose,
Grammatik der dokumentarischen Texte des Mittleren Reiches.
2014 (cloth, xx+553 pages), € 85 (subscribers' price: € 69)
ISBN: 978-3-943955-13-2

14   Andréas Stauder,
The Earlier Egyptian Passive. Voice and Perspective.
2014 (cloth, xviii+448 pages), € 69 (subscribers' price: € 59)
ISBN: 978-3-943955-14-9

15   Eitan Grossman, Stéphane Polis, Andréas Stauder & Jean Winand (eds.),
On Forms and Functions: Studies in Ancient Egyptian Grammar.
2014 (cloth, vi+366 pages), € 59 (subscribers' price: € 49)
ISBN: 978-3-943955-15-6

16   Julia Budka, Frank Kammerzell & Sławomir Rzepka (eds.),
Non-Textual Marking Systems in Ancient Egypt (and Elsewhere).
2015 (cloth, x+322 pages), € 59 (subscribers' price: € 49)
ISBN: 978-3-943955-16-3

17   Eitan Grossman, Peter Dils, Tonio Sebastian Richter & Wolfgang Schenkel (eds.),
Greek Influence on Egyptian-Coptic: Contact-Induced Change in an Ancient African Language. DDGLC Working Papers 1
2017 (cloth, viii+534 pages), € 89 (subscribers' price: € 69)
ISBN: 978-3-943955-17-0

18   Kristina Hutter,
Das sḏm=f-Paradigma im Mittelägyptischen: Eine Vergleichsstudie verschiedener Grammatiken.
2017 (paperback, x+289 pages, incl. 47 tables), € 49 (subscribers' price: € 39)
ISBN: 978-3-943955-18-7

19   Gaëlle Chantrain & Jean Winand (eds.),
Time and Space at Issue in Ancient Egypt.
2018 (paperback, viii+242 p.), € 55 (subscribers' price: € 39)
ISBN: 978-3-943955-19-4

20   Marwan Kilani,
Vocalisation in Group Writing: A New Proposal.
2019 (paperback, vi+150 pages), € 39 (subscribers' price: € 29)
ISBN: 978-3-943955-20-0
ISBN (OPEN ACCESS PDF): 978-3-943955-90-3 | doi.org/10.37011/studmon.20

21   Gaëlle Chantrain,
Eléments de la terminologie du temps en égyptien ancien.
2020 (paperback, xxxiv+344 pages), € 59 (subscribers' price: € 49)
ISBN: 978-3-943955-21-7

22   Kathrin Gabler, Rita Gautschy, Lukas Bohnenkämper, Hanna Jenni, Clémentine Reymond, Ruth Zillhardt, Andrea Loprieno-Gnirs & Hans-Hubertus Münch (eds),
Text-Bild-Objekte im archäologischen Kontext: Festschrift für Susanne Bickel.
2020 (cloth, xxii+293 p., 23 colour, 60 b&w illustrations), € 65 (subscribers' price: € 49)
ISBN: 978-3-943955-22-4

23   Simon Thuault,
      La dissemblance graphémique à l'Ancien Empire: Essai de grammatologie cognitive.
      2020 (paperback, xx+376 pages, illustrations), € 59 (subscribers' price: € 49)
      ISBN: 978-3-943955-23-1

24   Matthias Müller
      Grammatik des Bohairischen.
      2021 (paperback, xxiv+936 pages), € 49 (subscribers' price: € 45)
      ISBN: 978-3-943955-24-8

25   Helmut Satzinger & Danijela Stefanović,
      Egyptian Root Lexicon.'
      2021 (hardcover, viii+717 pages), € 89 (subscribers' price: € 69)
      ISBN: 978-3-943955-25-5

All prices include German VAT (7%).

For orders, standing orders and further information:

www.widmaier-verlag.de
orders@widmaier-verlag.de

North American customers may also contact the official distributor ISD
(for issues since volume 9):

www.isdistribution.com